Women's Experiences with HIV/AIDS

Women's Experiences with HIV/AIDS

An International Perspective

EDITED BY

Lynellyn D. Long and E. Maxine Ankrah

Columbia University Press

NEW YORK

Columbia University Press
Publishers Since 1893
New York   Chichester, West Sussex
Copyright © 1996 Columbia University Press,
except for article 11, "The Epidemiology of HIV and AIDS
in Women," which is in the public domain

Columbia University Press and the editors gratefully acknowledge permission
to reprint from Geeta Rao Gupta, Ellen Weiss, and Purnima Mane, "Talking
about Sex: A Prerequisite for AIDS Prevention," *AIDS* 1994 (8) : Supplement 1;
and Christopher J. Elias and Lori L. Heise, "Challenges for the Development
of Female-Controlled Vaginal Microbicides," *AIDS* 1994 (8) : 1–9.

Library of Congress Cataloging-in-Publication Data

Women's experiences with HIV/AIDS : an international perspective /
edited by Lynellyn D. Long and E. Maxine Ankrah.
p. cm.
Includes bibliographical references and index.
ISBN 0-231-10604-1 (cl : alk. paper).
ISBN 0-231-10605-X (pbk. : alk. paper)
1. Women—Diseases. 2. HIV infections—Sex factors. 3. AIDS
(Disease)—Sex Factors. I. Long, Lynellyn. II. Ankrah, E. M.
RC607.A26W653   1996
362.1'969792—dc20   96-31322

Casebound editions of Columbia University Press books
are printed on permanent and durable acid-free paper

Printed in the United States of America

c 10 9 8 7 6 5 4 3 2 1
p 10 9 8 7 6 5 4 3 2 1

Contents

Foreword

PETER LAMPTEY, M.D.

Prevention and treatment programs designed to curb the spread of sexually transmitted diseases, including HIV (human immunodeficiency virus), among women have not sufficiently addressed the complex web of cultural, economic, and structural constraints that hinder the ability of women, worldwide, to protect themselves from HIV/AIDS. Information about women's experiences and needs is limited and, consequently, many AIDS (acquired immunodeficiency syndrome) intervention programs to date have not adequately incorporated these critical insights into program design and implementation. Gender inequalities, social status, poor sexual negotiating skills, transactional sex, inequalities in education and employment, and socioeconomic disruption as a result of poverty and war put women at increased risk of HIV.

An urgent need exists to identify and understand the socioeconomic, cultural, and structural factors that favor HIV transmission and to develop innovative approaches to HIV prevention that draw not only on women's sexual experiences but also on the socioeconomic and cultural realities of their lives.

HIV transmission to women occurs in the context of complex sexual and social relationships between men and women and within much larger structural and environmental influences. Although it is important to address the neglected needs of women in designing AIDS prevention programs, we need to remember that for such programs to be successful, they need to address the roles of both men and women in their broader social environment.

Women's Experiences with HIV/AIDS: An International Perspective is a timely and important work that examines the experiences of women from diverse backgrounds in the context of the socioeconomic and cultural factors that facilitate

HIV infection. By combining international research data with compelling personal accounts of women's experiences worldwide, the authors explore these complex factors to define a cohesive policy agenda and plan for action.

Comprehensive in scope and poignant in its presentation of the human side of AIDS, this book complements and bolsters those few other significant works dedicated to revealing how AIDS irrevocably touches all aspects of women's lives. This book, which covers the experiences of women from many walks of life and widely divergent backgrounds and cultures, will appeal to educators, public health and public policy officials, designers of HIV prevention programs, and general readers who search for a better understanding of how to halt the AIDS epidemic.

Acknowledgments

This edited volume represents the insights and support of many anonymous women and men. The editors wish especially to thank those women living with HIV/AIDS who shared so generously of their time and whose experiences have taught us all so much.

We would also like to thank several people working in HIV/AIDS research who contributed many valuable ideas and suggestions for this volume. They include Barbara de Zalduondo, Lisa Messersmith, Elizabeth King, Mead Over, Gilbert Herdt, Margaret Bentley, Victor Barnes, Dale Rezabek, Paul Seaton, Debra Schumann, Ingrid Katz, Dominic Montagu, and Tom Kane. We also thank S. N. and Meena Sridhar for their valuable linguistic help and our editors, John Michel and Ronald Harris, for their patience, good advice, and excellent editorial suggestions.

The editors and authors owe much to the institutions in which they work or have worked and which made this volume possible. These include Family Health International, the U.S. Agency for International Development (USAID), Johns Hopkins University, the Population Council, the International Centre for Research on Women, Centers for Disease Control, Tulane University, and many others. The editors would especially like to thank USAID's Office of Women in Development, whose staff provided moral support, encouragement, and good advice on the initiation of this work. The editors also thank Panos for its support in ensuring that the proceeds from this volume will be used to benefit women living with HIV/AIDS and HIV/AIDS projects for, by, and with women throughout the world.

One individual deserves special mention for her tireless efforts to see this volume through from start to finish—Jane Schueller-Rosengren. She spent countless hours with the editors tracking down authors in far corners of the globe, helping to edit the material, and organizing meetings to review the work. Without her efforts this volume would not have been possible.

Finally, we wish to thank our spouses and children for their care and support. We know we could not have accomplished this work without them. It is also to our children and their generation that we dedicate this volume, in the hope that they may be the better for it.

Women's Experiences with HIV/AIDS

Introduction: Counting Women's Experiences

LYNELLYN D. LONG

Thousands of women in every corner of the globe are dying of AIDS yearly. Many more women are living with human immunodeficiency virus/and acquired immunodeficiency syndrome (HIV/AIDS) or caring for others—children, spouses, grandchildren, and friends—affected by this disease. By the beginning of the next century, women living with HIV or AIDS throughout the world are likely to outnumber men.

In the early years of the epidemic there was little recognition that women died of the disease, despite the 1985 Nairobi Conference on the Advancement of Women. One of the earliest reported cases was Dr. Grethe Rask, a Danish woman doctor who died in 1977 (Shilts 1988). Not until the late 1980s did health workers recognize, however, that heterosexual transmission existed. Before that, HIV/AIDS in women was largely invisible.

Women have recently begun to mobilize around the issue of HIV/AIDS in their lives. Early research and intervention programs for HIV/AIDS prevention in Western industrialized countries targeted adult homosexual males (La Guardia 1991). The first studies on women focused on commercial sex workers, who were seen as carriers of the disease to heterosexual men. Then, as men brought HIV/AIDS home to their wives, women suddenly became carriers to their children. Many research studies and interventions seemed to ignore that sex workers themselves could be mothers or that both infected wives and sex workers suffered from male "vectors" (Day 1988; Messersmith 1991). Most recently, prevention programs are focusing attention on young, adolescent girls as men seek out younger, "safer" sex partners. This focus of controlling female adolescent sexuality holds girls, but not their male partners, responsible for ensuring the moral and physical well-being of the next generation (Parker 1995).

Women and girls still play a very marginal role in many HIV/AIDS research programs, interventions, and policy debates, especially in large-scale efforts. Even when women are included in research trials, their participation often has to do only with research on children. For example, Kurth (1993:4) observes that in the United States, "two-thirds of the federal monies earmarked for research on AIDS in women and children has been used for research on children." Intervention programs often fail to take into account the particular situations and experiences that make women more vulnerable to HIV/AIDS than men. In policy debates and documents, it is popular to include women and gender considerations, but their inclusion usually has little effect on the scarce resource allocations or financial expenditures.

Over and above physiological differences, women's and girls' educational, economic, social, political, and cultural status in varying degrees and combinations affect their capacity to protect themselves and to demand that their partners do so as well. Despite an increasing recognition that women (particularly young women) will comprise a growing number of new AIDS cases worldwide, there has not been enough effort to enlist girls and women in setting research agendas and policies or in having them take responsibility for effective prevention and control efforts. Too often, medical and public health experts tell girls and women what they ought to do and ignore their contexts, social networks, and parameters of choice and action. At the same time, many interventions are equally insulting to boys and men by treating them (particularly those with a heterosexual orientation) as if they are incapable of practicing or modifying their sexual behavior to engage in safe sex.

A central argument of this book is that by taking women's and girls' experiences seriously, both men and women will be able to do a better job of preventing HIV/AIDS. The editors decided to write about women and HIV/AIDS because they were personally frustrated by how critical aspects of women's lives and their experiences are ignored in research, policies, and programs. They also believe that women and girls must have a greater voice in determining the agenda for action if this epidemic is to be countered effectively in the coming century.

Before editing this book, Maxine Ankrah lived in Uganda, where she has spent most of her adult life and considers her home. In Uganda she witnessed a situation in which "there was no denying that a real avalanche was rolling down into the valley." Ankrah observes that women were so busy weeding their crops, raising their children, and caring for their households that they did not have the time to look up or to gather the resources to stop the avalanche. She recounts, "There was no one to warn her or to pull her out of harm's way—to offer her a helping hand in a timely way. I wanted to stand in the gap and shout; both to the women themselves and to those who could help."

HIV/AIDs affected Ankrah personally when Chichonko, a girl who had grown up with Ankrah's daughter, died in August 1992. "I want her relatives to know that I have not forgotten what Chichonko gave to the life of my daughter," Ankrah explains. Shortly after that, a colleague who was working with Ankrah in a women's rights' organization and had contracted AIDS from her husband died, leaving behind two daughters. Ankrah recognized that her colleague's situation was not unique, and she hopes that women's efforts to organize will make it harder in future years for her colleague's two daughters to "fall at the hands of a man's behavior."

My own awareness of HIV/AIDS in women's lives came while interviewing refugee women in Nairobi, Kenya, in 1990. During the interviews, several women described how their economic situation had deteriorated because they had adopted the children of a sister or a friend who had recently died of the "disease." These same refugee women, burdened with more children to feed and clothe, found themselves forced in turn to sell sexual services to gain enough income to feed their expanded households. The women were uniformly knowledgeable about the symptoms of HIV/AIDS and how it was transmitted, but, given their economic circumstances, they said there was little they could do to protect themselves. As refugees they also could not officially obtain work permits, and the few international relief income generation and training activities were targetted at men. When I pointed out to policy makers the dilemma these women faced, they initially replied: "We can't publicize this problem because it would stigmatize these women and then no country would be willing to take them."

Ensuing refugee crises in Rwanda, Haiti, and Bosnia-Herzegovina have forced international recognition of HIV/AIDS and refugee women's reproductive health. Yet, although women's advocates, human rights organizations, and local nongovernmental organizations (NGOs) have increased international awareness, the financial and technical resources remain almost nonexistent in refugee settings. Refugee women themselves largely depend on local initiatives and their own economic and social strategies to survive.

Later, in informal conversations and semistructured interviews with adolescent girls and women in the urban United States, I recognized similar patterns of vulnerability among young American women—especially poor women, women of color, and recent immigrant adolescents. One 17-year-old immigrant girl I knew well said of her numerous sexual encounters: "I would never ask the guy to use a condom." Although she was quite knowledgeable about HIV/AIDS, traditional intervention programs and messages had little meaning in this young woman's life. Her own sense of self-worth was at stake in these sexual encounters, and her struggle with daily survival gave her little reason to take a long-term perspective about her own future.

In 1992, while working for the Office of Women in Development in the U.S. Agency for International Development (USAID), I was asked to help support a new "women and HIV/AIDS initiative." Through this endeavor, I realized how little funding was devoted to women worldwide and how difficult it was to ensure that girls and women were included in existing program designs. Early international intervention efforts focused on women as commercial sex workers, so-called core transmitters or the problem of orphaned children. Even though "pattern two" (heterosexual transmission) countries were soon recognized to be the predominant pattern in much of the nonindustrialized world (and eventually worldwide), most interventions ignored women's role in this process. Women were at best seen as "innocent victims" of promiscuous men. As Wagner and Cohen (1993:230) observe, "Globally, much less emphasis has been placed on developing education and prevention programs for women who are not sex workers. This lack of attention is based on the belief that women in the general population are not the 'core transmitters' of HIV infection."

Over the course of the next two years, several women and men working in donor and international organizations gathered both separately and at various meetings to discuss ways of putting "women and AIDS" on the international donor agenda. From these initial series of meetings, Maxine Ankrah and I decided to organize this volume of edited papers. We considered the process of organizing, meeting, writing, editing, and discussing our work with various women around the world as important as completing an edited volume, if not more so. We hope that the volume in turn will generate more communication, advocacy, and organization by and for women.

Resources and the Knowledge Base

When this project began there was a dearth of literature on women and HIV/AIDS, and many early discussions among the authors focused on the parameters of this topic. In the past three years there has been a marked increase in the literature on women and HIV and in what is known about how HIV and AIDS affects women.

As early as 1988, Shilts observed the public denial of women's vulnerability. However, as it became increasingly clear that women would constitute more than half of those inflicted with HIV/AIDS by the year 2000, a few studies began to consider the effect of this disease on women. Corea, a reporter, chronicles the "invisible epidemic" in the United States in the second decade of the disease from 1981 to 1990. She documents how slow the medical establishment and policy makers were to respond to HIV/AIDS in women. Rudd and Taylor (1992), through first-person accounts of Canadian women living with AIDS, demonstrate the importance of understanding women's experiences through their own stories of living with HIV. Schoepf (1992) conducted extensive research with women in Zaire and from their life histories uncovers the structural and gender inequalities that contribute to women's vulnerability there. In the United States context, Patton (1990) analyzed the way HIV/AIDS is represented in the media and in public discourse. She observes that women, especially sex workers, are treated as vectors moving HIV from the sex and drug underworld to heterosexual men, or as "innocent victims"—women who had unknowingly married an HIV-infected person (1990:38–39). In a similar vein, Seidel (1993) analyzes how medical and medico-moral rather than human rights discourses have dominated and shaped responses to the AIDS pandemic in sub-Saharan Africa. In her more recent account Patton (1994) analyzes in detail, in both U.S. and global contexts, how systemic practices and discourses pit "deviant" women against the general public (middle-class white women and adolescents) who "need protection."

Several edited volumes illuminate prevention, care, and treatment issues of women living with HIV. Chen, Amor, and Segal (1991), for example, examine the critical intersection between AIDS and women's reproductive health. The Center for Women Policy Studies (1992) provides a comprehensive guide to resources on women and AIDS for women in the United States, while Berer (1993) provides an international resource book that includes some personal accounts. Dorn, Henderson, and South (1992), in another edited volume, focus on the encounters that HIV-positive women who use drugs have with the British health care system. Bury, Morrison, and McLachlan (1992), from their studies of women in the United States and Great Britain, outline education and counseling, medical (including pregnancy and contraception), and support issues for women in these countries. Similarly, Squire (1993), in her edited volume, focuses on the psychological concerns that Western women with HIV/AIDS face.

In her seminal review, Day (1988:425) shows that the characteristics of prostitution vary regionally and that local practices and their possible role in the transmission of HIV cannot be understood through outsider's definitions of prostitution. She critiques the labeling of prostitutes as a high-risk group because such labeling allows other women to assume falsely that they are not at risk. Several researchers (Day 1988; de Zalduondo 1991; Herdt 1992; Messersmith 1991; Parker 1995) deconstruct the notion of "risk groups" and argue for examining locally specific risk behaviors, practices, and situations that increase women's vulnerability. In a recent edited volume, Reid (1995:ix) observes, HIV/AIDS "throws into stark relief the fault lines of a society: the way power is exercised, gender constructed, socioeconomic stratification exploited."

By the end of the second decade of the epidemic, Worth (1989) documented how condoms were not an effective or viable intervention for many women in the United States. For fear of being seen as promiscuous or unfaithful, many women were unwilling to ask or require their partners to use a condom. Rwabukwali et al., in Feldman's global anthology (1994), report similar findings among Baganda women in Uganda. Many Baganda women perceive they are at risk but have little control over their sexual interactions. Most women who have negative feelings about condoms have not even seen one! Rwabukwali and his colleagues observe that interventions to encourage condom use must include more than education. Counseling, social support, and structural changes are also needed.

There is increasing attention to the clinical symptoms of women with HIV (see Hankins and Handley 1992). Research primarily in Western countries shows that women have shorter survival rates than men primarily because they come later for treatment or are less likely to seek it (Bury, Morrison, and McLachlan 1992). Disease management strategies have also been less well developed for women (Kurth 1993). Recent studies suggest, however, that this survival gap has diminished (Anastos and Vermund 1993). In January 1993 the Centers for Disease Control (CDC) amended their case definition of AIDS to include invasive cervical cancer, recurrent pneumonia, and pulmonary tuber-culosis—conditions that tend to affect or are only seen in women (Kurth 1993).

Despite a growing literature on women and HIV/AIDS, coverage of women's issues at international AIDS forums suggests that women are still not at the fore-front of the international agenda. Coverage of women, as a specific concern or infected group in the plenary sessions, did not begin until the Seventh Interna-tional Conference on AIDS in 1991 in Florence, Italy. At that conference, women's specific issues were covered in three out of nine plenary sessions. The discussions focused on prostitutes, incidence, transmission, and health and pre-vention issues. At the Eighth International Conference on AIDS in 1992 in Ams-terdam, HIV/AIDS and women's empowerment became a major conference theme and generated publicity in the popular press. Seven out of twenty sessions addressed issues related to women and AIDS and the discussions covered a broad range of topics on prevention, control, access to health care, physiological man-ifestations, transmission issues, and so on, which related to all women. However, following the attention on women's empowerment, coverage of women's issues decreased at the Ninth International Conference in 1993 in Berlin. Only two out of some twenty-one sessions addressed women's issues, specifically prevention and care, and maternal-fetal transmission. The Tenth International Conference in 1994 in Yokohama devoted only three out of eight sessions to women's issues. The topics on women in these sessions covered control and prevention issues, mater-nal-fetal transmission, and prevention programs for prostitutes.

Early international prevention efforts and research also treated women as vectors transmitting HIV/AIDS to men or their children. Women as prostitutes, and not in their other roles, dominated the research agenda. Little discussion was given to how economic constraints—specifically recession, structural unemployment, and discriminatory labor practices—affected women's growing vulnerability in many locales. The so-called discussions of women's empowerment that came out of the Eighth International Conference rarely went beyond naming the problem. Little time was spent exploring the implications of empowering women, perhaps because such discussions invariably lead to changing social roles and addressing existing structural inequalities. It is far less threatening to pass out condoms to prostitutes than to provide the same women with joint title to property or access to employment and housing programs.

The areas in which women are positive role models and are working to address the effects of HIV/AIDS have received little funding or recognition. Numerous women are volunteering time and services to those sick with HIV/AIDS and are caring for sick children and grandchildren. Yet at international AIDS conferences and meetings, little attention is given to improving care and support systems or to lessening the burdens of care providers. Given limited resources and the magnitude of the epidemic, the international community will have to depend on volunteers. How to support the work of such volunteers or to enlist the aid of others remains to be addressed.

Unfortunately, whatever the approach, the efforts to slow the spread of HIV/AIDS in women of all ages and to lessen the new burdens of this disease on their lives have had little success. By the first half of 1992, women accounted for 50 percent of all new cases of HIV infection worldwide. That same year heterosexual transmission became the leading route of transmission of HIV in American women (Altman 1995:C7). In several countries, women already outnumber men in new infections. Conservative estimates suggest that by the year 2000, more than 13 million women will be infected worldwide (see Buzy and Gayle in this volume). In the United States AIDS is currently the fourth cause of death for women in their productive years (aged twenty to forty-four) and will rise to second place in the next few years (Altman 1995). It is also the leading cause of death in men and women in 79 of 169 U.S. cities (Altman 1995:C7).

Hopes of a vaccine still lie a decade or more away and cost-effective control technologies are not likely to be available for another generation or more. Advances in female-controlled barrier methods are slow because research in this area commands few resources. Although prevention efforts are often quite successful in informing women about HIV/AIDS and its effects, these efforts often fail to address the problem of why women cannot make male partners use condoms or simply refuse to engage in risky sexual practices. Knowledge alone is not sufficient when women do not have the power to act on it. Yet our understandings of the empowered woman are too often informed by what she is not.

In their recent volume, Schneider and Stoller (1995) address the issue of empowerment and provide practical feminist strategies for "women resisting AIDS." Although their work primarily focuses on working-class women and women of color in the United States, the themes they raise may have relevance to the conditions and situations women face in a global context. Schneider and Stoller argue for processes of feminist social change. Specifically, they observe the following:

> For HIV-positive women, empowerment begins when they change their ideas about the causes of their powerlessness, when they recognize the systemic forces that oppress them and stop blaming themselves for their situation, and when they begin to act to change the conditions of their lives. (Schneider and Stoller 1995:5)

Although many women in other parts of the world reject Western "feminist" discourses and ideologies, nevertheless similar processes are occurring as women's NGOs, community groups, and other support groups in many different parts of the world are recognizing that they must act to change the social, economic, cultural, and political forces that constrain their ability to address HIV/AIDS and its effects in their own lives.

Women's Experiences

The desire to inform and empower our own work on HIV/AIDS and women's health from an international perspective was a focus of many conversations surrounding this volume. The early discussions among both women and men focused on how little was being done within our own research, prevention, and control programs to address HIV/AIDS and women. We observed that despite the rhetoric, limited resources were available and most people did not know what could be done to make a difference. Yet even when research pointed in specific directions, the findings were often ignored in the design of large-scale prevention and control programs. Several authors observed that no forums existed to address the most significant aspects of our findings. For example, even when our work was peer reviewed, our colleagues sometimes asked why women's workload is relevant to HIV? Many also failed to see why housing shortages and costs might affect women's risk or that lesbian women could be at risk. At the policy level, we were often asked to insert a brief paragraph on women's issues but little discussion centered on how policies might change significantly to address women.

As a group we are involved in HIV/AIDS programs. Several authors conduct research overseas or domestically (domestic being defined according to the author's place of residence). Some are involved in direct service delivery, administer programs, or design large-scale prevention efforts, whereas others are engaged in determining policies in government and international organizations. Several have been and are involved in all three aspects—research, pro-gramming, and policy formation. Three authors are living with HIV. The contri-butions from these different perspectives demonstrate the centrality of women's experiences in preventing and living constructively with HIV/AIDS.

The authors represent diverse backgrounds, several regions of the world, and three to four generational cohorts. Men and women are involved in this project and contributed to its conceptualization and realization. As a group we share a common concern for the political aspects of HIV/AIDS prevention and control, wishing to ensure that more resources are made available to address HIV/AIDS in women and that existing scarce resources are allocated equitably. Several authors share a common concern of informing and advocating for sociopolitical change. All take the problem of HIV/AIDS in women seriously and believe that more should and can be done.

Five Themes

During the construction of this book, several authors along with others involved in HIV/AIDS research held two meetings about "HIV/AIDS and Women's Experiences." During the meetings, we discussed our own work and elaborated issues we believe are critical to a better understanding of HIV/AIDS and women. From these meetings and subsequent discussions, five organizing themes emerged.

First, women's experiences need to be taken seriously in preventing, con-trolling, and living with HIV/AIDS. By experience, we mean the routines and schedules of women's daily lives, including the time and resources available to them and their relationships to their families, communities, and one another. Women's own knowledge base and particular sets of experiences should shape and inform policies, research, and programs. From the perspective of experi-ence, it is necessary to consider the diversity of girls' and women's lives and how even within that diversity, particular lives change over time. No particular expe-rience can be representative of all women or even of a group of women but in-depth and cross-sectional analyses of different experiences provide insight into HIV/AIDS in women and inform programs, policies, and research.

The idea of taking experience seriously in large part comes from anthropol-ogists and interpretative anthropology. An "anthropology of experience" informs other subjects of research (Bruner 1986) and HIV/AIDS research itself (Farmer 1992; Rudd and Taylor 1992). Experience includes data that are not only sensory, cognitive, and having to do with reason—empiricism in its rawest form—but also feelings, beliefs, and expectations (Bruner 1986:4). However, the researcher can only describe an individual's behaviors and practices, not his or her experiences. Researchers cannot even fully characterize their own experiences. Yet expressions of experiences—writings, conversations, images, and performances—are available to be considered and interpreted.

The process of interpretation of experience is itself an artistic expression which, if treated as scientific fact, can distort or constrain the very material of experience. By interpreting from limited sets of experiences, researchers and practitioners often miss the most significant and insightful details (Sontag 1966). The longitudinal, multidimensional, and evolutionary aspects of particular experiences and situations are compressed and artificially constrained in "Knowledge, Attitude, and Practices" (KAPS) surveys or out-of-context focus groups. Much of HIV/AIDS research, in particular, constrains definitions of knowledge, attitude, and practices and even completely omits sexuality and differing sexual practices. Such constriction reflects a need to bring this disease under control and to create an illusion of more control into our own lives. Yet the cost has been limiting what we know and what we can learn from and about this disease; perhaps, more significant, it is narrowing the way we relate to one another, creating simplistic dichotomies of those with HIV and those without. As Sontag (1978:3) observes, "Although we all prefer to use only the good passport, sooner or later each of us is obliged, at least for a spell, to identify ourselves as citizens of that other place." In this book several authors make a serious attempt to become citizens of that other place, whereas others assess the experiential aspects of their own work or life situations.

A second organizing theme is that women must share a common political concern and recognition of their mutual vulnerability vis-à-vis this disease if they are to mobilize effectively for HIV/AIDS prevention. Recognizing the commonality of women's experiences means moving beyond concepts of risk groups or even risky practices to address the particular contexts of women's lives. For many women who have little control over their sexual decision making, it is important to examine those socioeconomic, cultural, and political aspects that constrain their autonomy (Parker 1995), as well as all women's potential vulnerability to HIV/AIDS. From a political standpoint, it is critical that women without HIV/AIDS recognize their own vulnerability—whether as daughters, wives, lovers, grandmothers, cousins, or friends of those living with HIV—in order to develop a larger political constituency. Portrayals of particular experiences may help in creating common recognition of mutual concerns. From this standpoint, this book has an advocacy role that goes beyond the desire to enlighten and inform.

Third, qualitative versus quantitative distinctions in setting research priorities and paradigms hinder good HIV/AIDS research. Both are needed. Although significant theoretical and epistemological distinctions exist in terms of knowledge bases assumed, relevancy, and truth claims, particular experiences need to be examined qualitatively and common aspects generalized quantitatively. To understand experience, many believe that the basic units of analysis must be established by those living the experience rather than by the scientific observer imposing his or her own external constructions of that experience (Bruner 1986:9). Again, this position would argue for long-term fieldwork rather than simply for "Knowledge, Attitudes, Beliefs, and Practices" (KABPs) surveys or focus groups with their social engineering bias and manipulation of others' lives. However, despite the need for an "anthropology of experience," surveys and epidemiological studies can also shed useful insights on people's experiential and subjective understanding, particularly when the research design and implementation explicitly involve those for whom such knowledge matters.

Runions, an author living with HIV, observes that a colleague's work on the epidemiology speaks to her own particular concerns. The point is that researchers have some obligation in this field to make their information accessible and open to criticism from those with lived experience. Participatory research methodologies, in the overall design, implementation, and reporting of projects and interventions help both to inform those for whom such knowledge is critical and the process itself. Reporting in ways that make critical information accessible to many women, especially those most affected, is also important. This volume represents a beginning in creating such dialogues between researchers, practitioners, policy makers, and woman living with HIV.

Fourth, HIV/AIDS research should be transdisciplinary (Lindenbaum 1992). Women's experience and their experiences with HIV/AIDS cannot be understood or fully represented from the perspective of one particular discipline or by adding together the insights of several disciplines. Most researchers and practitioners work on multidisciplinary projects and teams. Collaboration across and within disciplines or on projects is common but often not reflected in the bureaucratic control of resources whether in academic or governmental institutions. However, the commitment to social change and to developing new theories and understandings that go beyond particular disciplines and perspectives requires multi- and transdisciplinary approaches. All the contributors to this volume make a serious effort to communicate their findings across and beyond their own particular disciplines. This meant defining technical terms for one another, attempting to utilize one another's language where useful and insightful, eschewing jargon, and wherever possible, using specific examples, obvious calculations, and quotations.

Fifth, empowerment needs to become a meaningful concept. Despite the rhetoric heard at international meetings and among the donor community, little discussion focuses on the implications of empowerment in HIV/AIDS research, policy, and programs. As stated earlier, much of what people know about empowerment is its absence. Too often discussions and programmatic attempts suggest the contradictory notion that one can empower someone else.

Empowerment needs to be addressed in empowering terms by bringing girls and women directly into the debates about HIV/AIDS. The political activism of the gay community demonstrates how one community has been able to mobilize, inform, and act. Lessons can be learned from this experience, but invariably there are many communities of women with differing characteristics, life experiences, sexual orientations, and forms of empowerment.

What do an Afghan refugee woman who treks through the mountains with her infant and rifle on her back, an eighteen-year-old woman studying economics in Nairobi, a rural Brazilian woman whose every waking hour is filled with domestic and productive work, a commercial sex worker in New York City, and a former prime minister of Norway have in common?[1]

Gender is only one characteristic among many that people use to distinguish themselves from or unite with others. Skin color, sexual orientation, social class, occupation, lineage, national identity, geographic location, political ideology, and physical status are just a few other dimensions that may have a particular relevance in different women's lives and experiences with HIV/AIDS. Women who are prisoners of private domestic worlds or state-sanctioned violence cannot act until conditions of safety can be assured (Herman 1992).

Although important strategic benefits of global solidarity exist among women and especially among HIV-positive and -negative women (see Ankrah in this volume), the authors illustrate the vast range of women's experiences, priorities, expectations, and resources. Empowerment is also a process and women often need to invent new strategies given the particular circumstances of their lives in order to assert their autonomy. At the same time, international forums, such as those in Beijing and Cairo, provide important opportunities for women's NGOs and community groups to mobilize around issues of common concern and to assert some common human rights concerns.

The Lens of Women's Experience

For many, the experience of HIV silences. The particular social group with whom we spend our time may have a difficult time accepting this part of our lives. Parents and friends may distance themselves from the research we do, the programs we run, the policies we effect, or the illness we have by using medical and scientific jargon and euphemisms, that is, if we are fortunate enough to be heard. Others have to overcome silence and denial. HIV/AIDS is akin to leprosy and tuberculosis in our times. Fear and stigmatization are very much a part of HIV/AIDS and women's experience.

In part one of this book, "Living with HIV," Thomas begins by describing how being HIV-positive has changed her sense of self and forced her to reexamine her primary relationships and daily routines. Although recognizing how her social context and networks led to her intravenous (IV) drug use, Thomas claims full responsibility. She also shows that in coming out about her HIV status, she is more empowered to take responsibility for her actions and find greater meaning in her life.

In article 2, a university professor from East Africa, in contrast, chooses to remain anonymous in writing about her experiences of living with HIV. By her very anonymity she speaks eloquently to the fear and stigma many women face. The professor is angry at her husband who has given her this disease and at the society that silences her. Like Thomas, who has lost her boyfriend, the professor must develop a new support system. Both women experience the everyday aggravations of taking care of children, concern for their future, and dealing with other family members who are not very supportive.

In another personal account, Hunter and Alexander describe the experiences of women who sleep with other women. Hunter and Alexander confront traditional depictions of women's sexuality as "heterosexuality." Too often HIV/AIDS programs put women in rigid social categories of wife, mother, or prostitute—all framed in strictly heterosexual, middle-class Western perspectives. These categories, however, fail to capture the experience of most women, even those whose life-styles most closely approximate some normative, heterosexual ideal. Many women experiment with different ways of having sex with one or more partners, and a large majority have more than one sexual partner in their lives. The denial of women's diverse sexual experiences prevents men and women from relating to one another in more constructive ways—creating simplistic categories of heterosexual, bisexual, and homosexual. This denial also increases everyone's vulnerability.

Runions, from yet another personal perspective, recalls the fear and stigmatization she encounters from being HIV-positive. Her testimonial speaks to middle-class American women who do not identify with any so-called risk group yet do not practice safe sex. As Thomas does, Runions addresses the profound ways in which HIV/AIDS affects relationships and everyday aspects of one's life. Are the university researcher—despite her anonymity—and Thomas being more honest and attuned to their situations than Runions? Runions admits that as a Southern woman she cannot speak about her own anger. Such comparisons, however, ignore the social conditions and cultural contexts that frame each one's responses and interpretations.

Patton (1994:112) observes that an AIDS diagnosis for women usually does not cause the change in social standing or identity that it does for self-identified gay men. However, in these personal accounts, such changes in identity and social awareness (or empowerment) seem to occur or have already occurred.

Each writer describes her own experiences with HIV and what it has meant in her life. The process of analyzing and coming to terms with her experiences—refusing to be silenced or ignored—in itself seems to be a transforming experience for each woman.

Part two of this volume, "Economic and Sociocultural Perspectives," provides case evidence about why women contract HIV/AIDS and the different reasons for women's vulnerability. The first case study examines why women work as prostitutes for intermittent periods of their lives. Alexander, a founder of Coyote—a prostitute's rights organization—debunks the common stereotype of prostitutes as a "risk group." She points out that the average length of time that women engage in this profession is four to five years and that the primary reason women take up this profession is economic. Alexander also describes different strategies women use to protect themselves in this profession and points out that prostitutes have the requisite knowledge about different sexual practices to provide advice to policy makers and intervention planners in designing effective HIV/AIDS prevention and control programs.

From their research in Haiti, Ulin, Cayemittes, and Gringle argue that the taproot of AIDS lies deep in poverty. From a cultural and gender perspective, they observe in Haitian society that women are not expected to enjoy sex but that sex is a medium of exchange to support the woman and her children. Interviewing both men's and women's focus groups, they find that bargaining for condom use can be a logical extension of dispensing sexual favors. However, they advise that interventions cannot rest on the individual woman's ability to negotiate but that specific gender and structural inequalities must be addressed.

In Tanzania, Outwater observes that changing sexual norms and access to foreign men have increased women's vulnerability. However, she also points out actions that individual Tanzanian women have taken to decrease their vulnerability. Specifically, she observes that some women are decreasing the number of sexual partners, engaging less in prostitution, and changing their economic sources of support (e.g., becoming vendors and small business owners). She also observes that the epidemic has improved coordination between NGOs and the formal health care system (i.e., hospitals and clinics) as each sector recognizes that it cannot address this problem alone. She believes that women are gaining new respect in Tanzanian society as caregivers. Her observations support the position of several authors that women are not helpless victims vis-à-vis this disease but face certain vulnerabilities. Women demonstrate different strengths when they are engaged as full partners in control and prevention programs.

In Northern Thailand, Bond, Celentano, and Vaddhanaphuti show how the client-patron relationships of sex workers and brothel owners replicate the social relations of traditional Thai society. These relationships ultimately determine how a woman is able to protect herself from infection. Those working in well-established brothels are better positioned to protect themselves than are the young village girls who are sought after by men for casual sex. At the same time, Bond, Celentano, and Vaddhanaphuti, as does Alexander in her article, observe that girls and women engage in sex work—a life and death strategy— to cope with landlessness and poverty, to support parents and children (in some cases debt bondage), or to flee unhappy and abusive homes.

Klein-Alonso observes the rising incidence of HIV/AIDS among Brazilian women. She suggests that Brazilian women (of all social and economic classes) can no longer consider the consequences of sexual activity only in the context of reproduction but must consider it in the context of protection. Her analysis of women's internal representations suggests why women with a good level of knowledge about AIDS and HIV prevention do not change sexual practices that endanger their lives. Specifically, she analyzes certain feminine archetypes that res- onate in many Brazilian women's experiences. Klein-Alonso then shows how these archetypes may be invoked to elicit women's own deepest assumptions and feel- ings and to challenge existing conceptions of traditional attitudes and practices.

In the final case study, Kirmani and Munyakho address the effects of structural adjustment programs on women's vulnerability. Debates about structural adjust- ment programs (SAPs) in Africa in many ways raise the same issues as debates about social welfare reform and the role of government in the United States and Western Europe. Kirmani and Munyakho go beyond the simplistic debate about whether SAPs are necessarily detrimental or beneficial to analyze short- versus long-term effects of these reforms in the East African context. They see three short-term effects that affect women's vulnerability: (1) changes in public expen- ditures (particularly for health care and education); (2) changes in prices (espe- cially food); and (3) changes in income and working conditions. Similarly, in the United States and Europe, women's access to government benefits and services (social safety nets) and their access to the labor market and employment oppor- tunities affect their vulnerability. In East Africa the adverse effects of structural adjustment (at least in the short term) often fall on women, resulting in longer and harder working days for women. Kirmani and Munyakho emphasize the need to evaluate the gender effects of SAPs. From specific case evidence of women's experiences, they argue that "AIDS reflects to a large extent the real value of the uncompensated and often unrecognized social contribution of women."

Part three of this book, "Issues and Concerns," addresses particular problems that all women face in a time of HIV/AIDS (Herdt 1992). The first essay in this section, article 11, written by two epidemiologists, addresses how women worldwide are being affected by this disease. Buzy and Gayle provide evidence that women constitute an increasing number of the new cases and that by the year 2000, the majority of those afflicted with the disease will be women. They also discuss the geographical dispersion of HIV/AIDS—women in Asia and Africa are the most heavily affected—and the difficulties of obtaining accurate prevalence rates in many countries.

In article 12, Parker and Patterson show how the increasing rates of sexually transmitted diseases (STDs) (other than AIDS) contribute to the spread of HIV/AIDS. They cite estimates of 250 million new infections of STDs annually but point out that incidence and prevalence rates are much higher in most of Asia and Africa than in the United States or Western Europe. Parker and Patterson argue that preventing and treating STDs is critical to HIV/AIDS prevention and control worldwide. They also observe that low-cost investments in prevention in other countries have relevance to industrialized, Western countries as well. Specifically, they recommend identifying and treating vulnerable groups; informing, educating, and communicating with women and men about STDs; continuing to develop simple, inexpensive diagnostic tests; providing integrated health services (e.g., integrating STD diagnosis and treatment in family planning or maternal and child health programs); and creating one-stop shop services. The last recommendation is important for increasing access to health services given the numerous demands on women's time and responsibilities worldwide.

In article 13, O'Gara and Martin describe how HIV/AIDS affects women's choices about breast-feeding. They caution that misinformation and a lack of information about whether HIV-positive women should breast-feed may have a profoundly negative effect—particularly in resource-poor countries—on women's breast-feeding choices (comparable to earlier infant formula campaigns). O'Gara and Martin examine the current state of knowledge about how and to what extent HIV/AIDS is passed through breast milk. They point out that rates of transmission from HIV-positive mothers vary from 18 to 52 percent among breast-fed babies and 25 to 33 percent among bottle-fed babies. Transmission is most likely when the mother is experiencing viremia (explosive multiplication of the virus shortly after infection). O'Gara and Martin further observe that breast milk may also inhibit the bonding of GP120 to the CD4 receptor. They suggest that rather than recommending unilaterally that HIV-positive women should not breast-feed or that only HIV women in developing countries should breast-feed, all women need access to more and better information about their possible risks in order to make informed choices.

HIV/AIDS also affects women's relationships with their children. Auer's analysis of these relationships in article 14 covers an HIV-positive woman's decision to carry a pregnancy to term as well as her decisions about foster care for her children after her death. Auer provides several case examples from her work with women and children in a North Carolina clinic and with international programs. She points out the difficulties of detecting HIV/AIDS in newborns and the prohibitive costs of antiretroviral therapies. She also addresses the challenges women face in caring for their children who are HIV-positive. One of the most difficult experiences an HIV-positive mother faces is knowing that her own fate will be mirrored in her child and that she will not be there to help that child. Auer argues for the necessity of better support services for women and their families who are living with HIV/AIDS.

In the final essay of this section, article 15, Ankrah, Schwartz, and Miller examine care and support systems at a time when women themselves are making increasing demands on these systems. Women are often the primary care givers for HIV/AIDS patients in many societies, particularly when care options are limited. The authors define the difference between care and support, and point out that care and support systems need to function synergistically in order to meet women's needs. They also call for cooperation and solidarity between HIV-positive and -negative women to meet the challenge of HIV/AIDS.

In part four, "Promising Directions," several authors propose recommendations for improving women's experiences with HIV/AIDS, including prevention and control strategies for women. In article 16, Preble and Siegel review the experiences of women in the 1980s—the first decade of this disease for women—and outline promising interventions and directions for the second decade—the 1990s. They argue that lessons can and should be learned from family-planning programs in nonindustrialized societies. As other authors before them, they also argue for involving women in the design and implementation of policies and programs.

Along similar lines, Cash, in article 17, derives lessons from her experience in developing HIV/AIDS and public health programs in urban America, Malawi, and northern Thailand. From her work Cash believes that peer education programs for adolescent girls and women in workplace settings are very effective. Cash observes that the pervasive ideology that good girls do not get AIDS and the silence around women's sexuality increases girls and women's vulnerability in many locales. However, she also believes that educational strategies can be effective and outlines some exemplary materials and methodologies. In Thailand, for example, Cash developed a comic book that used humor to initiate discussions about condoms. This book helped educators to address sensitive topics in culturally appropriate ways and encouraged communication among peers.

Gupta, Weiss, and Mane, in article 18, summarize their important findings from the International Center for Research on Women (ICRW). ICRW's program on women and AIDS includes seventeen applied research studies in Latin America, Asia, and Africa. Using data from these studies, the authors outline what is learned by incorporating a gender perspective and accounting for gender roles and relationships. Globally, they observe that women's fears of violence often make it difficult for them to practice safe sex. The authors recommend a multifaceted approach for disease prevention aimed at improving women's economic status, providing information about sex and HIV prevention, and including fathers, sons, husbands, and parents in HIV/AIDS prevention programs.

In the next article, Elias and Heise summarize their findings about effective barrier methods for women and the development of female-controlled vaginal microbicides. They observe that typical prevention efforts aimed at partner reduction, condom promotion, and control of STDs are inadequate. Given widespread gender inequalities women need a prevention technology that does not depend on their partner's consent. However, several scientific challenges remain for developing an effective vaginal, noncontraceptive microbicide. These range from defining the chemical and physical properties of potential microbicides to elucidating the exact biological mechanism of HIV transmission. They also discuss the feasibility of designing clinical trials that are scientifically valid and ethically defensible. Elias and Heise call for public-sector leadership as well as collaboration between the public and private sectors.

Kendall, too, examines the ethics of research on HIV/AIDS and women. In article 20, he argues for ethical principles to ensure autonomy (i.e., freedom from coercion), beneficence (i.e., that the research will not cause harm), and justice (i.e., that the research benefits the participants, the community, and the society at large). He also evaluates several research approaches, including large-scale, structured surveys, focus groups, and ethnographic approaches and argues for those that inherently assume women's participation.

Finally, in the epilogue Ankrah and I outline an agenda for action. In this agenda we argue that women and men working together can do more to address the negative consequences of HIV/AIDS in women's lives. Given the escalating number of women affected and inflicted, governments and donors need to recognize that HIV/AIDS in women is and should be an urgent matter. Using the insights gained from women's experiences, however, it is possible to design innovative and creative approaches for addressing one of the most difficult social problems affecting all women and men.

Losing Ground?

Women worldwide appear to be losing ground on many fronts—economically, politically, socially, and personally. In their daily struggle with HIV/AIDS, they often lose ground as well. However, the belief that no one individual or community can make a difference is itself disempowering. Such pessimism reflects in large part the complexities of social existence. Even as women throughout the world grow closer through different forms of communication, political leaders, and the media, even some women's groups promote divisiveness and fear of others. A crisis such as HIV/AIDS challenges basic premises and assumptions, people's trust and faith in their future, and tolerance. The experience of living or coping with HIV/AIDS can also enlarge our differences as people distinguish themselves from others in order to create an illusion of greater control over their lives. Gender differences along with other social attributes, including class, ethnicity, race, and geographic location, may increase as more women are afflicted and this crisis deepens. Yet it will be a tragedy for everyone if we allow our differences to divide us in our willingness to respond. As this volume shows, the diversity of other experiences and ways of addressing this disease must be recognized and respected if we are to make any headway in preventing, controlling, and living with HIV/AIDS.

REFERENCES

Altman, Lawrence K. 1995. AIDS is now the leading killer of Americans from 25 to 44. *The New York Times*, January 31, 1995, C7.

Anastos, Kathryn and Sten H. Vermund. 1993. Epidemiology and natural history. In Ann Kurth, ed. *Until the Cure: Caring for Women with HIV*, 144–64. New Haven: Yale University Press.

Berer, Marge (with Sunanda Ray). 1993. *Women and HIV/AIDS: An International Resource Book*. London: Pandora.

Bruner, Edward M. 1986. Experience and its expressions. In Victor Turner and Edward M. Bruner, eds., *The Anthropology of Experience*, 3–32. Urbana: University of Illinois Press.

Bury, Judy, Val Morrison, and Sheena McLachlan. 1992. *Working with Women and AIDS: Medical, Social, and Counseling Issues*. London: Routledge.

Center for Women Policy Studies. 1992. *The Guide to Resources on Women and AIDS*. Washington, D.C.: The Center.

Chen, Lincoln C., et al. 1991. In J. S. Amor and Sheldon J. Segal, eds., *AIDS and Women's Reproductive Health*. New York: Plenum.

Corea, Jena. 1992. *The Invisible Epidemic: The Story of Women*. New York: Harper.

Day, Sophie. 1988. Editorial review. Prostitute women and AIDS: Anthropology. *AIDS* 2:421–28.

de Zalduondo, Barbara O. 1991. Prostitution viewed cross-culturally: Toward recontextualizing sex work in AIDS intervention research. *Journal of Sex Research* 28 (2).

Dorn, Nicholas, Sheila Henderson, and Nigel South. 1992. *AIDS: Women, Drugs, and Social Care*. London: Falmer.

Farmer, Paul. 1992. *AIDS and Accusation: Haiti and the Geography of Blame*. Berkeley: University of California Press.

Feldman, Douglas A. 1994. *Global AIDS Policy*. Westport, Conn.: Bergin and Garvey.

Hankins, Catherine A. and Margaret A. Handley. 1992. Review: HIV disease and AIDS in women: Current knowledge and a research agenda. *Journal of Acquired Immune Deficiency Syndrome* 5:957–71.

Herdt, Gilbert. 1992. Introduction. In Gilbert Herdt and Shirley Lindenbaum, eds., *The Time of AIDS: Social Analysis, Theory, and Method*, 3–26. Newbury Park, Calif.: Sage.

Herman, Judith Lewis. 1992. *Trauma and Recovery: The Aftermath of Violence from Domestic Abuse to Political Terror*. New York: Basic Books.

Kurth, Ann, ed. 1993. *Until the Cure: Caring for Women with HIV*. New Haven: Yale University Press.

LaGuardia, Katherine D. 1991. AIDS and reproductive health: Women's perspecives. In Amor and Segal, eds., *AIDS and Women's Reproductive Health*, 817–25. New York: Plenum.

Lindenbaum, Shirley. 1992. Knowledge and action in the shadow of AIDS. In Herdt and Lindenbaum, eds., *The Time of AIDS*, 319–34.

Messersmith, Lisa Jean. 1991. The multi-dimensionality of the lives of commercial sex workers in Bamako, Mali. Unpublished paper presented at the American Anthropological Association Annual Meeting, Chicago, Illinois.

Parker, Richard. 1995. Conceiving sexuality. In Richard Parker and John H. Gagnon, eds., *Conceiving Sexuality*, 3–19. New York: Routledge.

Patton, Cindy. 1990. *Inventing AIDS*. New York: Routledge.

——. 1994. *Last Served? Gendering the HIV Pandemic*. Social Aspects of AIDS Series. London: Taylor and Francis.

Reid, Elizabeth, ed. 1995. *HIV and AIDS: The Global Inter-Connection*. United Nations Development Program (UNDP). West Hartford, Conn.: Kumarian.

Rudd, Andrea and Darien Taylor, eds. 1992. *Positive Women: Voices of Women Living with AIDS*. Toronto: Second Story.

Rwabukwali, Charles B., et al. 1994. Culture, sexual behavior, and attitudes toward condom use among Baganda women. In Feldman, ed. *Global AIDS Policy*.

Schneider, Beth E. and Nancy E. Stoller. 1995. *Women Resisting AIDS: Feminist Strategies of Empowerment*. Philadelphia: Temple University Press.

Schoepf, Brooke Grundfest. 1992. Women at risk: case studies from Zaire. In Herdt and Lindenbaum, *The Time of AIDS*, 259–86.

Seidel, Gill. 1993. The competing discourses of HIV/AIDS in sub-Saharan Africa: Discourses of rights and empowerment vs. discourses of control and exclusion. *Journal of Social Science Medicine* 36 (3): 175–94.

Shilts, Randy. 1988. *And the Band Played On: Politics, People, and the AIDS Epidemic*. New York: Penguin.

Sontag, Susan. 1966. *Against Interpretation*. New York: Anchor.

——. 1978. *Illness As Metaphor and AIDS and Its Metaphors*. New York: Anchor.

Squire, Corinne, ed. 1993. *Women and AIDS*. London: Sage.

Wagner, Krystn, and Judith Cohen. 1993. Programs and policies for prevention. In: Kurth, Ann. *Until the Cure: Caring for Women with HIV*. New Haven: Yale University Press.

Worth, Dooley. 1989. Sexual decision-making and AIDS: Why condom promotion among vulnerable women is likely to fail. *Studies in Family Planning* 20 (6): 297–307.

PART ONE

Living with HIV/AIDS

1 | Negative in the Beginning, Positive in the End

CHRISTINE THOMAS (WITH LYNELLYN D. LONG)

Diagnosis

I was diagnosed with the virus in 1989. Andre, my baby of four months, and I were in DC General Hospital at the same time. We kept getting fevers. My son was hospitalized first and had been there about two weeks on the pediatric side, and I was on the adult side. I didn't even think about HIV. I just couldn't understand why we kept getting these infections. When they asked me, "Can we test you and your son for the AIDS virus?" I said, "Sure, why not. Okay." I never suspected we might test positive.

It took three days to get the results. Ten doctors—all men—showed up in my hospital room. There were so many of them, they couldn't all fit in the room. The chief said, "I have some bad news and some good news. Which do you want first?" "The good news," I replied. "You're only HIV-positive," he replied. "What's the bad news, then?" I asked. "Your son has full-blown AIDS." I felt like dirt, like the scum of the earth, when they brought all those students in there to tell me. I said to them, "Do all these people have to be in here?"

The head doctor tried to give me a lot of hope—false hope it turned out. He told me about another woman down the hall. "Her baby passed," he said, "But she went into remission and doesn't have the virus anymore." He was dumb about the facts. I questioned him about what could be done for my son. "He may live with AIDS. The fever is gone, the infection is gone," he told me, giving false hope. That was wrong as well. I went home, but over the next month Andre deteriorated rapidly. I used to go to the hospital every day to see him. He had so many IVs in him, there were no veins left. They even stuck IVs in his head. It was sad.

Andre's father and I had been together for six months. When I learned I was pregnant, the father told me he was married and went back to his wife. I never saw him again until Andre was in the hospital about to die. I didn't want to tell him that his son had AIDS. But a lady said, "You have to. You have to tell him that his son is dying." So I did, and he went to see his son a week before Andre died.

The day Andre passed, I was working at the uniform company. A lady called me at work. I knew it then, even before she told me. I felt so guilty when I saw Andre. I took my child and held him for fifteen or twenty minutes. "I'm sorry," I told him, "If I had known— " But I wanted a son. Later, in 1991, I had Larry. By then, a doctor at the National Institutes of Health (NIH) told me that even with HIV I could have a child and there would be a 70 percent chance that the child could live a healthy, normal life. Larry was planned.

My own reaction when I learned I had the virus was "Why me? How could this happen? When? What am I going to do now?" Even though I was HIV-positive, I didn't want to tell anybody.

At first I started out trying to take everyone I could with me. I didn't tell any of the men I slept with. Then I remembered when my son died, and I knew I couldn't do it to someone else. I started taking care of my health in 1992. Every guy I had slept with I went around and made amends. Most of them thought I was joking. A few, like the guy who had lived with me for three years, said, "Well, you've got to die from something." Some told me later that they tested negative.

I encountered a lot of prejudice with the virus. Doctors would walk into the room and when they found out what I had, they would walk out and never come back. Some friends never called me again. I was torn from my family, too. In the beginning I lived here and there with friends. I didn't want to tell anyone at first that I had the virus.

I got an apartment in Anacostia with the Very Low Income Purchase Assistance (VPAP) program—finally the first place of my own. Every year my mortgage went up until it was almost $500 a month, not including gas, electricity, telephone, and three children. Finally I couldn't afford it anymore and was about to be evicted. I became suicidal and called the suicide hot line.

I told the counselor at the hotline that I was HIV-positive and tired of living. I could see myself deteriorating. I saw my eyes sunken, my cheek bones thinning. I can often see the virus changing a person's appearance now, especially when they get to the last stages. I see their frames changing in their body, becoming like skeletons. The suicide hotline told me about the Whitman Walker Clinic. A case manager referred me to their housing, and in June 1994 I moved to McKinney House with my three children and my fiancé.

Sometimes I feel like an outcast living up here in the Northwest. Somehow

I never wanted to live here without other family members or friends. I feel alone, even though my family isn't very far away. They could easily come up on the metro, but they don't. I think it is because of their prejudice, their fear and ignorance of the virus. I still feel empty not having a family around—sometimes I go into bouts of thinking.

I wonder a lot about when and where I got the virus. Why can't they tell you how it is contracted? Why can't they tell by the infection you have how long you have had it? I often think about that. They recorded that I've had the virus since 1989, but I know it has been longer. It bothers me a lot not knowing exactly when and where and how long I've had it.

Drug Use

There are three ways I could have gotten the virus. I'm a former IV drug user. That's how I think I got it. I also had a blood transfusion in 1985 after a saline abortion. I could have gotten it from someone I slept with, too, but I don't think so.

I had the abortion at DC General. They gave me a saline injection and just left me there on a bed in the room. When the baby started to come, I was supposed to push that beeper. I delivered the baby myself. It was the most difficult delivery I ever had. After that, they came and cut the cord. I was sick for two or three weeks. They told me not to get up for anything, not even to go to the bathroom. But I thought I was strong enough and so I got up. I passed out. It was late at night, and the only way they knew I fell was that the IV pole fell over, too. Otherwise I would have hemorrhaged to death. They immediately gave me two pints of blood. That blood could have been contaminated. But I don't think so.

I think it was the drugs. In those years, I was living wild: dealing, using, having sex, everything. I was running the streets. I would be gone sometimes two weeks at a time. I didn't care about anything. Those were my wild years. I was wild on the drugs out there. It was 1982, right after I had my second daughter, and I was twenty at the time. I did drugs—heroin—for two years. Before that I was selling it.

Some of the people I grew up with, that was what they did. In our neighborhood, several big drug dealers passed out packages in the morning. The packages included a couple of bags for my own profit (or to use myself). After I sold my package, I would turn in the money and get a profit at the end of the night. It was nice to make $1000 on a Friday night. Every morning I used to give drugs to some lady, who was seriously addicted, from my personal profit bags.

One day I was curious and wanted to see what the drugs felt like. I knew how drugs made people look, but I wanted to see how people felt when they took them. Curiosity got me, nothing more. The lady I used to give the drugs to said to me, "You don't want to do this." But I told her that if she didn't let me try it, I wouldn't give her any more drugs. She injected them for me, because I didn't have a clue how to do it. I liked the way they made me feel. I didn't stop until I was arrested two years later.

I grew up in that life-style. Everyone was doing it. It was nice going out every night. I was working at a nursing home at the time and ran in the streets when I wasn't working. I started shooting up in the morning, continued all day, and then shot up again before I went to bed.

It was only when I was arrested that I stopped. I was arrested out in the street for possession of heroin. What that judge said to me stopped me from ever going back to drugs. When she locked me up, she said, "I'm not locking you up because you are a menace to society, but you do not have the willpower to stop." If I hadn't been arrested, I would have been dead in a month. My drug tolerance was 99.5 percent at the time. Later, I went back to the DC courts and found the same judge and thanked her for saving my life.

I only stayed locked up in jail for two weeks, after which they immediately transferred me to CADAC (Comprehensive Alcohol Drug Abuse Center), a long-term drug program at St. Elizabeth's. I went through eight months of treatment: "Admissions" for two months; "Intense Treatment" for three months; and "Transition" for three months.

I was bullheaded when I was in Transition. I went to the University of the District of Columbia (UDC) for an eight-week training program as a home health aid. Then I got a job, but my problem was managing my money. You had to show that you could budget and save money before you could leave the program. Finally I broke bad. At eight months I walked out at midnight with my boxes and never went back. All I had had when I arrived was one pair of jeans, a blouse, and a coat—the same clothes I was wearing when I was arrested. By the time I left, I had accumulated a lot of clothes, shoes, hair supplies, and other things, which I had bought shopping. I would go shopping every pay period, which was why I couldn't budget my money. For six months after that, I was on probation.

Early Years/Growing Up

My aunt looked after my two daughters while I was in CADAC. She was given custody of them by the court when I was arrested, because I had written her name down as next of kin, in case of an emergency. I raised my daughters on public assistance. After I was arrested, I signed my checks over to my aunt.

I know that she didn't look after my daughters as well as I would have liked.

She raised them the way she raised me. At least I know that my aunt treated the oldest one the way she treated me. The youngest got what she wanted. It was the same way my aunt treated me and my cousin.

My mother died when I was eight. She suffocated in a car with the motor running. She and the man with her died of carbon monoxide poisoning. It was June 1969. They said she committed suicide. I don't know if she did or not. My mother was also living with the same aunt at the time. We had moved in with her when I was about two years old.

I don't know who or where my father is. They used to tell a story in my family that when I was born, my mother was seeing an African man at the time who was black as soot. My mother brought him home and said he was the father. But when he saw me [light-skinned with sandy red hair], he gave my mother ten dollars, jumped over the fence, and never came back. He knew right away I was not his child.

When my mother died, my aunt raised me and my two brothers. There were six of us altogether. I was the youngest daughter. After me, there was only one younger brother. My oldest brother and sister never lived with my aunt. After my mother's death, my older sister moved out when she turned sixteen. My older brother, my younger brother, and I stayed with my aunt. Because of the separation, we were not a close-knit family.

My life as a child with my aunt is a Cinderella story. I had to do all the cleaning, grocery shopping, and picking up after everyone else. My cousin [my aunt's grand-daughter by her first marriage] was the princess. Later the princess left my aunt, moved to Chicago, and got married. My aunt has a lot of grandchildren, but her daughter and I are the only ones who keep in contact with her.

My grandfather also lived in my aunt's house. It was a three- or four-bedroom house. He was a diabetic. He had had his legs amputated because of the diabetes and sat in a wheelchair. When I was a little girl, I was afraid of him. He used to watch us from the upstairs bedroom window and tell my aunt everything we did. I had to go past his bedroom and would try to run every time I got to his door. He would whip us if we said we didn't want to come by. Because I was so scared of him and didn't want to see him, I got a lot of whippings. He died when I was about five years old.

I favor my mother a lot. Her face had a birthmark and was molded on the left side. My aunt used to say that my mother ran the streets a lot. "You're just like your mother; ain't nothing, never were nothing, and ain't never going to be nothing," my aunt would tell me. She says the same to my oldest daughter. My daughter, Quianda, also looks like me, which is why I think my aunt treated my daughter that way.

When I lived with her, my aunt was married to her second husband. He was evil. I really had a hard childhood. My aunt and uncle always had enough for my cousin. My cousin got whatever she wanted. Sometimes I had to wear the same clothes to school all week long. They never had any money for us. I could never be in the school pictures or things like that. "We don't have the money," my aunt said, even though she was getting our social security checks. Later I reported her to social security, but not until I was already sixteen.

My uncle beat us a lot—me and my two brothers—but not our cousin. Usually my cousin wasn't there. I was glad when she came over, because her visits saved us from the beatings. When she was there, they would want to party more than fight. After I turned fourteen, my uncle touched me sexually. When I told my aunt, all she said was "Well, what does he want with you? You ain't no good." Even though some people blame the past for their choice of a life-style, I'm not one to put that on my drug use. I made my own decision about drugs.

As long as I can remember, there was a whipping every Friday night. My uncle would get paid on Friday and come home drunk from work. My aunt would close the living room door and stay in her bedroom until she was tired of hearing the noise.

When he tried to abuse me sexually, I told my aunt. She didn't do anything. The next time he tried, I said, "If you ever put your hands on me again, I'll kill you." He had come home drunk and raised his hand to hit me again. He stopped when I stood up to him. "This girl is losing her mind," he said. But after that he left me alone and never hit me again.

At fourteen I ran away to live with my older sister. I walked across the South Capital Street Bridge to my sister's apartment in Anacostia. After the first three or four months, she kicked me out and sent me back to my aunt's. I had already stayed with my sister the summer before. When I ran away, I lied and told my sister that my aunt had sent me. But my sister called my aunt one day and my aunt said, "Oh, that's where she is." After my sister sent me back, I stayed another week and a half at my aunt's until she beat me with a telephone. When my sister saw the bruises on my face, she let me move back in with her. I didn't move back in with my aunt again until I was nineteen.

Relationships

I dropped out of school in the tenth grade when I became pregnant in 1979 with my first daughter. I was seventeen at the time. I was no longer interested in school when I got pregnant. I got pregnant with someone who lived in the same neighborhood. He picked our daughter up from the hospital. When he had a job, he bought her pampers and milk.

I named my first daughter "Quianda"—a name I made up. In 1982, when I was twenty years old, I had my second daughter, Raymonda, by the same father. I named her after their father, Raymond.

Raymond was later shot to death running his mouth off. I was working as a cashier supervisor at the Flagship Restaurant at the time. I worked at the Flagship a couple of years after working in a nursing home in Maryland. Raymond was having an argument with the owner of a bar-and-grill restaurant. He didn't get along with the owner. The owner threatened to kill him if Raymond messed with him. The owner told him, "If you don't get off my premises, I'll shoot you." Raymond answered, "Well, shoot me then."

A few days before he died, Raymond asked me to marry him. The night he was killed, I was supposed to pick up the engagement rings. We had been living together off and on. He was a part-time roofer when he wasn't running the streets. I didn't show up that night. To this day I feel guilty about that. I often think that maybe if I had shown up, he wouldn't have gone to the bar-and-grill. They caught the owner but he got off on self-defense. Raymond had worked long enough for his daughters to receive survival social security.

In 1985 I had the saline abortion. I was messing around with someone at the time. I didn't want to have any more children if they were not going to be taken care of by the father. In 1989 I had my son, Andre, the one who died from AIDS. Then, in 1991, I had Larry. The first year, his father did great. He was really interested in Larry. But that ended when he noticed that I had "another man around my son." That was my fiancé, Robert, who died this past February.

Robert was my soul mate. I had known Robert since I was eleven years old. We lived in the same neighborhood. I first started going with Robert just before I ran away. He gave me the confidence to talk back to the family, to stand up for myself. Robert would say, "Be aggressive." He was like my hero. When I was fourteen, he wanted us to get together. His mother, who was supposed to be my godmother, didn't approve of that. I was too young, she thought. Robert was seventeen and in and out of jail. He was mainly there for robbery. The last time he was arrested, it was for armed robbery. He did eleven years in the Maryland penitentiary that time, and that is what separated us.

We got together again when Robert ran into my eldest sister and asked how I was doing and where I was. I was living in my place in Anacostia at the time. He gave my sister his phone number and told me to call. I finally caught up with him through his mother. When I caught up with him we went out for three weeks, and then he moved in with me. I knew I had always wanted to be with him. I always used to tell other men, "You'll never be like Robert."

When I was young Robert told me how to hold my head up. He convinced me that I wasn't an ugly duckling. "You're so beautiful," he told me. Robert went to jail once trying to get me a winter coat. He also told me to report my aunt to social security.

Robert was a strong, firm man, kind and caring. I depended on him to take care of me. Robert had another child, a daughter named Robin, who we were raising. He had gone through a custody battle to get her. He also had a job as a cook's assistant. On top of that, he did everything for the family—cleaned the house, washed the clothes, cooked the food, helped the children with their homework, and chastised them when necessary. He was the only father they ever had. After my first experiences with doctors, I had stopped going for visits and taking care of myself. I was ready to die. Robert made me want to live again and was instrumental in my going again to the doctor.

This past February Robert was shot to death in my apartment. He got into an arguement with my niece's boyfriend. First they were fist-fighting. Then knives were pulled out, and the fight escalated. I saw Robert run to the utility drawer and I jumped between the two. My niece called the cops. When the DC cop walked in, she shot Robert in his neck, hip, and back. The coroner's report said that he died within the first thirty seconds.

The fight started as a verbal altercation over my oldest daughter. Quianda came home upset and ran downstairs. I don't know what upset her—one of those teenage moods. Robert followed her downstairs to find out what was wrong. My daughter kept saying, "Leave me alone." "What's wrong with her?" Robert asked. My niece's boyfriend said, "Why don't you just leave her alone!" Robert was very sensitive and emotional about my children. That started the fight.

When I lost Robert, I also lost Robin. The courts gave her back to the legal guardian who Robert had fought with to get her. She was all I had left of him, and they took her from me. I still have to go to a court hearing about Robert's case. I don't think they'll do anything to the cop. She's working in an office now while the case is pending. Quianda has low self-esteem since Robert's death. She's had very traumatic dreams about him. Larry is very protective of me. He won't sleep in his own bed now. He began bed-wetting after Robert died.

Robert died to keep me alive. When he was alive I let him take care of me. He did everything for me sometimes. I wasn't taking responsibility for going on. Because of Robert and all that has happened, I have to go on and I feel much stronger now.

Living with HIV: The Future

I still have mood swings and problems with my self-esteem. I have my ups and downs. Most of the time I feel pretty good. I'm kind of fortunate. My T-cell count is about 190/189, but it goes up and down. It has been down as low as 160, but it has also gone up to 215. I can tell whether a medication is working. I tell the doctor what kind of medications I want to take depending on the side effects. I tried AZT and felt fine, but then my white cell count dropped. I tried DDI, but it affected my pancreas. A medication works for awhile, but then I think one becomes immune. When I decided to stop taking DDI, I preferred to let the virus take its course. Now I'm on this experimental drug—3TC. So far it's all right.

I've drawn up a will. I decided that the two girls will go with their god-mother, Shirley. When everyone else threw me away, Shirley took me in. I met Shirley more than ten years ago down in front of Hechts at a bus stop. I was trying to catch a bus to the jail in Lorton to see an old friend of mine. Shirley saw that I didn't know how it all worked. There was a long line of people, and everyone was pushing and shoving to get on the bus. "Come on up here with me!" she said, and she got me in line. "Just stick with me—you'll be all right," she told me, and I've been sticking with her ever since.

After Quianda's and Raymonda's father died and I lost my job, I was living here and there. Shirley and I, along with her two children, slept on the sofa bed in her mother's living room. There were too many people in her mother's apartment, so we decided to go to a shelter called the House of Ruth. We went in, filled out the forms, and while we were sitting in the lobby area waiting for beds, we saw some pretty wild people dressed in chains and boots. We realized that we couldn't stay there and left before they found us a place. We went back to Shirley's mother's apartment. We stayed there until we found an apartment together on our own.

Shirley lives in the Southeast and has her own home now. She has two jobs: one as a legal secretary and the other as a special police officer for a security company. She is used to the girls, but it would be too much to have her take Larry, too. Quianda thinks it is fine to live with Shirley, but she says, "Mom, you're not going to die. I'll be out of the house before that happens." Raymonda is equally protective and always concerned about how I feel and that I eat properly. She loves school and I hope she keeps that with her. I know someday that all my children will make me proud.

In the will I wrote that Larry will go to my oldest sister. My sister works in a pediatrician's office and has an apartment in the Southeast not far from Shirley's. I'm not sure about that decision. My sister was recently diagnosed with diabetes. I'm not really worried about that because I know the Lord will make a way.

I have the children in counseling. We have family and private therapy. They are about to close our case with the family therapy. The therapist taught us how to put our feelings into perspective.

I'm not active in any church but I have a strong belief in the Lord and, on many days, that is where I get my strength, through my prayers.

I'm a strong woman, I know, but mentally I've lost a whole lot. Some days the virus makes me forget things. I have to write everything down. When I first started caring again, I was living for my children, but I realized that I had to live for myself. I started for my children, but now it is for myself.

My daughters say sometimes, "Mom, you're just selfish." I talk to them a lot about my past, the things I've done and the mistakes I've made. I tell my daughters, "There is no reason for you to follow in my footsteps." At first, I was holding on to them too tight and would get all stressed out if they got a C on their report cards. The kids see the change in me now. I used to holler and scream a lot, but now I don't let them stress me out as much. With teenagers there is a lot of stress and I can't let them get to me. Last year my second daughter was getting in trouble for fighting and was being put out of school. This year I told her, "If you get put out again, I'm not going to take you back." She doesn't believe me but she keeps staring, wondering what's wrong with me. I want her to take responsibility for her actions. My oldest daughter has a bet with her male friend. He's told her that he'll give her $20 for an A and $10 for a B. That's just between them, but Raymonda feels left out and is jealous of that. "Mom, can't I have $20 for an A?" she asks.

When they all start fighting, I tell them, "There will come a time when you will need each other. You've got to stick together. I wish I was raised with my family."

Since I've had the virus, I've met several friends who don't have the virus but have a lot of confidence in me. Because they believe in me, they are always pushing me to do something more. "Let's call Christine. She'll do it," they'll say. For example, the Whitman Walker Clinic put me on their Management Committee Board. I told them, "I don't think you all need me on this Board of Representatives." In the meetings we talk mostly about leases and financing—things I don't know much about. But they insist that I stay on the Board. So I'm the representative for McKinney House.

When the cure comes, I'll start over again. First I'll go back to school and get my GED. I always wanted to be a social worker. I don't have the patience for all that right now. Before, when I didn't care, I'd think I'm dying anyway. But now I'm living with this virus. Who's to say that I'm going to die with this? I'll be here when the cure gets here.

ACKNOWLEDGMENTS

My life has not been a bed of roses, but there are people in my life that made me feel just that special, so I would like to take this time to say thanks to all. But first I would like to thank God for being my higher power. Then there are those who let me know I am loved and not alone and will never be as long as I have life. Like I said, negative in the beginning, positive in the end, my belief is that I will be here when the cure gets here. Thank you Stephanie McAllister, Eric Faggan, Rob Micheals, Fenner Urghart, Thereasa Abell, Sallie Crowder, and a host of other people who know who they are. I love you all and thank you for being there for me.

2 I Have a Life, I Will Live

ANONYMOUS

I was born in a small remote village in East Africa, where sharing and collective activities and actions were the norm. Children were supposed to listen to every adult member in the community, and, in return, their well-being was the responsibility of every adult. Except for a few families that had been influenced heavily by Christianity, education was not a priority for girls or boys, although boys usually were considered first if there was any chance for schooling. My parents had been exposed to some Christian influence, and I guess it was because of this that most of the children in our family had a chance to go to school. My father's dream had always been for one of his daughters to be a teacher, so that the rest of the community would envy him for the decision he had made. It was a bit of a disappointment for him when I opted to pursue further studies, because this meant I was lessening my chance of getting a marital partner. The ideal I was raised with was that a girl should get a certificate and then get a husband.

I want the reader to understand that I am still very attached to the small village where I was born. Part of my strength to live comes from my feeling of indebtedness to them. They expect a lot from me, and I have always tried not to make them lose hope in me.

My school life was very smooth, although, as I already indicated, it was against many odds. I had to prove myself capable of competing with boys to win my father's support and to convince him willingly to sell something in order to raise the money to pay my school fees. I did it, and managed to sift through the educational system which was predominantly male. In 1983 I graduated with honors from the oldest university in my country, married a year later, and had a baby boy within the first year of marriage. By any standards, therefore, I had proved myself a very successful woman.

After my graduation, I got a job with a very good and reputable organization, but my desire had been to further my studies. It was a dream I had shared with my husband before we got married, and since we were both interested in pursuing further studies, we agreed that we would be supportive of each other in the event one of us had the chance. Although we both had well-paying jobs, the cost of living was rising because of poor economic conditions.

The Partner

The deteriorating economic conditions in most African countries, especially resulting from the implementation of the International Monetary Fund (IMF) and the World Bank Structural Adjustment Programs, led to a brain-drain in the hardest-hit countries. The final years at the university were mostly concentrated on making contacts with those who had already left for "greener pastures," mostly to Southern Africa. The common arrangement was such that the man, as the head of the family, went first to establish himself and to make arrangements for his family to join him later. Everyone who went down south expected a better standard of living whenever they would decide to go back to their countries. Such was the dream I shared with my husband.

In 1986 my husband left for "greener pastures" where he had already made contacts through his friends. That time it seemed as if everything was working in our favor. Just before he left, I was admitted into a university in Scotland where I had applied for further studies. We decided that he would take the children with him and that I would join them later, after completing my course, which would take one year. The months I spent without my family were very lonely, but this motivated me to work hard so I could complete the course quickly and join them.

Two months before completing my course, while I was in the final stages of writing my dissertation, I received a letter from my husband telling me that he was sick, which was why he had not communicated with me as often as possible. He told me he had been sick on and off and that in fact he had had one long bout of fever that turned out to be typhoid fever. I hoped to God he would be all right. At the time we had left home, the incidence of AIDS had increased so much that it had become, by now, everyone's concern. However, I took him at his word and prayed it was not what I feared it was. A week before I received his letter, a friend had confided in me that her husband was very sick at home and that she had learned from her sister that he might be suffering from AIDS.

AIDS in the Family

I had heard of people who were dying of AIDS before I left home, but not many people close to me had been affected by the disease. Most of the affected were from Uganda, and though it was not a distant country, the disease itself seemed so distant. So, as far as I was concerned, and I believe most people felt the same way at the time, it was a distant disease that was affecting only white homosexuals. As to how our people were being infected at that time, no one bothered to find out.

The first person close to me to die of the disease was my aunt's son-in-law. Even then, we did not know he had died of AIDS until after his death when many people had become affected and the government started an anti-AIDS campaign. I remember sitting in the hospital with the patient's wife, and during the discussion, someone made a "humorous" comment about the patient, and said, "Man, I hope you are not suffering from this disease I have heard about called AIDS." We all laughed it off but did not end the "good discussion." One woman commented that if the disease is spread through sex, then people should stick to one partner. Maybe a cure would not even be welcome, she continued, because men should stick to their wives. When I remember all this, I imagine that perhaps most of the people who were discussing a seemingly humorous topic were already harboring the virus and were sitting on a time bomb.

A month after my husband wrote to me that he was sick, his friend wrote to tell me that his condition had deteriorated and that he was to be admitted into the hospital. When I talked to him later on the phone, he said that the doctors hoped he would improve but that, as the next of kin, I had the right to be informed by the doctor about his condition. My fears became worse then, but I still tried to think of the "easy possibilities." I decided I was not going to carry this burden alone. I told my tutor that I had gotten a message that my husband was very ill and had been admitted to the hospital. The tutor was very understanding and supportive. I still had a dissertation to write, and it was not going to be easy.

I also decided to tell one of the professors with whom I had become friends. She had been to my country a year before I went to the university. I told her I was very scared of the possibility of my husband having AIDS. She told me not to worry too much. She was also so helpful. She allowed me to use her telephone to talk to my husband's doctor at her expense.

During the discussion with the doctor, he first told me that my husband was suffering from tuberculosis but that his condition was not improving even though he was responding well to the treatment for tuberculosis. He then asked me whether I was alone in the room. I said there was one other person with me.

When I said that, my friend sensed I needed privacy and politely went into the bedroom. The doctor then told me the history of my husband's sickness: he had first been diagnosed with tuberculosis but did not improve even after treatment. Then he had resisted having an HIV test, but the doctor insisted on it. After giving me a lengthy background, which I believe was preparing me for the worst news, he said, "Your husband has AIDS." I went numb. Despite the fact that I had feared all along that he might be suffering from the disease, I was still hoping against hope that I was wrong. For a moment I could not speak. The doctor kept asking, "Are you there?" After a long pause I said, "Yes, I am here." He then said he wanted me to come there. I replied that I was in the final stages of writing my dissertation and that I was not going to give it up. He told me not to worry too much. There was, the doctor said, a possibility that I was not infected since my husband and I had been apart for quite some time.

After the conversation, when my friend returned from the bedroom, she asked me what the doctor had told me about my husband's illness. I said, "Well, it is tuberculosis." I was very worried, though, and she sensed it was something worse. I told her the doctor said it was indeed very bad. She tried to cheer me up and suggested we go for a ride in the mountains. She drove me through the most beautiful terrain of Scotland I had ever seen. She had always promised me a ride, but the time had never come. I will never be able to describe what went on in my mind during that ride. I was like a moving picture—very absent-minded. My friend realized I was not telling her something, and she said to me, "Why are you more worried than before when you already knew he was sick?" I had no way of explaining to her that it was more than sickness. I wanted to tell her that this was a disaster, but I somehow sympathized with her. What could she do? Say she was sorry? Was this what I needed at the time? Would it not instead make her so sympathetic that she would not even want to take me for a ride for some time, a ride that was aimed at making me forget my troubles? Anyway, I decided to keep it to myself for awhile, knowing full well that I would tell her and my tutor at the appropriate time. When she finally brought me back to where I was staying, she asked me whether I was sure I was going to be all right. She even suggested that I stay at her house, but I refused. Believe it or not, I was feeling very dirty. I did not want anyone to touch me, because I thought I was contagious. That night was one of the worst nights of my life, and I do not think there can ever be a worse one. I cried all night. How could this happen to me?

At the time I felt that my life would end any day, any minute. I put a halt to all my plans. Within two days, however, I had managed to pull myself together. I have always been a very determined woman, fighting to get what I want in life. Knowing how much I had sacrificed to get this far, I was determined to stay and obtain the qualification that I had come to the university to pursue. I was not going to give up—at least not before I got my masters degree.

For a moment, though, I wanted to die. Not because I was afraid of the disease, but because I knew I was about to lose the man I loved. I felt angry, betrayed. I did not know whether I was angrier at the thought of losing him or at his "infidelity."

Amid tears, I managed to complete my dissertation. The day after I submitted it, I told my friend the truth. I told her why I had not told her after my telephone conversation with the doctor, and she looked at me and said, "You are right. I do not know what to say even now. I wish everyone was as strong as you." I then asked her to tell my supervisor for me. I have always wanted to let them know that whatever I have achieved is to a large extent because of their caring attitude after I learned of my husband's illness. Surely, had they not been supportive then, I would never have been able to make it through to the final stage. My tutor advised that I be tested for the disease before I left, but from the time I was told of my husband's diagnosis I was prepared to live like an infected person, and I did not see the use of having the test done.

The Unspeakable

At the doctor's advise, I went to see my husband, hoping he would not be as badly off as I was imagining. His friends met me at the airport, and they were as supportive as any friends could possibly be. I did not ask them immediately how my husband was doing. I was now becoming somewhat evasive and did not want to know the truth; yet it was the naked truth that I was going to see!

When I entered my husband's hospital room, he struggled to appear happy to see me but he was too weak to express his happiness. I could not help but cry when I saw him. I first stood in the window gazing outside before I gathered courage to greet him. He had deteriorated so much that it was very difficult to recognize him. He then struggled to tell me the nature of his illness. He thought he had me convinced that he had a badly infected liver. I then learned from his doctor that he had warned him not to disclose the results to me, because he did not know how I would react. I hoped that with time he would bring himself to tell me what he was suffering from, but he never did.

I was angry that he had refused to tell me. Every day I waited for him to open up to me but he never did, right up to the day he died. It still pains me even today. I keep wondering whether he even would have told me were we still sexually active after he knew about his infection. When I later talked to a friend of mine, who was convinced that her husband infected her when he knew he had the disease, I felt even angrier. Yet the very worst anger one can have is the anger one feels when there is no one to direct it at. When the person is dead and all the infidelity begins to unfold, it is too late. In some instances, children can get caught up in the middle of this.

Since many friends were looking after him, they suggested I go home with the children and prepare for his return home. I was not sure at the time whether he would return home as a person or as a body. It was the most painful good-bye of my life. I knew I was leaving my husband at a time he needed me most. Yet conditions were such that I had to go home and report to my job, from which, fortunately, I had not resigned.

Returning

When I first reported to my place of work, those who knew I had made arrangements to join my husband were surprised. I tried the best I could to keep his illness to myself, save for a few friends and close relatives. The disease was associated with promiscuity, and many believe that anyone who got it deserved to die because they had brought it on themselves. At my workplace, I disclosed it to one colleague who was not even a friend, but who later proved the most helpful friend in my time of need. She was amazingly supportive, and to me this was very consoling. Just one person who would be able to understand what I was going through was almost enough. I told her my husband would soon be returned home, and I would be away from my job. She promised to be as supportive as she could. She then advised that if I was going to be leaving soon, it would be better not to report back to work officially but just to report that I had completed the course and was ready to come back at some future time. She was the second person to assure me that there was a possibility I was okay.

My most difficult task was how to tell my parents about the disease. They were so happy to see me back home, and I found it difficult to break the news to them. Somehow I managed to do it. Since they did not know about the disease, they hoped he would be all right. Sometimes ignorance helps. It does not always kill.

The waiting period was very traumatic. I kept in touch with my husband's doctor, and when my husband was stable enough to travel, he was flown home, accompanied by a nurse. He went straight to the hospital. He was glad to be back home, although I do not know for sure what was going on in his mind. Surprisingly, his condition improved tremendously. He even thought of going back to work, if there was a job. This seemingly good health did not last, however. He deteriorated again, and this time he asked to be taken to the village. I had to go with him. This became one of the most trying periods of my life. The conditions in the village were so poor that it was very difficult to even follow the basic rules of hygiene. But I tried.

The time we spent in the village reminded me that a group of people existed that was still so caring no matter what the cost. I do not recall a day going by without three or more people coming by to check on us. All would come, of course, with suggestions of possible medications, and some would travel long distances in search of the "recommended herbs." It worked, and his improvement was even greater than the one he had made in the hospital. It was amazing. The caring atmosphere also helped a great deal. When I remember that tremendous improvement, I gain a lot of strength, knowing that a positive attitude is the greatest medicine. He was determined to live, and at one time I told him I would not mind even if he lived as an invalid. His eventual death remains the worst memory for me, and I have failed to get over it.

Carrying On

After my husband's death, one of the most important decisions I had to make was whether to go back to my original job or maintain my dream of pursuing an academic career. One reason I wanted to change jobs was, of course, because I wanted a completely new environment, where hardly anyone knew my history. When I finally received my papers, I was offered a teaching job at the university. Somehow I felt more comfortable working with people who understood. There was, however, another snag ahead. What was the use of staying in academics when there was almost no possibility of advancement? At first I considered it a remote possibility that I would be able to pursue further studies. There was the fear of being required to have the HIV test if I were to pursue further studies in most of the developed countries that commonly offer scholarships, namely, Great Britain, which is not as nasty as the other three, Canada, the United States, and Germany. I later learned that the difficulty of obtaining entry visas to these countries had been a dreadful experience for most of my colleagues who had wanted to travel abroad. A friend came to me one time expressing regret at having agreed to have the test done in order to get a visa to Canada. She had not gotten the visa, yet she had been told of her status, for which she was not prepared. I remember how agonizing this was for her, and I opted not to undergo such an ordeal myself. What hurts is that this woman, who was refused entry more than three years ago, is still well and, had she been admitted, would perhaps be nearing the end of the course. Does it make sense to refuse someone further studies because he or she is infected? Is the fear rooted in the possibility of contagion? If that is the case, surely these countries cannot claim immunity to the disease! And do they test when they travel to these "other" countries? It then becomes difficult to live "positively," when all positive plans are hampered by one's sero status. If indeed it has been scientifically proven that the virus is not spread through casual contact, why should one be refused entry to any country?

In any case, I know many women and men who opt to live celibate lives when they learn of their infection, because they know there is a likelihood that having sexual relationships may shorten their life span. Although I had resolved to live a normal life, there was an aspect where I decided to compromise, and that was my sexual life. I was determined to live a celibate life. I know this is difficult for many people to believe, and I had friends who laughed it off as a joke. I had many proposals, and many times I was tempted to give in. But I cannot help but think about the possibility of either infecting someone else or being reinfected myself. I have almost come to associate sex with AIDS. Sometimes I wish everyone thought that way; maybe that would check the spread. I hate the virus so much that I do not want to hear any other person telling me they are infected. Perhaps what strengthens me, and what keeps me going, is that I realize I do not just miss sex but I miss it with my husband. I guess the fact is that to me he is irreplaceable.

Life with HIV

Four years after my husband's death, most of my friends became concerned that I was "wasting my life." "Why can't you go on living?" was a common question. Did I need a man in order to live? I convinced myself that I didn't. I needed my children's love, and I wanted to give them the love they needed. Melina, one of the senior members of the staff, reminded me quite often that I should take an HIV test and not remain ignorant.

I finally agreed to take the test, and when I went back for the results, the man told me, "Well, the results are positive," and then he quickly added, "That doesn't mean you have AIDS, only that you can pass on the virus to someone else." Believe it or not, I was not shattered by the result. My grief had ended with my husband's death. Of course I had imagined at times I was safe, but still I had always known there was a possibility I was HIV-positive.

When I told Melina of the test results the following day, she was more disappointed than I. Just remembering the expression on her face gives me the assurance that people really care. This means a lot to me. It is comforting to know that people are with you in very difficult situations. Melina is someone I do not want to disappoint; I know she cares a lot. I would not distinguish her love from that of my family.

During that same week, a colleague, who had been given a scholarship to study in Germany, received a letter informing her that she was required to undergo a medical exam. An HIV test was one part of the exam. In fact, although it is called a general medical exam, the HIV test is the determining factor. Some people with other complications have been given visas, whereas others who are healthy but who test positive for HIV are refused entry visas. My friend was worried because she had heard of colleagues who had been denied visas. Her fears were justified; she went for the medical exam and was never given a visa. She is still healthy, two and a half years after she was refused a visa for a one-year course.

Because I was determined to live on, I decided not to undergo the trauma of being barred from entering any country because of my sero status. I decided to register for a doctorate in an African country, and luckily I got sponsorship. Knowing what achievements I had made thus far, I was determined to make the best of it. HIV was not going to stand in my way. I looked at my high school colleagues, and I was definitely one of the few who had made it to that level. I knew many of them were struggling with other life stresses, which were even worse than being HIV-positive.

When I decided to disclose my status to a few friends, the choice of who to tell was based on a careful calculation of who would provide encouragement and support. This to me meant those who would not debate my living on. I did not want to confide in anyone who would "advise" me to rethink my priorities. If I was determined to live on, then this was without any compromise. I was determined to deal with the virus, for I know that the strength within me is greater than the virus.

I know that many women need encouragement because they have the will to live on. I have met many young widows who are desperate after losing their husbands. Others are ready to struggle on. They do not sit passively and wait for fate to take its course, contrary to what many outsiders would like to believe. They may be helpless when it comes to protecting themselves because of cultural entrapments, but they still have the will and determination to live when they are faced with challenges.

There are challenging moments when I think about my children, who are still too young to understand and who have the confidence that their mother is there for them even though they do not have a father. Their innocent faith gives me the courage to live on. I depend on courage, perseverance, and faith. A preacher once said in his sermon, "To make your life small when it could be great is a sin." It is always best to bring out the best in ourselves. This is only possible in an environment that is caring and understanding.

3 | Women Who Sleep with Women

JOYCE HUNTER AND PRISCILLA ALEXANDER

I'm a gay woman, living with AIDS. Nobody out here believes I'm real.
—Martina Brown (Women's National Network 1993)

There's no category for lesbian women with HIV. Like we don't exist. Nobody's looking at lesbian couples with one HIV-positive and one HIV-negative to see if the virus is passed. It's like our lives don't matter.
—Gloria, an HIV-positive lesbian (Women's National Network 1993)

The AIDS crisis has affected women who sleep with women— a category that includes both women who identify as lesbian or bisexual and women who do not—in many ways: as friends of people infected with HIV, as caregivers for people with symptomatic disease, as activists in the AIDS political community, and as women infected with HIV or ill with AIDS. It is this last category that is the most hidden, the most denied, by lesbians as well as by epidemiologists.

In this article we first examine the vulnerability of women who sleep with women to HIV infection and AIDS, and then we examine the context within which they are vulnerable, including the range of lives, identities, and behaviors represented among them. Finally, we consider some issues involved in developing HIV/AIDS prevention interventions for women who sleep with women.

Vulnerability to HIV Infection

Although lesbians are thought to be the group least vulnerable to HIV infection, some have been infected since the beginning of the epidemic. In a study of 1,122 women diagnosed with AIDS in eleven U.S. states between January 1990 and September 1993, 5.8 percent reported having had sexual contact with a woman in the previous five years, 86 percent of whom had also had sex with men during that period (Chu, Diaz, and Schable 1994). In general, the behaviors that put lesbians and bisexual women at risk for HIV infection in industrial countries are the same as those that affect heterosexual women: (1) injecting drug use; (2) unprotected vaginal or anal intercourse, and in some cases fellatio, with a man, particularly if the man is an injecting drug user or bisexual (Chu 1990); and (3) donor insemination, especially if performed outside a clinic or if the donations are not screened (Eskenazi et al. 1989). In developing countries, additional risk factors may be the use of unscreened blood for transfusions (e.g., to treat malaria or following childbirth) or the use of unsterile injecting equipment in health care settings.

Examining the risk of infection through sexual transmission, a growing number of studies suggest that there is a fair amount of heterosexual behavior among women who have sex with women. In a study among 594 black women in the United States who self-identified as bisexual (65) and lesbian (529), 31 percent were formerly married and 2 percent were currently married (Cochran and Mays 1988). Another U.S. study of lesbians found that 30 percent reported having had sex with men in the previous five years, and 14 percent in the previous two years. This same study found that 11 percent had had one or more sexually transmitted diseases (Michigan 1991). A third U.S. study of 141 women who identified as lesbian found that 80 percent had engaged in penile-vaginal intercourse, 72 percent in oral sex, and 23 percent in anal sex with men (Hunter et al. 1992). Showing the possible impact, another U.S. study found higher rates of HIV infection among 19 women who had had sex with women (89.5 percent) than among 96 exclusively heterosexual women (51.0 percent); an interesting note is that the primary risk factor for women who had sex with women was anal intercourse with men (Weiss et al. 1993). Lest anyone think this phenomenon is unique to the United States, a study of women in public lesbian meeting places in four major Italian cities found that 35 percent reported vaginal penetration and 18 percent anal penetration with male partners; 22 percent had had oral sex with men during menstruation (Sasse et al. 1992).

A factor often ignored in studies of lesbians is their involvement in the sex industry. Sex work is a major source of income for poor women—in both developed and developing countries—either on a casual basis between other income-producing efforts or full-time. In both developed and developing countries, a significant proportion of female sex workers have sex with women, professionally or in their personal lives (Case 1993; Delacoste and Alexander 1987; Harsin 1985; St. James 1985). Some lesbians, particularly adolescents, are forced out of their homes and find themselves on the streets having to fend for themselves, perhaps trading sex for a place to sleep, perhaps for money to pay for food or drugs. In Eastern Europe unemployment is much higher among women than among men—for example, 70 percent of the unemployed in Russia are women (Lissyutkina 1993)—at the same time that access to abortion and child care have been sharply curtailed. As a result prostitution has increased sharply in many Eastern European countries, and many women, including those who have sex with women, have migrated to Western countries in search of work, often including sex work.

The association between sex work and HIV infection varies from country to country, and from one class of sex workers to another, but in general, vulnerability to HIV infection is greatest among lower-income sex workers, no matter what the country. In industrial countries the risk is primarily associated with either injecting drug use or noncommercial relationships with injecting drug users, and not with prostitution per se, although there is some evidence of increased vulnerability associated with trading sex in the context of crack use (Edlin et al. 1994; Porter et al. 1994; Weiner et al. 1992; Weissman, Sowder, and Young 1990). In developing countries the risk is less clearly defined, although poor access to health care, a high prevalence of untreated ulcerative STDs (sexually transmitted diseases), and a dearth of sterile examining and injection equipment appear to be major factors for HIV infection, especially in high-seroprevalence communities or where access to condoms and the ability to insist on their use are poor.

On the other hand, lesbians' sexual risk may not be exclusively from sexual contact with men; for example, one small study of lesbians attending a genitourinary clinic in London found a relatively high prevalence of other viral STDs, including herpes simplex, which can be transmitted through cunnilingus and human papilloma virus (Edwards and Thin 1990). Although there are no clear statistics on female-to-female transmission, and the U.S. Centers for Disease Control (CDC) does not publish such data in its periodic surveillance reports, there are two published case reports and an increasing number of anecdotal accounts of lesbians who have contracted HIV through woman-to-woman sex. Meanwhile, it is not yet clear whether female-to-female transmission can occur through contact with ordinary vaginal secretions via cunnilingus and hand-genital contact (i.e., if there are cuts on the hand), or if direct contact with blood is necessary (e.g., through sexual contact during menstruation or activities that involve blood-letting).

What Is a Lesbian: Identity versus Behavior

The most obvious definition of the term *lesbian* is also the simplest—that a lesbian is a woman who has sex with women. However, a more complex definition would have to include behavior in the context of a committed relationship lasting for many years, one-night stands with a series of partners, lifelong monogamy, serial monogamy, and concurrent relationships and partnering, as well as connections along the continuum from exclusive and lifelong homosexuality to a point just short of exclusive and lifelong heterosexuality. Moreover, sex between women can be an act in furtherance of deeply felt love, merely the response to physical desire, or an act performed in the context of earning a living.

As an example of the complexity of this subject, although both authors currently identify as lesbians—to themselves and to the world—and focus their emotional and sexual energies on their relationships with women, both lived as heterosexuals at an earlier stage of their lives. Thus Joyce Hunter married and raised children, although she knew from early childhood that she was a lesbian, in a conscious effort to conform to society's (and her therapist's[1]) expectations of her and to be "like other people." Priscilla Alexander was far less conscious of her feelings for women and lived a rather active heterosexual life as a young adult, only coming out as a lesbian at the age of thirty-four. Indeed, the world of women who sleep with, or have sex with, women includes women who knew as children that they were different, that their sexual and emotional desire was for other women, whether or not they acted on it, women who for most of their lives have been drawn to both women and men, and women who assumed themselves to be straight, only fully recognizing their desire for women well into their adulthood. There are also women who identified as lesbian or sought out only women as sex partners when they were young, who later explored their feelings or transferred their emotional and sexual energies to men. Although these internal perceptions of sexual desire and emotional connection may be similar from one culture to another, the social, political, and legal context in which they transpire varies tremendously from one country to another, along with the amount of room a society provides for exploration or recognition of same-sex desire.

Nonetheless, women have sex with women in virtually every society, as the variety of words in the world's languages attests. The official words often are derived from the Greek island of Lesbos, where Sappho led a group of women poets, philosophers, and lovers in ancient times. Examples include *lesbiana* (Spanish); *lesbica* (Italian and Portuguese); *lesbierin* and *lesbe* (German); *lesbienne* (French); and *lesbisk* (Swedish). Many languages also have slang terms such as *marimacha*, *tortillera*, and *tortilla* (Spanish); *gouine* and *goudou* (French); *warmi* (Swiss); and *daiku* (a Japanese transliteration of the English word *dyke*). In some cases, specific words express a kind of crossing of gender as well as sexual orientation; for example, in Quecha the term *mamaku* means mannish woman whereas *qharincha* means tomboy, and in English there are the terms *butch* and *bulldager* (Global Lesbianism 1982).

Often a significant dissonance exists between behavior and identity, however, generally as a result of the widespread homophobia and stigma that reinforce denial of sexual identity and behaviors. Lesbians across cultures and classes feel the impact of homophobia, especially as they have become more visible in society. Therefore many women still feel compelled to lead isolated or "closeted" lives. Once one leaves the urban centers of developed countries, the majority of women who love other women are married, and their efforts to establish intimacy with the women they love continues to be hidden in the cracks of their lives.

Looking at the United States, it is more than forty years since Alfred Kinsey and his colleagues found that a large proportion of people in that country have had both homosexual and heterosexual feelings, ranging from an occasional fantasy or feeling of arousal to full and intimate relationships. In terms of actual behavior they found that 4 percent of men were exclusively homosexual at the time they were interviewed and 37 percent had had at least one homosexual experience (Kinsey, Pomeroy, and Martin 1948), whereas 2–3 percent of women were exclusively lesbian at the time of the interview and 13 percent had had lesbian sexual experiences to the point of orgasm (Kinsey et al. 1953). In 1987 the Kinsey Institute found that 46 percent of four hundred women who identified themselves as lesbians had in fact had sex with men in the previous seven years (Reinisch, Sanders, and Ziemba-Davis 1987). More recently a national survey of 3,432 adults in the United States found that 4.9 percent of men and 4.1 percent of women had engaged in sex with at least one person of the same gender since the age of eighteen, 2.1 percent and 1.3 percent, respectively, within the past year, although in the top twelve central cities, 10.2 percent and 2.1 percent, respectively, had done so (Laumann et al. 1994). Similar data have been reported in studies conducted in France (Spira et al. 1993) and Britain (Wellings et al. 1994), suggesting some similarity across Euro-American cultures.

The gender differential in how often homosexuality is expressed, especially as an overt and conscious identity, is likely to be affected by (1) the enormous weight of societal assumptions that women have less sexual drive than men, and thus less sexual desire, which might prevent many from even recognizing their sexual desire for other women; (2) the fact that women do not have to feel any sexual desire in order to engage in a sexual act; and (3) the level of repression of homosexuals in society, which could discourage women, who already experience societal repression because of their gender, from acknowledging their homosexual desires. Nonetheless, women do have sex with women in virtually every society, in many cases while having sex with men at the same time.

For example, during adolescence and early adulthood, when young people are discovering their sexuality for the first time (coming out), those who think they may be attracted to people of their own gender are likely to explore their sexuality with the opposite gender as well (Hunter et al. 1992; Savin-Williams, 1990; Reinisch, Sanders, and Ziemba-Davis 1988). Moreover, although coming out usually begins in adolescence, in some cases the process begins, or at least is recognized, only in middle or late adulthood. The process is developmental, consisting of a series of physical and emotional stages through which the person moves, rather than a discrete state of being. As a result personal identity (i.e., how one sees oneself) is often different from social identity (i.e., how others might define your behavior, on the one hand, or how you might present yourself to others) (De Monteflores and Schultz 1978; Hetrick and Martin 1984). Thus, during this process of establishing a consonant identity, an individual may indeed be sexual with both women and men.

However, even after establishing a "lesbian" identity, some lesbians who participate in gay rights or AIDS activist or service organizations, and who spend many hours working alongside gay men, have sex with their gay male friends. And despite their high awareness of AIDS, such behavior often involves risky sex. For example, in the 1988 Kinsey Institute study cited above, 32 percent of the lesbians who had had sex with men in the previous seven years knew their male partner to be bisexual, yet despite all the knowledge about AIDS in the lesbian and gay communities in the United States, *only six percent reported using a condom every time* (Reinisch, Sanders, and Ziemba-Davis 1987).

In countries where homosexuality is heavily repressed, it is likely that one of the few places where lesbians will be able to meet and to find each other will be in bars, often sharing those protected spaces with sex workers, as they did in the United States in the years before the Stonewall Rebellion catapulted the gay rights movement into prominence[2] (Garber 1992; Miller 1992). However, as contact with less repressive societies increases—through tourism, the media, and the internet—more women who have sex with women are recognizing that they are part of a distinct community. In the former Czechoslovakia, immediately after the fall of communism, one woman said, "We were all isolated, so isolated—I always knew I wasn't the only lesbian in the world, but it was wonderful to actually see with my own eyes that there were so many of us" (Miller 1992).

Where the lesbian and gay rights movement has not had a significant impact, or in cultures with strict gender expectations within countries with public gay activism, the overwhelming majority of women who have sex with women will also have sex with men, and many lesbians are married, sometimes to a bisexual man, or in formal or informal polygamous unions. For example, one author (Alexander) attended a meeting of lesbians in Israel, in 1983, at which almost all the women were married. The other author (Hunter) attended a similar party in a suburb of New York City as well as an Orthodox Jewish lesbian/gay festival; in both cases many of the women were married. Moreover, in suburban or rural areas, even in countries with high lesbian and gay visibility and activism, many women who identify as lesbian are married and therefore functionally bisexual. "There were . . . 'housewife lesbians' who visited the bars on occasion. These were women who had opted for marriage as a social inevitability and means of surviving economically, while they continued to have secret homosexual affairs, whether intermittent or long-term, taking advantage of the room to maneuver that their institutional heterosexual status provided" (Chamberland 1993).

In many parts of the world, gender-gradience, in which one partner assumes a more traditionally masculine role while the other takes on more feminine characteristics, at least in their outward appearance, is a common feature of lesbian life, and there is a growing body of research on the historical record of cross-dressing and other aspects of lesbian and gay life (D'Emilio and Freedman 1988; Davenport-Hines 1990; Garber 1992; Grahn 1984; Kennedy and Davis 1993; Nestle 1992). While in the Philippines, one of the authors (Alexander) saw women who were clearly lesbian, many of whom were in classic butch-femme couples.

Another form that lesbian relationships often take in more rigid societies is strict age-gradience, in which one partner is significantly older than the other. For example, a few reports have been published of female-to-female marriage in Africa, reportedly nonsexual in nature (Amadiume 1987), as well as one study of lesbian relationships in Mombasa, in a part of Kenya where a traditional form of male transvestism has also been documented (Shepherd 1987). In both examples one partner is usually significantly older than the other, as the relationships are formed to cement economic relationships and involve the accumulation of capital (White 1990). In Nigeria, as a consequence of the AIDS crisis, homosexuality has been publicly acknowledged among the Hausa, and lesbian relationships are beginning to be acknowledged as well, particularly in urban areas among educated women (Berer and Ray 1993).

Lesbians' Health in the Background

In considering lesbians' risk of HIV infection, it is important to understand something about lesbians' other health concerns, including their engagement with the health care system. In the United States, for example, lesbians as a group have alarmingly high rates of breast cancer, estimated to be three times that of other women, especially if they have never been pregnant or have not breast-fed and if they have smoked (Haynes 1992). Some studies have suggested that lesbians are more likely to smoke than heterosexual women, which may be a temporary artifact of being the first women to challenge conventional femininity codes, which results in higher rates of lung cancer. Moreover, there is a relatively high prevalence of obesity among lesbians, which may in part be an effort to cope with or ward off male attention, which, when combined with smoking, contributes to a greater risk of heart disease. In addition, higher rates of alcohol abuse—associated with the historical reliance on bars to provide safe meeting spaces, as well as the need to cope with the stress of living in homophobic societies—means that lesbians are likely to be more vulnerable to such alcohol-related diseases as cirrhosis of the liver than are their heterosexual sisters.

An additional factor contributing to stress among lesbians and bisexual women, and to a dependence on alcohol and other psychotropic drugs, may be a history of child abuse—at least as prevalent among lesbians as among heterosexual women, and possibly higher if parents sexually or physically abuse daughters who are tomboys or otherwise act in ways considered inappropriate for daughters. Numerous studies of women who inject drugs have found a high prevalence of a history of child sexual abuse, and some have also found that a disproportionate number of women who inject drugs are women who have sex with women. For example, one Australian study found that 32 percent of 325 injecting drug users were either bisexual or lesbian (Ross et al. 1991).

The stress of living double lives—out to one's friends in the lesbian and/or gay community, closeted to one's family, coworkers, and heterosexual friends—can have a profound impact on lesbians' emotional and mental health. Although lesbians and bisexual women who live in major cities in developed countries are increasingly open about the gender of their life partners, in small towns and rural communities they have to at least pretend otherwise. In countries with more defined role divisions—for example, Mediterranean countries—the pressure to conform to heterosexual role definitions is even stronger.

When the fear of disclosure is high, even therapy and other forms of mental health care offer little release from this stress if lesbians feel unable to talk about the issues closest to their lives. Moreover, both authors have known many lesbians whose parents committed them to psychiatric institutions in an effort to "cure" their homosexuality. In many cases the women were given extremely toxic psychotropic drugs, with long-term physical consequences. It is an experience that both leaves long-lasting emotional scars and engenders a profound distrust of mental health care providers.

Indeed, as a result of the stigma associated with homosexuality, negative experiences with health care providers, and a lack of access to lesbian-sensitive health services, many lesbians are anxious about disclosing their sexual orientation to health care providers, including (or especially) those providing gynecological care. As a result, a number of studies have found that lesbians are less likely to seek regular health care than are other women (Cochran and Mays

1988; Smith 1988). Looking at the situation from the viewpoint of the health care providers, one study of nursing students found that more than half considered lesbians to be "unacceptable" and 15 percent thought lesbian sexual behavior should be illegal (Eliason and Randall 1991). In view of this, it should not be surprising that some studies have found that lesbians obtain fewer screening exams and are less likely to be educated about signs and symptoms of serious diseases than are other women (O'Hanlan 1993).

HIV Prevention and Control among Lesbians

"We need the education to know how to keep ourselves healthy," (Women's National Network 1993). If we are going to help women who have sex with women protect themselves and their partners from HIV infection, our campaigns will have to recognize that lesbians are at risk in at least three dimensions—their own injecting drug use, unprotected sex with men, and, although to a much smaller degree, unprotected sex with each other (Hollibaugh 1995). We will have to recognize that women who sleep with women are as diverse as other women throughout history and that they come from every economic strata, race, and culture, from every part of the world. In every culture, moreover, lesbians who are members of ethnic minorities struggle with the same race and class problems as other women face in their larger cultures.

With women who have sex with women, the widely held assumption that lesbians are not at risk will be a major obstacle to effective interventions, and most interventions will have to include a significant education component. However, as we know from experience with all other AIDS prevention efforts, education is not enough: it takes much more to achieve significant changes in behavior. The task will differ according to whether women are in the early stages of exploring their sexuality or have a well-developed identity and life-style; whether they see themselves as lesbians, bisexuals, or heterosexuals; and whether they are married or single, rich or poor. Community organizing will be central to the effectiveness of any program and must be rooted in the involvement of the women themselves, at all stages of the development and implementation of the intervention.

Any project will have to address such issues as the prevalence of bisexuality, whether by identity or situational, whether open or covert, and how to raise the issue of safer sex with both categories of partners. In high seroprevalence communities, it will be essential to involve lesbians who are already infected with HIV to both clarify the risks and serve as a model of the necessary behavioral changes. Projects will also have to heed the social, structural, and legal constraints on women's behavior, and especially the impact of law enforcement on

lesbians—whether because they are lesbians in countries that continue to prohibit same-sex relationships, because they use illegal drugs, or because they
work in the sex industry. Many women who have sex with women are mothers,
so that projects will have to consider the women's children—both providing
child care for women who participate in the project's activities and helping
women infected with HIV to plan for their children's future.

The materials given out by a project will have to include not only educational
information but also practical items, including some kind of barrier for cunnilingus (e.g., latex dental dams or condoms that can be split along one side to
create a barrier or plastic wrap), as well as water-based lubricants. Pharmaceutical companies that are working on the development of a nonirritating, intravaginal, and intra-anal microbicide should also consider the issue of odor and
taste, so important for oral sex. In addition, where injection-related infection is
an issue—whether from sharing needles to inject psychoactive drugs or because
clinics and other health care facilities cannot be relied on to have sterile
syringes—projects should provide sterile needles and/or bleach with which to
clean them. Written materials must be relevant to the culture of the women
involved but should always include information about both heterosexual and
woman-to-woman sex and about sex work as well as sex as part of a relationship.

In the end, though, what is most important to remember is that love is an
essential part of our being, no matter who we are on this earth—young, middle-aged, old, whether we are heterosexual, bisexual, or homosexual. The need
to express ourselves sexually is an innate part of who we are: "It was as if I had
been sleeping all my life until that very instant when I reached out and she met
me with her heart" (Madrón 1987).

REFERENCES

Amadiume, I. 1987. *Male Daughters, Female Husbands: Gender and Sex in an African Soci-
ety*. London: Zed.
Belinda. 1987. It took everything I had (an oral history). In J. Ramos, ed., *Compañeras:
Latina Lesbians (An Anthology)*, 44. New York: Latina Lesbian History Project.
Berer, M. and S. Ray. 1993. *Women and HIV/AIDS: An International Resource Book*. Lon-
don: Pandora.
Case, P. 1993. Personal communication with Priscilla Alexander.
Chamberland, L. 1993. Remembering lesbian bars: Montreal, 1955–1975. *Journal of
Homosexuality* 25 (3): 231–69.
Chu, S. Y. 1990. Epidemiology of reported cases of AIDS in lesbians, United States,
1980–1989. *American Journal of Public Health* 80 (11): 1380–81.

Chu, S. Y., T. Diaz, and B. Schable. 1994. Risk behaviors among women with HIV/AIDS who report sex with women. *International Conference on AIDS* 10 (1): 311 (abstract no. PC0173), August 7–12.

Cochran, S. D. and V. M. Mays. 1988. Disclosure of sexual preference for physicians by black lesbian and bisexual women. *Western Journal of Medicine* 149:616–19.

Davenport-Hines, R. 1990. *Sex, Death, and Punishment: Attitudes to Sex and Sexuality in Britain since the Renaissance*. Glasgow: William Collins Sons.

Delacoste, F. and P. Alexander. 1987. *Sex Work: Writings by Women in the Sex Industry*. San Francisco: Cleis; London: Virago, 1988. (*Sex Arbeit: Frauen in der Sexindustrie*. Munich: Wilhelm Heyne Verlag, 1989.)

D'Emilio, J. and E. B. Freedman. 1988. *Intimate Matters: A History of Sexuality in America*. New York: Harper & Row.

De Monteflores, C. and S. J. Schultz. 1978. Coming out: Similarities and differences for lesbians and gay men. *Journal of Social Issues* 34:59–72.

Edlin, B. R., et al. 1994. Intersecting epidemics: Crack cocaine use and HIV infection among inner-city young adults. *New England Journal of Medicine* 331 (21): 1422–27.

Edwards, A. and R. N. Thin. 1990. Sexually transmitted diseases in lesbians. *International Journal on STD and AIDS* 1 (3): 178–81.

Eliason, M. G. and C. E. Randall. 1991. Lesbian phobia in nursing students. *Western Journal of Nursing Research* 13:363–74.

Eskenazi, B., et al. 1989. HIV serology in artificially inseminated lesbians. *Journal of Acquired Immune Deficiency Syndrome* 2 (2): 187–93.

Garber, M. 1992. *Vested Interests: Cross-Dressing and Cultural Anxiety*. New York: Routledge.

Global Lesbianism. 1982. In *Connexions: An International Women's Quarterly*, no. 3 (Winter).

Grahn, J. 1984. *Another Mother Tongue: Gay Words, Gay Worlds*. Boston: Beacon.

Harsin, J. 1985. *Policing Prostitution in Nineteenth-Century Paris*. Princeton: Princeton University Press.

Haynes, S. 1992. Lesbians and Cancer. Presentation at the National Lesbian and Gay Health Foundation Conference, July, Los Angeles, California.

Hetrick, E. S. and A. D. Martin. 1984. Ego-dystonic homosexuality: A developmental view. In E. S. Hetrick and T. Stein, eds., *Innovations in Psychotherapy with Homosexuals*. Washington, D.C.: American Psychiatric Association.

Hollibaugh, A. 1995. Lesbian denial and lesbian leadership in the AIDS epidemic: Bravery and fear in the construction of a lesbian geography of risk. In B. E. Schneider and N. E. Stoller, eds., *Women Resisting AIDS: Feminist Strategies of Empowerment*, 219–30. Philadelphia: Temple University Press.

Hunter, J., et al. 1992. Sexual and substance abuse acts that place adolescent lesbians at risk for HIV. *Ninth International Conference on AIDS* 8 (2): D421 (abstract no. PoD 5208), July 19–24.

Hunter, J., M. Rosario, and M. J. Rotheram-Borus. 1993. Sexual and substance abuse acts that place lesbians at risk for HIV. *International Conference on AIDS* 9 (2): 790 (abstract no. PO-DO2–3432), June 6–11.

Kennedy, E. L. and M. D. Davis. 1993. *Boots of Leather, Slippers of Gold: The History of a Lesbian Community*. New York: Routledge.

Kinsey, A. C., et al. 1953. *Sexual Behavior in the Human Female*. Philadelphia: W. B. Saunders.

Kinsey, A. C., W. Pomeroy, and C. E. Martin. 1948. *Sexual Behavior in the Human Male*. Philadelphia: W. B. Saunders.

Laumann, E. O., et al. 1994. *The Social Organization of Sexuality: Sexual Practices in the United States*. Chicago: University of Chicago Press.

Lissyutkina, L. 1993. Soviet women at the crossroads of Perestroika. In N. Funk and M. Mueller, eds. *Gender Politics and Post-Communism: Reflections from Eastern Europe and the Former Soviet Union*, 274–86. New York: Routledge.

Madrón, C. 1987. Poem. In J. Ramos, ed., *Compañeras: Latina Lesbians (An Anthology)*, 119. New York: Latina Lesbian History Project.

Michigan Organization for Human Rights. 1991. *The Michigan Lesbian Health Survey: Results Relevant to AIDS*. Lansing, Michigan.

Miller, N. 1992. *Out in the World*. New York: Vintage Departures.

Nestle, J., ed. 1992. *The Persistent Desire: A Femme-Butch Reader*. Boston: Alyson. See especially L. MacCowan, Re-collecting history, renaming lives: Femme stigma and the feminist seventies and eighties, 299–330; M. R. Desquitado, A letter from the Philippines, 295–98.

O'Hanlan, K. 1993. *Lesbians in Health Research*. Office of Women's Health Research, National Institutes of Health: Scientific Conference on Recruitment and Retention of Women in Health Research.

Porter, J., et al. 1994. Crack smoking methods as risk factors for HIV infection. *Tenth International Conference on AIDS* 10 (1): 391 (abstract no. PD0170), August 7–12.

Ramos, J., ed. 1987. *Compañeras: Latina Lesbians (An Anthology)*. New York: Latina Lesbian History Project. See especially C. Madrón, Poem; and Belinda, It took everything I had (an oral history).

Reinisch, J. M., S. A. Sanders, and M. Ziemba-Davis. 1987. Self-labeled sexual orientation, sexual behavior, and knowledge about AIDS: Implications for bio-medical research and education programs. In *Proceedings of the Workshop, "Woman and AIDS: Promoting Health Behavior."* Washington, D.C.: National Institute of Mental Health. September.

Ross, M. W., et al. 1991. Sexually transmissible diseases in injecting drug users. *Genitourinary Medicine* 67:32–36.

St. James, M. 1985. Personal communication with Priscilla Alexander.

Sasse, H., et al. 1992. Potential routes of HIV transmission among women engaging in female-to-female sexual practices. *International Conference on AIDS* 8 (2): D421 (abstract no. PoD 5209), July 19–24.

Savin-Williams, R. 1990. *Gay and Lesbian Youth: Expressions of Identity*. New York: Hemisphere.

Shepherd, G. 1987. Rank, gender, and homosexuality: Mombasa as a key to understanding sexual options. In P. Caplan, ed., *The Cultural Construction of Sexuality*, 240–70. London: Tavistock.

Smith, E. M. 1988. Health care attitudes and experiences during gynecological care among lesbians and bisexuals. *American Journal of Public Health* 20:69–73.

Spira, A., N. Bajos, and ACSF (Analyse des Comportements Sexuels en France Investigateurs). 1992. AIDS and sexual behavior in France. *Nature* 360:407–9.

Weiner, A., et al. 1992. Intravenous drug use, inconsistent condom use, and fellatio in relationship to crack smoking are risky behaviors for acquiring AIDS in streetwalkers. *International Conference on AIDS* 8 (2): C338 (abstract no. PoC 4560), July 19–24.

Weiss, S. H., et al. 1993. Risk of HIV and other sexually transmitted diseases (STD) among lesbian and heterosexual women. *International Conference on AIDS* 9 (1) (abstract no. WS-D04–4), June 6–11. The conclusions about anal sex were included in the oral presentation but not in the abstract.

Weissman, G., B. Sowder, and P. Young. 1990. The relationship between crack cocaine use and other risk factors among women in a national AIDS prevention program—United States, Puerto Rico, and Mexico. *International Conference on AIDS* 6 (3): 126 (abstract no. S.D.124), June 20–23.

Wellings, K., et al. 1994. *Sexual Behavior in Britain: The National Survey of Sexual Attitudes and Lifestyles*. New York: Penguin.

White, L. 1990. *The Comforts of Home: Prostitution in Colonial Nairobi*. Chicago: The University of Chicago Press. Cf L. White. 1986. Prostitution, identity, and class consciousness during World War II. *Signs: Journal of Women in Culture and Society* 11 (2): 255–73.

Women's National Network of the AIDS Coalition to Unleash Power (ACT UP). 1993. *Briefing Report: Lesbians Living with HIV/AIDS Deserve Health Care Not Death Care*. Prepared for the Office of the U.S. Department of Health and Human Services, April 23.

4 | HIV / AIDS: A Personal Perspective

DEBBIE RUNIONS

I remember the first time I heard about AIDS. It was 1982. . . . There was this joke: "What's the worst part about having AIDS?" The answer: "Convincing your mother you're Haitian."

Back then AIDS was a disease that hit three main categories of people: (1) Haitians, (2) intravenous (IV) drug users, and (3) gay men. As I recall, no one really cared much that these people were dying from a mysterious disease that resulted in a horrendous physical deterioration. Many considered the illness to be God's retribution for their sins.

Rock Hudson, Liberace, Halston, Tina Chow, Howard Ashman, Tony Perkins, Rudolf Nureyev . . . the list of deaths within the arts community began to grow. Middle America winced, but still celebrities were only slightly more familiar to them than those other AIDS casualties.

In the mid-eighties, the virus began to show up in surgery patients and hemophiliacs who had received transfusions. It was then we learned with horror that our blood supplies had been contaminated.

Until then, most Americans had never known anyone personally who had HIV or AIDS. AIDS was still, for the most part, a disease of the socially disenfranchised.

I am a forty-three-year-old widow and the mother of two adult children. By day I am an executive assistant for the Tennessee Business Roundtable, a membership association of about 250 CEOs across the state. Two nights a week I teach journalism at Nashville State Technical Institute. I am a native Tennessean and a graduate of a private, religious university. I do not smoke. I rarely drink. I have never used either recreational or intravenous drugs. I am not a person with hemophilia. I have never had a blood transfusion. I am heterosexual. I do not consider myself promiscuous. I have never had anonymous sex or even a "one-night stand." I believed that I fell into no high-risk category.

I had one sexual encounter in 1992. On October 18 I came in contact with the AIDS virus and by November I was in the hospital.

I was the first child and the only daughter in my family. My daddy always had a multitude of jobs. He owned and operated a taxi cab service, as well as a game room and vending machine company. He also farmed and worked for the post office. Daddy's father died when he was two, and his mother followed when he was nine. Being orphaned at such an early age during the Depression taught him a great number of survival tricks. By the time I came along, Daddy could make money sitting on a rock empty-handed. His early losses also caused him to realize exactly how important a family was. We never doubted that we were the most important part of his life.

Momma was a staunch Southern Baptist stay-at-home mom. She was young and beautiful and wore shirtwaist dresses and pearls just like Donna Reed. She even vacuumed in high-heeled cork weggie shoes. It was the fifties, after all. Twelve years younger than Daddy, she didn't learn to drive until she was almost thirty. I volunteered her for "Room Mother" at school every year.

I had two younger brothers and a strong extended family. My grandmother lived across the road, and we children spent every night with her. The cousins visited so often that we grew up more as brothers and sisters.

My childhood was filled with infrequent but unusually intense illnesses. One of my most vivid memories of third grade was when my teacher, Mrs. Capps, took me into the cafeteria and pulled my shirt up over my head to show my back and chest to the cooks.

"Can you believe this?" she asked. "Debbie has the chicken pox for the third year in a row." That had never happened in the history of Waverly Elementary School.

Two years later, my cousins and I played on an oak tree felled by lightning. There were nine of us. When the morning came, every inch of my skin, including the insides of my eyelids, was swollen and itching. I was the only one who had an allergic reaction to the poison oak that covered the fallen giant.

When I was sixteen, I was hospitalized for a month and out of school for four more with mononucleosis complicated by mumps. I was unconscious for six days as my fever raged to 106 degrees. I almost died. It was the worst case the doctors had ever seen. It was then that I became allergic to penicillin and all its family. My hair fell out for the first of what was to be three nearly bald episodes in my life. Two years after that, when I had an unusual emergency gall bladder surgery, I became allergic to the Mycin drugs.

I was a good student. I was a member of the band, the Beta Club, the math honors club, and the yearbook annual staff. I was a 4-H all star, a Future Teacher, and was elected "Friendliest" by my senior classmates. I graduated in the top 15 percent of my class.

While I was book smart, I knew little about my body or my sexuality. There was only so much a person could learn from a book back in those days.

Three days after my sixteenth birthday I had my first date. At age seventeen, two weeks before my eighteenth birthday, I married Harry Runions, the first boy I ever dated, the first boy I ever kissed, and the only boy with whom I had been sexually intimate.

I know it sounds unbelievable in this day and age, but we did not realize that we had "done it" until I began to have morning sickness. Harry took me to the doctor to discover why I was ill. When the doctor informed me that I was pregnant, I said, "No, I can't be. I'm still a virgin!"

"No, hon," he shook his head with a smile, "you're not."

Dazed, I went out to the car where Harry sat waiting and told him I was pregnant. His response was, "No, you can't be. You're still a virgin!"

"No, hon," I assured him, "I'm not."

Harry and I married. After the wedding my mother gave me the one bit of advice her mother had given her on her own wedding day: "Close your eyes and think of England." Now tell me, how many generations back did that gem of wisdom precede me?

Our firstborn was a daughter, and our son followed two years later. We decided to attend college when our children were ages two and four. We both took twenty credit hours each semester, held down part-time jobs, and coparented. We graduated in three years.

We were both nominated for Who's Who among Colleges. Harry was chosen social work student of the year and graduated with honors. I was chosen history student of the year for two consecutive years and graduated with high honors—sixth in my class. Harry continued his education at the University of Tennessee School of Social Work and I took postgraduate studies at Middle Tennessee State University in journalism.

Harry received his MSW and was offered a position at a church-sponsored children's home in Lubbock, Texas. Once again, I became a full-time, stay-at-home mom. But this time I was also a part-time freelance writer. In 1980, two years after our move, at age thirty-two, Harry died in a car accident. I returned to Nashville where I had family, friends, and a professional network support system.

I was a thirty-year-old woman with a daughter about to enter puberty and a son who had celebrated his ninth birthday only days before his father's death. I had never been on my own before. I left my father's house to go directly into my husband's. Where once we had been a family that soared like an eight-winged being, without Harry we careened, plummeted, and recovered (barely), with six wings and deep scars.

It was during this healing time that I did things that would prove to be my saving grace in the years to come. I chose not to take a job outside our home or to further my education. Instead, I stayed at home with my children, actively developed, cultivated, and nourished friendships, studied theosophy, and built my reputation as a writer of magazine articles.

In the years following Harry's death, I dated sporadically but had only two significant long-term relationships. Neither resulted in marriage. Then, in 1989, I met a man who was like no one I had ever encountered. Twelve years older than I, Luke (the name has been change for protection) was wealthy, cultured, charismatic, and powerful. Unfortunately, I found out only after I had fallen in love with him that he had a cold stone where his heart should have been. A stormy seven months into the relationship, I ended it. Through the following years we were, on infrequent occasions, lovers.

Our last encounter was October 18—more than a year since I had last heard from him. It was the only time I was sexually active in 1992. It was also the first and only time in our three-and-a-half-year relationship that we had ever had unprotected sex. You see, I had previously received the herpes virus from the man with whom I had my second long-term relationship. I had made Luke aware of my condition before we ever became sexually intimate. He always protected himself from becoming infected by me. But not this night. I did not even realize that this night was different until after the fact.

Within three weeks, I developed flulike symptoms and a case of vaginal herpes that was like nothing I had ever experienced. Within two days I couldn't eat or walk. I moved in and out of sleep that left me feeling drugged. My fever soared to 104 degrees and stayed there for four days. My daughter, fearing that I would die, took me to the emergency room. I spent two days in the hospital. Blood tests determined that my infection was viral, but we could not pin it down. My doctor believed that I was just experiencing a wicked case of the flu.

Two weeks after the onslaught of the illness, however, I was only minimally better. I still could not walk without bracing against the wall. My fever stubbornly refused to leave me cooler than 102 degrees ten days after my hospital stay. I couldn't work a full day and I couldn't concentrate when I was there.

I could not eat. I had no appetite. This terrified me. In forty-two years I had never looked at food without genuine affection. The smell made me nauseous. There was no taste. The small amount I was able to ingest gave me severe diarrhea. Frightened, because of continued illness, past experience with my

immune system, and my unconventional medical history, I asked my doctor to
test me for mononucleosis, the Epstein-Barr virus, and HIV.

I have since learned that it is common for women to have to request an HIV
test—no matter what their symptoms. Because of the shame factor inherent in
HIV and AIDS, some doctors find it personally embarrassing and potentially
humiliating to ask their patients who appear to fall into no high-risk category to
take the test.

Both the mononucleosis and Epstein-Barr proved negative. The ELISA HIV
blood test indicated a "low positive" for antibody activity. We were not too
alarmed because similar readings often occurred when the person tested was
suffering from the flu or some other severe viral infection. We then did a Western blot blood test, which has a much higher rate of accuracy but is significantly
more costly than the ELISA. It suggested the possibility of an HIV presence but
remained indeterminate.

I phoned Luke, telling him it looked like I might be HIV-positive and asked
him if he would take the test as well. He said that he would do it immediately
and call me with his results. I was momentarily relieved. If Luke tested negative,
I knew that I would too. A call from him would mean not having to agonize for
three months before I could take more blood tests to determine my status.

That was November 20, 1992. He never called.

My HIV tests came back positive in January 1993. The progress of HIV in its
contamination of the blood system is judged by the number of one's T-4 cells. A
healthy person has from 700 to 1,200. When one's count falls below 200 and
has at least one opportunistic infection, he or she is considered to have full-
blown AIDS. My T-4 cell count was 468. My doctor assured me that I would feel
great for years—perhaps up to ten—before the virus would deplete my
immune system enough to produce the dreaded symptoms. By then there could
be a cure. He told me how sorry he was.

My mind spun. How could I have been infected such a short time and have a
T-cell count of only 468? I knew that I was HIV-negative in March 1990 because
I took a test, not because I believed I had put myself at risk but to bring closure
to the seven-month relationship with Luke. I began to wonder if I had actually
contracted the virus sometime after the test.

With one exception, Luke was the only man with whom I had been intimate
since that time. The exception happened in May 1990. Before I discussed the
possibility with my doctor, I called the former lover with whom I had spent one
night and asked if he would take an HIV test. He agreed and tested negative.

When I asked my doctor if it was possible that I could have gotten the virus
in 1990 or 1991, he was quite firm that I had not contracted it then. If I had
received the virus at any time six months before my illness in November, he

said, the ELISA would have shown a high positive as would have the Western blot. He was convinced that the reason my first tests were indeterminate was because the virus had only recently been introduced to my system and I had just begun to seroconvert.

I suppose I was in shock from November through the end of January. My first thoughts were of the things I feared I would lose—health, family, friends, jobs, and insurance. I had visions of every good aspect of my life being taken from me by the disease itself or my world's response to the disease. During those first days it never occurred to me that HIV might be a stranger bearing gifts.

I told my children and my four closest friends as soon as the first ELISA came back with suspicious results. My daughter, Jamie, seemed to accept the possibility of my infection from the first. Jeremy, on the other hand, said, "Don't worry about it, Mom. I'm sure they got your lab work mixed up with someone else's." My friends and their spouses met me at my home after work, and we sat around remembering the last twenty or so years we'd been together. Although I was scared, I also felt loved and mightily supported.

The next day I visited my licensed practical social work (LPSW) counselor. Judy Eron began with our family when we decided we needed help working through the grief we all endured with Harry's death. For about ten years she had been observing, interviewing, and guiding our family. She had seen us through numerous traumas, including the children's brushes with the police during their adolescence; a nasty accident that involved my son, a pedestrian, and a $1,250,000 lawsuit; the financial loss of my public relations business; the sale of our home; rape at knife point; robbery at gun point; car theft; an accidental drug overdose; codependency counseling; the death of Harry's father and mine; Mrs. Runions's Alzheimer's disease and my mother's leukemia. We had history. Lots of it.

As providence would have it, Judy also worked with many people living with AIDS and with the hospice center. She had even co-authored a musical play called *Deadlines* dealing with the issues that face people with old age and terminal diseases. Judy knew me as well as anyone.

Unfortunately she had some unnerving news herself. She and her husband were going to retire early. Judy would be leaving her practice and the state in four months. Her concern was that I find support within the HIV/AIDS community. After we discussed all the possibilities, we decided that the best place for me to go was within my own spiritual fellowship. Patricia Reiter, a minister of First Church Unity, led an HIV/AIDS healing and support group. Judy had met one of the group members when he won a leading role in her play. She gave me Michael's name and number. I called him immediately and we chatted.

"This group is different," he warned. "We talk about living life to the fullest.

We are on a quest for healing—not just the infected body but the wounded soul. We discuss health, nutrition, and medicines, both those of the Western allopathic tradition and of the Eastern and Native American homeopathy—vitamins, minerals, enzymes, herbs, and flower essences. We deal with tough issues—family of origin, sexuality, relationships, ethics, addictions, and spiritual progress."

I told him it sounded perfect for me and on February 3, 1993, my forty-third birthday, I attended my first meeting. That night I became the group's first infected heterosexual member and also its only positive female. Group members encouraged me to begin to confront my fears of loss by looking into my health insurance coverage. To my relief I found that though the Roundtable paid for it, the group membership was in my name and would be mine no matter if I lost or changed my job, as long as I kept the premiums current. The first of my great fears died.

I had known since I took notes during my grandmother's funeral when I was fourteen and presented the family with a "death report" that I was going to work through the emotional storms of my life by writing and sharing my observations. My refusal to keep a secret is renown. If it makes a good story and someone might benefit by it, I am going to tell it.

By the end of February I had written a magazine article on my experience and a fairy tale dealing with the perceptions of "good" and "bad." In March I told my brothers. By April I had given my initial "first-person" speech before a crowd of 250 health care professionals and had been asked to become a board member on the United Way's Community AIDS Partnership. Everyone who was personally involved in my life knew of my HIV status except my boss, Dave Goetz, and my mother.

In April United Way called and asked if I would be willing to do a television spot for their season's kickoff in August. I agreed, thinking to myself, "You are getting too public with this. You are going to have to tell Dave and your mother before they hear about it from someone else or, God forbid, see you on TV."

I waited a good long time to tell my boss. I had wanted to tell him since I first found out about my condition, but November through May are our busiest months at the Roundtable. One of the major services we provide our members is legislative tracking and updates. Dave, as the executive director, lobbies and attends legislative sessions. I manage the office and give administrative support. We hardly even see each other during those months.

I had a lot of fears about telling Dave. The primary fear was that he would fire me.

I had never intended to become a secretary. In fact, I did just about everything I could to keep that from happening. In the small town I'm from, the most anyone ever expected from a woman was that she become a homemaker, a secretary, or a teacher. That hacked me off. As an alternative to taking home economics, I enrolled in Spanish. In place of shorthand, I took physics. Instead of typing, I played the clarinet.

It was not until I entered journalism classes, after I received my BA, that I was forced to learn to type. I was thirty-nine before I ever sat in front of a computer. My typing speed, minus my errors, was twenty words per minute. I never did learn shorthand.

Sooner or later I became all three of the things I had tried to avoid becoming. Only a wry twist of fate placed me in my first secretarial position in 1988. By the time I began working for the Roundtable in December 1990, my typing speed had increased to about sixty words per minute and I was literate, if not fluent, in a few core computer programs.

Bound by the financial constraints of the business, Dave could only afford someone with my skills. As a result, I was not as proficient, as he came to discover after two years of experience, as what he required. Our relationship had been ambivalent and fraught with frustration. I was afraid he was only waiting for a good chance to fire me. I feared HIV would afford him that opportunity.

Tennessee is an employment-at-will state. That means you can be fired for any reason without being given an explanation. The employee has no recourse unless she is a member of a union or she believes that she has been released because of her gender, race, national origin, or religious creed. Then she may file suit under the Civil Rights Act. The American Disabilities Act, which protects the jobs of persons with HIV/AIDS and demands that an employer make reasonable accommodations for them, applies only to companies with twenty-five or more employees.

If I had been an outstanding secretary or if I had been with the association for many years, I might not have been so fearful. But I was not and I had not.

I withheld my secret from Dave until the end of April. On Secretary's Day I told him of my infection and of my desire to go public and take an advocacy role. I explained to him how important it was for me to keep my job.

Later, when someone asked him what his feelings were when I told him of my illness, he said he felt as though he were sitting next to a person who had been struck by lightning. To my surprise and great relief, he immediately expressed compassion and sorrow for my situation. He began directly to educate himself on the virus and on what his responsibilities as an employer were. Neither of us had ever known anyone personally who had HIV or AIDS. We didn't have a policy or procedure for this challenge. There were only two of us. He was married, and I only had sex once a year. I guess we thought we didn't need one.

In June Frank Ritter, a personal friend and an editor at *The Tennessean*, Tennessee's largest newspaper, called and asked me if, in light of the mushrooming statistics on HIV and AIDS infections in women, I would be willing to go public. He suggested a front page topic cluster of articles for a Sunday edition, circulation 285,000. Pictures included.

I still had not told my mother. I had been trying for weeks, but the punch line of the first joke I ever heard about AIDS is true. The worst part about having HIV infection is telling your mother. I had the additional problem of her weakened condition from leukemia.

This was the same woman who removed her cork weggies and pearls, took to her bed in shame, and vomited up her guts in a darkened room for a week following my marriage. The same woman who asked me, after I had been dating a man for three years, if I was celibate. When I told her I was not, she threw herself onto her bed sobbing, "Why do I live?"

You have no idea what it is like to have Olivia De Havilland as a mother.

Actually, she took it much better than I could have ever hoped. Her first response was, "I am so sorry. Just do not tell your boss or anyone else and we will manage." When I explained to her that I had already told Dave and just about everyone I knew except her, she said, "Well, just do not go on television or write about it." When I told her I had plans to do a TV spot for United Way, she said, "Well, I really would appreciate it if you would not write about it. It would not help anyone else, and it could hurt you a lot."

At that point I decided I had given her as much as she could take at one time. I could talk to her about that front page article later.

When I told Dave that I had an opportunity to "come out" in *The Tennessean*, he said, "You have been fortunate so far. You have not lost your insurance, your jobs, or your apartment. No one has rejected you. Are you sure you want to push your luck one more time?" His question was valid. I told him I'd have to think about it some more.

I went home and talked with my children. Jeremy immediately gave his approval. "We have got to make something good come out of this," he said. "Maybe if you tell your story it will save someone's life."

My daughter was not as keen on the idea. She is a nanny for two little girls by day and a third one on some nights and weekends. She feared that the parents would be uninformed about how the virus is spread and be afraid to have her taking care of the girls. After we discussed it for some time, Jamie agreed that we needed to seize the opportunity. She told the parents of my infection before the article ran. They responded with kindness.

I polled my friends and members of my family. They had mixed opinions on the wisdom of doing the story, but they all said that they would support whatever decision I made.

The last person I asked was a member of my Unity healing group. Mark Ryan had been infected with HIV in the early eighties. He developed AIDS in 1990. When I met him in March, his T-cell count was 7. He had Karposi's sarcoma on his skin, in his mouth, and on his liver. He had been on AZT and the other AIDS drugs for years. They had stopped being effective.

Mark had had chemotherapy and radiation treatments for the cancer and had volunteered to take experimental AIDS medication through Vanderbilt Hospital's medical research division. In May he developed MAI, commonly known as the "wasting disease." When I went to visit him, he weighed about ninety pounds and was yellowed by jaundice. Notwithstanding, he was dressed in shorts and a T-shirt, sitting up in the middle of his bed listening to an Enya CD.

I hugged him hello and told him how lovely it was to see him even though it had only been two days since I had last seen him at church. One thing we learn quickly once we enter the land of AIDS is that we never take our time together for granted. I told him that he looked beautiful and asked him what he had done that day. "I have been to see my doctor and to shop at the mall," he said.

Knowing that the doctor had given him no more than two weeks to live, I asked him what he had bought. "A cellular phone," he held it up for me to examine. I had to laugh. He had bought a red sports car only weeks before (on credit, of course) but had been too sick to drive it.

"And who do you intend to call?" I questioned him.

It was his turn to laugh. "Anyone I want to."

I loved Mark with a depth of passion that neither of us could understand. After all the death and loss and sickness that had circled through my life, I thought that I had my emotions under control. I never mourned after I was diagnosed with HIV. When my friends cried I said, "I will give you five minutes to weep, then you have to get a grip. If I can take this, so can you."

Mark taught me better. The first night he missed group because of his illness, I fell apart. As I sobbed uncontrollably, I came to understand that you never get death down. Each time it is different. I also learned that it is easier to accept your own death than to watch a friend succumb to it.

That day I asked him, "Mark, sitting there where you are, near the end of this journey and looking at me just barely onto the path, what is your advice regarding 'coming out' by media exposure? What do you think I should do?"

"First, let me say, I understand your concern," he began. "Telling even one person, considering the shame-based nature of the disease, demands a great risk. If you choose not to do the story, I will support you wholeheartedly in that decision and love you just as much as if you go ahead and do it. Having said that, I must tell you that I would love to see you go public. You are a woman, a heterosexual, a respected member of the business community, a teacher, and a person who has touched thousands of people through radio, television, and the print media. You are the mom next door.

"What you would be saying to society by telling your story is that this is not a gay men's disease," he continued. "This is not a virus that consumes only the 'untouchables' of society. By going public, you tell this community that AIDS is everyone's problem. Maybe if more 'regular' people come forward, others will begin to see that they are not bullet-proof. If you, Little Miss Pollyanna, can have this virus, anyone can."

I made my decision on the spot. Mark died three days later.

I told Dave that I wanted to do the article. "We will have to inform the executive committee," he said. "You have got more experience in telling this than I. How do you suggest I approach them?"

"I believe that people are hungry for chances to forgive. I think they yearn for the occasion to show compassion. If you approach any person, as if you are giving them a great opportunity to do just that, their attitudes will mirror yours," I told him.

He followed my lead and the executive committee responded positively. They were supportive of my place in the organization. They called and visited me. They sent cards and letters. They also suggested to Dave that he send an Executive Memo to the membership to alert them to my condition and the upcoming *Tennessean* article.

I cannot express to you what the support of the Tennessee Business Roundtable has meant in my life. Dave wrote a beautiful piece that brought absolutely no negative response. On the contrary, we both received kind and encouraging words from the membership.

The Roundtable shares office space with the Tennessee Trucking Association. After we sent out the memo, I told TTA's president and each of the office staff one at a time. I gave them individually a copy of the article I'd written about my experience and a brochure with some facts and myths about the disease and how one gets it. Without exception, they gave me kindness and compassion.

I then sent a copy of both materials and a cover letter to the community college where I teach, and to the landlord of my apartment complex. I did not want anyone who had the power to take anything away from me to read the *Tennessean* article without my having told them about my HIV status first. Again, I was met with encouragement and support.

The story appeared on August 8. I got calls from everywhere—from people I knew and folks I did not. My very first Sunday School teacher, Miss Norma Mitchum, called long-distance to tell me she loved me and she knew Jesus did, too. A woman called saying her sister was HIV-positive but that she had small children and for their sake did not feel that she could reveal the nature of her illness. She thanked me for speaking out in her sister's place.

I received more than fifty letters, all of them positive and encouraging. One letter came from a woman who had been one of my very best friends in grade school. She had left Waverly at the end of the seventh grade, and we hadn't been in touch since. That was 1962.

Several letters came from people who knew me from my days as a fundamental Christian. I had left that fellowship with great sadness when the church expressed disapproval of the breadth of my spiritual explorations. The letters were warm and accepting and forgiving. Bridges that I thought had been damaged beyond repair appeared to have been strengthened by the shock of my illness.

Every one of my in-laws, cousins and all, wrote or called or both. Considering that I had been a widow for thirteen years, I found this extraordinarily beautiful.

In my hometown, my mother and brothers were receiving the same treatment. They had calls from old friends, faraway relatives, and church members. People visited Momma, brought food, and stayed awhile to talk about how sad the situation was and how brave she was to encourage me to go public. I knew then that we were all going to survive this experience.

Looking back, it seems that I have been preparing for this moment my entire life. It may seem strange to you that I could move from despair to gratitude so smoothly. I have not always been such a quick study. Over and over again I have been given opportunities to grow in faith, hope, and forgiveness. There is an old Sufi proverb that says, "When the heart weeps for what it has lost, the Spirit laughs for what it has found." I've come to recognize this experience as yet another chance to grow.

The virus has been quite a teacher. First it showed me just how quickly a fairly healthy body can succumb to disease. Though I have only experienced the initial illness, the virus has indicated how sick I can be and still live. Having HIV in my body forced me to reevaluate my life-style. I have adjusted my life so that I have become more health conscious. I have made changes to relieve much of the stress around me. *No* is now an active word in my vocabulary.

I have changed my diet. I eat fewer of my momma's pork chops and consume more vitamin-rich foods. I'm learning about different vitamins, minerals, and herbs that strengthen the immune system and am investigating other alternative sources of healing. I feel better and look healthier than I have in years.

With this situation, as with any other health crisis, I believe it is important that we play an active part in our own healing. Not all doctors appreciate a curious and questioning client. And certainly insurance companies refuse to

pay claims on any experimental, nutritional, or food supplementary procedures.

I believe that it is important to keep nontraditional health options available.
There is no such thing as false hope. That is an oxymoron. Hope cannot be false
because of its intrinsic nature. And even if there were such a thing as false hope,
when you've been told you're terminal, any hope at all is better than none.

Second, AZT, ddI, and DDC, medicines designed to combat AIDS, have never
cured one person. Although in some cases they have improved the quality of life,
in others they have created numerous side effects that have often led to complications that brought about death. And they are expensive. It is not unusual for
an AIDS patient to spend more than $2,000 a month for prescribed drugs. I have
rarely run into an alternative healing therapy that costs anywhere near that.

In addition, there are long-term survivors of this plague. Along with the
research monies we spend trying to develop new drugs and a vaccine, we should
be studying them—mind, body, and spirit—to learn how they continue to
maintain their good health. It probably would consume a fraction of the cost of
drug research and produce a wealth of useful information to those of us who
have just begun to live with HIV or AIDS.

While teaching me about taking care of my body, my new companion has
taught me how dear and supportive my family can be. I am especially proud of
my children's reaction to my contracting the virus. Having lost their father
when they were so young, they could have reacted with fear or anger or even
despair. Instead, they have been my greatest supporters and my most enduring
sources of joy.

HIV continues to remind me of how many deep and sustaining friendships I
have been given during my life and has opened the door to introduce me to an
extended family—people who, like me, loved others too well and ourselves too
little one too many times. My fellow travelers on this path have taught me that
romance does not necessarily die in the presence of this disease. Indeed, many
found the special relationship they always wanted after they contracted HIV.

I have discovered that there is nothing like perceiving strong restrictions in
your life to bring it into sharp focus. It is as though I saw only in black and white
and now have been granted the opportunity to experience color. Although each
of us knows in the back of our minds that our future is not guaranteed, discovering that you have an illness that is generally believed to be fatal brings that
reality to the forefront of one's consciousness.

I am reminded of the story of a man who fell from a cliff. On his way down
the side of the embankment, he grabbed a bush that kept him from being cap-
tured by a tiger below. As the roots gave way an inch at a time, he spotted a plant
bearing a strawberry growing in a nearby crevice. He plucked the fruit, and as

the roots released their grasp of the soil, placed it in his mouth as he fell to his fate. It was the best strawberry he ever tasted.

Although I received the virus from one "low-risk contact," I have learned that HIV is difficult to transfer. According to my doctor, the odds of my getting the disease from one unprotected sexual episode is somewhere in the neighborhood of five hundred to one. In my healing group, I've met numerous couples who have had unprotected sex for years while one partner had the virus and didn't know it. The other mate remains HIV-negative. There are other pairs who have done intravenous drugs together, shared needles, and had unprotected sex. One is positive and the other is negative.

It appears that the virus has less to do with bodies or sex than it does with lessons in love. My experience reflects that the virus seems to find those who have not found love outside themselves or cannot find enough love inside themselves or both.

The virus is still new to me and I do not know everything about it on any level, but this I have come to believe: HIV attached itself to me because I was willing on some level to receive it. Although I was neither physically nor emotionally conscious of my choice, I believe that I have agreed to this experience for my own soul's growth and perhaps for the spiritual evolution of humankind.

I realize that this is not a belief held in common with the majority of people who have HIV or AIDS. Because of the unusual number of challenges my family and I have been called on to withstand, I began a quest to answer my questions of "Why?" "How?" and "What now?" The process I discovered on my expedition to understand how to survive and even thrive no matter what the physical, mental, or emotional circumstances, ended up being something I'd heard about all my life. It was called faith.

The faith I am talking about is not just intellectual belief. I am talking about *knowing* that whatever the situation appears to be, no matter how physically painful, how mentally debilitating, or how emotionally devastating, it is a point of spiritual growth, a place of grace and a lesson in healing.

To truly believe everything that happens is for the good and is delivered in love demands a nontraditional, maybe even unorthodox perspective. It means changing your vocabulary to remove the words *victim* and *blame*. The faith I am talking about requires a suspension of belief in the "facts" as presented by the five senses. It necessitates the activation of hope in the face of sorrow-filled experience. It compels you to ignore the edge of the physical/emotional cliff and entreats you to take a spiritual leap. This is what nineteenth-century Danish theologian Soren Kierkegaard termed the *leap of faith*.

I have been given many cliffs and many opportunities to leap. I am now attempting to live consciously within the leap—every day, all day long. Because of this I am empowered. I am no longer a helpless recipient of fate's whims but a co-creator with God. That joyful acceptance is the element that gives me peace and makes me unusual. It is the very thing that causes people from all walks of life experiencing all kinds of challenges to approach me and say, "I want to be where you are. I want what you have."

Dr. Elizabeth Kübler-Ross, who has worked with death and dying for decades and AIDS since the early eighties, has said that one day humanity will come to view AIDS as one of the greatest gifts of our history for the relational bridges it builds and the understanding and compassion it develops.

She further predicted that those who received the virus will be recognized as souls who were prepared to accept a challenge equal to spiritual physics.

The question I am asked most often is, "How do you feel about the man who transferred the virus to you?" My answer has changed over the course of a year. When Luke did not return my call to tell me he had taken a test, I felt as though he had discarded me and my request as unimportant. I became concerned that he was knowingly spreading the virus to other unsuspecting women and putting their lives in danger.

I went to two different attorneys to see if I could file criminal charges. I found that there is no law in Tennessee against transmitting HIV. In the few states where such a law does exist, one must prove that the person knew he was infected when he spread the virus. I then asked if I could file a civil suit, not because I wanted any money but because I wanted to provide a binding date that might serve as "proof of knowledge" should he transmit the virus to another individual after my infection. Neither attorney wanted to take the case.

In retrospect, I am glad. I believe it is best that we have no criminal statutes against the transmission of HIV. If we enacted such laws, they might become the first legal steps toward social restriction or physical quarantine. On a personal level, a civil lawsuit would have held me in an emotional frame of bitterness and blame that could have only hurt and never healed me.

For certain people, being able to file legal claims gives them a feeling that they are doing something in a situation where we are essentially told nothing can be done. The anger and sense of righteous zeal for "saving" someone else by persecuting another gives some people a feeling of control when most of life appears to be held in the hands of chaos. My philosophy, however, is that we are all responsible for our own behavior. Although Luke was no doubt extremely infected with the virus, and he may indeed have known that he was infected, I was a grown woman who had heard about AIDS, knew what it took to protect myself, and did not.

I feel deep pain when I think that a man that I loved with a great passion did not care enough about me to call and see how I was feeling, what my medical prognosis was, or how my friends and family were adjusting. I have an equally intense sense of loss because I have no way to know how he is feeling or where he is in his process.

Since I believe that we all are co-creating with God opportunities to grow in love, I no longer feel responsible for his behavior or for the well-being of the other women with whom he may be having sex. I do, however, feel responsible for educating as many people as possible about the way the disease is contracted and for developing within the community at large a sense of compassion for those already living with the virus.

Although my own personal ethics demand that I no longer engage in sexual intercourse, I do not hold Luke responsible for my infection. I give him the respect he deserves as one of the greatest teachers in my life. The disciplines I have learned through him have been extremely difficult—trials by fire. But the lessons have also taught me that like a phoenix, the spirit rises triumphant from death and pain's ashes.

HIV has changed me and every single person around me. It has brought me joyous new relationships and has helped heal old ones. I do not have one relationship in my life that is not better and stronger today than it was a year ago. I choose to view my HIV as a gift to help me live my life in the heart of love.

The virus has instructed me in the elements of abundant living: (1) no drugs, alcohol, or smoking which damage the physical immune system; (2) proper diet, exercise, and regular emotional workouts with trainers; (3) no sex when what I want is love (no unprotected sex—ever—unless in a marriage of faithful commitment); and (4) a course of spiritual investigation, development, and growth.

My friends have chosen to view my contracting HIV as a lesson for them in awareness. They look into my face—my middle-aged, ordinary, mother-next-door face— and see their own reflected back at them. They look at me and say, "But for the grace of God go I." Then they hug me and tell me we are all going to be okay.

Those of us who meet each Tuesday night in the HIV-positive support group know, "*Because* of the grace of God go we." Not one of the people in that group is the same person he or she was when first infected with the disease. Our lives were changed forever in the instant it took for the doctor to say, "I'm sorry. Your test came back positive."

Each of us knows that our time is precious and that our lives must be meaningful. For us HIV/AIDS became our guide and teacher. The virus gave us the intense edge that drives us painfully to scrape away the sorrow and disappointments of our existence to reveal the innate integrity of our spirits. We began to learn from one another about the goodness within us and the forgiveness of God.

We bravely dig into our childhoods, face the demons of our families of origin, our adolescent experiences, and our psycho/spiritual core beliefs, and many, many times we walk away stronger, cleaner—with something of our original innocence restored.

That is why we have turned the acronym of our virus into Healing Inner Values. We laugh, we live, and we learn from one another how to mine the riches of each day that often go unnoticed and unappreciated by those not gifted to see life's boundaries or to truly taste wild strawberries.

Joan Baez sings a song that has these lines, "My house stands on the edge of glory. Steady as the seasons change. Dreams of grace arise before me and call me home again." We who are infected with HIV have been given an amazing gift. Every time we share one another's lives or another's death we realize that we are standing on the edge of glory and that we are facing toward home.

AIDS is a horrible, horrible disease that has taken many of the brightest lights of the world. It has become a metaphor for the time and energy we waste in guilt, hate, bigotry, and shame. There appears to be no cure anywhere near us, and a vaccine seems just as distant. The extraordinary part about this debilitating and deadly disease is that it is preventable. All a person has to do is care for and respect himself enough to protect himself.

The most important lesson I have learned from life is that an individual can respond in different ways to any given situation. We can contract, isolate, blame, and hide in shame and anger or we can expand, unite, and stand with courage and love. We can become victims or victors. We can lash out at the world in our pain and die. Or we can forgive ourselves and our world, find peace, and be healed.

As paradoxical as it may seem, we believe that the virus, which may destroy our bodies and take the lives of many millions of others in the next decades, is healing us as individuals and may in fact usher in a global transformation. That is the best part about it. That is why we call it AIDS.

PART TWO

Economic and Sociocultural Perspectives

5 | Making a Living: Women Who Go Out

PRISCILLA ALEXANDER

There are a thousand, ten thousand, a hundred thousand words for it and for its practitioners. Multiple words in multiple languages name this profession, said to be the oldest in the world: prostitutes, sex workers, hookers, whores, malayahs, femmes libres, bar ladies, geisha, putas, beshas, ladies of the night, hostesses, night walkers, ashawahs, call girls, escorts, guides, masseuses, streetwalkers, entertainers, strippers, dancers, guides, watembezi.[1]

Not always a "profession" really, often something not quite recognized—a way to survive between one job and another, or to supplement another wage when the rent is due, or school fees have to be paid, or prescriptions must be filled. Sometimes it is a way to pay one's way along the route from the farm to the city, from the South to the North, from the outlying world to the centers of commerce and culture.

Whether in San Francisco or Paris, Nairobi or Rio de Janeiro, the average length of time women work in the sex trade is four to six years. Some only do it for a week or so, many for a year or so, some for twenty or thirty years. Although it is said to be a young trade, I know one woman who began sex work at the age of fifty-five and another who continues to work at the age of sixty-two in order to supplement her retirement pension in a country that recognizes her work (Metal 1987; Réal 1993, personal communication). In any case, far more former than current sex workers exist in the world, and most go on to something else, despite the common mythology that they all die of disease, murder, or suicide.

Why do women become prostitutes? I always think of the line so many customers use, "What's a nice girl like you doing here?" One could just as easily ask, "What's a nice man like you doing here," but the cultural stereotypes don't allow it. The primary motivating factor, whether in Manila, Calabar, Ciudad Juarez, Frankfurt, or Toronto, is money—the need to earn a living, to pay for an education, to support one's children, to support a husband or lover, to send money home to parents still living on the farm. Even when managers—pimps, madams, mamasans, bar owners, landlords, police—take an outrageous part of the income, a woman can still make more as a prostitute than as a street vendor, a rickshaw driver, a retail clerk, a fast-food cook, a file clerk, a switchboard operator, a cotton picker, a waitress, or an elementary school teacher. In some countries, some prostitutes make more money than doctors and lawyers.

Other factors play a role as well. Some women begin sex work when they are still teenagers. They may have run away from homes filled with intolerable physical and sexual abuse, and the only work they can find in the big city is prostitution on the street or, if they are lucky, in a club or bar (Filgueras 1993, personal communication).[2] Sometimes when they run, they look for other prostitutes or pimps to "turn them out"; sometimes they are duped into the life by men who promise them love and happiness, and sweet talk them into going out on the street, beating them if they resist. And some are teenagers sent by their families to pay off debts, the debt bondage that keeps some young women captive in brothels in Thailand and India and perhaps other countries as well. Still others volunteer to pay off debts, proud that they can help their families. Sometimes they know what they are getting into; all too often their ideas about what prostitution is like pale next to the reality. Sometimes they think they will wait on tables or sit at desks in hotels, deluded by false promises because to tell the truth is to risk arrest.

Most women, however, begin sex work as adults, as defined by their cultures.[3] Some have been married, in some cases without their full consent, and the marriage has gone wrong; perhaps it was violent. Some rebel against the female role they are expected to play, do not want to marry, and leave home to avoid it. Some are lesbians—by desire, by behavior, only sometimes by identity—and prefer to have sex with many men, as a job, to avoid having sex with one, as a wife. Some are drawn by ideas of the excitement a city offers and make a calculated gamble that prostitution will enable them to take advantage of the new city, the new country, and will not be too hard on them. Others are forced to migrate—by war, famine, chronic unemployment, or political repression. If they migrate, they are often dependent on brokers—to front them money for tickets, to arrange travel documents that will let them stay in countries that do not want them—brokers that cannot say, up front, that the work they will do is prostitution, so they lie and say it is other things and charge incredible amounts of money to make up for their own risk of imprisonment.

Migration as a Central Issue

Prostitution has always been associated with migration. The oldest records of prostitution have been found in the legal codes of ancient cities—religious and mercantile centers that drew people from miles around. In fact, wherever there have been markets, there have been prostitutes, whether the markets and fairs of ancient Mesopotamia or Elizabethan England or the market days of small towns in today's Ethiopia. Prostitution has also always been associated with religious festivals, again magnets for people from outlying areas (Lerner 1986a, 1986b; Bullough and Bullough 1987; Roberts 1992; Tannahill 1992; G/Kidan 1990, personal communication).

During the Crusades or the Hundred Years War, Marco Polo's travels, or the Conquest of the Americas, for example, tremendous numbers of people, mostly men, migrated to alien countries. Similar migrations occurred during the colonization of the North American West, East and West Africa, Latin America, and the Indian Subcontinent. During the Industrial Revolution hordes of people migrated from farms to cities in North America and Europe, as today people are migrating from countryside to city in Africa, Asia, and Latin America, or—with or without papers—from poor countries to rich ones, including the escape from Eastern Europe. There has always been migration—often men traveling alone at first, working in the new place, sending money home, looking for female companionship until (and if) they sent for their wives and children. Women, too, have always migrated—to escape war, famine, and unemployment, to take advantage of the "modernity" of the city, or to break out of traditional roles that confined them (Tong 1994; Yamazaki 1985). It is impossible to stop migration. Prostitution always has been, and probably always will be, one of the adaptive strategies to cope with the stress and dislocation of migration: surcease for the men, an income for the women.

The Laws and the Label

In no country in the world is prostitution completely legal, a fully recognized occupation, offering the same rights and privileges guaranteed other workers. Some aspects are always illegal. In the United States every aspect is illegal— soliciting, engaging, running a business, living off the earnings, crossing a state border for the purposes of prostitution, renting a premises for the purposes of prostitution, loitering—except in a few rural counties in the state of Nevada where women can legally work in little prison camps called brothels. In many countries, engaging in prostitution has been removed from the penal codes, often in response to the 1949 United Nations Convention that called for decriminalization of prostitution per se but recommended leaving as criminal all activities that profit from the prostitute's labor (Convention 1949). In most developed countries women are arrested day after day, night after night, for standing on street corners, for offering or agreeing to provide sex for a fee, for placing an ad in a newspaper, and/or for discussing sex and money on the phone—because soliciting has remained a crime. If two women work together, one is vulnerable to arrest on the more serious charges of living off the earnings of a prostitute or running a disorderly house. In some countries (e.g., the Netherlands and Germany), cities set aside zones where soliciting is legal, sometimes also tolerating brothels or parallel businesses, visible within those zones, invisible outside them. Some countries (e.g., China, Japan, and the United States) bar prostitutes from entering their country even if they have no intention to do sex work while they are there, even if they no longer work in the industry. Many of those same countries allow prostitutes to enter for specified periods of time—six months is common—on "artists' visas," pretending that sex work is not the artistry involved.[4] Many countries have carved out exceptions to prohibitions of prostitution, using such euphemisms as massage parlors or saunas, escort services, entertainment or hospitality businesses, periodically arresting women on prostitution charges, or closing the euphemistic businesses, to prove that "prostitution" is not allowed.

As a result, it is rare that sex workers can use such strategies as collective bargaining or strikes to improve poor working conditions. In Germany, where prostitution is legal in specified zones, brothels that improve their working conditions in response to pressure from prostitutes get closed by the police because they are defined as "encouraging women to become prostitutes," which is illegal. The houses with poor conditions are allowed to remain open (Representatives 1991).

To avoid arrest, many women migrate from one establishment to another, one city to another, and across national boundaries, which prevents them from establishing networks of support where they live or ongoing relationships with health care providers and other service agencies. Migrating frequently, they become isolated from any sense of community except the brothel-like businesses where they work or the specific group of prostitutes and pimps with whom they migrate.

Being arrested on prostitution charges can be quite traumatic—the sex worker must first check out the potential client, decide whether it is safe to work with him, get into a car with him, and let him into her work space. To get arrested she must first decide to trust, only to have the trust violated. Sometimes she does not even have to trust or to solicit or to agree; it is her word against that of a police officer, and in a world in which prostitutes are routinely denied human rights, she can get arrested anyway.

In 1989, when I was working for COYOTE, a prostitutes' rights organization, a woman who was desperate just to talk to someone called the office. She had just been released from jail that day, she told me. She was walking down the street, and the police officer who had arrested her on the previous case called to her from his car. She recognized him but felt she had no choice but to go over to him. He asked if she would do a blow job. She, not knowing what to do, agreed, and was arrested.[5]

Twenty-one states in the United States have enacted laws requiring anyone convicted of prostitution, or in some cases merely arrested, to be tested for antibodies to HIV. In eleven states anyone who is arrested again after testing positive is liable to be charged with felony prostitution (prostitution is usually a misdemeanor), carrying prison terms ranging from three to twenty years, depending on the state (AIDS Policy Center 1994).[6] Many of those arrested under these provisions have tried to stop working, but because their infections are relatively new, so that they are too healthy to receive the social security payments to which people diagnosed with AIDS are entitled, and because they are unable to find other employment, they have no option but to continue working. They are charged with felony prostitution even if they carry condoms with them at the time of the arrest or inform the "client" that he will have to use a condom. As late as 1994, prosecutors in San Francisco used possession of condoms as evidence in felony proceedings, because they felt they could not obtain a conviction without such evidence (Kingston 1993).[7] Unfortunately this problem is not unique to the United States, as there are reports of police confiscating condoms from prostitutes in England, Kenya, and India, and it is likely to be a common form of harassment in many countries.[8]

In countries where street prostitutes are arrested repeatedly, sometimes several times a year, each time spending time in jail, they become increasingly isolated and depressed. If they use drugs to make it easier to work, which some do, their drug use is likely to increase with each incarceration (inside the jail as well as out), as their feelings of powerlessness increase. With the constant dislocations, many women lose their children, as families or the state sues to deprive them of custody, which only increases their despair and feelings of worthlessness.

But it is not just that they are arrested. Whether they work in Manila, Bombay, Nairobi, New York, or San Francisco, to a greater or lesser extent they are forced by police to comply with demands for "free sex" or "sex in exchange for not being arrested" and sometimes regular financial donations to one police officer after another. Women working in a massage parlor in central Manila told me that as many as fifteen police officers came by every week to demand sex and money.[9]

Sometimes the police own the brothels where the women work; sometimes they just have cozy relationships with the brothel owners (Asia Watch 1993:5), who also must provide sex (usually someone else's services) and money to stay in business. One woman who worked independently in New York City told me of friends who worked in brothels routinely raided by police who then gang raped all the women working at the time.[10] When I was in Kisumu, Kenya, on the shore of Lake Victoria, women told me that police were "rough clients" and did not pay.[11] In New York City one woman told me she had had sex with half the officers in the local precinct.[12]

Once arrested, a woman is labeled a "prostitute," a woman beyond the pale of womanhood. For women who only work casually, the first arrest can push them across the line into full-time prostitution, labeled and shamed, afraid their families will know. For many who are arrested again and again, they come to see arrests as just a part of the job, like rape, something to be tolerated because "what else can you do?"

Occupational Safety and Health Hazards

The occupational hazards associated with prostitution are many. First, dealing with clients in such an intimate way can be stressful, especially to the novice who has not yet learned methods of control. Dealing with managers who pressure the workers to take on every client who chooses them, regardless of how drunk or abusive or whether the official shift has ended, is also stressful. The inability to turn down clients can mean that some clients feel free to use physical violence to have the kind of sex they want or just to express hatred, while the woman has no legal recourse (not to mention that most police believe that, by definition, a prostitute cannot be raped; she is, after all, a public woman, a woman held in common by any and all men, under the law). Most prostitutes are in fact raped at least once in the course of their work. With experience, many learn how to control their clients, but some never do and are raped and beaten repeatedly.

Again, if management is always pushing them to accept more clients, to do what the client wants, no matter what, women have little or no ability to protect themselves from sexually transmitted diseases. Far too many men, in too many countries, still refuse to use condoms fourteen years after the first AIDS-related opportunistic infections were described in the medical literature. Some countries require that all prostitutes register—with either the police or public health agencies—and regularly report for examinations for sexually transmitted diseases, in order to guarantee "clean" women to clients, as if that were possible. Far from helping the women to remain free of disease, registered prostitutes in some countries have a higher incidence of sexually transmitted diseases (STDs) than unregistered workers. In Singapore the unregistered women both provided different and safer sexual practices and used condoms more often than registered and tested workers, despite the "education" the registered prostitutes had been receiving (Chan 1992, personal communication). In Indonesia, women who were regularly tested, and given a penicillin shot whether or not they had an infection, had a higher incidence of STDs than women who avoided the system (Horton 1990, personal communication). German prostitutes have complained that clients use the fact that prostitutes are required to be tested as justification for their refusal to use condoms, often saying, "You're clean, I don't have to use one!" (Pheterson 1989). The end result, of course, is that neither the sex worker nor the client is safe.

In many prostitution businesses—bars and nightclubs, for example, but also sometimes brothels—managers require the women to drink alcohol with their clients, indeed to convince the client to buy them expensive drinks. As a result some become addicted to alcohol. In other situations, in order to deal with the stress of the job some women use stimulants while they work, depressants when they want to go to sleep, and eventually become dependent on those drugs. If drug use comes to dominate her life, the prostitute may end up working to pay for the drug or exchange sex for the drug, by which time she may be even less able to control what happens during a transaction.

Vulnerability to HIV Infection

In all countries, some sex workers are more vulnerable to HIV infection than others, usually in inverse proportion to their economic status; that is, women who work at the higher-per-transaction price level are at less risk, whereas women who earn the least-per-transaction are at the greatest risk. However, the risk is not always from the prostitution per se. In Western, industrialized countries, the prevalence of HIV in sex workers is directly related to the prevalence in injecting drug users—that is, the women become infected because of their own drug use involving needle sharing or through unprotected sexual activity with men who inject drugs, usually their lovers or husbands, rarely their clients (Darrow 1992). Women who work on the streets earn the least per client, are the most likely to be arrested or raped while working, and are the most likely to inject drugs or live with men who do. Women who work indoors earn more, generally have safer working conditions, and are less likely to use drugs or have sex with men who do.

The situation in developing countries is less well documented. However, in Thailand, the highest rate of HIV infection in prostitutes is in the northern provinces, near the border with Myanmar, in the Golden Triangle, which is the center of opium production. Many come from families in which heroin injection has replaced the more traditional opium smoking, often with shared needles. Their clients often come from those same communities, both in Thailand and from across the border. In addition, many work in very low-cost brothels and must see many clients to pay off their parents' debts, as well as their own debts added on for room and board. It is likely that their vulnerability to HIV infection is from both drugs and sex, and may be compounded by unsterile conditions in the "clinics" where they must be tested regularly or even more when doctors come into the brothels to examine them.[13] The women who work in Bangkok, however, or in the resorts that cater to "sex tourists," have lower rates of infection. They earn more per client, are less likely to use drugs or to have sex with men who use drugs, and may be in a better position to choose which health provider they use.[14]

In Bombay, India, where more than a hundred thousand women work in brothels in the impoverished Kamathipura district, rates of HIV and other sexually transmitted infections are also high and climbing rapidly. These high rates are again likely to be the result of a combination of risks, including drug use, sex with men who are infected, and unsterile conditions and inadequate treatment in "STD clinics" staffed by "quacks." Even in Bombay, however, some women with better working conditions and more power to negotiate are less vulnerable to disease (Oostvogels 1992–93, pers. comms.; Mark 1981; Raghuramaiah 1991; Nanda 1990).

In Nairobi, Kenya, the women who work in the poorest bars, in the poorest neighborhoods, earn the least and have the highest rates of infections. On the other hand, among the poorest workers in Nairobi, older women, who have more clients per day and who have worked the longest, had the lowest rates of HIV infection (Kreiss et al. 1986; Piot et al. 1987; Simonsen et al. 1990). Although Plummer et al. (1993) theorize that women who remain seronegative after repeated exposure are able to resist the virus because of biological factors, another element may be that because of their experience, they are better able to control the client and the transaction. When I met with a group of older prostitutes in another Kenyan city, Mombasa, they told me that they never let a client stay for more than two-and-a-half minutes; if he wasn't finished in that amount of time, they just told him his time was up. In addition they shared work spaces, so that if any client resisted using a condom, the other woman could reinforce the demand.[15]

In all developing countries, the women who work with well-off businessmen and tourists are healthier, again because their clients are less likely to use drugs or have other risks for infection. Another possible factor is that the upper-income workers are more able to sidestep the behaviors most likely to put them at risk, replacing vaginal and anal intercourse with fellatio and hand jobs, modern and Western in the public mind, and much less risky for both the women and their clients.[16]

The subject of prostitution is being debated in many parts of the world, including within the women's movement. Many women who are not prostitutes, and who do not know any prostitutes, are appalled by the whole concept of prostitution—some because they feel that women are degraded and abused by prostitution, some because they resent prostitutes being available to their husbands, and some for both reasons. Some former prostitutes who have survived particularly bad experiences think the only solution is to abolish prostitution, and they support continued legal repression to do so.[17] Other prostitutes, including some whose experiences have been horrendous, as well as others whose experiences have been tolerable—even positive, look at the range of abuse and danger for women in the sex industry, and are convinced that the only way to end the abuse is to bring prostitution out of the shadows. They are working for the repeal of all existing laws and the legitimization of the workers, the prostitutes. They want to force the institutions that surround sex work to change so that working conditions are safe, so that no one works in the industry who does not want to, so that a history of working in the industry does not result in travel restrictions, exclusion from certain kinds of jobs, denial of the right to raise one's children, or any of the other consequences that now are common.[18]

Whether the abolitionists or the sex workers' rights advocates are correct in the long run, the reality is that prostitution is not going to go away in the foreseeable future, if ever. Women will continue to turn to the sex trade to pay their bills, to support their children or parents, and to survive. The issue that confronts us then is how to change the conditions of prostitutes' work so that what has always been a coping strategy, a temporary occupation between one thing and another, does not carry a death sentence (Schoepf 1992, personal communication).

Sex Work-Related Interventions

In the early 1980s, as more and more reports of HIV/AIDS were published about this frightening new syndrome, with its killing opportunistic infections, prostitutes in the Western, industrial countries began to worry. If, as epidemiologists began to hypothesize, this syndrome was caused by some agent that could be sexually transmitted, clearly prostitutes would be at risk. At the same time epidemiologists, most of whom were men, began to panic, fantasizing that prostitutes were dirty "reservoirs" or "pools of contagion," waiting to infect unwary and "innocent" clients (and even clients' babies and sometimes their wives). Prostitutes in the West, being rather practical, realized that condoms, which traditionally they used when they could or else bargained for higher prices when clients resisted, were literally all that might stand between them and this disease. In the United States, Canada, Germany, Italy, the United Kingdom, Australia, and New Zealand, prostitutes formed organizations and applied for government and foundation funding to start reaching out to their colleagues in the business to ensure that all sex workers knew about the need to use condoms with all clients. Studies done in those countries showed an early rise in consistent condom use among female sex workers, which has stabilized at between 70 and 80 percent.

Ongoing street and in a few cases brothel outreach projects have made an enormous difference. In addition to educating and distributing condoms to all sex workers, and needles or bleach with which to clean the needles to those who inject drugs, these projects have advocated for prostitutes with public health officials, police, and lawmakers, to try to improve working conditions in general and to fight mandatory testing and other repressive measures. In a few countries, most notably Australia and the Netherlands, the government has begun the process of legal reform, a process in which prostitutes' groups have played a major part.

In far too many countries, in both the North and the South, the first response of policy makers is to test prostitutes for HIV and keep those who test positive from working, despite the fact that this approach has never been very successful in controlling other STDs. Instead, this approach pushes prostitution, and prostitutes, underground and away from health services. Some countries passed new legislation (e.g., twenty-one states in the United States) and some simply added HIV testing to already existing mandatory testing programs (e.g., Germany, Senegal, Thailand, and Peru). In a few developing countries, public health officials, working with donor agencies, followed the lead of the prostitutes' groups in the North and designed interventions that took advantage of sex workers' wide range of skills (e.g., acting, music, negotiation, physical skills) and knowledge (e.g., about male sexuality, about ways to take care of themselves) in order to develop peer education projects. And some of those projects transformed what originally was only intended to be education and distribution of condoms into complex community organizing, addressing many aspects of sex workers' lives. Striking examples include projects in Nigeria, Zimbabwe,

Thailand, the Philippines, and Mexico (Esu-Williams 1993; Apisok 1993; Wilson et al. 1990). Over the years representatives of some of those projects have met prostitutes from the northern countries, especially during the International AIDS Conferences, and both groups learned from each other. Those from the South bring back new skills and ideas about prostitution to share; those from the North return home better able to approach and organize immigrant women working in their countries.

One of the most profound lessons that has come from the meeting of prostitutes and nonprostitute representatives of projects from many different countries is that no matter how different the cultures within which prostitutes work, their work is not so different, and the women who trade sex for money have much in common with one another. They are, for the most part, strong women because they have to be. They know more about male sexuality than almost anyone else in the world, including most men, and they also know a lot about their own sexuality, again because they have to. This means that in any country, women with experience in the sex trade can make invaluable contributions to the fight against AIDS—and not just in the context of prostitution. They can share some of their knowledge and skills with other women, for example, how to have their own pleasure as well as how to eroticize using condoms so that sexual pleasure with men can be safer. Indeed, the age-old division of women into whores, who are sexual but not reproductive, and madonnas, who reproduce but are not sexual,[19] must be overcome if all women are to be able to protect themselves from HIV and other sexually transmitted diseases.

REFERENCES

AIDS Policy Center. 1994. Intergovernmental Health Policy Project, George Washington University, as of December 1994.

Apisok, Noi. 1993. *Removing Structural Barriers to HIV Prevention in the Sex Industry*. Ninth International Conference on AIDS, Berlin, Roundtable RT-18, June 10.

Asia Watch. 1993. Women's Rights Project, *A Modern Form of Slavery: Trafficking of Burmese Women and Girls into Brothels in Thailand*. New York: Human Rights Watch.

Brandt, Allan. 1985. *No Magic Bullet: A Social History of Venereal Disease in the United States since 1880*. New York: Oxford University Press.

Bullough, Vern and Bonnie Bullough. 1987. *Women and Prostitution: A Social History*. Buffalo: Prometheus.

Chan, Roy. 1992. National Skin Centre, Singapore. Personal communication.

Convention for the Suppression of Traffic in Persons and the Exploitation of the Prostitution of Others. 1949. United Nations.

Darrow, William W. 1992. Assessing targeted AIDS prevention in male and female prostitutes and their clients. In F. Paccaud, J. P. Vader, F. Gutzwiller, eds., *Assessing AIDS Prevention*, 215–31. Basel: Birkhäuser Verlag.

Esu-Williams, Eka. 1993. *AIDS Prevention: A Guide for Working with Commercial Sex Workers, Experiences from Calabar, Nigeria.* Durham, N.C.: AIDSTECH, Family Health International; Calabar, Nigeria: Cross River State AIDS Committee.

Filgueras, Ana. 1993. SOS Crianca E Edolescente. Personal communication.

G/Kidan, Almaz. 1990. Department of AIDS Control, Addis Ababa, Ethiopia. Personal communication.

Harsin, Jill. 1985. *Policing Prostitution in Nineteenth-Century Paris.* Princeton: Princeton University Press.

Horton, Meurig. 1990. World Health Organization, Global Programme on AIDS. Personal communication.

Kingston, Tim. 1993. Criminalizing AIDS: DA Arlo Smith's office targets HIV-positive prostitutes (Can you say scapegoat?). *San Francisco Bay Times*, September 9.

Kreiss, Joan K., et al. 1986. AIDS virus infection in Nairobi prostitutes. *New England Journal of Medicine* 314:414–18.

Leigh, Carol. 1993. Personal communication.

Lerner, Gerda. 1986a. The origin of prostitution in ancient Mesopotamia. *Signs: Journal of Women in Culture and Society* (Winter): 236–54.

———. 1986b. *The Creation of Patriarchy.* New York: Oxford University Press (especially chap. 6, pp. 123–40: Veiling the Woman).

Lockett, Gloria. 1983–89. Personal communications.

Mark, Mary Ellen. 1981. *Falkland Road.* New York: Knopf.

Metal, Phyllis Luman. 1987. Not huarachas in Paris. In Frederique Delacoste and Priscilla Alexander, eds., *Sex Work: Writings by Women in the Sex Industry.* San Francisco: Cleis; London: Virago, 1988. (*SexArbeit: Frauen in der Sexindustrie*, 35–36. Munich: Wilhelm Heyne Verlag, 1989.)

Nanda, Serene. 1990. *Neither Man nor Woman: The Hijras of India.* Belmont, Calif.: Wadsworth.

Oostvogels, Rob. 1992–93. Personal communications.

Pheterson, Gail, ed. 1989. *A Vindication of the Rights of Whores.* Seattle: Seal Press. (*Nosotros, Las Putas.* Madrid: Talasa Ediciones, 1992.)

Piot, Peter, et al. 1987. Retrospective seroepidemiology of AIDS virus infection in Nairobi populations. *Journal of Infectious Diseases* 155 (6): 1108–12.

Plummer, F. A., et al. 1993. Evidence of Resistance to HIV among Continuously Exposed Prostitutes in Nairobi, Kenya. Ninth International Conference on AIDS, June 6–11, Berlin, WS-A07–3.

Quindlen, Anna. 1993. *New York Times.* October 3, sec. 4, p. 15.

Raghuramaiah, K. Lakshmi. 1991. *Night Birds: Indian Prostitutes from Devadasis to Call Girls.* Delhi: Chanakya.

Raphael, Rachelle. 1995. Personal communication.

Réal, Griselidis. International Documentation Centre on Prostitution. Personal communication.

Representatives of German prostitutes' rights organizations. 1991. European Prostitutes Congress. Frankfurt, Germany.

Roberts, Nickie. 1992. *Whores in History: Prostitution in Western Society*. London: Harper-Collins.

Schoepf, Brooke Grundfest. 1992. Personal communication.

Simonsen, J. Neil, et al. 1990. HIV infection among lower socioeconomic strata prostitutes in Nairobi. *AIDS* 4:139–44.

Stuart, Carol. 1994. Personal communication.

Tannahill, Reay. 1992. *Sex in History*. Rev. ed. Scarborough House Publishers.

Tong, Benson. 1994. *Unsubmissive Women: Chinese Prostitutes in Nineteenth-Century San Francisco*. Norman: University of Oklahoma Press.

Wilson, David, et al. 1990. A pilot study for an HIV prevention programme among commercial sex workers in Bulawayo, Zimbabwe. *Social Science and Medicine* 31 (5): 609–18.

Yamazaki, Tomoko. 1985. *The Story of Yamada Waka: From Prostitute to Feminist Pioneer*. Tokyo: Kodansha International.

Suggested Readings

Prostitution

Developing Countries

Day, Sophie. 1988. Editorial review. Prostitute women and AIDS: Anthropology. *AIDS* 2:421–28.

Lee, W. 1991. Prostitution and tourism in south-east Asia. In N. Redclift and M. T. Sinclair, eds., *Working Women: International Perspectives on Labour and Gender Ideology*, 79–103. London: Routledge.

Mark, M. E. 1981. *Falkland Road*. New York: Knopf.

Maurer, M. 1992. *Tourisme Prostitution SIDA*. Geneva: Centre Europe Tiers Monde.

Nanda, S. 1990. *Neither Man nor Woman: The Hijras of India*. Belmont, Calif.: Wadsworth.

Neeguaye, A. 1990. Prostitution in Accra. In M. Plant, ed., *AIDS, Drugs, and Prostitution*, 175–85. London: Tavistock/Routledge.

Nelson, N. 1987. "Selling her kiosk": Kikuyu notions of sexuality and sex for sale in Mathare Valley, Kenya. In P. Caplan, ed., *The Cultural Construction of Sexuality*, 217–39. London: Tavistock.

Onstenk, A. 1989. A visit to Burkina Faso. In G. Pheterson, ed., *A Vindication of the Rights of Whores*, 260–63. Seattle: Seal Press.

Phongpaichit, P. 1982. *From Peasant Girls to Bangkok Masseuses*. Geneva: International Labor Office.

Pickering, H., et al. 1992. Prostitutes and their clients: A Gambian survey. *Social Science Medicine* 34 (1): 75–88.

Raghuramaiah, K. L. 1991. *Night Birds: Indian Prostitutes from Devadasis to Call Girls*. Delhi: Chanakya.

Shepherd, G. 1987. Rank, gender, and homosexuality: Mombasa as a key to understanding sexual options. In P. Caplan, ed., *The Cultural Construction of Sexuality*, 240–70. London: Tavistock.

Tabet, P. 1989. I'm the meat, I'm the knife: Sexual service, migration and repression in some African societies. In G. Pheterson, ed., *A Vindication of the Rights of Whores*, 204–26. Seattle: Seal Press.

Truong, T.-D. 1990. *Sex, Money, and Morality: Prostitution and Tourism*. London: Zed.

White, L. 1990. *Comforts of Home: Prostitution in Colonial Nairobi*. Chicago: University of Chicago Press.

———. 1986. Prostitution, identity, and class consciousness during World War II. *Signs: Journal of Women in Culture and Society* 11 (2): 255–73.

Wilson, D., et al. 1989. Sex workers, client sex behaviour, and condom use in Harare, Zimbabwe. *AIDS Care* 1 (3): 269–80.

———. 1990. A pilot study for an HIV prevention programme among commercial sex workers in Bulawayo, Zimbabwe. *Social Science and Medicine* 31 (5): 609–18.

Developed Countries

Carmen, A. and H. Moody. 1985. *Working Women: The Subterranean World of Street Prostitution*. New York: Harper & Row.

Cohen, B. 1980. *Deviant Street Networks: Prostitution in New York City*. Lexington, Mass.: Lexington.

Delacoste, F. and P. Alexander, eds. 1987. *Sex Work: Writings by Women in the Sex Industry*. San Francisco: Cleis; London: Virago, 1988. (*Sex Arbeit*. Munich: Heyne Verlag, 1989.)

French, D. and L. Lee. 1988. *Working: My Life as a Prostitute*. New York: E. P. Dutton.

Jaget, C., ed. 1980. *Prostitutes, Our Life*, trans. A. Furse, S. Fleming, and R. Hall. London: Falling Wall Press.

Perkins, R. 1991. *Working Girls: Prostitutes, Their Life and Social Control*. Canberra: Australian Institute of Criminology.

Perkins, R. and G. Bennett. 1985. *Being a Prostitute: Prostitute Women and Prostitute Men*. Boston: Allen and Unwin.

Pheterson, G., ed. 1989. *A Vindication of the Rights of Whores*. Seattle: Seal Press. (*Nosotros, Las Putas*. Madrid: Talasa Ediciones, 1992.)

Réal, G. 1992. *La Passe Imaginaire*. Levallois-Perret, France: Éditions Manya.

The Historical Record

Bullough, V. and B. Bullough. 1987. *Women and Prostitution: A Social History*. Buffalo: Prometheus.

Connelly, M. T. 1980. *The Response to Prostitution in the Progressive Era*. Chapel Hill: University of North Carolina Press.

Otis, L. L. 1985. *Prostitution and Medieval Society: The History of an Urban Institution in Languedoc*. Chicago: University of Chicago Press.

Roberts, N. 1992. *Whores in History: Prostitution in Western Society*. London: Harper-Collins.

Rosen, R. 1982. *The Lost Sisterhood: Prostitution in America 1900–1918*. Baltimore: The Johns Hopkins University Press.

Tannahill, R. 1992. *Sex in History*. Rev. ed. Scarborough House Publishers.

Tong, B. 1994. *Unsubmissive Women: Chinese Prostitutes in Nineteenth-Century San Francisco*. Norman: University of Oklahoma Press.

Yamazaki, T. 1985. *The Story of Yamada Waka: From Prostitute to Feminist Pioneer*. Tokyo: Kodansha International.

STD and HIV/AIDS: Policy Considerations

Lessons from History

Brandt, A. M. 1985. *No Magic Bullet: A Social History of Venereal Disease in the United States since 1880*. New York: Oxford University Press.

———. 1987. A historical perspective. In H. L. Dalton and S. Burris, eds., *AIDS and the Law: A Guide for the Public*, 37–43. New Haven: Yale University Press.

———. 1988. AIDS: From Social History to Social Policy. In Elizabeth Fee and Daniel M. Fox, eds., *AIDS: The Burdens of History*, 147–71. Berkeley: University of California Press.

Davenport-Hines, R. 1990. *Sex, Death, and Punishment: Attitudes to Sex and Sexuality in Britain Since the Renaissance*. Glasgow: William Collins Sons.

Harsin, J, 1985. *Policing Prostitution in Nineteenth-Century Paris*. Princeton: Princeton University Press.

Mort, F. 1987. *Dangerous Sexualities: Medico-Moral Politics in England Since 1830*. London: Routledge and Kegan Paul.

Walkowitz, J. R. 1980. *Prostitution and Victorian Society: Women, Class, and the State*. Cambridge: Cambridge University Press.

Contemporary Discussions

AIDS Action: Special issue on the Sex Industry. 1991. September 15. Available from the WHO/GPA Documentation Centre, Geneva, or from AHRTAG, 1 London Bridge Street, London SE1 9SG, United Kingdom.

AIDS Health Promotion Exchange. 1992. Number 1, focusing on sex work-related HIV/AIDS prevention projects. Available from the WHO/GPA Documentation Centre, Geneva, or from the Royal Tropical Institute, Department of Information and Documentation, Mauritskade 63, 1092 AD Amsterdam, The Netherlands.

Alexander, P. In press. *Making Sex Work Safer: A Guide to HIV/AIDS Prevention Interventions*. World Health Organization, Global Programme on AIDS.

———. 1995. Sex workers fight against AIDS: An international perspective. In B. E. Schneider and N. Stoller, eds., *Women as the Key: Practice and Politics in the HIV Epidemic*, 99–123 (Philadelphia: Temple University Press).

Cohen, J. B. 1988. Overstating the risk of AIDS: Scapegoating prostitutes. *Focus: A Guide to AIDS Research* 4 (2): 1–2.

Cohen, J. B., P. Alexander, and C. Wofsy. 1988. Prostitutes and AIDS: Public policy issues. *AIDS and Public Policy Journal* 3 (2): 16–22.

Consensus Statement from the Consultation on HIV Epidemiology and Prostitution, Geneva, 3–6 July 1989. WHO/GPA/INF/89.11.

Darrow, W. W. 1984. Prostitution and sexually transmitted diseases. In K. K. Holmes et al., eds., *Sexually Transmitted Diseases*, 109–116. New York: McGraw-Hill.

———. 1992. Assessing targeted AIDS prevention in male and female prostitutes and their clients. In F. Paccaud, J. P. Vader, and F. Gutzwiller, eds., *Assessing AIDS Prevention*, 215–31. Basel: Birkhäuser Verlag.

Decker, J. F. 1987. Prostitution as a public health issue. In Harlon L. Dalton and Scott Burris, eds., *AIDS and the Law: A Guide for the Public*, 81–89. New Haven: Yale University Press.

Miller, H. G., C. F. Turner, and L. E. Moses, eds. 1990. *AIDS: The Second Decade*. Washington, D.C.: National Academy Press. See especially Interventions for female prostitutes, 253–88.

Packard, R. M. and P. Epstein. 1992. Medical research on AIDS in Africa: A historical perspective. In Elizabeth Fee and Daniel M. Fox, eds., *AIDS: The Making of a Chronic Disease*, 346–76. Berkeley: University of California Press.

Plant, M., ed. 1990. *AIDS, Drugs, and Prostitution*. London: Tavistock/Routledge.

Report of the Workshop on Strategies for the Prevention and Control of AIDS among Commercial Sex Workers, Regional Office for the Western Pacific of the World Health Organization, Manila, Philippines, 23–27 September 1991. (WP)CDS(P)/ICP/GPA/003-E, Report series number: RS/91/GE/33(PHL.

Scambler, G., et al. 1990. Women prostitutes in the AIDS era. *Sociology of Health and Illness* 12:260–72.

Scambler, G. and R. Graham-Smith. 1992. Female prostitution and AIDS: the realities of social exclusion. In Peter Aggleton et al., eds., *AIDS: Rights, Risk, and Reason*, 68–76. London: Falmer.

Treichler, P. A. 1992. AIDS and HIV infection in the third world: A first world chronicle. In Elizabeth Fee and Daniel M. Fox, eds., *AIDS: The Making of a Chronic Disease* 377–412. Berkeley: University of California Press.

6 | Bargaining for Life: Women and the AIDS Epidemic in Haiti

PRISCILLA R. ULIN, MICHEL CAYEMITTES, AND
ROBERT GRINGLE

Roots of an Epidemic

AIDS arrived early in Haiti. Before most of the world had awakened to the first signs of the approaching pandemic, mysterious uncontrollable opportunistic infections had already begun to appear in Haitian clinics (Pape et al. 1983). From one documented case of what was diagnosed as immunodeficiency disease in 1979, the epidemic grew to approximately five thousand AIDS cases identified by the end of 1992—and it continues to escalate (World Health Organization 1994). Recent estimates of seroprevalence in high-risk groups, such as urban prostitutes, their clients, and STD patients, run around 42 percent. In the urban population considered not at risk, the probability of infection is about 5 percent (Ulin, Cayemittes, and Metellus 1993).

It was evident even in the early stages that the taproot of the AIDS epidemic in Haiti lay deep in poverty and whatever transient relief the exchange of sex as a commodity could bring to desperately poor people. In Haiti, as in many other countries where the epidemic was taking hold, urban prostitutes and their male clients became the focus of AIDS prevention programs. However, efforts to contain the spread of infection had little impact as the epidemic moved out from these primary risk groups to Haitians not at first regarded as populations at risk. In contrast to the early years when cases of AIDS were observed almost exclusively in men, HIV infection has now shifted to women and children, and today the sex difference in reported AIDS cases has largely disappeared.

Efforts to trace the natural history of the epidemic have recently focused on asymptomatic populations, among them pregnant women, mothers of hospitalized infants, and the wives and partners of HIV-infected men. Studies conducted

by the Haitian Study Group on Kaposi's Sarcoma and Opportunistic Infections
(GHESKIO) have found seroprevalence rates ranging between 7 and 10 percent
in urban antenatal clinics (Cornell-GHESKIO 1992) and evidence of HIV in 12
percent of a sample of mothers of sick children (Pape and Johnson 1988). In a
1992 study of postpartum women, researchers from the Haitian Child Health
Institute noted seroprevalence rates in urban and rural areas, of 7.4 percent and
1.9 percent, respectively, with concentrations in young women aged fourteen
to nineteen (6.0 percent) and twenty to twenty-four years (7.0 percent)
(Cayemittes, Hankins, and Maynard 1993). On the basis of their findings, the
authors of this report conclude that approximately seventy thousand seropositive women in Haiti will give birth to between twenty-eight hundred and forty-
five hundred HIV-infected infants a year, or an average of eight to twelve new
cases each day.

Reciprocity and Exchange: The Social Context of AIDS

Without question, the sociocultural environment in Haiti is having a profound
influence on the spread of the epidemic, especially to women in the general
population. Throughout its history a succession of political crises has burdened
this already impoverished country with massive unemployment and loss of
access to the most basic resources for education, job training, and health care.
Nearly everyone suffers, but women pay the greatest price in terms of low
income, low literacy, high fertility, and high infant and maternal mortality. Yet
it is the Haitian woman who is expected to provide stability and harmony in the
family, earning her subsistence by serving a husband or sexual partner and raising children often under conditions of profound deprivation.

Reciprocity and exchange define most sexual relationships in Haiti: the man
is expected to provide a woman with a house and money for day-to-day
expenses in exchange for household services, childbearing, and sexual satisfaction. Although Haitian law can require a married man to support his wife and
children, a wedding is a luxury few Haitians can afford. Less than 25 percent of
Haitian men and women aged fifteen to forty-nine are married (Comité Inter-
Agence Femmes et Développement 1991): the majority of Haitians live in common-law relationships with customary rules of mutual support similar to marriage or in a variety of casual (nonbinding) sexual unions that assume neither
cohabitation nor economic support—although even in these the norms of reciprocity define the relationship in terms of a loose exchange.

These multiple forms of sexual union are a critical factor in the spread of
AIDS in Haiti, encouraging multiple partnerships and diminishing personal
responsibility for the mutual protection of health. Indeed, in their sample of

1,245 postpartum women, Cayemittes and his colleagues found seroprevalence rates of 0.7 percent among married women and 5.6 percent among women in common-law and other less stable relationships (Cayemittes, Hankins, and Maynard 1993).

Writers (Allman 1980; Lowenthal 1984; Comité Inter-Agence Femmes et Développement 1991) on the social construction of sexuality in Haiti have observed that sexuality has distinctly different meanings for men and women. Men, on the one hand, are reputed to have insatiable sexual appetites that oblige them to have multiple female partners at considerable cost to themselves in order to support their several households.

For women, on the other hand, sexuality is dissociated from pleasure—in public, at least (Lowenthal 1987; Comité Inter-Agence Femmes et Développement 1991). Women are not supposed to enjoy sex but only to provide it for the pleasure of men. Women commonly refer to their sexual organs in economic metaphors: "my property" (*interè-m*), "my capital" (*mammanlajan-m*), thus defining sex in terms of a marketable commodity. Sexual relations are women's work, not pleasure—and women view engaging in sexual intercourse as their part of the bargain, deserving of compensation (Lowenthal 1987:75).

Thus, in an environment of perpetual material scarcity for nearly everyone, sex becomes a medium of exchange that a woman may use to bargain for the support she needs for herself and her children. Although men may enjoy a freedom of behavior that amounts to polygyny, women's strategy for survival may better be described as serial polyandry, or union with a succession of partners, each one providing her with one or more children, along with the hope that the father may offer some support (Comité Inter-Agence Femmes et Développement 1991). However, since men have no legal obligation to provide child support outside marriage, more often than not the responsibility ultimately falls entirely on the woman's shoulders.

Lowenthal (1987:87) describes the conjugal relationship in rural Haiti in terms of confrontation and exchange of resources in a "field of competition" between men and women. In what amounts to a contractual arrangement, men depend on women for domestic labor and reciprocate by providing material support in a long-term relationship. In Lowenthal's analysis, the public ideology that governs sexuality puts men at a disadvantage by supporting the notion that sex as a medium of exchange is valued by men but not by women. As long as women are able to claim not to want what men have to offer, they have a theoretical advantage in negotiating access to sexual services. Privately and among themselves, women may acknowledge their desire for sex but for bargaining purposes choose to maintain the appearance that sex is an unwelcome burden.

Although women in Lowenthal's study have the upper hand in sexual negotiation, they have significantly less influence on the physical encounter itself.
Once in the sexual act, men assume the dominant role in relation to female
partners, whom they tend to view as objects in the transaction. The juxtaposi-
tion of roles in the two arenas is fundamental to the double standard of sexual
conduct that holds women responsible for the conditions under which a sexual
encounter takes place and exempts men on the grounds that they are less able
to control their desires and therefore are rarely accountable for their sexual
exploits.

Lowenthal's work suggests that women are accustomed to negotiating sexual relations to promote their own welfare but have little influence on their
partners' other sexual affairs. If this is the situation, perhaps women have
merely looked the other way when their men disappear from the house without
explanation, accepting as fact that men have greater need for sexual gratification. At the same time, some women may feel free to pursue their own additional sexual agendas. This pattern of behavior may once actually have been
functional for the stability of the union, but today it is fuel for the AIDS epidemic.

Any effort to change sexual behavior in Haiti, even in the face of the new
threat of incurable disease, can expect to meet strong resistance. As long as
mutual monogamy with an uninfected partner and condoms provide the only
available means to prevent HIV infection, the woman's bargaining position will
continue to be weak. If the male partner is unable or unwilling to exercise
restraint or accept protection, resources traditionally available to women may
be inadequate for negotiating the transition to new norms of sexual behavior.
On the other hand, the contractual nature of male-female relationships in Haiti
may prove to be the basis for such negotiation if partners have a common understanding of AIDS and a mutual interest in protecting both their own lives and the
lives of their children.

Such is the social context of AIDS in Haiti. But how aware are women of the
risk they face from one day to the next? The investigators in a 1989 survey of
AIDS knowledge, attitudes, and behavioral risk among twenty-six hundred
Haitians aged fourteen to forty-five conclude that virtually everyone in the
country at least knows about AIDS and that more women than men believe it can
be prevented (Adrien and Cayemittes 1991). Male respondents (21.5 percent)
greatly outnumber female respondents (1.5 percent) in the number who report
having partners outside marriage or a monogamous union in the month pre-
ceding the survey. Yet women feel only slightly more secure from AIDS than
men. Forty-one percent of women and 50 percent of men believe that they
themselves are—or might be—at risk of acquiring the disease. The irony here

stems from traditional norms and values of sexual behavior that for generations have supported the "contract" between men and women in Haitian society.

Understanding the Impact of AIDS Prevention on Women

Moser (1989) argues that development planners often fail to recognize the different roles men and women play in society and hence to plan for their different needs. Her critique is especially relevant to health planners and educators who may be promoting AIDS prevention without understanding the implications of their messages for women. A woman's ability to protect herself from HIV transmission is intricately woven into social institutions that determine the balance of decision making in sexual relationships. As Mason (1994:5–6) puts it, "Simply to examine women's or men's material or social conditions without reference to the normative orders affecting these conditions is inadequate." To understand the impact of AIDS prevention programs on women, it is essential to examine institutional norms associated with sexual behavior and their differential effect on women and men.

The discrepancy between reported behavior and perceived personal risk among women described by Adrien and Cayemittes (1991) may reflect women's awareness of the risk that their partners' sexual behavior poses. The extent to which Haitian women perceive themselves to be passive recipients of a fatal yet preventable disease is a key issue in understanding their response to AIDS prevention campaigns that emphasize safer sex. If AIDS prevention measures, specifically condom use and partner reduction, are largely under the control of men, then what will be the impact on women of intervention programs that direct women to exercise control over their own and their partners' sexual practices?

In 1992 researchers from the Haitian Child Health Institute and Family Health International's AIDSTECH Project conducted a qualitative study to explore the gap between women's reported risk and their sense of vulnerability to the AIDS virus (Ulin, Cayemittes, and Metellus 1995). The authors of this article are indebted to the 105 women and 54 men in the study who were willing to talk about their experience with the AIDS epidemic and specifically the vulnerability of women. These participants come from two study sites: an inner-city neighborhood in the capital, Port-au-Prince, and a peri-urban settlement in Les Cayes, a provincial city located 112 miles to the south. Both sites are known as *bidonvilles*, neighborhoods of extreme poverty with high population density, substandard housing, low literacy, and high unemployment.

Twelve focus groups of women and six groups of men from the two communities met with researchers to share their perceptions of the AIDS epidemic and the effect it could have on the lives of people like themselves. Discussions focused primarily on sexual decision making and communication between partners, with particular emphasis on the risk to women and the capacity of women to negotiate protection.

Consequences of Vulnerability in an Age of AIDS: Women's Beliefs

Most Haitian women who participated in the Women and AIDS Study recognize AIDS as a familiar illness and fear it for a variety of reasons. Women frequently expressed this fear in terms of inevitable death and the suffering it would cause the family. Many spoke of the economic costs when the breadwinner dies, the breakup of the family unit, poverty, destitution, ostracism, and even the spread of the disease to other family members. A thirty-six-year-old woman factory worker reveals how conscious she is of her own responsibilities when she says: "It [AIDS] has many consequences if you are the one helping out the family and taking care of a household. Mother, father, brothers—they all depend on you. Then the disease comes, and all that is left is death."

Women participants focused particularly on the effect of AIDS on surviving children. Certain phrases were common, such as "AIDS crushes families," "kids have no future," and "children in misery." A woman with a husband and two children warned that "if both mother and father die of AIDS, the family is finished. With no parents, children can become wanderers (*vagabon*), thieves, or drug users." Single mothers expressed doubt as to the willingness of their children's fathers to fill the void. As a woman in a common-law relationship said, "If the woman dies, the man will simply go and live with his other women," leaving the children to manage on their own.

Although women concur strongly that "anyone can get AIDS," some feel that they are exceptions to this rule. Many qualified such remarks, implying that people do not need to be afraid if they do not "fool around" (*viv deyo*) or participate in sexual encounters outside the regular partnership. Remarks such as, "If a woman has confidence in herself (*fe respe*) and the husband she is living with, she knows she will not contract the disease" illustrate this cautious optimism. Some women offered personal testimony of their own responsible behavior and sometimes also the fidelity of a husband or regular partner, but there is less conviction about the latter. Others base their confidence on religious belief: "I am not afraid, because my husband is a Christian. The true Christian has one wife, and his wife has one husband. They don't fool around."

The belief that the righteous have divine protection is reflected in such assertions as "God will not let me contract AIDS unless I go around looking for it." Then, as if to suppress an edge of doubt, this woman added, " Even if my husband is promiscuous, I would know if he were coming to give it [AIDS] to me. God will see to it that he does not transmit it to me." However, few share even the guarded confidence of some of these women. It is more common to hear women speak of the unpredictability of AIDS, turning to several recurrent themes: You can't tell who has it; you can't trust your partners; men won't listen; and, finally, if you refuse your partner, you only increase your risk, because he will find what he wants on the streets.

Not surprisingly women in the less stable relationships spoke of another dimension to the problem—dependency on men for economic support. One woman with five children and no steady income summarizes the fears of other economically dependent women when she observes: "You have less chance of catching the disease [AIDS] if someone is taking care of you and feeding your children. If you are poor and trying to survive by living in the streets, you have no protection. It can happen to you more easily."

Women's sense of vulnerability is compounded by their awareness that infected people who do not appear ill may still transmit the disease: "When the disease first penetrates the man's system, he may not know he has it. You, as his wife, won't know—you will contract it no matter what, because it doesn't appear full blown at first [*li pa vin ak fos*]. You will always get the disease, because neither person knows."

Individually some women volunteered that their own husbands were faithful to them, but the underlying consensus seems to be that monogamous unions are rare. Women commented frequently that, married or not, men leave the house to have affairs with other women who may be infected. As a married woman puts it, "The wife at home knows she is sleeping only with her husband and trusts him—so she gets AIDS." Issues of trust and distrust arose with painful frequency in the discussions as women recounted experiences that have left them uncertain and fearful. "We are afraid," explained a married woman, "because even if you want to live (monogamously) with men, they do not want to stay with one woman." Another married woman volunteered that, "for myself, I would not be afraid, but the person I am with is not seeing just me, so I will always have fears." The uncertainty expressed by these and other women is an important element in their fear of AIDS. They have heard and taken seriously the public health messages warning of the dire consequences of promiscuous sex, but they lack any sense of personal empowerment to act on their own behalf.

The Status of Women's Rights in AIDS Prevention Strategies

When prevention was raised as a topic for discussion, women recited, as if in unison, the rules of safe sex as presented in posters, in the mass media, at health centers, and at workplaces. However, beneath this veneer of superficial knowledge are deep-seated contradictions and conflicts between old norms of behavior and new prescriptions for change. Women are clear that they would prefer monogamous partnerships, but repeated references to the sexual freedom of men uncover a sense of powerlessness to influence their partners' behavior. Sexual freedom is a privilege that men enjoy at women's expense. In a typical exchange on this issue, married women spoke resentfully about the ability of men to make their own decisions about leisure time and money:

> Life is easier for the man, because the woman has to stay home and take care of the children. The man has more free time.
>
> The man is always out. He does what pleases him. He may be giving money to other women while his woman and children go hungry.

Although some women make allowances for individual men who may behave differently, women almost uniformly do not trust men when it comes to sexual relationships. Many women commented that men as a whole believe they are in command, "the chief of the woman" with little or no accountability for sexual behavior outside the home. At the same time women observed that to avoid "problems," it is better for a man to think that his woman at home does not know. One of the many ironies for Haitian women is that they are not supposed to know what their men do outside the house, but not knowing may open them to ridicule and often to unprotected sex with an HIV-infected partner.

Defining and Negotiating Rights to Protection

What can a woman do when she suspects her man of having other partners who may infect him with the AIDS virus? There is wide consensus that women not only have a right to protection for their own sake but for the sake of their children, and must do everything possible to avoid getting AIDS. At the same time women express ambivalence about whether women have a right to demand that men use condoms and under what circumstances—arguing that men have an obligation to protect their partners by using condoms yet at times imposing stringent conditions on a woman's right to confront her partner with such a bold request. One such criterion is that the woman be certain of her risk. Women who have a "right" to demand condoms are those who "know" that their husbands have other partners. Most seem to feel that without "proof" of their partners' infidelity, women are not entitled to bring up the subject of condoms: "If the woman knows that her man is frivolous, she is right to ask him to use a condom, but if she has no proof of that, she shouldn't ask him."

Often the same women who would require proof of infidelity were those who earlier had said that women do not know what their partners do outside the home. However, asking a husband or common-law partner to use condoms amounts to a charge of infidelity, and whether the accusation is indeed warranted, most women hesitate to raise such a volatile issue. An irony in the *rules* that determine a woman's right to ask for condoms is that women often do not know—and are not supposed to know—whether their men are frequenting prostitutes or having affairs with other women. But, as one woman bluntly put it, "There are no women who should not ask men to use condoms, because there are no men who do not 'fool around' [*viv deyo*]."

Many have doubts about the safety of condoms, recounting stories they have heard of suffering and death when condoms burst or remained inside women. Nevertheless, most women view condoms as a necessary last resort, the only hope of protection for a woman who wants to continue a sexual relationship with a man who has refused to give up his other partners. With little clear consensus on men's willingness to remain faithful or use condoms, women's strategies for dealing with the problem vary from tactful persuasion to ultimatum. They proposed and debated several alternatives, but for every solution there are new risks. A woman can reason with her partner, attempting to convince him of the wisdom of fidelity or the prudent use of condoms; she can bargain, offering sex on the condition of protection from disease; or she can refuse outright, resorting to abstinence or even abandonment as the last resort when a partner is unwilling to change his promiscuous life-style.

To some women, reasoning with a man or cajoling him into giving up the other women in his life offers a viable solution. As one woman hopefully remarked, "A woman can talk to a man, and if he is a person who listens he agrees and gives up what he used to do." Women who spoke in support of this strategy argue that by explaining the danger of AIDS transmission to a man, his wife or common-law partner could appeal to his sense of duty to protect her life and the welfare of his family. A woman who doubts her partner's fidelity must also do more to satisfy him so that he will cease to think about other women. This position sometimes has overtones of self-blame: "We are women, so there's not much we can do except ask them why they have other women—is it because we don't give you enough affection that you leave us? Or is it because we have too many children? We have to talk to them in a way that touches their sensitive spot."

Some women believe that gentle persuasion will also induce a man to use condoms:

> You start to call him pet names even if you don't usually, and you tell him the condom will be good for both of you.

You call the man to you and you say, now that there's a disease out there, when you go out—and I don't know where you go—you must use condoms. It's protection for me and you.

Other women were doubtful that soft words would ever change a man's behavior. They countered with the argument that, in general, men do not listen. They do not listen, explained one woman, because they never want to give up the women they have: "The other woman knows that he would never throw away the old pot for a new one. He will stay with the old one, but he will also not leave the new one."

Women who responded with skepticism to the notion that men could be persuaded by reason were more likely to advocate bargaining: "If I need something and my man does not give it to me, I will not make love with him. He has to give me what I want for me to do it."

References to the use of sex as a bargaining tool are common across all types of partnership. Women in marriage and common-law relationships said they might refuse to sleep with a man who was not supporting them adequately, especially if money were going to another woman. "If I need something," said one married woman, "I ask my husband for the money, and if he doesn't give it to me, I do not make love with him. Then he gives me the money right away." Bargaining for condom use therefore seems to some women a logical extension of their customary reliance on dispensing sexual favors to obtain what they needed.

The Double Edge of Refusing Sex

Given the reality of sexual freedom for the men in their lives, women are also giving serious thought to abstinence as a solution to the risk of acquiring AIDS from a promiscuous partner who declines the use of condoms. However, despite many comments that discovering a partner's infidelity would justify refusal because of the threat of AIDS, refusing sex to prevent disease still seems to be a relatively new and even frightening idea for most women. In general, the women do not regard refusing sex as an unusual event in a relationship, but the reasons they give for refusing a partner's sexual advances suggest that it is acceptable behavior only if denial is infrequent. Common reasons for refusal are fatigue or illness, menstruation, preoccupation with financial or other household worries, and an argument between the partners. Women also cite pregnancy prevention and disaffection, abuse and neglect as justification for at least trying to avoid sexual contact.

Although a sense of responsibility to the conjugal relationship makes it unthinkable for most women at first to refuse a partner, introducing the risk of

AIDS into the focus group discussion usually caused the same women to reverse their position. There were many references to sleeping in separate beds or on the floor. Some women said that being alone would be preferable to the risk of AIDS and advised that women who could not avoid a risky sexual relationship should try to find domestic work or street vending to support themselves. Unlike fatigue, illness, anger, and even family planning, however, using AIDS risk as an excuse to avoid sex is not a woman's prerogative and carries no assumption that the relationship will ever return to normal. Consequently, even women who recommend refusing a promiscuous partner recognize that this is a dangerous strategy and likely to backfire. They are saying, in effect, that in principle a woman has a right to refuse sex for fear of contracting AIDS, but in reality her right may not be recognized by her partner.

The greatest fear that women expressed is that in refusing sex they will send the man back out to the streets to find a more compliant woman who will infect him with HIV, which he will then carry back to the woman at home. Women tend to agree that refusing sex amounts to little less than a death warrant for themselves:

> People say that when you like the skin, you should like the seed. In these times—with AIDS in the streets—you have to accept when your husband says, "Let's make love."
>
> If the man wants me to make love and I refuse—and that happens to me sometimes—I just think about what happens in the streets and I accept.

Women also fear other reprisals, including loss of spending money for food and clothing, and physical retaliation, which is a reality shared by some women:

> When men want to sleep with you, you can't refuse. If you try, they force themselves on you, and you know what has happened before, so you do what you have to. I have already experienced that.
>
> I have a man living with me. As soon as I stop breast-feeding the babies, he always gets me pregnant, but if I refuse to have sex I get beaten up.

Overall, women have a strong sense that they must inevitably accede to men's sexual desires in order to protect themselves and the welfare of their children. The retaliation that many women fear seems a greater and more immediate risk than the threat of HIV infection itself. Although some women believe that "men who are not beasts" would agree, a stronger voice argues that few if any men will ever be willing to give up their other women or use condoms.

In this study women who take a negative stand on the issue of partner response to condoms were the more numerous and the more vocal. For the most part their concerns center on issues of denial and trust. They contend that men refuse to admit having other partners and instead turn the blame on the women at home. Men want to know why they are being asked, whether it is because the woman is sick herself or because her own behavior is putting him at risk. If a man wishes to take her request for condoms as evidence of infidelity, he may then respond with physical abuse, withdrawal of economic support, or abandonment.

The specter of economic neglect or abandonment emerges in discussions more often and with more intensity than the fear of physical abuse. Women feel that they can be manipulated by men who have the power to deprive them of the resources for basic survival. Many women express their powerlessness to change sexual behavior in terms of their dependency on satisfying men—women who do not work are not perceived to have the right to make demands; women with jobs earn that right because they have other options for themselves and their children:

> If the man is making money and you are not, he never pays much attention to you, but if both people are working, the woman is worth something. I have experienced this in my own house, and I realize my husband would not treat me the way he does if I had a job.
>
> A woman can make decisions only when she works; otherwise they (men) call her useless.

Comments such as these take the problem of AIDS prevention to a more fundamental level: the direct link between women's fear and frustration in the face of the epidemic and their sense of powerlessness to control their own lives. For the women in these focus groups, money is as much a symbol of freedom as it is a material resource for achieving independence from male domination. Without access to income, they lack the self-esteem and the financial security to be full partners in critical decisions that could determine their chances of survival in the AIDS epidemic.

Despite the disastrous prospect of women losing what little economic security they may have had, many participants are still convinced that if a man with other partners rejects condoms, a woman should refuse sex or even leave him. It is clearly a painful issue and one that illustrates the women's struggle to resolve contradictions inherent in an old way of life that has left them with the personal resolve but neither the material nor interpersonal resources to act effectively.

Validating the Status Quo: Men's Perspectives

Focus group discussions with men in the two communities validate many of the women's observations, adding stark illustration to some of women's greatest fears; however, important differences also appear. Remarkable parallels exist between men and women in their views on women's rights to protect themselves from HIV infection, to refuse sex, and to ask that the partner use a condom. Male participants in the study speak of monogamy as an ideal, but they also accept multiple sexual relationships as a fact of life, at least for men. Men in both communities seem to take for granted a double standard that grants sexual freedom to men and denies women the right to question their partners' activity. They frequently prefaced their remarks with "if" clauses—"*If* the woman suspects her husband has another woman" or "*If* she realizes that you live dangerously"—suggesting that it is not normal for women to know about steady partners' sexual affairs, but that they sometimes find out. The following comment illustrates the thinking of many men on male responsibility for transmitting HIV to women who do not necessarily know their partners are at risk: "When the woman [wife] thinks that her husband has only her, she will not have an affair with another man, but the husband's mistress may have other men, and those men will contaminate her."

Male participants are well aware of the chain of transmission and men's position as the link between HIV-infected women and women at home. However, they are also anxious to preserve their independence without one woman interfering in their affairs with another. A married man explained how he would attempt to control such a dual relationship: "I can decide to have another woman. I can give that woman certain conditions. I can tell her, 'My wife does not know about our relationship. If you let her know, and you tease her when you pass her in the street, I will leave you.' "

On the other hand, men are equally emphatic that the woman they call *fanm* (wife or common-law partner) has no right to have other men. If they allude to the possibility of their own wives' infidelity, they do so in terms of a man's obligation to control a woman's behavior. Men expect "loose women" (*fem lib*) to have multiple partners, but this norm does not apply to the woman who by law or by custom has agreed to exchange sexual fidelity and domestic labor for a long-term relationship and the economic protection that such a relationship traditionally offers. Men sometimes warn, however, that even in these more stable relationships, women are in need of surveillance and discipline: "It is normal that if I have a woman at home, I keep her from having sex with another man. You [the man] can decide that. If she has sex with another man, I will leave her or I will beat her."

The extent to which women are able to control access to their bodies is obviously a critical element in their capacity to protect themselves from contracting AIDS. Men debated the circumstances under which women should have the right to refuse sex and the range of reactions they might expect from male partners if they did refuse. Sharp differences of opinion polarized these discussions, highlighting the struggle men have to resolve a basic contradiction between their right to demand compliance and the right of women to refuse.

One perspective is that women who are well treated by their partners actually have no reason to deny them sexual gratification. Their use of words such as *joy* and *understanding* highlight the importance of personal relations and material well-being in the conjugal agreement:

> The man is the master of the house. He is in command. When he asks the woman to have sex, she cannot refuse, because there is joy and there is money in the house.
>
> The woman is human, but if there is understanding in the home, she can never refuse to have sex. You can [always] have sex with the woman; even if she does not feel happy about it, she has to do it anyway.

For the most part, however, men tend to grant women the right to refuse sex—under certain conditions: fatigue, ill health, menstruation, and family planning are the most commonly mentioned but often with little enthusiasm. Men also cite hunger, unhappiness, and financial neglect as reasons women can sometimes refuse, but they resent what they perceive as manipulation on the part of women:

> Sometimes the woman could refuse because she is hungry or has no money to eat or buy things, but a woman is an animal with ambition. If you give something to her and she likes it, you can have sex with her every night, but if she is unhappy, you can't touch her.
>
> You can give from A to Z, but once she knows you have another woman, she will refuse to make love with you.

Although men make little direct reference, positive or negative, to women's economic dependence, they acknowledge the unhappiness of those who feel neglected or abandoned by men seeking their own pleasure. A vivid description by one man illustrates a general awareness of women's economic plight:

> Another reason a woman can refuse to make love is that sometimes her husband works and she doesn't know what he is doing with the money. She thinks he is having fun with it. She thinks he is spending his money outside and can get AIDS and infect her. Meanwhile, she is dying from hunger at home. She knows that her husband is spending money, but she doesn't get any, and when he comes home she has to make love to him.

Even though participants tend to agree that most men will overlook a partner's occasional refusal, their comments also offer numerous examples of valid objection by a man to any such decision on the part of a woman. Frequent disclaimers such as, "Women have the right to refuse, but" reveal the difficulty men are experiencing as they struggle to resolve competing issues of freedom and responsibility. There is clearly a limit to most men's tolerance for sexual rejection:

The woman has the right to refuse, but if I want to make love, I will do it any-way. If she refuses, I will say, "Cheri . . . this or that," I will run outside to get her a soft drink, I will caress her. There is no way I would not have inter-course.

If she really is in love with the man, she has a responsibility. And why does a man go out with a woman? It is for affection and other things. But if I offer to make love each day and she tells me it is impossible, I will pressure her.

Although most men do not openly advocate violence against women who refuse their partners' sexual advances, their remarks reflect subtle differences in degrees of coercion, with only a fine line separating the force of persuasion from undisguised violence:

A woman may have reasons for not making love that day, but men have secrets for making her accept anyway.

I will caress her until she obeys, because this [her refusal] may bring divi-sion in the home.

When I start to caress my wife and she refuses, I want to fight with her. If I caress her and she still refuses, I become angry, because I am excited. She may refuse, but I can fight.

She will have to accept.

Refusing sex because of a partner's promiscuity provides a different kind of jus-tification from refusal for some temporary indisposition like menstruation or fatigue. Despite their insistence that under normal circumstances women's sex-ual compliance is an obligation they expect, men almost without exception con-cur on the danger of sex with multiple partners and agree that women have a right to protect themselves from AIDS at any cost, including anger and even retaliation from a possibly infected partner:

The woman can refuse to make love with her husband if she finds out that he has sex with another woman. She thinks about how in this time of many dis-eases there is one called AIDS. She might be thinking that if her husband has sex with another woman he could get AIDS from that woman and give it to her. It could be the cause of her death. She should take the precaution of avoiding sex with him that day.

This comment is significant for several reasons. It represents the view of most male participants that when women discover that sexual contact with their part-ners puts them at risk of contracting HIV, they are right to protect themselves. When the issue is redefined to include the possibility of HIV transmission, men who earlier condemned the woman who refused sex for what they considered trivial reasons reverse their position. The issue of refusal now takes on a temporal dimension. The speaker above seems to suggest that the woman's decision to refuse sex is relatively recent, linked to the appearance of a new disease and a fear that did not exist in the past. The phrase "she can avoid sex with him that day" raises a question about participants' understanding of transmission. Similar comments of both men and women in other groups suggest that some people still do not fully appreciate the nature of the risk.

Although most men said that they believe women have a right to refuse sex with a promiscuous partner, they also warn that this strategy could backfire, lead the partner to accuse her of infidelity, and give him reason to return to his other women. As one man explained it: "If the man feels like making love and the woman does not, he can go out and have sex with anyone. He can get AIDS, which he can bring into the home, and everybody, including the newborn, will get it."

The logical conclusion seems to be that a woman who refuses sex is, in reality, increasing the chance that her partner will become infected by other women: "If I tell the woman that I feel like making love and she doesn't agree, well! I will go out! Then who is responsible that I get AIDS? She is, because I am not used to living with another woman, I am used to living with her."

Based on such reasoning, men tend to want to resolve the issue by increasing, not decreasing, sexual contact with the primary partner. Their rationale is that if the woman at home pays more attention to his needs, the promiscuous partner may forget his other sources of sexual pleasure.

The number of times men propose such a solution reveals a tendency on their part to shift blame to the wife or common-law partner for creating the problems that could result in AIDS, with its inevitable threat to the household stability which they profess to value. By resuming the customary role of compliant, nurturing wife, a woman supposedly solves the problem of HIV risk with no cost to domestic harmony, helping to preserve the balance of power that sustains a man's sense of freedom. This perspective is analogous to the anxiety that many women express concerning the retaliatory behavior of an angry or dissatisfied partner who "can always go to his other woman."

Condoms: Whose Responsibility, What Rights?

Discussion of condoms provokes controversy among men, just as it does among women. In general, men viewed condoms as an unfortunate but sometimes necessary alternative to giving up one's sexual freedom. However, men express sharp differences of opinion among themselves on most condom-related issues, including their reliability as protection against HIV, women's rights to ask men to use them, men's reactions to being asked, and women's attitudes toward using them.

Despite the fact that condoms seem to provide a reasonable solution in some situations, men are divided on the rights of different categories of women to demand that their partners use them. Most men reveal their ambivalence by including the prior condition that a man should already have the number of children he wants. Men frequently combine contraception and disease prevention in their remarks on condoms and sometimes shift the focus of the discussion from AIDS to family planning. The Creole word *planin* is often substituted for the word *kapot*, or condom. Not surprisingly, men appeared more at ease putting the emphasis on contraception, rather than disease prevention. In fact, several men suggested that a woman who is trying to convince a partner to use condoms will be more successful if she uses the argument that having fewer children will enable them to provide food and pay school fees for those they already have. Moreover, it would be *in*appropriate, they said, to use condoms if the couple did not already have "three or four" children.

Thus, in the eyes of most men, condoms are unquestionably appropriate for couples who wish to avoid pregnancy. Several men also alluded to the right of schoolgirls to demand condoms to avoid pregnancy so that their parents do not learn of their sexual relationships. This example is used often enough to suggest that adolescent girls are a familiar source of sexual entertainment for older men: "My wife at home cannot ask me to use condoms, but sometimes you sleep with a young girl. This young girl can ask you, because she doesn't want to get pregnant and have problems with her parents."

As the above quote implies, men are seldom willing to give women in long-term relationships the right to ask for condoms, except for family planning. A prototype of the woman who is *not* entitled to ask, according to the following remark, is "a woman who is yours, who lives honestly, and who does not yet have children. Now, she will not use condoms at all, and she does not want you to ask her to, whatever the circumstances."

Most remarks on this topic suggest that the longer the union, the less power women have to initiate behavioral change, because conjugal expectations are stronger and women therefore are under more constraint to ignore their partners' extramarital behavior.

In addition to schoolgirls, prostitutes, and women in bars, other women with multiple partners are also entitled to insist on condoms. For such women, fidelity may or may not be an issue, but a wife or long-term partner who suggests using condoms will, by so doing, shatter the "understanding" that has sustained their union. To raise the issue seems to many men an admission of guilt. A woman who has "good behavior" and is faithful and respectful in the presence of her husband will not ask, because she will not want him to think she is HIV-infected or has another man. Men commonly remarked in the focus groups that if one partner brings up the subject after many years in a stable relationship, the other will have a right to begin "asking some questions, since we are not used to using condoms."

Condoms and Beyond: Negotiating Change

When they believe the woman has a right to ask for condoms, male participants generally expect less resistance on the part of men than do female participants. In both study communities there were men who said that some men who should use condoms will refuse, whereas others who have more than one partner will comply *if* their partners use discretion and tact to convince them. The success of strategies for convincing their partners seems to depend heavily on a woman's skill in communicating the message that because "there is AIDS out there" her man will have to take precautions if he wants to continue their relationship. Male participants, playing the role of the woman to demonstrate how she might influence a male partner, constructed messages like the following: "The woman can often talk with the man. She should say, 'Cheri, I love you. AIDS is a plague. It destroys lives. If we should stay together and you cannot live only with me, you will have to use condoms.' That's what she has to say, because she can't just throw the man out."

Many men agree with some of the women, that with soft words and firm resolve a woman can induce a man to reflect on his life-style and consider a change. Avoiding the necessity of a condom may be sufficient incentive, they said, to convince a man to give up other partners; or, he may be willing to use a condom if the alternative is losing his primary partner. In such situations, participants are acknowledging women's bargaining skill to make the point that at least some men can be convinced.

Male participants allude occasionally to distrust and the fear of disclosure that a woman might cause by raising the question of condoms, but the possibility of inciting anger and retaliation is mentioned much less often in discussion of condom use than in similar discussions of refusal to engage in sex. Nevertheless, men express doubts as to the sincerity of those who agree to use condoms. "A playboy (*vagabon*) is born a playboy," said one married man. The danger he sees is that "even though the woman tells a man to use a condom, he will still have his other women. Someday he will cheat and have sex with his wife without it."

On the other hand, a number of men gave examples of women's resistance to condoms. Several men told stories of girlfriends who had refused condoms.

Others explained that fear of raising suspicion about her own behavior might influence a woman, and she might decline a man's offer of protection.

Although the range of male opinion on couples' responsibility for HIV prevention reflects widely divergent opinions within the group as a whole, the central tendency is one of compromise. It is consistent with the majority point of view that men may have to compromise if their wives discover their sexual exploits. On the other hand, an equally strong tendency is to lay the major responsibility for behavioral change squarely on the woman's shoulders. The latter position is consistent with customary expectations shared by both sexes of the woman's role in the conjugal relationship.

Renegotiating the Conjugal Contract

Despite—or perhaps because of—the fragmentation of Haitian life, the family remains the principal base of emotional and economic support for its members. The strict separation of roles that is the basis for the conjugal union, whether legal or consensual, is embedded in family values, however inegalitarian the relationship may be. Simply stated, a man enjoys and protects his right to the domestic and sexual services of a woman for whom he can provide a roof and basic household amenities, particularly if she is the mother of his children. For women, however, this uneven exchange may amount to little more than bondage. Nevertheless, both partners in the transaction accord high priority to the stabilizing role of the woman, who has the responsibility to assure the integrity of the home, protect the children, and balance the impulsive and sometimes irresponsible behavior expected of men.

The AIDS epidemic may now be eroding some of the basic norms and assumptions that have served to perpetuate the conjugal contract in Haiti. Men must confront the increasingly apparent contradiction between two irreconcilable values: their sexual freedom and their duty to protect their homes and families. Women meanwhile struggle to resolve the conflict between economic dependency and personal survival, recognizing in what they view as their traditional obligations as sexual partners the risk that they may someday die themselves and be unable to meet the needs of their children.

Countless women in Haiti continue to live with a pervasive but poorly defined sense of impending disaster from AIDS, not knowing from which direction the disease will strike and fearing the means of prevention as much as the disease itself. The well-intended messages of AIDS prevention programs often contradict deeply rooted norms of Haitian gender behavior, creating a painful conflict for women who feel powerless to negotiate the behavioral changes they know could lower their risk of contracting the disease. Women are caught in a double bind, fearing that attempts to protect themselves will in fact increase their risk by giving partners justification to seek other women.

AIDS prevention efforts directed at individual behavioral change have thus far had little impact on the relentless pace of the epidemic. Evidence presented in this article indicates that both research and intervention need to focus on the impact of gender-based norms on behavioral maintenance and change. Mason's (1994) conceptualization of women's status suggests that selection of relevant norms will depend on the social context; in the case of women at risk of HIV in Haiti, this study suggests that gender discrimination is deeply embedded in access and control over material resources, decision-making autonomy, and the norms that govern sexual freedom. However, as Mason (1994:2) points out, "individuals are not just passive recipients of society's rules for behavior, but rather engage in reinterpreting and renegotiating these rules." Social researchers have an opportunity to contribute to efforts to slow the spread of AIDS in Haiti by exploring the rules that influence sexual decision making and applying their findings to strategies for intervention at the level of institutional change. AIDS control programs that build on an understanding of fundamental gender differences in HIV risk will be better equipped to foster open communication between women and men, strengthening the power of women in sexual negotiation and helping to reshape the conjugal contract in Haiti.

REFERENCES

Adrien, Alix and Michel Cayemittes. 1991. Le Sida en Haiti: Connaissances, Attitudes, Croyances et Comportements de la Population. Bureau de Coordination du Programme National de Lutte contre le SIDA, Port-au-Prince.

Allman, James. 1980. Sexual unions in rural Haiti. *Journal of Sociology of the Family* 10:15–39.

Cayemittes, Michel, Catherine Hankins, and James Maynard, Jr. 1993. Séroprévalence de l'Infection au VIH-1 Chez les Femmes Qui Viennent d'Accoucher: Haiti 1991–1992. Centre de Recherches pour le Développement International, Ottowa.

Comité Inter-Agences Femmes et Développement. 1991. La Situation des Femmes Haitiennes. UNICEF, Port-au Prince.

Cornell-GHESKIO. 1992. AIDSTECH Project 1991–1992, Final Report. Port-au-Prince. Unpublished.

Lowenthal, Ira Paul. 1984. Labor, sexuality, and the conjugal contract in Haiti. In C. R. Foster and A. Valdman, eds., *Haiti—Today and Tomorrow*, 15–34. Lanham: University Press of America.

———. 1987. Marriage Is 20, Children Are 21: The Cultural Construction of Conjugality and the Family in Rural Haiti. Doctoral dissertation. Johns Hopkins University, Baltimore.

Mason, Karen Oppenheim. 1994. Conceptualizing and Measuring Women's Status. Paper prepared for the 1994 Annual Meeting of the Population Association of America, Miami, Florida, May 5–7.

Moser, Caroline O. N. 1989. Gender planning in the Third World: Meeting practical and strategic gender needs. *World Development* 17 (11): 1799–1825.

Pape, Jean, et al. 1983. Characteristics of the Acquired Immunodeficiency Syndrome (AIDS) in Haiti. *The New England Journal of Medicine* 309 (16): 945–50.

Pape, Jean and Warren Johnson. 1988. Perinatal transmission of Human Immunodeficiency Virus. *Boletin de la Oficina Sanitaria Panamericana* 105:73–89.

Ulin, Priscilla R., Michel Cayemittes, and Elisabeth Metellus. 1993. *Ecart entre les Connaissances et le Changement de Comportement dans le Domaine du Sida: Role des Femmes Haitiennes et Pouvoir de Décision en Matière Sexuelle.* Institut Haitien de l'Enfance, Pétion Ville, Haiti.

———. 1995. *Haitian Women's Role in Sexual Decision-Making: The Gap between AIDS Knowledge and Behavior Change.* Family Health International Working Paper No. WP95-04. Durham, N.C.: Family Health International.

World Health Organization. 1994. *Weekly Epidemiological Record*, no. 26 (July).

7 The Socioeconomic Impact of AIDS on Women in Tanzania

ANNE OUTWATER

Tanzanian women are not seeking to liberate themselves from the traditional roles of wife, mother, and caregiver. However, under the impact of AIDS, the way society interprets these roles exposes women to great risk. Women themselves are asking how they can continue to fulfill traditional roles in a manner that allows them to win respect without the threat of death. This article describes how women are adopting coping strategies that empower them to address this challenge.

Economic and Social Decline

Tanzania's flag symbolizes the country's wealth: the blue represents the water of the Indian Ocean, lakes, and rivers; the green, its land; the yellow, its minerals; and the black, its people. The country is bounded by the Indian Ocean on the east and three major lakes to the west. From the lakes and the mountains run rivers to the sea. The port at Dar es Salaam, Tanzania's capital, is connected by rail and road to the landlocked countries of the African interior. Twenty-five percent of the nation's land, including Mt. Kilimanjaro, Ngorongoro Crater, and the Serengeti Plains, is gazetted to protect the wildlife and preserve the ecosystems that sustain it. Gold and gems, including diamonds, rubies, and tanzanites, are resources still largely untapped.

Tanzania's first president, Mwalimu Julius K. Nyerere, helped to unify the country. Tanzania is one of the only countries in Africa in which an indigenous language, Swahili, is the official language. This has served to ease communication and unite more than a hundred different tribes so that people are citizens of Tanzania, first, and members of their respective tribes second.

In the midst of this potential wealth, Tanzania is nevertheless undergoing great pressure. It is a country at peace; yet economically and socially, times are difficult. Intertwined, threatening the benefits of all its wealth, is the AIDS epidemic.

The economic stress is profound. With a gross national product (GNP) in 1990 estimated at $90–100 per capita, Tanzania is one of the world's poorest countries. Devaluation of the local shilling, virtual wage freezes, cutbacks of social services and food subsidies, and reductions in public employment have all taken place in the last decade. Formerly, low wages were supplemented by official food subsidies and other social services. With the removal of subsidies as part of the economic structural adjustment program (SAP), poverty at the individual as well as the community level is being felt more acutely.

The economic situation is reflected in the malnutrition of the children. One in every five children is born with a low birth weight. Almost half the children under five years of age are stunted, representing a failure to receive adequate nutrition over a long period (Ngallaba et al. 1993). The economic problems are further reflected in poor housing, lack of clean water, relatively high child mortality, one of the shortest life expectancies in the world at fifty years, lack of good health services, and inadequate opportunities for education.

The health infrastructure remains relatively strong. Tanzania has established wide and equitable coverage of heath care for its people. Around 72 percent of the rural population lives within five kilometers of a government dispensary or rural health center, and 93 percent of the total population lives within ten kilometers of some health facility (World Bank 1989). But quality of care suffers. Staffing, running water, gloves, and drugs are often lacking. In 1990 about 10 percent of the government's recurrent budget went to the health sector, which translates into an expenditure of only about U.S.$2 per capita.

Similar patterns are found in schooling. The government's aim is to provide accessible education for all. Since 1961, the number of girls receiving no education whatsoever has dropped from 74 percent to 15 percent. At Independence only 0.1 percent of girls had achieved some secondary or higher education, and the figure today is 6.4 percent (Ngallaba et al. 1993).

Yet parents and guardians must provide substantial payments to teachers, as incentives, and for books, building funds, and uniforms. Many schools lack desks, chairs, books, and paper or pencils. Some teachers have had only minimal preparation for teaching.

Although the government is currently trying to privatize failing public enterprises, options for employment are minimal. For most women, especially those without education, their employment options are farming, petty trading, and domestic work (barmaids and housemaids).

Demographic patterns are also changing. A few generations ago, in many tribes marriages occurred shortly after puberty and women married as virgins. According to the 1991 Demographic and Health Survey, of women aged forty-five to forty-nine who were mature at the time of Independence, 27 percent were married by age fifteen, and 60 percent had married by eighteen. This correlates closely with the fact that 31 percent had had intercourse by age fifteen and 67 percent by eighteen years of age. Of the cohort of women aged twenty to twenty-four in 1991, one generation later, only 7.2 percent were married at age fifteen and only 37 percent by age eighteen. The age of first sexual intercourse had also risen, so that at age fifteen only 17 percent were no longer virgins, and at age eighteen 60 percent had become sexually active.

Many old people claim that in the past married partners remained faithful to each other and usually did not have multiple partners outside marriage. They maintain that AIDS is not a new disease but that people died of a disease with the same symptoms. However, because multiple sexual partnering was uncommon, the slow rate of spread limited its impact.

A generation ago, men also earned more than their children and helped to support their children as they matured. Within the newly opened economy of the 1990s, the skills their children have learned, such as speaking English, often bring the offspring into the world market. With such money more readily available through the modern sector, children can often earn more than their parents. Thus the authority of the older generation over important aspects of behavior, such as sex, is greatly weakened. A young girl with access to foreign men can bring home in an evening more than the father or mother earns in a month. Because of this, traditional norms and intergenerational relationships are turned upside down. If a family is having trouble making ends meet, parents are tempted to look the other way when the daughter helps support the family by selling sex.

HIV/AIDS and Tanzanian Society

"AIDS is believed to have recently surpassed malaria as the leading killer among diseases in adults, and is likely to do so for children in the very near future" (World Bank 1992). Tanzania is one of the countries hardest hit by HIV/AIDS. The Ministry of Health (1993) claimed that by 1995 there will be 1.6 million HIV-infected Tanzanians. By the year 2000 there will be 800,000 AIDS patients and 750,000 orphans. Eighty percent of HIV infection is believed to be the direct result of heterosexual transmission. High-risk women in Morogoro call AIDS "the greatest ghost of all ghosts."

Education campaigns have been successful in that more than 95 percent of the population is aware of HIV/AIDS (Muhondwa 1991). However, condom use is still low, with only 9 and 4 percent of the male and female population, respectively, using condoms. A recent study on "partner relations" concludes that 20 percent of the sexually active men and 15 percent of sexually active women have sexual partners other than their spouses (World Bank 1992).

HIV/AIDS is spreading across the country. Cities and towns serve as centers for social and economic networks and AIDS radiates from them. The farther away from the transport routes and from access to towns, the lower the rates of HIV prevalence, as shown in a study reported on Mwanza, a town situated on Lake Victoria in the northwestern part of the country. This phenomenon is also seen in Kagera Region, one of the hardest hit areas of the country (see table 7.1). Tanzanians are aware of this connection. A European official, working with the Dutch Development Agency with Songea Development Action, reports that some villagers refused the offer of a revamped road because "it will bring AIDS."

Deaths and funerals of men attract more attention than do those of women. Men's funerals are often larger because they have control of more resources, and people from the workplace, as well as from the community, attend their funerals. Political and business leaders are mostly men, and their deaths are associated with a great outpouring of grief and shock. Moreover, men appear to be dying at a faster rate than women, although the male/female ratio of AIDS cases is 1/.09. That ratio is also narrowing. More women than men now have HIV (1:0.89), and at an earlier age (Ministry of Health 1993).

Women's Traditional Vulnerabilities

Traditions that have contributed to the vulnerability of women in the past are enhanced by the AIDS epidemic. The traditional professions of caregiver, mother, prostitute, and wife all leave women vulnerable to the virus in ways that men are not.

TABLE 7.1.
The Effect of Locality on HIV Prevalence Rates

Area	Year	Category	Total %
Kagera	1987	Total	219/2172 = 10.08
		Urban	133/542 = 24.54
		Rural	86/1630 = 5.28
Mwanza	1990–91	Total	256/4135 = 6.19
		Urban	140/1130 = 12.39
		Rural	65/976 = 6.66
		Village	51/2029 = 2.51

SOURCE: Republic of Tanzania, Ministry of Health.

In most cultures caregiving falls almost exclusively on the shoulders of women as wives, mothers, sisters, daughters, aunts, and grandmothers. At Muhimbili Medical Center in Dar es Salaam, the major referral hospital in the country where 50 percent of the medical patients are HIV-positive, women supply the extra care needed beyond the treatment regimens of medical specialists. This includes preparing food and spending their scarce funds on medicines that the hospitals can no longer provide free of charge. The care of AIDS patients is time-consuming and difficult. The World Bank (1992) estimates that the care burden for an HIV-infected child in Tanzania totals about two hundred days on average per patient over the year prior to death.

The economic demands of AIDS care are also burdensome. The World Bank (1992) calculates that each adult AIDS case treated in the hospital absorbs U.S. $290 in nursing and drug costs, and each pediatric case costs on average U.S. $195. As the hospitals are increasingly unable to cope, the government is moving to decentralizing care of the patients to the home. The potential cost savings are important to the government; but this transfers the cost directly to the family, and the actual burden of care usually falls directly on women.

As patients, relatives, friends, and others spend more of their scarce resources on AIDS-related expenses, and as some of them already also earn less because they work less, all people involved have less income and resources for other purposes, such as their children's schooling as well as for providing for their own futures. A vicious downward cycle ensues.

After the death of the person with AIDS, care must be provided for the children left behind. Women usually take responsibility for the care of orphans (Mukoyogo and Williams 1991). Specific data about AIDS orphans in Tanzania are scarce. But by 1991, 23 percent of Tanzanian households included foster children who were living without the presence of their biological mother or father (Ngallaba et al. 1993).

Many parents find it difficult to meet the basic needs of their families, and in particular, the needs of children. School children and teenagers pressure parents to provide them with the latest fashions. Children need their school fees paid. They need a lift home. How will they get them? There is unfortunately often an answer to this dilemma for a young girl in dangerous liaisons with men (Zewdie 1993).

The Tanzanian abortion data illustrate the consequences of the "sugar daddy" phenomenon. During a study of factors associated with induced abortion in public hospitals in Dar es Salaam, women were asked: "Who made you pregnant?" Forty-nine of 62 girls in a study said their unwanted pregnancy was the result of having sex with a man older than themselves. Of these 49, 39 percent said their partners were 45 years or older (Mpangile 1993). The appeal of such sexual encounters is, in part, that adolescent girls are accessible for a relatively small amount of money, and that they are perceived as being free from the AIDS virus.

For single women, the risks are especially poignant. A quarter of the households in Dar es Salaam are headed by women. According to the 1991 Demographic and Health Survey, only 6 percent of women reported having multiple sexual partners in the previous month. This percentage, however, rose to 19 percent among separated, divorced, and widowed women (Rutenberg et al. 1993). Women who perceive themselves to be economically vulnerable may seek out more than one partner to help make ends meet. Each extra partner makes the woman more susceptible to HIV infection. The story of Neema illustrates the vulnerability of many women.

> Neema was once married to a rich man and they had several children. When the husband died, the relatives came and took away all their personal possessions—the land and the house that he had owned. Neema became destitute and went away with her children. (Women, even those without access to adequate resources, have to earn food for themselves and their children.) Neema settled in the nearest town and has turned to prostitution to support her children.   (Romocki et al. 1992)

Commercial sex workers are aware of the risks of HIV transmission and AIDS. They know that such activity exposes them to disease and early death. In the town of Morogoro, women who were interviewed for an ethnographic study conducted by Health for All Volunteers Trust and FHI/AIDSCAP (Family Health International/AIDS Control and Prevention Project), explained: "We were many in this business, but so many women have died. We were about two hundred people. At present we are only about forty . . . Frankly speaking, this disease will wipe us out" (Outwater et al. 1995).

Women are at risk and will largely remain in that condition as long as their economic dependence and lack of education leave them few options for leading a secure and independent life. However, not only the poorest women are at risk of acquiring HIV. Even if the women are not economically vulnerable, they may still be socially vulnerable. A wife cannot refuse her husband's sexual advances too many times, if she wants to keep him at home. A double standard also applies. A woman is supposed to be faithful to her man. In contrast, the man is sometimes more free to have sexual relationships with other women.

AIDS is not just a disease of the poor but also a disease of the rich. Many believe that the men are bringing AIDS into the home. This is borne out in a study carried out by Kapiga et al. (1994). At family-planning clinics in Dar es Salaam, 2,289 women not known to be members of high-risk groups were interviewed through the use of a structured questionnaire. Overall HIV prevalence was 11.5 percent. HIV risk increased with both the woman's level of education and her partner's education. Although the number of sex partners in the last five years was positively associated with HIV risk, the median number of sexual partners of HIV-positive women was only two. It was found that there is a "high prevalence of infection among educated women; a similar relationship was seen with the husband's education, despite the fact that education was inversely associated with women's reported number of sexual partners." The researchers hypothesize that "high education is almost certainly associated with higher socioeconomic status; thus it may increase the ability of men to support or acquire multiple sex partners."

Emerging Coping Strategies

A strong culture is one that is flexible enough to respond and adapt to challenges. Even in the midst of intense societal and economic pressure, positive trends are emerging in Tanzania because of the AIDS epidemic. For example, the blood supply is being made safer against contamination by the HIV virus. The scarcity of assured blood is forcing the medical establishment to look at more far-reaching ways of treating the causes behind anemias, and thus decreasing the need for blood transfusions altogether. Principle areas of concern are the impact of malaria and nutrition on children and pregnant women.

Cooperation between diverse institutions in Tanzania is also occurring at an unprecedented level. With the increasing inability of hospitals to meet the demands of growing numbers of AIDS patients, cooperation is increasingly sought between these and nongovernmental organizations (NGOs) that assist patients at home. NGOs are also coordinating their efforts among themselves and are cooperating on a wider range of activities. If one institution can offer HIV-testing and another counseling, for example, the two work together in ways not seen in the past so that each uses its strengths to complement the other in order to support the patient or client.

It is common to hear that "behavior change is difficult to accomplish." In Tanzania, change is taking place on all fronts. Change is hard to measure, however; it is far easier to identify the problem than to see which aspects of the same problem are diminishing both in intensity and substantively.

Muhondwa (1991) reports that over 70 percent of the respondents to a national WHO/GPA (World Health Organization/Global Programme on AIDS) survey on knowledge and practices claim to have made relevant changes to reduce the risk of HIV infection. Most said they had reduced the number of sexual partners; others said they used condoms. There is anecdotal evidence that people are beginning to wonder why it should be acceptable for "successful" men to engage in casual sex, to have many lovers, and to keep mistresses and concubines. Muhondwa (1991) observes, "Such behavior is increasingly being labeled as promiscuous and hence a hazard, not just to the men concerned but through them to their wives and to their unborn children."

Recognizing women's vulnerable but vital position, the government of Tanzania has recently enacted legislation that protects women's rights to inherit property. Now women are entitled to retain half of all land, housing, or other possessions acquired during the marriage, even if the marriage is never formalized. Simplified wills have also been developed so that they can be ratified without a lawyer. Increasing numbers of people are now willing to write wills.

Knowledge in Tanzania about AIDS is high. Internalizing that knowledge is the key to sustained behavioral change. Through the AMREF (African Medical and Research Foundation) Trucker's Project, it has been found that targeted groups do respond (Mwizarubi et al. 1991). Women at truck stops say that the men are their economic base. Truckers, however, point out that the women are just *matunda* (fruits), "something sweet, something nice, but not essential." Now with AIDS, men are beginning to forgo the *matunda*. The truck drivers are hearing, "Pesa zako, zitatumika kuninunulia sanda" (Your money will be used to buy my burial cloth).

Dr. Deogratius Mtasiwa, District Medical Officer of Ilala District, Dar es Salaam, observes that "prostitute communities are shrinking." These communities are reported to be decreasing in size throughout the country. The one exception is a group of young girls, newly emerged in Dar es Salaam, who by their own report are servicing "European diplomats." Brothel prostitutes in Morogoro are finding that their customers have largely disappeared. "We had ten clients a day formerly while at present we get only one or two clients a day; other days no clients come at all. Now, we have hard times; life is very tough. AIDS has led us into a bad situation." Many former prostitutes have returned to their villages because of fear or because they are dying. Contrary to expectations, they are not being replaced. "In the past all the rooms had people, but currently many are vacant because when one leaves, there is no replacement," reports Dr. Lucy Nkya of the Health for All Volunteers Trust in Morogoro.

Evidence of change includes changing patterns of income generation. Tanzanian women are having to expand their economic base. One woman says: "When I first came here, my work was this prostitution to get the necessities of life. The price was Tanzania shillings 50, and that was a lot of money. I was able to save money in the bank. I bought a farm at home. But now the situation is really bad because of AIDS, meaning we agree to settle down with one man and continue business by selling liquor." Others are selling soup, bananas, dried fish, used clothes, and makeup. Still others are opening small restaurants.

Four years ago the subject of condoms was almost taboo. Over a six-month period (June–December 1992) advertisements could be heard on the radio at prime time. A social marketing specialist, working for AED/AIDSCOM (Academy for Educational Development/AIDS Prevention through Communication Project), said: "We had been warned by experienced health communication experts to expect a backlash, and were ready with canned responses for a range of complaints. The only criticism we ever heard was 'Why didn't you use the word *condom?*' "

Among groups that practice high-risk sexual behaviors, especially those who have been targeted for AIDS prevention interventions, condom use is no longer an issue. For customers of commercial sex workers, it is part of the way they do business. In Morogoro, a woman said, "We are forced to do it (stay in prostitution), but we are using condoms. I tell my customer to wear it for his safety and mine. Some customers refuse to wear condoms; then you have to miss the money because at present we are frightened by the rate at which people are dying."

Formerly, horror stories were reported about the treatment of persons with AIDS. It was said that other passengers left the bus if someone with AIDS boarded, and that husbands left their infected wives. Although these events may still occur, these reactions are atypical. Stories are now told of family members and friends caring for AIDS patients, despite all its challenges, until the person dies.

According to Scholastica Ndunguru, a counselor at WAMATA (a Tanzanian organization dedicated to the care and counseling of people with AIDS), their first client was a man whose relatives had abandoned him. The relatives told the neighbors that he had died, and they publicly mourned him for three days. The deception was discovered when a neighbor saw the man in town and thought he was a ghost. When the patient finally died, he was buried by the City Council and WAMATA, and no one came to the funeral. Ndunguru now reports: "We do not have that problem anymore. A big change has occurred in only a few years. AIDS can even make families come closer."

An astonishing amount of care is being given at home. Whereas at one time AIDS patients were shunned, now it is common for an HIV-infected patient to participate in household tasks, even tending small children, as long as he or she is able. Ms. Halima Shariff, NGO Program Officer at AIDSCAP/Tanzania reports:

> Women are struggling to meet the needs of people with AIDS, and although it adds a burden to their lives, it is also empowering them. Caring for HIV-positive people and assuming the role of the main caregiver is taking on new dimensions and is a contribution that cannot be overlooked by society. AIDS

makes women realize that the burden being carried is something only women can undertake and carry well. Though it is stressful, it is winning women a respected position.

In 1992 an incident occurred in which the parents and husband fought over who would tend a woman sick with AIDS. The parents decided, without consulting the husband, to take their daughter back to her home village. When the husband found out, he refused to let his wife go. He said it was his decision, and he wanted to take care of her at his home. The man was a businessman and could not leave his work, yet he did not want his wife to go back to her village where he could not care for her. He had already spent several hundred thousand shillings, searching for a cure for her. The woman sided with her husband.

Changes in Family Life

One hears stories again and again that HIV/AIDS is bringing about changes in family life. AIDS can make family ties stronger not just in the sense of the heroics of someone caring for afflicted members and for taking in orphans. In having to cope with AIDS, the bond between family members is strengthened. It is reported frequently that quarreling within families decreases because spouses are not wandering from one sexual encounter to another. Fathers are staying home with their children. Stronger allegiances are forming between brothers and sisters because they spend more time together.

As the epidemic in Tanzania persists and with such intensity, the normative stories reflect new understandings. Many people have bereaved and mourned not only the dead person but the loss of intimate and valued associations. They have had to undergo entirely new experiences. As more *wakubwa* (well-known personages) die, AIDS becomes a shared story, rather than a tale of a single person's transgressions.

Living in Tanzania amid this tragedy is very sobering. Few people can seriously doubt that change is occurring on both the personal and the societal level. Especially with an improvement in educational standards, it is becoming apparent that within the tragedy of the AIDS epidemic are opportunities for the strengthening of women, families, and the society as a whole.

Legislation has brought in new inheritance laws that benefit women. New behavioral norms, or some would say, a return to traditional ways, have been measured in partner reduction. Condoms are increasingly acceptable to both men and women and are being used. Women themselves are pushing for economic security in new roles in business. The need for nursing is becoming so acute that the caring historically provided by women is being supported institutionally in new and innovative ways. All this holds out the chance that the ancient vulnerabilities of women are being recognized and that measures are being put in place to ensure that these are indeed removed, especially in light of the AIDS epidemic.

REFERENCES

Kapiga, Saidi H., et al. 1994. Risk factors for HIV infection among women in Dar es Salaam, Tanzania. *Journal of Acquired Immuno-Deficiency Syndrome* 7 (3): 301–309.

Ministry of Health, The United Republic of Tanzania. 1993. *National AIDS Control Programme: HIV/AIDS/STD Surveillance*. NACP Epidemiology Unit. Report No. 7. Dar es Salaam.

Mpangile, G. S., M. T. Leshabari, and D. J. Kihwele. 1993. Factors Associated with Induced Abortion in Public Hospitals in Dar es Salaam, Tanzania. *Reproductive Health Matters* (November).

Muhondwa, E. 1991. The social implications of AIDS. *The Courier*, no. 126: 53–54.

Muhondwa, E., M. T. Leshabari, and Y. Batwa. 1991. *The Joint KABP/PR Surveys: Preliminary Communication*. Submitted to WHO/GPA Geneva and MOH/NACP Dar es Salaam.

Mukoyogo, M. Christian and Glen Williams. 1991. AIDS orphans: A community perspective in Tanzania. "Strategies for Hope," no. 5. Actionaid, AMREF, World in Need.

Mwizarubi, B., et al. 1991. Targeting truckers in Tanzania. *AIDS and Society* (April–May).

Ngallaba, S., et al. 1993. *Demographic and Health Survey 1991/1992: Tanzania*. Bureau of Statistics, Planning Commission: Dar es Salaam.

Outwater, Anne, et al. 1995. Morogoro focused ethnographic study of commercial sex workers, final report. Family Health International/AIDSCAP and Health for All Volunteers Trust.

Romocki, LaHoma S., et al. 1992. *STD/AIDS Peer Educator Training Manual*. Family Health International/AIDSTECH, AMREF, NACP/Tanzania.

Rutenberg, Naomi, Ann K. Blanc, and Saidi Kapiga. 1993. Sexual behavior, social change, and family planning among men and women in Tanzania. Paper presented at IUSSP Seminar on "AIDS Impact and Prevention in the Developing World: The Contribution of Demography and Social Science." France.

World Bank. 1989. *Tanzania Population, Health, and Nutrition Sector Review*. Africa Regional Office.

World Bank. 1992. *Tanzania AIDS Assessment and Planning Study*. Africa Regional Office.

Zewdie, Debrework. 1993. The rapidly increasing HIV/AIDS infection rates among young girls. Paper presented at the Thirteenth International Conference on AIDS in Africa.

8   "I'm Not Afraid of Life or Death": Women in Brothels in Northern Thailand

KATHERINE C. BOND, DAVID D. CELENTANO, AND
CHAYAN VADDHANAPHUTI

The rapid spread of the HIV epidemic in Thailand has been attributed to its widespread commercial sex industry linking high-risk groups to the general Thai population (Weniger et al. 1991; Brinkmann 1992). International attention on the number of prostitutes in Thailand, estimated to be between 200,000 to 800,000 (Sittitrai and Brown 1991) has stirred considerable national and international controversy, with studies and reports of the commercial sex industry tending to focus on establishments geared toward foreign tourists. This focus may in part be the result of the easy access Western journalists and researchers have to these establishments, as well as to a willingness on the part of Thai authorities to present commercial sex as a foreign phenomenon (Muecke 1992). However, it is the actors in indigenous commercial sex establishments, particularly in the lowest price scale, who appear to be experiencing the greatest impact of HIV infection (Ford and Koetsawang 1991; Celentano et al. 1994; Pyne 1992).

The social, economic, political, and cultural institutions that contribute to the Thai commercial sex industry have been widely explored by foreign and Thai academics. Prostitution has been illegal in Thailand, following a period of regulation from 1905 to 1960. Since 1960 a series of laws have been implemented, including the Anti-Prostitution Law, which intended to "rehabilitate" prostitutes; the 1966 Entertainment Places Act, requiring licensing of entertainment establishments; and the Penal Code, penalizing procurers of women for prostitution, with stricter punishments for women under eighteen years of age (Asia Watch 1994). The 1994 Asia Watch Report outlines legal efforts to control prostitution, especially as it relates to women who have been trafficked, and charges complicity on the part of the Thai government. Newly proposed legislation would hold procurers and clients responsible (Asia Watch 1994:36); however, these laws have yet to be passed.

In her landmark study of peasant girls from the northern and northeastern provinces of Thailand who migrated to work in Bangkok massage parlors, Phongpaichit (1982) cites poverty as the primary reason for entering sex work, as expressed by young rural women. She shows how the migration of rural women into urban sex establishments may be seen in the context of rapid socioeconomic changes facing rural households in the late 1970s to early 1980s. Since her publication, these forces of change have strengthened over the ensuing decade, with rural people experiencing exacerbated problems of land ownership, and even more pronounced debt (Ekachai 1991).

The economic contribution of daughters to the household economy has been well documented (Phongpaichit 1982; Gray 1990). Gray posits that choices for off-farm employment, such as factory, office, and service work, relate to the social and economic differentiation of young village women based on varying access to strategic resources such as land and investments in education. Intragenerational differences also exist, as older sisters engage in activities such as commercial sex work to support the educations of their younger siblings (Gray 1990).

In addition to poverty, reasons for entering sex work relate to lack of education and individual life experiences, including divorce or abandonment by husbands; sexual abuse and rape; and alcoholism, drug addiction, and gambling by family members. A study of 410 women working in a range of commercial sex establishments in the north found that nearly half had previously been married, and 77–80 percent had at least one child. Most women had only four to five years of primary education and 22 percent were illiterate (IPS 1993:21).

Gender expectations have been raised as a contributing factor to sex work. Muecke (1992) interprets women's involvement in sex work as being related to the role of women in the cultural continuity of Buddhism and the maintenance of the household. Women are viewed as lower in the karmic order, and therefore destined to suffer. Making merit (building temples, providing donations to the order of monks) is viewed as a means to alleviate suffering. Prostitution provides a channel for mobility that does not violate these gender expectations. Women are engaged in worldly, economic activities to uphold the household economy, they experience suffering through their work, and they donate funds to build temples to alleviate the suffering (Muecke 1992). The cultural obligation and gratitude of women to repay their parents, *bounkhun*, exerts additional pressures on daughters to enter sex work (Muecke 1992; Yoddumnern-Attig 1993).

The "sexual double standard," which holds premarital sexual relations taboo for women but acceptable and even encouraged in men, has also been discussed (Ford and Koetsawang 1991). Concepts of "good woman" versus "bad woman" continue to stand in the way of AIDS prevention efforts for women (Cash, cited in Ekachai 1993). The accepted norm that men can have multiple sexual partners has lead to the establishment of sexual networks, with men acting as bridges between various populations of women (Nopkesorn et al. 1993b; Havanon, Knodel, and Bennett 1992).

Ideals of "good women" require no premarital or extramarital sexual relations on the part of women. In reality, multiple sex partners for rural women previously existed in the context of remarriage (Vaddhanaphuti 1993). The ethnographic literature of northern Thailand indicates that female premarital sexual activity has long been practiced under the social controls of the worship of local spirit cults (Mougne 1981; Gray 1990; Turton 1975; Narujohn 1980). With the increase in migration and sale of land, this form of sexual control has significantly diminished. Young women who migrate from villages to towns have new opportunities for developing sexual relationships in dormitory, workplace, and entertainment settings.

Several northern Thai scholars have framed the sexual transmission of HIV within the context of circular migration and changes in the rural economy and local power relations (Singhanetra-Renard 1994; Vaddhanaphuti 1993). These power relations between ethnic groups, with minorities playing subservient roles to the lowland Thai, extend into the realm of sexual relations in villages as well as in commercial sex establishments.

Community studies of recruitment into sex work examine the impact of remission of funds on the family and community at large. The acceptance of sex work by the community is linked to the success of the sex worker in raising the family's economic, and thereby social status. The contribution of money to village development in the form of merit-making is also regarded by the community as a benefit of "going south" (Phongpaichit 1982; Limanonda 1993; Santasombat 1991).

The term *tok khiew* or "green harvest" has been adopted in discussing the prosperity brought to rural families by their daughters (Hengkietisak 1994). It connotes an elaborate system of village-based recruitment into sex work, where agents provide loan contracts to families in exchange for their daughters' labor. In the context of Burmese women lured into sex work, this system is referred to by the Asia Watch Report as debt bondage (1994:53).

These discussions of sex work in Thailand maintain a general tone useful in understanding the existence and perpetuation of the commercial sex industry. However, with few exceptions (Pyne 1992; Asia Watch 1994), they have yet to examine closely the social environments within different types of commercial sex establishments. Such a discussion of the social environment is useful in considering intervention approaches.

The issue of diversity in sex work is also important for intervention planning. Interventions should account for variations in meeting place; facilities; degree of control the female sex worker has over her own work and over the specific encounter; prices for service and percentages surrendered to others; sexual practices and other services provided; and the sexual culture and social meanings of commercial sex (de Zalduondo, Avila, and Zuniga 1990:11). The Thai Ministry of Public Health has devised a classification system for commercial sex establishments based on whether the sale of sex takes place on the premises as the primary transaction ("direct establishment") or whether another service is provided, with women taken out of the establishment for sex ("indirect establishment"). This classification has been adopted by other researchers in examining risk for HIV infection.

In 1989 the first HIV seroprevalence survey conducted among female brothel prostitutes in Chiang Mai, Thailand, revealed an alarming rate of 44 percent seroprevalence. A follow-up study found associations between HIV infection and frequency of sexual intercourse, low prices for sexual service, and postsexual cleansing with water alone (Siraprapasiri et al. 1991). As of June 1992, the Thai Ministry of Public Health documented HIV infection rates among brothel sex workers in Northern Thailand at over 20 percent, whereas those among higher-class sex workers were greater than 5 percent (MOPH 1993).

Several epidemiologic studies of HIV infection among young Northern Thai military conscripts point to commercial sex patronage as a prominent risk factor for HIV infection (Weniger 1991; Nelson et al. 1993; Nopkesorn et al. 1993a). Other risk factors included rural geographic origin, sexual initiation at a younger age, more frequent sex with prostitutes, low price, low condom use, and high rates of HIV infection among low-priced brothel prostitutes in upper north Thailand.

A cross-sectional survey of female commercial sex workers identified by military conscripts in Chiang Mai Province indicated that significant factors for HIV-1 included nonurban location of the sex establishment, ethnicity as lowland northern Thai, and lower price and history of genital warts and dysuria (Celentano et al. 1994). Condom use, number of partners, and duration of employment were not significantly associated. Condom use in urban commercial sex establishments was found to be higher than in rural establishments (Celentano et al. 1994).

Women in direct brothels had significantly higher rates of sexually transmitted diseases (STDs) such as gonorrhea and chlamydia than women in indirect establishments (*Preparation for AIDS Vaccine Evaluation*). Women in these establishments were younger, worked for a shorter duration, and were more poorly educated (Khamboonruang et al. 1993).

Aspects of sex work that have been shown as significant HIV risk factors from epidemiologic seroprevalence studies in northern Thailand include "direct" and "indirect" establishments, low price, number of customers, and rural location. These factors have more to do with structural features of the establishment than with the individuals working there. Critical to the adoption of safe behavior at the individual level is the degree of choice and control a woman has within that structure (Ulin 1992; Carovano 1991; Campbell 1991).

Interventions to control HIV transmission in the commercial sex industry include health education to increase condom use, policies regarding condom use and child prostitution, forced closure of establishments, and educational and occupational development projects aimed to deter women from entering the commercial sex industry. These interventions indicate that a variety of options have been tried or suggested to decrease women's risks of acquiring or transmitting HIV in the commercial sex encounter.

Northern Thailand Study

As part of a collaborative study of social mobility, sexual behavior, and HIV in northern Thailand conducted by the Johns Hopkins University and Chiang Mai University's Social Research Institute, we collected qualitative data on female commercial sex workers in northern Thailand. We focused on aspects of women's choices and control in the context of these intervention strategies. We conducted in-depth interviews with fifty-six commercial sex workers, nine establishment owners, and public health workers in four districts of Chiang Mai Province; two districts of Mae Hong Son Province; and one district of Lamphun Province, all in upper north Thailand. These small-scale establishments, located in urban, periurban, and rural areas, included fifteen brothels and three restaurants, ranging in price for service from 50 to 200 baht (U.S.$2–$8) in brothels to 200 to 1,500 baht (U.S.$2–$60) in restaurants. The ethnic background of women in these establishments included lowland northern Thai, Shan, Lahu, Akha, Lisu, and central Thai.

Commercial Sex Establishments

"Official" classifications of sex work are based on epidemiologists' perceptions of risk. Issues that women in small-scale brothels and restaurants describe as important to their work lives include the number and types of customers, services or tasks that they must perform, living conditions, and relationships with the establishment owner.

Brothels, referred to as *song* in central Thai and *baan saaw* (women house) in northern Thai dialect, where the sale of sex is the primary transaction, are referred to by the Ministry of Health as "direct" establishments. Brothels in Chiang Mai city and surrounding areas tend to cluster in districts, some in or near slum areas. Within these districts, related businesses such as small huts selling whiskey and beer, snooker halls, and small food stalls abound. In several districts, the brothel proprietors rent land from the same landlord and split the rent costs. The structures are cement buildings with one common area and attached smaller rooms. These rooms serve as the women's bedrooms in which they also provide sexual services. Brothels located further out in rural areas are constructed as bamboo bungalows.

Gae, an informant working in a restaurant/brothel outside Chiang Mai City who has worked for ten years in a total of nine places, explains: .

> Brothels are like houses—they are divided into different rooms. Some houses are nice. The rooms are wide open and clean, with a lot of customers. Some houses are bad. The rooms are narrow and too close together so they feel crowded. Brothels have some freedom. You can go out where you want, if the owner is understanding. They are not afraid that we'll escape, even if we still have debts. A good brothel owner is not fussy and lets us go where we want. In brothels, there are a lot of customers.

Another form of "direct" establishment is the *tu krajok*, or glass-encased room with levels of benches, like carpeted steps. Women refer to working in these establishments as *nang tu*, or sitting in the glass case. A customer enters these establishments and finds women with numbers pinned to their dresses, sitting on tiers of carpeted stairs. There is usually a television inside for them to watch while waiting for customers. The glass is dark on the inside and lighter on the outside. According to one woman:

> When we sit in the glass case, we can't see them but they can see us. In the one I worked in, there were more than thirty women, and they paid us a monthly salary of 1,500–2,000 baht. They also paid us per diem. For every customer we got 10 baht. We got this once a week. Here we weren't imprisoned, but they didn't want us to go out. If we hadn't stayed for a month, we weren't allowed to go out at all. People on the inside couldn't go out, people from outside couldn't come in. They had things for sale there, too. Like soap and toothpaste. They fed us twice a day, morning and evening. Many of the customers there were soldiers. On Friday and Saturday they'd come and

reserve to stay the night. They'd tell the *khon cheer khaek* [manager; one who cheers on customers] who they wanted, go out and drink, and come back around midnight or after the party ended.

Tu krajok exist in a variety of establishments, from rural brothels to urban massage parlors, and vary in price, service, cleanliness, comfort, and size. Women in the cases share the experience of isolation and inability to see and therefore select customers. Recently, glass cases have been removed from most establishments as part of the policy to eradicate child prostitution.

To the outsider there appears to be a contradiction in Gae's description of imprisonment. Although she denies that she was imprisoned, she describes a situation in which women were unable to go out. This contradiction may in part be the result of the perception of young women that they are under a system of debt which was agreed upon by their parents. Also, young women who have previously been sheltered close to home, or Burmese and hill tribe women who do not know where they are, fear "the outside" and may have some sense of protection by staying inside.

In December 1992 Prime Minister Chuan Leekpai initiated a policy to eradicate child prostitution. A series of police raids and crackdowns followed. In the process young women were arrested and, in the case of Burmese women, deported or detained, and brothels were closed (Asia Watch 1994). No legal action was taken toward procurers or owners. The process of closure varies according to the police in each locality. In some areas establishments are required to close for a specified period according to a rotation schedule. Owners bring the women, still indebted, to work in other brothels until they can reopen. Brothels in several districts have been shut down completely; however, owners maintain that they will continue to provide services to regular customers only. The movement of a woman from one establishment to another doubles her debt each time.

Another response to the crackdown is to shift businesses from brothels and glass cages to licensed restaurants, which become "indirect" sex establishments. Restaurants are licensed to provide food and drinks but may also have waitresses who can be taken "off" for a price after working hours, with a percentage going to the owner. In others, "service women" sit and drink with customers, thereby receiving a commission from the sale of drinks. Some restaurants have adjacent rooms where sex is sold directly. A restaurant worker describes her working conditions:

A restaurant is a place that sells whiskey, beer, food, and *jin-jin* (women). In one place I worked we had to serve food. The restaurant was bigger and cleaner than the brothel. It was not crowded and we felt we could breathe.

The *khon cheer khaek* was okay—not too fussy. Sometimes we got 20 baht a day for expenses. We got breakfast around noon and an evening meal around 5:00 or 6:00 PM. Another kind of restaurant had "boy" or male waiters. We only had to sit behind the restaurant. This was more comfortable; my legs didn't hurt. During work hours, we couldn't sit with customers. We only sat with them when we went up to the room. In this place the manager was a woman, around thirty years old, and still single. She was a lot fussier than the men—she talked too much. There the price was 100 baht for short-term and 300–400 baht for all night. It was expensive because it was in Bangkok. There were lots of customers—adolescents, adults, police.

The focus of the Ministry of Public Health's ''100 Percent Condom Campaign" has been HIV-prevention activities primarily among "direct" establishments.

The shift from brothels to restaurants has implications for disease-control efforts. First, as the sale of sex becomes "hidden" or indirect, owners are no longer open to the efforts of public health officials to conduct health education and screening. Second, in the establishments where owners may be sensitive to the health needs of the women, the sale of sex occurs outside their domain, and they are no longer able to oversee health checkups or protect women from violence. Third, condom use in "indirect" commercial sex establishments may diminish. On the other hand, women who are taken "off" may assert more authority in screening and refusing customers.

Social Relations

A discussion of social relations in commercial sex establishments would be incomplete without mentioning the patron-client relationship and kinship in the Thai context. Widely discussed in Thai studies, the patron-client relationship is "a hierarchical one in which the patron occupies a superior position and the client is subservient" (Terwiel 1984:19). A patron is expected to be benevolent and protective of his clients, who owe gratitude and servitude in exchange for protection. This relationship can be traced to the historic system of bondage and servitude under the feudal system (Terwiel 1984). Also important is the manipulation of kinship and kinship terms in social exchanges in which age determines the hierarchical order (Kemp 1984:60; Davis 1984:69). Relations in commercial sex establishments are linked to these social systems.

Hierarchies established by owners, pimps, and police contribute to a woman's sense of obedience or determination, exploitation or support and protection. In small-scale establishments, owners may play the role of patron, and young women and their families are "clients," people of lesser status willing to perform services for their patron. Many establishments operate as "family" businesses, with relatives owning several brothels in the same districts, owners as married couples, or children of previous owners. Many owners view their work as helping young women and their families out of poverty. The women working in these establishments refer to one another using fictive kinship terms based on age—*phii* (older sister) and *nong* (younger sister)—and to the owners as *phaw* and *mae* (father and mother). The provision of room and meals contributes to a feeling of being looked after which, for many women, was lacking in their own homes. They evaluate the owner based on how well he or she "takes care" of them. One young woman reports:

> Here, the owners are relatives. But in the other restaurant, the women don't have any freedom. The owners didn't trust the girls. I met this owner at the STD clinic. The owner of my place is nice, he lets us go anywhere. If I tell him first, he doesn't mind. I have a lot of freedom. Last year, they closed the restaurant during Songkraan for one day and had a celebration and treated all of us. They had a roast pig. When I go home to Chiang Rai, he sends me. He gives me three days. I arrange the day to pick me up. But today the manager took me to the clinic because there was no car available. He's very nice. If there are any problems, he talks to us. He teaches us to make good money.

The owner establishes his range of control in several ways. First, the debt system by which women are procured requires a form of bondage; they are kept in the brothel until their debts are paid. One brothel owner described the system of procurement and debt in his brothel as follows:

> I know a brothel in Fang [a northern district]—we used to exchange girls. The girls still had debts so I had to help. I had to pay transportation costs and an agent fee of 1,000–2,000 baht, depending on how beautiful the girls were. They collected 20 percent interest. I had to pay both the down payment and the interest, so the girl's debt was transferred to me. I didn't charge the girls for the agent fee or the car cost.
>
> I arrange a contract with the girl's parents and the agent, like a deposit. I don't want to give an ordinary loan because that is only covered under the civil law. If we have to go to court, they'll only tell them to pay the money and who knows when it will be paid. If something happens, I want them to go to prison. I go through a third party, an agent. If the agent doesn't give the money to the parents, I can charge him with embezzlement. But most agents don't cheat us because this is their occupation, their business. If they cheat us they can't survive.

> In the case of most of the girls here who have debts, I will keep their iden-
> tity card so they don't dare to escape anywhere. If I find girls on my own, I
> have to get to know their families, see what kind of people they are and how
> they live. When I pay them, I'll make a loan contract with them.

In addition to the women's identity cards, many owners use land titles as collateral. Immigrant and hill tribe women are particularly vulnerable to these
forms of collateral because they lack legal rights afforded to ethnic Thais.

Second, the owner establishes rules, regulations, and punishments by
which to assert his authority. "Uncle Thong," a fifty-year-old villager in a district about fifty kilometers north of Chiang Mai, owns a brothel in which
approximately ten women work. He explains how he initiates women into the
house:

> I train the girls once a week. First I explain the rules to them: (1) They can't
> take marijuana or amphetamines into the house [brothel]. If they are found
> with these they are kicked or hit; (2) They can't ride on the back of a cus-
> tomer's motorcycle and go out without asking permission. If caught, I will
> fine them 1,500 baht per time; (3) They are forbidden to argue and fight with
> each other. If caught, they are fined 1,500 baht per time. Anyone contribut-
> ing to or encouraging such a fight will be fined 2,500 baht; and (4) No drink-
> ing of alcohol. The fine increases according to frequency of the offense.

In other establishments, owners may prohibit the women from refusing customers. Kai, a young Lahu woman, works in a brothel in a district just outside
Chiang Mai. She explains, "If the owner is here, we can't choose or refuse customers. We'll get cut 500 baht if she finds out."

The owner teaches new women the rules and techniques for serving customers or entrusts a woman to do so who has worked in the brothel for a considerable length of time. This woman, regarded as *lun phii*, or older sister, is
responsible for looking after the younger girls, for which they are expected to
return admiration and respect. Both the owner and the *lun phii* have perceptions
of safe behavior and risk, such as washing or getting checkups, which may not
necessarily contribute to women's health. As such, they must be included in
health promotion efforts. One owner explains:

> I teach the girls about serving customers and using condoms every three
> days. The new ones do not know anything so I have to teach them. These girls
> aren't the ones spreading the infection because they go for regular checkups.
> The ones in restaurants, like singers who sleep with customers, will spread it
> because they don't wash inside. Women in brothels are cleaner—they know
> how to wash, they see the doctor regularly.

While strict controls over women may contribute to an inability to refuse customers or to initiate behavioral change, alternative support structures may involve owners who assist by refusing customers who don't use condoms, taking women for health checkups, assisting with the cost of medication, and protecting women from violent customers. In sum, owners exert control by developing a system of strict regulations and punishment, and influence by "taking good care of" women in their brothels.

These strategies are similarly employed by the pimp, or *mengdaa* [literally, water bug], who serves to assist the owner. The pimp is euphemistically referred to as a *khon cheer khaek*, or a person who cheers on customers. These terms are used interchangeably by two informants. One reports:

> *Mengdaa* are usually men. But they don't like being called *mengdaa*—they like to be called *khon cheer khaek*. Before, the *mengdaa* used to beat girls. But not nowadays. If they do this now, we can get the police to shut the place down. Most *khon cheer khaek* are between twenty-eight and thirty-two years of age. I don't really know why they're in this age group. Their responsibilities are to call customers, lift things like whiskey and beer, sweep the house, take out the trash. He says, "Big brother, which one do you want, whichever one you like, take her. All night or short term. Short term is 100 baht, all night is 200. All our girls are good." Some brothels have *mengdaa*, others couldn't be bothered. It's better if the owner looks us over, rather than a *mengdaa* who tries to control us. In some places the owner will control the women or have relatives look us over, like younger in-laws. The *mengdaa* scolds us. When customers complain, they hit the customers and scold us. They teach us to do this and that. If we don't speak nicely to customers, they'll teach us how.
>
> There's usually only one *khon cheer khaek* in the brothel. There are no factions or preferential treatment. He treats us all the same because we sit in the glass case. The *mengdaa* recognizes all the old faces. If a new customer comes in, he cheers. Some are close to the customers, so they'll cheer the best girls, the ones who can handle any kind of customer and *len thaa* [play positions].

The relationships between the women and the *mengdaa* are complex. Some women regard them with disgust and resent the control exerted over them; others develop more intimate relationships or view them as a vehicle for escape. Many of the *mengdaa* have sexual relations with women in the establishments, ostensibly to "check the goods." As one *mengdaa* (twenty-one-year-old male), who also served as agent, explained, it is usually another means of exerting control:

> I had an older friend who introduced me to a woman who was an agent. She sent women to sell sex abroad [in Japan]. I helped my older friend find

women in different districts. I got paid 500 baht per day when I went to find women. I used it for transportation expenses [a pick-up truck]. It was difficult to find girls during the planting season. It was easier after the harvest. We used good public relations techniques to talk to them at home. Most of them had already gone off to sell sex, and had come back home. There were some new girls, around eighteen to twenty years old. If I could find around ten girls, I would take them to Bangkok all at once. First we would take them to a beauty parlor for facial treatments. The owner would lend them the money to do this. They paid off the debt later. The main agent in Bangkok would send the women on to different places or have them work in Bangkok. The girls in this network all went voluntarily; there was no force. Some girls would take the money first and escape home. During the time that I took them, I had sex with them too, to establish intimacy and to make them feel that they weren't being controlled.

Although the *mengdaa* views the sexual relationship as a means to establish intimacy and trust, many of the women interpret the act as rape or coercion (Asia Watch 1994). This interpretation may also be linked to the willingness of the woman to enter sex work.

In a few cases, attachments are formed between the *mengdaa* and the sex worker. Om is a Shan woman from Burma who has worked in a number of geographic areas and different types of establishments. She explains: "I stayed in a brothel for three months but escaped—they kept us locked up. A pimp took me out because we liked each other. We planned to live together. I escaped first and the pimp said he'd follow, but he never did."

While a hierarchy exists between the owner, the *mengdaa*, and the women, all these actors operate under the control of the police. The problem of police exploitation of commercial sex workers is common wherever prostitution is illegal (Campbell 1991; Delacoste and Alexander 1987; Asia Watch 1994). There have been allegations of a locally based police system that "enforces" the antiprostitution laws in various ways. Most "collect fines" from owners and threaten women with arrest. One male owner describes the system of payments:

> They come to collect the second of every month. The head department comes the ninth of every month. One brothel used to collect the money from all the "houses." We had a problem because some houses didn't give the money. Later, every house would pay on its own. We'd meet at that house and gather the money. Aside from paying the regular fee, they like to collect money if there's a promotion or transfer; they ask us to help pay to celebrate, to buy a bottle of whiskey or some appetizers. We have to be a bit stubborn. If not, they'll bother us often.

The owner is responsible for the brothel's "fines," between 2,500 and 10,000 baht, in order to remain open. Some local police may pressure owners to close; however, only one owner has ever been arrested.

Individual women, especially those without identity cards, are also targeted by police for fines or favors. One woman from Burma explains:

> I was arrested, so I had to borrow 12,000 baht from a friend to pay off the police. I still owe my friend 4,000 baht. I told my friend that she needn't pay off the police. If they arrest us for eighteen days, they'll let us go because they can't afford to buy us food. Every month I have to pay them 500 baht. They don't bother me anymore.

The health authorities are expected to cooperate with the police in the closing of brothels. These "raids" are not sustained and some establishments reopen. The closing of small-scale brothels because of police crackdowns and problems of profitability have led to a process of screening for businesses; that is, small-scale owners are going out of business, whereas larger establishments become more developed. Meanwhile, women are shuffled from one place to another until their debts are paid, while at the same time the debts increase exponentially.

Money Management

The system of financial management in the brothel is another indicator of the degree of control women have over their work. If a woman enters into the brothel under a debt, an initial payment or a loan is usually paid directly to her parents. Once the debt is paid, she may leave the brothel or continue to work. If a woman enters with no debt or works off the debt, she can save her earnings and send money home, usually monthly.

Many brothels use a system of colored, plastic chips to keep track of earnings. Whenever she serves a customer, the woman will be given a chip, depending on the price and service, which varies from place to place. A male brothel owner explains:

> If we have all-night customers they can stay until 8:00 AM. After that they have to leave. If anyone stays longer they have to pay another chip. There are two types of chips—50 baht and 100 baht. We give the chips to the girls when they go up to the room. Then every ten days we take the chips and figure out the accounts.

A brothel in Pai, a remote town, operates similarly. As one woman explains: "Every time I get money I give it all to the owner. At the end of the month we count the chips. If my daughter needs money beforehand, we can count it early."

In a small brothel just north of Chiang Mai City, women earn an average of 1,000 to 1,800 baht per month (approximately U.S. $40–$70). Currently, most workers are highland girls and women who have no schooling and are unable to speak much Thai. A Lahu worker describes the system of management:

> When we need money to spend, we get it from "mother" [the brothel owner]. When we work we collect the chips. At the end of every month, "mother" will figure out the accounts. We keep the money with her and only know what she tells us. She does this with everyone because no one has gone to school. We don't know how she figures out the amount. She only tells us the amount but we have never seen the money. "Mother" hasn't figured out the amount for two months now. We haven't seen her around lately.

The owner of the brothel avoids the police, who are threatening to close it. If it closes, the women working will go home with no savings, not knowing how much money they should have earned.

Jiap, a lowland Thai, works in a restaurant nearby. She received a 10,000-baht advance for her mother to pay for the care of her child. Jiap says: "I am still in debt 5,000–6,000 baht because I asked him [the owner] to buy a video machine for 9,000 baht. I don't have to pay interest on it. Other girls also get advances."

As do many Northern Thai women, Jiap views the system as a means of accessing finances in order to purchase goods not otherwise available, and of achieving social mobility. She does not face the same degree of exploitation as the highland women in brothels next door.

Deductions are also made by the owners when money is loaned to buy medicine, clothes, and other necessities. In some establishments, women are expected to pay back double or triple the amount originally loaned.

Remittance of Funds

The system of remittance of funds sent home varies from place to place. Once the original debt is paid, the woman's parents may come to the brothel to collect money. A female restaurant worker who previously lived in Bangkok explains: "Sometimes my mother would come to get the money. She came three to four times; I'd give her 5,000–7,000 baht each time and take her out to the zoo or shopping. Once father came to get the money; he didn't even stop to see me."

Money may be sent home in several other ways: (1) taken by the brothel owner or agent; (2) sent home through the mail or delivered by a friend; (3) brought home in person; or (4) sent via a bank. Uay, a Lahu woman in a rural brothel, reports: "The owner sent 3,000 baht to my house once. My mother was ill, and she called here to ask for money. The owner sent money to her but I don't know where. She said she sent it to the bank."

When asked if her mother had a bank account at home, Uay acknowledges that no one in the village understood the banking system and that she did not think her mother knew about banks. Uay has never deposited money in the bank before because she cannot write her name.

Another young women in the same brothel told us, "I can only count to nine. When I buy something, I give the money to them and they give me the change, but I don't know how to count."

Women with little or no formal education and illegal status are particularly vulnerable to exploitation by owners. One local nongovernmental organization, EMPOWER, teaches language and math skills to women in the brothels as a means of minimizing such exploitation.

Women with no debts purchase gold as an alternative to depositing money in the bank. Unfamiliar with or distrustful of the modern banking system, many people regard gold as a form of currency. It is purchased by weight, and as more money is saved, it may be exchanged for a more valuable piece. The display of gold necklaces, bracelets, earrings, and rings is also an important symbol of wealth and status. Women who put all their savings into purchasing gold are vulnerable to theft by low-income customers.

Customers

Aside from structural controls in the establishment, the relationship between customer and sex worker ultimately determines how a woman is able to protect herself from infection. Women in brothels and restaurants with whom we talked categorized customers in terms of age, length of service (short term or all night), regular or one-time, cleanliness (appearance, smell), degree of alcohol consumption, and treatment of women (tipping, violence, sweet talk, and types of sexual acts). According to one worker:

> There are two types of customers. The first are *wairoon* [adolescent], aged nineteen to twenty-seven. Most *wairoon* at this restaurant don't go up to the room. They just drink. They don't have much money. Some give us tips of 20–30 baht, but most *wairoon* don't tip us. Some are nice, not too fussy. Some cause a lot of problems—they don't know what they're talking about. I don't like *wairoon* customers. The second type are middle-aged, from twenty-nine to fifty years of age. They're better than *wairoon*—they talk nicely, give us 50–100-baht tips. Some are stingy and don't tip us at all. Some are picky and greedy—they want to do it several times, no matter if they're paying for tem-

porary or all-night service. Some are at ease with me, we understand each other. I would choose this type of customer. They're more mature, know when they've had enough. *Wairoon* don't know when enough is enough. Sometimes there are old people, fifty to sixty years old. I'm afraid they'll go into shock. Sometimes they look like my father. Before we had this type, but nowadays I don't see many. When they come into the restaurant, friends will tease me that "father" is here.

Given the degree of control the owners and customers have over them, women in brothels develop strategies to protect themselves. These include the exchange of information and shared experience between women, collective or shared bargaining power, and the acquisition of negotiating skills, including techniques or practices taught among women to improve the work environment by increasing the customers' sexual pleasure, thereby reducing the time spent with each customer, increasing condom use, and washing after customers.

Toy, a forty-two-year-old Northern Thai woman, works in a brothel in a remote town near the border of Burma. She entered sex work to flee her husband, a gambling addict and an alcoholic. Many of her customers are ethnic Shan from Burma or men from local Lisu tribe villages. She has several regular customers, mostly adolescent laborers, almost every night. She earns 200 baht per each all-night customer. The regular customers take her out of the brothel to stay in a hotel. Because Toy is older than most of her customers, she is able to negotiate with them.

> If customers get out of control, the owner will tell them, "Look, you have the girl there, why not just get on with it?" Some customers will force them, like the Shan customers. These men are afraid of the police because they are here illegally. I tell them if they don't behave, I'll call the police. If they become violent I'll yell at them, "Don't you have a mother or sisters? If they came to you and cried like this, how would you feel? Don't you have any empathy? However strong you like it, remember I only get 30 baht out of this. Have a little consideration." I'll remember these customers and won't service them anymore. The owner is sympathetic about this.

This strategy of negotiation is based on manipulating the vulnerability of the customer. In this particular brothel, the owner supports women to refuse customers who do not use condoms. Ethnic and age differences between customer and sex worker are important aspects of the power relationship. For the young Shan women servicing older Thai or foreign customers, the same strategies would not work. The women are more in danger of being exposed and arrested than is the customer.

Feelings toward customers range from contempt to affection; these attitudes also reflect how a woman feels about herself and her work. Although they view many customers with disdain, a woman's self-esteem is tied in with her commodity value. Lat reluctantly entered a brothel to pay off her father's hospital bill and to support her son. She had only been working for a week when we spoke with her. Lat told us:

> Who wants to be sincere with women who work like this? Women who work like this—no one wants us for a wife. I don't have any desire to sleep with these customers. I never even had an orgasm with my husband. But at least I had a feeling that I wanted to be close to him, to give to him. But with these men, I don't have any desire. Especially since I've had to work like this.

Nit came from a family of eighteen brothers and sisters. At the age of nine, her parents divorced so she went to live with her sister, who worked in a brothel. She lacked affection, warmth, and support from family. She says:

> When I sleep with some customers, I sometimes feel desire. I like older customers. If a customer comes to see me often and then he picks someone else I feel jealous and cry. If he comes here, I only want him to sleep with me. I don't want him to sleep with anyone else. Sometimes if I sit in the glass cage and no one picks me, and I'm left all alone, I feel ashamed, awkward. I just sit there and cry.

Women in brothels also set limits as to the sexual services they will provide. Services such as oral sex may be specific to the establishment, for which a pricing scale is developed. In lower-priced brothels with a set cost per service, the sexual practice is up to each woman. Many women are reluctant to provide oral sex (*chai pak*) and to accept customers who change positions (*len thaa*). One informant says, "Some customers ask us to use our mouths on them. We have mouths for eating, not for sucking them. It makes us feel low." Oral sex requires the violation of standard spatial relationships—a woman must place her head, the most sacred part of her body, below a profane part of the man (Davis 1984:97).

Toy does not like accepting customers who change positions or incise pearls or broken glass into the end of their penises (*fang muk*), a practice intended to increase the woman's sensation. Toy says: "It hurts because some are too big. Some customers also incise pearls into their penises. This causes the condoms to break and gives us sores that can get infected. If these customers come back, I will refuse them." Changing or playing positions is regarded by men as a practice to be conducted specifically with prostitutes, for whom vigor, and even violence, should be accepted (Bond 1994).

Condom Use

Since the early 1990s, the Ministry of Public Health introduced the "100 Per-cent Condom Campaign," which requires the closing of establishments in which STDs are contracted. As one woman told us, "Health officials tell me I have to use condoms. Any place that finds gonorrhea gets shut down." However, we are not aware of any establishments that have been expressly closed because of STDs. They have also initiated innovative health education activities such as the Super-star Program. This health education model, based on social influence models, is promoted as a provincial health project that trains female sex workers selected as natural leaders from each establishment. The project aims to increase con-dom use among sex workers and provides opportunities for women to exchange information with one another.

There are two problems with the 100 percent condom policy. First, its enforcement is irregular and often tied in to the local system of vested interests. Second, it is ultimately the private act between the sex worker and the customer that determines whether a condom is used. Most women in brothels now insist on condom use with the customers, as confirmed by owners, women, cus-tomers, and health officials.

Initially, the biggest obstacle to the program was the customer's offer to pay extra not to use a condom. Health officials evaluated the program by sending "vol-unteers" to see if women would accept extra money not to use a condom. Many women caught on to these "customers" and now refuse. In more isolated areas, where intervention efforts have not been as intensive, women are more willing to accept additional payment. As a woman in a more remote rural area said, "One customer paid me 200 baht (U.S.$8) to not use a condom. I'm not afraid."

Customers may become violent if a woman insists he uses condoms or refuses to accept extra payment. Women have had to develop negotiating skills with customers and to face the ever-present possibility of violent reprisal. One woman reports:

> Some customers don't want to use them so I tell them, "younger brother" [fictive kinship term], if you don't use them you'll get diseases. If you get AIDS, then what will you do?
>
> Some customers won't use condoms. Sometimes they hit us and say, "You're nothing but a whore so what are you afraid of?" One friend had a customer who wouldn't use a condom. He took a knife to her throat. She was so afraid.
>
> I once had a drunk customer who wouldn't use a condom so I pushed him off the bed. Once I had a *farang* [Western] customer who wouldn't use a con-dom. He grabbed my wrists and forced himself on me.

Although women have every intention of using condoms and protecting their health, in these circumstances they must weigh the risk of immediate danger against the possibility of infection. These risks will not diminish until women have legal protection and customers are held responsible for such acts of violence.

A widespread media campaign focused on the risks of HIV transmission in brothels, coupled with the increasing number of deaths from AIDS in villages, has resulted in changing attitudes about brothel patronage and condom use, and has led to new impressions that risk is associated with the type of partner one has. One woman told us:

> Most customers are afraid of disease, so they all use condoms, even several layers. One customer used eight layers. A few still refuse—about one in ten or one in twenty. They say, "I haven't even used it with my wife. I'll never climax." Lately there have been very few customers. We all want to go home because there's no money.

Male customers also say that they are afraid of AIDS and have reduced the frequency of brothel visits. However, public health workers warn that the problem of condom use exists more between a sex worker and her regular customers or boyfriend than with short-term customers. Likewise, former brothel patrons now seek sexual contacts with women outside brothels.

Despite problems convincing customers to use condoms, women face other problems and discomforts with this technology. Condoms distributed by the Ministry of Public Health contain spermicides such as nonoxynol 9. Women have complained of itching, burning, and swelling, particularly those with more customers. Toy explains,

> I use condoms with customers every time, even with regular customers, because I'm afraid of getting diseases. But we have problems with condoms. Some break, some burn or itch. Some brands are better than others.

Toy has developed techniques to eroticize condom use, and to help other women in the brothel negotiate with customers. She puts them on in layers to create a ribbed effect.

> If the customer is large, it will hurt; if he's small, all the condoms will slip off. The one inside will get stuck in the outer layer. Sometimes younger women complain that customers don't use condoms so I will go and talk to their customers on their behalf. Some put condoms on for them—it takes them hours. When you use condoms, they become soft so you have to take it off and start again, and then it gets soft again.

Condoms are currently the only technology available to women. Many women have expressed interest in the addition of lubricants to facilitate condom use and decrease irritation. Nonuse of lubricants is attributed to slippage among smaller customers. There is also a danger that water-soluble lubricants (60–80 baht per tube) may be replaced by cheaper, oil-based lubricants. Elias and Heise (see their article in this book; see also 1993) present a strong case for the development of affordable, female-controlled technologies such as microbicides, which are needed given the lack of control faced by low-priced sex workers in the sexual encounter.

Vaginal Cleaning

Sex workers we interviewed believe that cleaning will deter infection. This belief is linked to the physical and emotional feeling of being polluted or dirty. Male customers expressed negative attitudes toward sex workers; they view them as dirty because they are felt to carry disease and have frequent contact with male genitals, a low part of the physical hierarchy.

Vaginal cleaning is a standard practice in nearly all commercial sex establishments. Women wash before and after each customer with abrasive or antiseptic soaps and douches: "I used condoms that itched and burned so I bought medicine to clean my insides. I bought it from the pharmacy for 180 baht per bottle. I use it every time after sex with customers." Many highland women use toothpaste to clean the vagina. They describe the soft texture and cool sensation as soothing, particularly if they have open wounds.

The perceived effectiveness of cleaning is also linked to the time elapsed after the sexual encounter. Washing must immediately follow intercourse. One young woman told us, "I once had a customer, a guy who came from the mountain (hill tribe). When he was finished, there was blood and puss everywhere. I had to rush over to wash myself." Customers wash themselves with soda, alcohol, or other acidic or abrasive substances that are believed to kill infection. These strategies are adopted given the existing risks beyond which women have any control or as postpreventive measures in the event condoms were not used.

Birth Control

Pregnancy is another work hazard that women go to great lengths to prevent. Most women in brothels use hormonal birth control, distributed at government family planning and STD clinics. There is a common practice of taking birth-control pills continuously to manipulate the menstrual cycle. Om, a Shan woman from Burma, was widowed and left with an eight-year-old child. She traveled all the way to Cambodia to work as a seasonal laborer. She says that she suffers daily because she has to provide for her child. She took birth-control pills to stop menstruating.

Kai, a young Lahu woman, was advised by the brothel owner to take birth-control pills continuously. She explains:

> The owner advised me not to take the yellow ones. Once the white ones are finished, I throw it away and start another packet. Since I've started working, I've only had my period once. It was heavy. On the second day, I took five pills to stop it.

Nit manipulates her cycle and uses a sponge during menstruation to enable her to continue working.

> I take birth control pills continuously for two to three months so my period doesn't come. Then I stop so it comes once every few months. There is a lot of blood—I use two or three boxes of sanitary napkins. Once it's flowed for two or three days I take pills to make it stop—I have to take five or six pills but it still won't stop. I continue working when I have my period—I put in a sponge. The customers don't know because we turn off the lights. They use condoms so they don't know it's messy. If I feel like there's a lot of blood but the customer isn't finished yet, I ask to go to the bathroom. I wash myself and change the sponge.

Many brothels require women to work while they are menstruating, although some allow women to stop for the first two to three days. Toy told us that when menstruating she only goes with regular customers and informs them that she has her period. The misuse of birth control pills is adopted as a coping strategy to enable women to continue receiving customers and to increase their income and is encouraged by the owners and by the older women themselves. Intervention efforts that tend to focus on infectious diseases must also include the range of other reproductive health issues.

Drugs and Alcohol

Women in brothels must cope with considerable physical and emotional pain. In her survey Limanonda found only a small minority acknowledged using drugs and alcohol before sex (IPS 1993). From in-depth interviews, we learned that drugs, including amphetamines and pain killers, are taken medicinally, not as a stimulant before sex. Gae described using pain killers to cope with work,

My uterus is shallow so it hurts if I have a lot of customers. I get swollen. I went to the hospital once when I was in Bangkok. At first the doctor said that I had an ectopic pregnancy, but it turned out not to be the case. If I have five to six customers, I feel a lot of pain so I buy pain killers from a pharmacy. They sell two pills for 5 baht. Sometimes if it really hurts, I'll stop work for three days.

At the owner's recommendation, Kai and her friends in the brothel take white pills believed to be amphetamines or ecstasy. These pills, on which the letter *E* is printed, are widely available in rural areas and are taken by other laborers as well.

The first time, I took *yaa kae nguang* [literally, medicine to cure sleepiness] because I didn't feel well. The owner bought it for me; it cost 200 baht per pill. Once I took the pills I felt better—my illness went away. One day I was feeling unhappy so I bought this medicine. The guy who sells it is never in the same place. I have to walk through the market to find him. If he doesn't know you he won't sell it to you. Sometimes if I don't feel well, if I have a fever, I buy medicine from the same guy. He arranges the medicine for me. Before I go to sleep I sweat but once I wake up it's gone.

When we take these pills we feel really well. It doesn't hurt when we work. The customer can do whatever he wants to me and I don't feel a thing.

This process of numbing oneself to pain and fatigue extends to the consumption of alcohol. Some brothels prohibit sex workers from drinking alcohol. However, alcohol consumption by sex workers is high in establishments such as restaurants, where women receive a commission on the number of drinks sold. The link between alcohol consumption and low condom use has been documented among male customers of commercial sex workers (Nopkesorn et al. 1993b; Nelson et al. 1993). Customers expect the sex worker to insist on using condoms so if the sex worker is drunk, the likelihood of condom use is low.

Gae works in a restaurant/brothel in which alcohol and beer are sold. She had worked for nearly ten years without being infected with HIV. She drinks with customers every night and has even jumped over the fence of the restaurant to drink in neighboring places. Gae described drinking up to a dozen large bottles of beer and seven bottles of whiskey in a night, and becoming unconscious. She says, "Sometimes it's good to drink. That way we don't feel what the customers are doing to us." The last time we saw her, we learned that she had seroconverted.

Self-Esteem, Control, and the Future

Given the working conditions, the lack of control, the number of sex partners, and the prevalence of HIV among commercial sex customers, it is easy to share the feeling of many brothel-based sex workers that they will inevitability become infected with HIV. As a twenty-nine-year-old Shan widow from Burma who has worked for two years so poignantly says, "I'm not afraid. We work like this—we are bound to die from some related disease. I'm resigned to that. I'm not afraid of life or death. I don't have parents. So what if I die."

The majority of young women in brothels are already infected, in some cases without knowing it. Tip has worked in brothels since the age of fourteen, more than eight years. She left a brothel to live with a regular customer; she regarded him as her husband for more than two years. She talked about being unable to conceive children with her husband, which resulted in her husband's family rejecting her and her returning to the sex industry. She receives regular check-ups but has never asked the nurse about her health conditions. She asked, "Do you think I can ask if I can have children? The nurse tested my blood and told me I have to use condoms all the time. Do you think I can ask the results? I really want to know."

Tip reflects the attitude held by most women, and Thai society at large, that their health is in the physician's domain and they need not know their results. Doctors have traditionally consulted with a patient's family regarding the status of health in order to protect the patient from additional anguish. However, the introduction of anonymous testing and counseling programs is initiating a shift toward notifying and counseling the patient in private.

Those who do know they are HIV-positive must consider the implications for their futures and their families. They are working in brothels because of the need to contribute to the family's economy. This responsibility does not end when they become infected, but rather intensifies as they realize that their productive years are diminishing and they will need to cover health care costs. Thus they feel an urgent need to save more money, yet desire alternatives to sex work. Gac considers her alternatives:

> I am still in debt 10,000 baht. Once it's paid, I'll stop working and go to sell things at home. I'll buy things in the Chiang Rai market and sell them at the evening market at home. Or maybe I'll open a small liquor store because they're building a dam at home. It'll be finished this year. I'm not sure if I'll work in this profession again. Some customers advise me to work at the Industrial Estate. Some people ask if I can speak English. They'll take me to apply for work at a department store in Chiang Mai. But I can't speak a word so I don't know what I'll do. I'm still in the dark.

HIV-positive sex workers face double stigma when they return home. As a result many disappear. Northern Thailand is only now beginning to face the deaths of family members and neighbors. It remains to be seen how much of a deterrent the impact of these deaths will have on future generations of potential sex workers and their families.

Life and Death Options

Commercial sex work in Thailand must be understood as a strategy employed by young women and their families to cope with landlessness and poverty, to support parents and children, and to flee from unhappy or abusive homes. As women enter into a situation where they must work under constraints imposed by police, owners, and customers, they develop ways to deal with health risks. Their options include: (1) escaping; (2) increasing the number of customers in order to pay off debts quickly or save money; (3) insisting that customers use condoms, despite risks of violent reprisal; (4) employing cleaning techniques to cope with feelings of pollution and fear of infection; and (5) numbing the pain with drugs and alcohol. Women turn to one another for support and advice. Those infected in the workplace then have to consider how to cope with HIV infection, stigma, and health costs when they return home.

Intervention efforts must continue to focus on the root causes for entry into these high-risk settings by increasing educational opportunities and occupational choices available to young women, and to improve the situation of debt and loans in rural areas. Those planning interventions must also consider the decision-making processes made by women and other actors who influence those decisions.

ACKNOWLEDGMENTS

Partial support for this work was provided by Family Health International (FHI) with funds from the United States Agency for International Development (USAID) and the National Institutes of Health Grant No. A133682. The views here, however, do not necessarily reflect those of the funding agencies. The authors would like to thank Somnaek Chachawan, Chainarong na Chiang Mai, Prasit Leeprecha, Sukanya Pornsapakul, Kanitta Phongsri, Vichulada Matanboon, Chakrit Taburi, Boripat Pongviset, Thanaphan Na Chiang Mai, and Monica Scandlen for their invaluable contributions to this work. We would especially like to thank the Thai Ministry of Public Health for their assistance, and the women in brothels and restaurants who generously shared their lives with us.

REFERENCES

Asia Watch and the Women's Rights Project. 1994. A modern form of slavery: Trafficking of Burmese women and girls into brothels in Thailand. Human Rights Watch, New York.

Bond, Katherine C. 1994. Sexual Culture of Northern Thai Men: A Preliminary Interpretation. Paper presented at the Workshop on Sociocultural Dimensions of HIV/AIDS Control and Care in Thailand. Chiang Mai.

Brinkmann, Uwe K. 1992. Features of the AIDS Epidemic in Thailand. Department of Population and International Health: Working Paper Series No. 3.

Campbell, Carole A. 1991. Prostitution, AIDS, and preventive health behavior. *Social Science and Medicine* 32 (12): 1367–78. Great Britain.

Carovano, Kathryn. 1991. More than mothers and whores: Redefining the AIDS prevention needs of women. *International Journal of Health Services* 21 (1). 131–42.

Celentano, David D., et al. 1994. HIV-1 infection among lower class commercial sex workers in Chiang Mai, Thailand. *AIDS* 8 (4): 533–37.

Davis, Richard B. 1984. *Muang Metaphysics: A Study of Northern Thai Ritual*. Bangkok: Pandora Press.

Delacoste, Frederique and Priscilla Alexander. 1987. *Sex Work: Writings by Women in the Sex Industry*. Pittsburgh: Cleis.

de Zalduondo, Barbara, Mauricio Hernandez Avila, and Patricia Uribe Zuniga. 1990. Intervention Research Needs for AIDS Prevention among Commercial Sex Workers and Their Clients Responding to Diversity in Actors and Settings. Paper presented at the meeting of the AIDS and Reproductive Health Network. Italy.

Ekachai, Sanitsuda. 1991. *Behind the Smile: Voices of Thailand*. Bangkok: Post Publishing.

———. 1993. AIDS and the Double Sexual Standard. *The Bangkok Post*, June 4, p. 25.

Elias, Christopher J. and Lori Heise. 1993. The Development of Microbicides: A New Method of HIV Prevention for Women. The Population Council Programs Division Working Paper No. 6.

Ford, Nicholas and Suporn Koetsawang. 1991. The sociocultural context of the transmission of HIV in Thailand. *Social Science and Medicine* 33 (4): 405–14. Great Britain.

Gray, Jennifer. 1990. The road to the city: Young women and transition in northern Thailand. Unpublished Ph.D. dissertation, Macquarie University, Sydney, Australia.

———. 1994. The Social and Sexual Mobility of Young Women in Rural Northern Thailand—Khon Muang and Hill Tribes. Paper presented at the workshop on the sociocultural dimensions of HIV/AIDS control and care in Thailand, Chiang Mai.

Havanon, Nappaporn, John Knodel, and Tony Bennett. 1992. Sexual Networking in a Provincial Thai Setting. AIDS Prevention Monograph Series, Paper 1. Bangkok: Family Health International, AIDSCAP.

Hengkietisak, Kamol. 1994. A Green Harvest of a Different Kind. *The Bangkok Post*, March 20, p. 17.

IPS (Institute of Population Studies). 1993. Chulalongkorn University. The Demographic and Behavioral Study of Female Commercial Sex Workers in Thailand. Institute of Population Studies, Bangkok.

Kemp, Jeremy. 1984. The manipulation of personal relations: from kinship to patron-clientage. In Han ten Brummelhuis and Jeremy H. Kemp, eds., *Strategies and Structures in Thai Society*. Anthropological-Sociological Center, University of Amsterdam.

Khamboonruang, Chirasak, et al. 1993. Baseline Prevalence of Selected Sexually Transmitted Diseases in Direct and Indirect HIV-1 Seronegative Commercial Sex Workers in Northern Thailand. Abstract Presented at the Conference on Advances in AIDS Vaccine Development Sixth NCVDG.

Limanonda, Bhassorn. 1993. Female Commercial Sex Workers and AIDS: Perspectives from Thai Rural Communities. Paper presented at the Fifth International Conference on Thai Studies. London.

Mougne, Christine. 1981. The Social and Economic Correlates of Demographic Change in a Northern Thai Community. Ph.D. dissertation, SOAS, University of London.

Muecke, Marjorie A. 1992. Mother sold food, daughter sells her body: The cultural continuity of prostitution. *Social Science and Medicine* 35 (7): 891–901. Great Britain.

Narujohn, Idahuchiracharas. 1980. The northern Thai peasant supernaturalism. In *Buddhism in Northern Thailand*, Thirteenth Conference of the World Fellowship of Buddhists. Chiang Mai. November.

Nelson, Kenrad E., et al. 1993. Risk factors for human immunodeficiency virus infection among young adult males in Northern Thailand. *JAMA* 20 (8): 955–60.

Nopkesorn, Taweesak, et al. 1993a. HIV-1 infection in young men in Northern Thailand. *AIDS* 7 (9): 1233–39.

———. 1993b. Sexual Behaviors for HIV-Infection in young Men in Payao. Research Report No. 6. Program on AIDS, Thai Red Cross Society. November.

Phongpaichit, Pasuk. 1982. From peasant girls to Bangkok masseuses. *Women, Work and Development* 2. International Labor Organization, Geneva.

Pyne, Hnin Hnin. 1992. AIDS and Prostitution in Thailand: Case Study of Burmese Prostitutes in Ranong. Unpublished master's thesis, Massachusetts Institute of Technology, Boston.

Santasombat, Yos. 1991. Mae Ying si Khaitva: chumchoa lae kankhaapraweni nai Sangkhom Thai. In *Newsletter of the Thai Association of Qualitative Researchers* 5 (12).

Singhanetra-Renard, Anchalee. 1994. The Meaning of Migration in the Socio-Cultural Context of the HIV/AIDS Epidemic in Northern Thailand. Paper presented at the workshop on the Socio-Cultural Dimensions of HIV/AIDS Control and Care in Thailand. Chiang Mai.

Siraprapasiri, Taweesap, et al. 1991. Risk factors for HIV among prostitutes in Chiangmai, Thailand. *AIDS* 5 (5): 579–82.

Sittitrai, Werasit and Tim Brown. 1991. *Female Commercial Sex Workers in Thailand: A*

Preliminary Report. Institute of Population Studies, Chulalongkorn University and Program on AIDS, Thai Red Cross Society.

Terwiel, Barend J. 1984. Formal structure and informal rules: An historical perspective on hierarchy, bondage, and the patron-client relationship. In ten Brummelhuis and Kemp, *Strategies and Structures in Thai Society*, 19–38.

Turton, Andrew. 1975. Northern Thai Peasant Society: A Case Study of Jural and Political Structures at the Village Level and Their Twentieth-Century Transformations. Ph.D. dissertation, University of London.

Ulin, Priscilla R. 1992. African women and AIDS: Negotiating behavioral change. *Social Science and Medicine* 34 (1): 63–73. Great Britain.

Vaddhanaphuti, Chayan. 1993. Changing Sexual Behavior in Northern Thailand. Paper presented at the Fifth International Conference on Thai Studies. London.

Van Landingham, Mark J., et al. 1993. Sexual activity among never-married men in Northern Thailand. *Demography* 30 (3): 297–313.

Weniger, Bruce, et al. 1991. The epidemiology of HIV infection and AIDS in Thailand. *AIDS* 5 (supplement 2): 571–85.

Yoddumnern-Attig, Bencha. 1993. Northern Thai Women and the AIDS Crisis: Family, Community, and Societal Determinants. Paper presented at the Fifth International Conference on Thai Studies, London.

9 | Women's Social Representation of Sex, Sexuality, and AIDS in Brazil

LUIZA KLEIN-ALONSO

Background

AIDS is increasingly infecting women in Brazil. The ratio of infected men to infected women has fallen rapidly. In 1985 thirty-six men were infected for every woman. By 1994 this ratio had fallen to four to one. Most of the increase in female infection is the result of intravenous drug use, but heterosexual transmission is also increasingly common. In 1995 AIDS represents the major cause of death for women from twenty to twenty-eight years of age.

These data suggest that women must consider the consequences of sexual activity, no longer just in the context of reproduction, but also in the context of protection against disease and death.

Brazilian culture in relation to sexual activity is very ambiguous. On the one hand it is still restrictive and oppressive, particularly in relation to women and their social roles. Brazilian men on the eve of the twenty-first century still distinguish between the "wife," the woman they marry who bears their children and whom they betray, and the "lover," the woman with whom they can have fun and sex in an erotic way.

Brazil is at the same time the country of Carnaval, where women go to the beach almost naked, where having a beautiful body is a must among young women, and where a man who kills a woman because of emotional involvement rarely goes to jail. Brazil has several Women Police Stations (WPS) whose role is to provide support for women to denounce sexual discrimination and aggressions. However, the majority of the women who denounce their husband, lover, or boy-friend ask the WPS to drop the charges after only a few days.

The power dynamics that operate in most Brazilian sexual relationships do not encourage one partner to open a dialogue about protection with the other. According to previous studies, women and men talk about their sexuality in very few situations (Alonso 1992:93). There is a general consensus that one has sex, one does not speak about sex. Couples that are formally married may talk about protection in the context of reproduction, but even in such situations the responsibility for that is entirely understood as the woman's duty. Brazilian men are considered to be too macho to refrain from their sexual drive, and women must be pleased to have a man who is so dominated by his manhood, since masculine identity is closely related to sexual performance.

Muraro (1983) in her work on women's sexuality in Brazil, concludes that the more dominated the man the more he dominates the women of his social class. Among all different social classes—workers, countryside workers, the middle class, and the wealthiest class—the man's body is commonly perceived as being centralized in the genital parts and more specifically in the penis. In contrast, a woman's body is perceived as having a diffused sexuality. Muraro's research shows that women still think that men have a better life than women, mainly because men can make their own decisions, do what they want, go wherever they like, and have more sexual pleasure.

In my own work from data gathered in 1992 and 1993, I find that women do not envy the penis, but they resent that being a woman represents more work. They constantly mention the "double journey" and observe that they have less professional and sexual opportunities than men. In contemporary times, women are very much divided between performing traditional roles and answering modern demands. Women know they must work outside the home to contribute to their families' income (for many women, this is no longer a choice), but they still feel that marrying and having a family is necessary. These beliefs are reflected in such comments as: "My marriage will be different, I'll be happy" or "My husband will help me, he will love me."

Women in our time are also aware that they no longer can be like their mothers or grandmothers. Some are nostalgic for the old days, saying: "Women were happier when they had someone that took care of them" and "Women had a more comfortable life when they did not have to work in two places as they do today." What is evident is that Brazilian women are very confused by the costs and benefits of being a woman in the 1990s. That confusion, which is not likely to be resolved for several generations, leads them to engage in old patterns of dominance in their relationship with men. Where power is concentrated on only one side and not shared, these patterns of dominance are enforced. For some women, power is also very threatening.

Brazilian men's dominance over women in the heterosexual relationship is nearly universal. This dominance permeates the area of sexual decision making, with specific reference to protective behavior. Several research and intervention programs have been implemented that try to empower women in negotiating protective behavior, since women's relative inability to control their sexual lives clearly increases their vulnerability to disease and unwanted pregnancy. Although not all empowerment programs succeed, some present very good initial results. In Brazil, starting in the 1970s with the Mother's Group of Basic Ecclesial Communities and increasing in the 1980s with feminist organizations, the practice of empowering women shows, however, that after six or eight months, most women involved in the programs present the same behavior they had before the beginning of the program.

Since AIDS is such an important topic when discussing sex and sexuality, I will focus on gender relations in Brazilian society in the context of the following:

1. male-female relations in a society and subcultures;
2. gender relations as they exist in the area of sex, with a specific focus on communication about sexual matters, and gender-based differentiation in areas over which control is exercised in sexual matters;
3. the potential for and direction of change in gender relations in a climate of increased awareness and concern about HIV/AIDS and the availability of protective options.

The purpose of my analysis is to describe women's social representations and how such representations affect women's ability to protect themselves. I begin with a brief theoretical framework.

Theoretical Framework

My research falls within the general line of investigation of concept and category formation (models of cognitive structures) related to internal representations. Through this line of investigation, I offer possible reasons for why people say one thing but behave to the contrary. The primary question that directed my research was why women who are highly knowledgeable about AIDS and HIV prevention do not change their sexual behavior? Specifically, why do women not practice HIV prevention during sexual intercourse?

Current research in Brazil, with different groups of women, demonstrates that knowledge of AIDS is high (varying from 60 percent up to 90 percent); however, condoms are used by less than 10 percent of women. Lurie et al. (1995) report that among commercial sex workers interviewed, 96 percent say they always use condoms with clients; however, only 6.5 percent report using a condom with their boyfriends. This finding indicates the existence of an emotional barrier to prevention.

In their review of the literature on concept formation, Markova and Wilkie (1987:399) observe that "the acquisition of concepts and social representations must be redefined as a cognitive-emotional process." In this sense, a phenomenon such as AIDS must be understood "in the context in which the concepts of social representations are used and on the personal and social circumstances of the knower." Although the distinction between concepts and social representations is still under discussion, most researchers understand the formation of concepts associated with the acquisition of knowledge, which is related to truth, certainty, and facts. On the other hand, social representations are associated with practices, sentiments, values, images, social stigma, beliefs, and myths (Markova and Wilkie 1987).

It is generally believed that scientific concepts are formed in a systematic and rational manner, based on one's ability to reason. In contrast, social representations rely more on convention and memory and are the result of the relationship between society and the individual. However, several studies in child development indicate that this is a meaningless distinction, no longer useful for studies concerned with behavioral change.

With regard to AIDS, researchers such as Markova and Wilkie state that a major factor influencing the formation of its concept and representations is the publicity given to AIDS by the mass media. Facts, figures, myths, and half-truths about AIDS appear daily in the popular press. AIDS sells newspapers today. The media has given support to the popular notion that the AIDS problem could not have arisen but for a permissive society; in other words, the epidemic could have been avoided if traditional family values had been respected. This implies a criticism of the last three decades that have been marked by a revolution in women's roles, what constitutes a family, and the way we perceive and have sex.

Given this background, I decided to design an intervention program taking into consideration the relationship between knowledge and values, and the assumption that learning a cognitive activity is an essential emotional practice. The social representations of being a woman, being in love, and of prevention were the focus of the discussions in women's groups, which I formed for this research study.

Focus Groups

Three focus groups were formed in São Paulo, Brazil. Each group had nine women ranging from twenty-five to thirty-five years of age. The women earned salaries ranging from U.S. $120 to U.S. $600 per month and had more than five years of schooling. Of the women in the three groups, nineteen were married, eleven had children (one out of wedlock), and twenty-one had migrated from other Brazilian cities outside São Paulo.

In their discussions the women stated that being a woman is strongly related to traditional assumptions. They observed that the woman is the one who takes care of the children, the elderly, and the home, who not only cooks, cleans, washes, and gets pregnant but now has to work outside the home. Being a woman is defined mainly by duties. The general consensus in the groups was that it is very difficult and tiring to be a woman. Notably, no one commented in the groups about their own sexuality.

Being in love, however, was a topic that elicited much comment. Most women told stories of being in love. Over time, that became a topic that women wanted to talk about more and more. The commonality in the stories is that women are rarely loved in the same intensity as they love, meaning that men love less than women do. The majority also felt that they had been betrayed. Most of the experiences brought about depression, suffering, misunderstandings, and sadness. However, women also viewed being in love as the only time they can experience happiness. Therefore all women in the group wanted to be in love again, believing that the next time it would be different. Only one woman said that to be in love for her was like being hooked, that she was a love addict, and that she felt it was not a good thing. When she said that, the rest of the group (eight women) disagreed and said it was normal. They also stated that being in love is a state in which there is only one important thing in life—the object of your love—nothing else matters.

With regard to the prevention and cure of AIDS, the first reaction of women in all groups was to say that they do not need to protect themselves, and that a cure for AIDS would be a good thing for those who are infected. I observed, however, that the women believe they can protect themselves by not allowing the discussion to be too revealing. Although they knew that the group was formed with the purpose of discussing AIDS, one of the participants said that AIDS is not related to being in love or being a woman. Instead, AIDS is related to sexual intercourse, and in this case only those who have sex without love have to protect themselves. No one contested this idea in her group.

The three groups linked the social representation of being a woman and being in love to the idea of prevention and cure of AIDS. In their conclusion the groups showed that although women are working outside the home, have several responsibilities, and have sexual relations outside marriage, the traditional image of woman dominates. Several women commented that they expect to stop working after getting married. Alienation from "things of this world" is seen as a prize of being in love, since you do not have to be busy or concerned with what is happening. Fantasy, along with the search for the right guy, still occupies a lot of time for most of the women who participated in the groups.

Social Representations and AIDS Prevention

The results of the analysis of the groups' discussions showed that Brazilian women strongly link sexual intercourse to love and tenderness, believing that once you are in love, by magic, you are vaccinated against sexually transmissible diseases, including AIDS. Given these findings I decided to develop an educational program aimed at promoting a guide for safer sex through a variety of educational strategies, including role-playing and lectures in a constant and interactive dialogue. My goal was to promote the understanding and the assessment of intentional behavior.

The program was offered to 117 women. Those who chose to participate were divided into six groups of 9 women each. Four groups had the educational program and two acted as a control group.

It is well understood that gender identity is constituted by cultural factors: the designation of sex by the parents when the baby is born, the influence of parent's attitudes, the ways one uses his or her own body, and the corporal and genital sensations that confirm or not the designation given by the parents. But in addition to the differences between biological sex and gender identity, there is another problem. Neither the biological sex nor the gender identity determine the sexual behavior of a person. This behavior involves something more.

For this intervention I decided to carry out a program based on the discussion of feminine myths. Campbell (1994) observes that for human beings in their eternal search for identity, the myth—as a symbol that calls forth and orients the psychological energy and as a vehicle of communication between the consciousness and the unconscious in the same way as dreams—is always fundamental. Campbell (1994) also observes that when modern Western civilization destroys its myths, it suffers from a rude interruption of this process of communication. The contemporary ambiguity that women live could be the result of a lack of opportunities to elaborate, at an internal level, the old mythological assumptions that orient their place in society.

The use of oral stories is appropriate because these stories provide more than information; they provide a way of thinking and an opportunity to think about their implications. By discussing the symbolic meaning of each story, in addition to its psychological impact, one can possibly discern how human beings behave. Interacting with a story also allows a person to relate his or her own history and experience through a universal medium. The meaning and the significance is not in the story itself, but in the way it acts on our own perception of it. The imaginative experience, as an exercise of hope and as a transgression of time and death, creates a possibility of what one could be and affirms the power of what it means to be a human being.

Based on the material from the focus groups and from the literature about intervention programs for women, I decided to try a program based on feminine myths. I chose three feminine myths that portrayed universal archetypes: Eve, Lilith, and Psyche.

In the intervention we did not discuss the three myths academically nor did we give lectures explaining them (although the literature, especially Jung, is very interesting and abundant). We explored the myths through the use of role-playing techniques. Women in the group were invited to act the roles of Eve, Lilith, and Psyche.

The myth of Eve was clearly understood. Some of the participants said that it was like being Maria, the mother of Jesus, and others said it was the myth of Amelia (a Brazilian elaboration of the archetype). This myth was seen as the traditional role women have played for generations. Eve was seen as the woman who depends on the man (father, husband, son, or brother), is not very smart, does all the domestic chores without complaining, and takes care of the children, husband, parents, and parents-in-law. Eve was seen as a sad and tired woman whose major source of happiness was her kids. Eve was also seen as a woman who loves and because of this suffers.

The myth of Lilith was translated as the "other one." Lilith was played as the woman who does not have children because she wants to keep her body in good shape. She is a woman who drinks and smokes, goes out at night, dresses in a fancy way, likes to dance, is very good in bed, knows how to keep a man, and yet is not dependent. Lilith was seen as the woman who uses a man, especially his money. Lilith was also the woman who has sexual pleasure (sometimes because she has sex without love); she is a woman who does not know how to love and is therefore very lonely.

After the role-playing of Eve and Lilith, the participants were invited to discuss what they had done. Speaking freely, the participants explained what they had done and what the role-playing had in common with their daily lives and thoughts. Some 56 percent of the participants said they were Eves, 27 percent said they would like to be a mixture of Eve and Lilith, and 7 percent did not express their opinion.

The role-playing and the discussion consumed three sessions, and all the women in the program were actively involved. Only one woman dropped out in the middle of the program because of a medical appointment. After the third session everyone agreed that being Eve or Lilith was not enough, although these myths are responsible for most of their attitudes and behavior. For some women it was a shock to realize that their ideas and thoughts were not the result of an individual choice but culturally and socially constructed. Therefore a discussion about what they would like to be was the topic for the fourth session.

In the fourth session I introduced the myth of Psyche, as the myth of the woman who, through a process of self-knowledge, decides what is best for her. That process involves a lot of work, happiness, and suffering. I related the Greek story about Eros and Psyche to the participants, who liked it very much. In the discussion they realized that Psyche's courage to love was basically the courage to have an individual experience. For Psyche, being in love was an opportunity to know herself and her identity; it was the time for her to experience the pain of being alive. Psyche concluded that love is greater than death and pain. But the most important aspect of the myth of Psyche was the ability to have an individual experience.

Women's Representations

The discussion about the feminine myths introduced gender relationships and cognitive experience beyond the traditional sociological framework. Currently many women in heterosexual relationships complain about men. There is a consensus that Brazilian women in the last decade developed and changed, whereas men maintained traditional expectations about relationships based on those of their parents and grandparents. After the discussions 68 percent of the women in the intervention groups as opposed to 31 percent in the control groups saw aspects of the psychosocial and cultural variables related to gender roles and conceptions of love and sexual drive as barriers to AIDS prevention.

An analysis of the discussions in the intervention program also demonstrates that Brazilian society no longer accepts the notion that it is natural and logical for men to have all the privileges; that they do is made obvious by their salaries and wages and their opportunities to develop professionally, despite women's sacrifices. The nonconformism that starts at the workplace is gradually reaching other spheres of women's lives.

In contemporary society, women are divided between traditional and new roles, which can be summarized as follows:

1. All agree that a woman who gets married and does not have children is a failure.
2. Until a woman finds the man of her life, she is not supposed to have sexual pleasure, which is a "modern" way to be pure (a virgin).
3. A woman is not supposed to show interest in a man openly, because men view that as a threat.

4. When a woman works outside the home or when she earns money, she should make less money than her husband.
5. It is inappropriate for a woman to voice her feelings and emotions, particularly regarding sex.

The women also made judgments about what it is to be a man. They concluded that men are sexists, because most of the women want them to be that way. All agreed that a female machismo influences the way mothers raise their sons and wives' expectations.

The assumptions that women in the groups held about men and their roles can be summarized as follows:

1. A man can argue and be aggressive and competitive, but he should never expose his feelings, cry, or admit that he has failed.
2. Domestic chores are seen as something unnatural for men to do; even simple tasks done by men are sloppy and careless, since "men have no skills at this."
3. Demonstrations of affection and tenderness are to be shown only among family members and close friends, never in public.
4. It is easier for a man to make sex without love than it is for a woman.

It was a revelation for the majority of the women (64 percent) to see themselves as the ones who help maintain the social construction of the macho man. This led to a discussion of women no longer being victims but rather partners who also create and legitimize a way of life that in the era of AIDS place them at risk for HIV infection and death.

Such traditional beliefs now accompany women who struggle for a good job and equal pay for equal work in the workplace, participate in the decision-making process in professional activities, buy cars and houses (no longer only clothes and perfume), participate in sports, and have extramarital sexual relations. From a socioeconomic perspective one could say that the practical life women live today should change the way they engage in a sexual relationship. But what is seen from these groups is that as long as women believe that sex can be done only if one is in love, an assumption tied to the myths of Eve and Lilith, there will be little change in women's ability to protect themselves from HIV.

Currently the situations related to sex, gender, and affection have many faces. Some women would like to return to the "good old days." Fifty-eight percent of the women view the idea of a loving relationship as an individual's privileged space. A loving experience is seen as the condition needed to overcome problems and to achieve happiness. Most women in the groups (74 percent), however, are conflicted and live with ambiguity. Some (42 percent) do not want to be dependent on men, and others (59 percent) do not want to be their "mother," albeit they do not know how to act differently. The thinking of 62 percent of the participants was affected by the myth of Psyche, providing them an opportunity to rethink their relationships and roles. Few women (less than 3 percent) in both the control and experimental groups differ in their ability to actually act differently and show positive attitudes, as well as in their intentions to act differently, indicating that these variables are most influenced by cultural values related to gender.

Applying an intervention program based on the discussion of archetypes demonstrates that being highly educated about AIDS can have an impact on prevention, if the discussions are related to an intervention where variables such as emotions, beliefs, sex-role perceptions, and self-image are considered. Women as well as men want to be loved. The recipe that has been in practice for years has not worked very well, but everyone thought it was the best he or she had. The challenge now is for women and men to re-create this idea in their own way.

REFERENCES

Campbell, J. 1994. *As Transformações Do Mito Atraves Do Tempo*. São Paulo: Editora Cultrix.
Lurie, P., et al. 1995. Socioeconomic status and risk of HIV-1, syphilis and hepatitis B infection among sex workers in São Paulo, Brasil. *AIDS* 9 (supplement 1): S31–S37.
Markova, I. and P. Wilkie. 1987. Representations, concepts, and social change: The phenomenon of AIDS. *Journal for the Theory of Social Behaviour* 17 (4): 387–409.
Muraro, R. M. 1983. *Sexualidade da Mulher Brasileira*. Rio de Janeiro: Editora Vozes.

10 | The Impact of Structural Adjustment Programs on Women and AIDS

MUBINA HASSANALI KIRMANI AND
DOROTHY MUNYAKHO

The World Bank and the International Monetary Fund (IMF) responsible for implementing the Structural Adjustment Programs (SAPS) have often been held accountable by those within and outside the health community. The economic policies on adjustment that these international organizations have introduced are perceived as increasing poverty in some regions, especially in sub-Saharan Africa. The spread of AIDS is claimed to be closely related to this growing poverty. Two hypotheses are put forward to explain this:

1. The effects of adjustment are most severely felt by the poor (especially women) with increases in both the extent and severity of poverty. Reduced economic power promotes prostitution and high-risk behavior, and poverty makes condoms less available and decreases the chance of seeking treatment for sexually transmitted diseases.
2. Structural adjustment leads to reduced social spending, thus curtailing the government's response to the AIDS crisis (Whiteside 1993).

Structural Adjustment Programs are aimed at putting a distorted economy back on track. Although all regions have been impacted by SAPS, in this article we focus largely on sub-Saharan Africa to which the literature has given considerable attention. In the case of Africa, SAPS were introduced in the context of a decade-long depression that resulted in sharp declines in Africa's terms of trade. Its economic performance was particularly dismal, with an average annual growth rate of only 0.4 percent during 1980–87. In the 1980s, development experts and donor agencies agreed on the importance of macroeconomic policies to the development of sub-Saharan Africa. Following the 1981 Berg Report, policy reforms for new structural adjustment loans and grants were introduced, and since 1982 saps have been adopted by more than thirty African countries (World Bank 1981).

Many adjustment packages include devaluation of overvalued currencies, increases in artificially low food prices and interest rates, a closer alignment of domestic prices with world prices, and emphasis on tradables / exportables and the gradual withdrawal of restrictions on competition from abroad. Other ways to invigorate stagnating economies include trade liberalization, privatization policies, a decrease in government spending, wage and hiring freezes, reduction in employment in the public sector or a decrease in the minimum wage, the removal of food input subsidies, and across-the-board reduction in budget deficits (United Nations Economic Commission for Africa 1989).

Although adjustment programs are important to improve countries' macro-economies, the positive effects, as indicated by experts and donor agencies, are to be felt in the long run. What is of concern in this discussion, therefore, is the harmful effect of adjustment on the poor and vulnerable groups in the short-term economic stringency, which in some cases may last several years, and its linkages to the spread of HIV.

Correlating AIDS to Socioeconomic Issues

The design of structural adjustment packages, and the assessment of their impact on the behavior of economic agents, be they individuals, households, or firms, tended not to consider gender as a distinguishing factor (World Bank 1994). Although both men and women participate in and are affected by economic adjustment, what is often not recognized by policy makers, and certainly not explicitly, is that this occurs in distinct ways for men and women, because men and women play separate roles and face different constraints in responding to policy changes and to shifts in relative prices and incentives.

Structural Adjustment Programs more explicitly mean change, not only at the macro level where policies are implemented but more significantly at the micro household level where women are most affected. Schoepf (1992), in some of her case studies of women in Zaire, suggests there is evidence that structural adjustment may also affect intimate relationships between men and women within the household. In a case study of a woman she calls "Nsanga," Schoepf portrays how the economic effects of an SAP create tension in Nsanga's marriage and ultimately lead to divorce.

In 1983 the International Monetary Fund instituted a series of "structural adjust-ment" measures designed to reduce government expenditures so that Zaire, like other Third World countries that had borrowed heavily in the 1970s, could make payment on its international debt. More than 80,000 teachers and health workers were made redundant. Nsanga's husband was one of those who, lacking a powerful patron to intercede for him, joined the ranks of the unemployed. After six fruitless months of waiting in offices, he began to drink, selling off the household appliances to pay for beer and then lutuku, the cheap home-distilled alcohol.

Nsanga tried many things to earn money. Like most poor women in Kinshasa, she has had only a few years of primary schooling. Because she has no powerful friends or relatives either, she was unable to find waged employment. She cooked food for neighborhood men, she sold uncooked rice in small quantities and dried fish when she would obtain supplies cheaply. These efforts brought in only pennies at a time. Her husband left and Nsanga does not know where he is. The children ate into her stocks and she went in debt for the rent. She asked her elder brother for a loan, but he refused, pleading poverty. Although he has a steady job as a laborer on the docks, he has two wives and nine children.

Without new start-up capital, exchanging sex for subsistence seemed the obvi-ous solution. The first year Nsanga became a deuxième bureau, "occupied" by a lover who made regular support payment. She also had a few "spare tires" to help out. Then she got pregnant and the "occupant" left. His salary could not stretch that far, he told her. So Nsanga had to take on more partners—a fairly typical down-ward slide. The neighborhood rate was 50 cents per brief encounter in 1987, and Nsanga says that if she is lucky she can get two or three partners per working day, for a total of $30 a month (at most). Many men now avoid sex workers because the mass media have identified "prostitutes" as a source of infection.

Nsanga's baby was sickly and died before her second birthday, following pro-longed fever, diarrhea, and skin eruption. Nsanga believes it was because semen from so many men spoiled her milk. Nsanga reports that she has had a few bouts of gonorrhea, for which she took tetracycline pills on advice from the drugstore clerk. About a year ago she had abdominal pains for several months but no money to con-sult a doctor. She says that the European nuns at the dispensary in her neighbor-hood do not treat such diseases. Diagnosis at the nearby university clinic costs the equivalent of 30 encounters, so none of the women she knows can afford quality care.

Asked about condoms, Nsanga said that she has heard of but never actually seen one. She has heard that men use them to prevent disease when they have sex with prostitutes. Nsanga rejects this morally stigmatized label and, if a lover were to pro-pose using a condom, would be angry: "It would mean that he does not trust me." In her own eyes Nsanga is not a prostitute because she is not a bad woman. On the *contrary, as a mother who has fallen on hard times through no fault of her own, she is trying her best, "breaking stones," to meet family obligations. In the presence of AIDS Nsanga's survival strategy has been transformed into death strategy. (267–68)*

The structural adjustment process affects households in several ways (Elson 1989). These are via:

- changes in public expenditure, particularly health and education;
- changes in prices of purchases, especially food;
- changes in income and working conditions.

The question is what do all these changes mean for the poor women and their household members and to their vulnerability to HIV transmission?

Changes in Public Expenditures

One aspect of the social impact of adjustment has been the deterioration of social services, particularly as experienced by women in sub-Saharan Africa in the mid-1980s, and which has been at the core of their concern over the past several years. It is generally agreed that the social cost of SAPs has weighed heavily on low-income groups, of whom women constitute the majority. In spite of this realization, few studies have addressed the gender dimensions of SAPs. With the exception of UNICEF's *Structural Adjustment with a Human Face*, little data exist to determine the effects of SAPs on women. Nevertheless, there is a widely growing consensus that SAPs hurt women more than men.

Nzomo (1994) accuses the World Bank of subscribing to the dominant patriarchal ideology that pervades the international political economy and marginalizes and ascribes to women a role subordinate to, but yet supportive of the male gender. According to Nzomo, all rhetoric about mobilizing women for social change translates into greater utilization of women's energies and time, to protect and promote the interests of the rich and the powerful, who are predominantly men. "It would appear that SAPs, as designed by the Bank as well as other bi- and multilateral agencies, seem to count on women's special capabilities for coping with the crisis, namely, endurance, perseverance, and ingenuity. It is women's coping mechanisms that both the male-dominated governments and the Bank have exploited in implementing structural adjustment policies that clearly hurt women more than men" (Nzomo 1994).

This gender-specific social cost of adjustment is not easily measured and therefore not counted in macroeconomic indicators. Such indicators not only ignore the gendered division of labor but also wrongly assume, for example, that changes in income, food prices, and public expenditure accompanying

SAPs affect all members of the household in the same way. The focus is on the gross national product (GNP), on imports and exports, balance of payments, and efficiency and productivity. Employment is defined principally in terms of formal sector goods and services, whereas the informal work of child care, gathering fuel and water, preparing and processing foods, housecleaning, and nursing the sick are excluded from the definition of economy and work (Nzomo 1994).

Nzomo (1994) perceives adjustment policies as only achievable at the cost of longer and harder working days for women who have to increase their labor both within the market and the household. The negative impact of SAPs on women in general and on those affected by AIDS, both directly and indirectly, is further intensified by marginalization of women and the rising phenomenon in developing countries of women-headed households. In Kenya, for example, over 60 percent of urban slum households are headed by women. Since these women form the majority of the poorest of the poor in adjusting countries, in comparison with other women, they have tended to suffer the most from SAP packages.

Data on the use of time indicate that women almost always face more severe constraints and harsher choices in this area than do men, a difference that has been magnified by the combined effects of economic recession and the implementation of SAPs. As individual and family incomes fall, women feel obliged to devote more time to their role as producers; they have to earn some income in cash or kind. This, in effect, means that they have to intensify their efforts in other directions, as their other roles must be carried out in less time. They put in more effort to provide for their families on lower incomes. They shop around and spend more time identifying the cheapest sources of basic goods. At the same time they must also safeguard their children's health and education at a time when SAPs have constricted government expenditure on social welfare, notably health provision and education.

Health, SAPs, and Women

Most of the activities funded under the basic social services component of SAPs are in the health and education sectors. Health-related activities focus on rehabilitating primary health care facilities and the provision of essential medicines, as well as basic training for health workers.

In per capita terms, real expenditures on health and education worldwide stagnated or declined between 1983 and 1989. Studies sponsored by UNICEF in the mid 1980s found that indiscriminate cuts in government health expenditures, often part of an adjustment program, led to declines in the health status of the population. Although these findings are controversial, one of the acknowledged problems of early adjustment programs has been the failure to specify protection of core social expenditures (World Bank 1994). According to some researchers (Gladwin and McMillan 1989; Elabor-Idemudia 1991, chap. 5), as health care costs increase, both in urban and rural areas, care becomes less and less affordable to poor women and children who make up 90 percent of health center clientele.

The removal of subsidies for health, education, and welfare because of SAPs results in diminished support for services previously available to women in their reproductive roles, while SAPs increase their productive roles and the demands on their time. It has been documented that SAPs tend to off-load the work burden of health and other costs of adjustment on women, "as if women's labor is infinitely elastic" (Nzomo 1994). This tendency could, on the contrary, stretch poor women to the breaking point, leading to the collapse of their capacity to reproduce and maintain human resources (Nzomo 1994).

The increase in health costs have several implications on women's health and their vulnerability to HIV. Because women are in charge of reproduction (within their household) as well as management of their family's health, they suffer from increases in health costs and the lack of medicines in the village dispensary (Due 1986; Meena 1991, chap. 7). In Zaire the SAP package requires that all health care be delivered on a fee-for-service basis; consequently, more women report that they are giving birth at home. Traditional Birth Attendants (TBAs) and other female members of the family often attend the birth. This raises an important question about the safety of these attendants. Unsterile conditions within the home environment and the attendants' direct contact with blood increases their risks for HIV transmission.

High health care costs also mean that fewer women receive screening and treatment for sexually transmitted diseases (STDs). Research findings in Africa and elsewhere have determined that untreated STDs are one of the crucial factors for HIV transmission in women. With rising health costs, cuts in both family planning and STD services are likely to further increase women's vulnerability to HIV. High health costs also mean that fewer men and women will undergo blood screening and HIV tests, thus enhancing the risks for unsafe sexual behavior and consequently HIV transmission within a community. In addition, cuts in health expenditure may lead to eliminating the purchase of "luxury" health items such as disposable gloves and syringes which in fact are basic necessities in the fight against AIDS.

Use of condoms is currently one of the key preventive measures proposed by many international organizations. Information, Education, and Communication (IEC) activities and counseling services for women are often established to convey the message for safe sex through the use of condoms. However, as adjustment programs often increase prices and the overall cost of living, access to condoms becomes almost prohibitive for both men and women, thus further accelerating their risks of HIV transmission.

Health is strongly correlated with economic development. A healthy population is more productive and has a greater capacity for learning. AIDS is distinct from other diseases and its effects can be quite severe: the disease undermines improvements in health status, and in turn may reduce the potential for economic growth, particularly within local economies.

As part of SAP reforms, many African countries have introduced user charges in the health sector. The rationale for user fees is that they facilitate cost recovery, generate additional revenue, improve equity, and discourage frivolous demand (Odada and Odhiambo 1989). In Kenya, where cost sharing has in effect existed since independence through *Harambee*, the late President Kenyatta's rallying call for development through self-help, the introduction of cost sharing through SAPs raises legitimate concerns (ibid.).

In Kenya, for example, sexually transmitted diseases are among the most common complaints of adults attending outpatient health facilities. They account for 5 to 10 percent of the case load at many clinics. Kenya's Ministry of Health began charging fees for patients attending public sector outpatient facilities in December 1989. The outpatient charge at government health centers was ksh (Kenya shillings) 10 and the fee for an initial visit to the Special Treatment Clinic (STC) was ksh 50. Diagnosis and treatment required ksh 60, excluding costs incurred in seeking care, for example, loss of income or transport.

For the majority of the poor, this is an enormous price to pay for health. In Nairobi more than 70 percent of households have a monthly income below ksh 2,000 and more than 20 percent of those have a monthly income below ksh 1,000. Most STC users are below this level, and the introduction of user fees constitutes a very real impediment to their seeking health care.

Although the cost-sharing scheme was temporarily interrupted in 1990, pending final institution, the following observations were made during its operation. The mean monthly attendance of men decreased by 40 percent of that before the fees were introduced. For women attendance dropped even more drastically, by 65 percent of the preuser charge period, implying greater inability on the part of women to cope with the new charges (Munyakho 1994). It can be concluded that the introduction of user fees in health increased the number of untreated STDs in the population, with potentially serious long-term health implications resulting from the rapid spread of HIV/AIDS (ibid.).

Education

Public expenditures on education have also been affected by saps. The implications of cuts in education on female participation can be particularly serious. Despite long-established findings on economic and social benefits to female schooling, data from sub-Saharan Africa (World Bank 1993) demonstrate the lowest participation of female schooling and training compared to Latin America, Asia, and the Middle East. Furthermore, the net primary enrollment ratio for the Africa region has declined from 68 percent in 1970 to 48 percent in 1991. A large number of children remain outside the formal educational system. Data from unesco/unicef (1993) show that about 26 million girls are out of school in the sub-Saharan Africa region. In secondary schools, the level of female participation has declined significantly. Of 63 percent of school-aged females who enter school at the primary level, only 14 percent go on to the secondary level.

Several constraints have been identified as keeping girls away from school. Among these, the most significant are the economic costs, particularly the direct costs of schooling such as fees, textbooks, and uniforms. These are critical in family decisions about sending daughters to school. With saps negatively affecting the incomes in households, together with the increasing costs of schooling, fewer girls attend schools in an already gender-biased educational system.

Data from sub-Saharan Africa also indicate that hiv spread is highest among adolescent girls. More research is needed to establish whether a correlation exists between adolescent girls' low educational levels and the spread of hiv. A clear conclusion may be drawn from available information that female adolescents, because of lack of access to higher schooling, fail to develop marketable, professional skills. Young women resort either to early marriage or entering into sexual relationships mainly for economic reasons with older, sexually experienced men, and thus are becoming more vulnerable to hiv infection. Family planning programs in many parts of sub-Saharan Africa also do not provide services for unmarried adolescent girls.

Adult female literacy in sub-Saharan Africa remains among the lowest, with only 38 percent of adult women being literate (Donors to African Education 1994). With saps advocating reduction in educational expenditure on basic formal education, African governments are less willing to finance nonformal educational programs for adult women. In view of the increase in female-headed households and the lack of necessary income-generating skills, women are likely to engage in sexual relationships with one or more male partners for reasons of survival. Unfortunately these family survival strategies often increase vulnerability to hiv infection and death.

The educational components of Social Action Programs and Social Funds focus on rehabilitation and, in a few instances, on the construction of primary schools and the provision of teaching aids and furniture. But for girls and women, escalating school costs make it impossible for many people to keep their children in school. When resources are scarce, the preference for sending boys to school is exacerbated by the need to tap girls' labor in large households to care for sick family members. There is also societal pressure on girls to marry early to replace the pool of older women, who either fall ill or die, as men seek younger, uninfected spouses (Panos Institute 1993).

Information is power, and by the same corollary its absence implies powerlessness. Women, highly affected by AIDS, may have less access to HIV/AIDS information than men. Many women live in areas where health care services are their only source of information. In poor communities, even these resources may be nonexistent. For many others information may exist, but circumstances such as distance from health care facilities, lack of money, and husbands' attitudes serve to deny them access.

Changes in Food Prices

African women provide most of the labor required to produce the food consumed in Africa. The estimates of women's agricultural production across sub-Saharan Africa range from 46 percent to high estimates of 58 percent (Dixon 1982). In addition, the proportion of African smallholders who are female household heads is very high by international standards (Due 1986).

In theory, SAPs should benefit African women producers because SAPs emphasize renewing agricultural production, eliminating an urban development bias, and aligning farmgate prices with world prices. However, the success of this strategy depends on how the policy is implemented and whether rural women are in fact selling food crops in a market or buying food crops to feed their families. Although SAPs assume that food price increases should benefit all producers equally, they generally reflect the existing sexual division of labor which is unfavorable to women.

According to several researchers working on structural adjustment and African women farmers (Due 1986; Elabor-Idemudia 1991; Gladwin et al. 1991; Lele 1991, chap. 2), the answer to whether women benefit also lies in the reality of social stratification and differentiation at the village and household level. Negative effects often reflect the imbalance in power relations which affects who gets access to the means of production and who controls the surplus or profit that results from added incentives to produce. Because of social stratification at the village level and inequality in gender relations at the household level, women rural producers are not in a position to benefit from supposedly gender-neutral effects of structural adjustment policies. Women-headed households tend to be the smallest of the smallholder; they are often consumers as much as producers of food products. Thus they suffer when food prices rise.

Ethnographic case studies on structural adjustment among African farmers by Gladwin et al. (1991, chaps. 4–10) show that SAPs can have adverse effects on African women—be they farmers, traders, or consumers, or live in rural or urban areas. SAP policies that increase food prices and reduce job opportunities may increase malnutrition and reduce immunity levels, making all family members more susceptible to diseases. In addition, the need for female head of households to provide food for their families' survival, where men have a more powerful position within the agricultural sector, may force these women into risky sexual behaviors. Gendered differences in access to resources, including land, labor, and capital, contribute to the spread of AIDS during periods of deepening crisis, as more women are forced to use sex with multiple partners to make ends meet (Schoepf 1988; Schoepf and Walu 1990). Other consequences for women's health are expected to be felt in the first decade of the twenty-first century as women try to manage their own and their families' health amid the AIDS epidemic.

Changes in Income and Working Conditions

Any attempt to examine empirically the effects of adjustment on women's work is complicated by the lack of continuous gender-disaggregated, time-series data for many countries, especially in sub-Saharan Africa which might reveal trends. However, a number of more or less systematic approaches have been attempted, including the use of matching pairs of adjusting and nonadjusting countries (International Labor Organization [ILO] 1994) or of control groups, an approach generally favored in World Bank studies.

Several major studies attempt to provide a framework for the analysis of the impact of adjustment on women, including the impact on their paid and unpaid work. Overall, these studies suggest that the most adverse impact of adjustment on women, particularly poor women, is negative. Women are increasingly pushed into the labor force, often at highly disadvantaged terms, because of the lowering of household incomes as real wages fall or unemployment rises (ILO 1994). The removal of subsidies on basic foods and services and the introduction of charges for health and education under adjustment programs may lead to the increased participation of women in paid employment in the informal sector, including working as sex workers when they are forced to meet the increased expenditures. Schoepf and Walu's (1990) study of household budgets in Kinshasa, for example, documents the substantial contributions of women to family survival. Longitudinal data collected by Schoepf and Walu between 1985 and 1989 show that many poor women's enterprises failed as a result of the pressures of inflation, often mediated by the women's subordination to husbands and lovers (ibid.).

The general picture of wage trends under adjustment is also one of falling real wages, particularly in sub-Saharan Africa and, to a lesser extent, in Latin America (ILO 1994). Currency devaluation, a major component of SAPS, has eroded the real wages of both rural populations and urban populations alike. When devaluation erodes the real income of peasants, there is a tendency for the male population to migrate to urban areas to seek wage employment (Meena 1991, chap. 7). Away from home for long periods, men engage in sex with other partners, thus increasing the risks of HIV transmission among their partners both away and at home.

Devaluation may also sharply reduce the real price of women's labor, their principal nontradable good, and the primary asset of most poor women. Those women who avoid being laid off from cutbacks in the public sector may still find that the real value of their wages has eroded. By lowering minimum wage levels, SAPS may also increase malnutrition, illness, and absenteeism, as well as lowering the performance of the women who are employed.

Employment and Income-Generating Activities

Many Social Action Programs and Social Funds attempt to support small-scale income-generating activities for the poor through community programs or through support to individual microenterprises. These programs typically have three components: technical assistance, training, and microcredit. Some examples in this regard are the Chad Social Dimensions of Adjustment (SDA) Project and the Cameroon SDA project.

Most Social Action Programs and Social Funds, with the exception of those in Senegal and Ghana, are multisectoral. This approach helps to address the concerns of a broad cross-section of the population. A combination of components can create positive synergies, such as infrastructure rehabilitation in the social sector coupled with training for microenterprises to undertake the work, or nutritional programs for young children coupled with support for income-generating activities for their mothers.

The Unquantifiable Costs

The cost of AIDS reflects to a large extent the real value of the uncompensated and often unrecognized social contribution of women. There is a broad consensus that the "social" cost of SAPs is most heavily borne by low-income groups, the majority of whom are women. Women struggling to survive bear the brunt of adjustment since they are the main providers of food and care for their families. They are forced to "adjust" economically, socially, culturally, and politically. The following case studies describe the difficult situation of Kenyan women with HIV/AIDS in a period of structural adjustment. Although the circumstances are based on real-life interviews, the women's names are changed to protect their identity.

Jane Kamau

Jane Kamau, forty-two, believes she contracted AIDS through her work as a traditional birth attendant. "Through these services, I have been able to earn an honest living for myself and my family, although I am now sliding into destitution," says the mother of four children between the ages of seven and fifteen.

With the little income she earned, Jane supplemented her husband's meager earnings as a casual worker in Nairobi's Industrial Area.

Jane recounts the genesis of her present predicament:"As TBAs, we were not using gloves then. When we heard about AIDS, three years ago, we became worried.We were advised to take HIV tests, which turned out positive." It took Jane two weeks to pluck the courage to reveal the results to her husband. The disclosure changed her life completely."He sent me away together with the children."

Jane quit working as a TBA, and until now she has not found another job. Life has been very difficult ever since. Her husband only pays the rent, after being forced to do so by the area chief. She lives on handouts from good samaritans, sympathizers, and friends who bring her flour, rice, and a little money. But life is tough on everyone, and often she and her children go hungry.

At the time of the interview, Jane's health was not too bad. She feels staying at home is better than being hospitalized. "I stay with my children, give them the motherly love they need, and share whatever little there is for us. I only visit the hospital when I have diarrhea."

Jane goes to the Kenya Medical Research Institute (KEMRI) when she has diarrhea, which happens once or twice a week. She is given antidiarrheal drugs, antibiotics, and other drugs free of charge. But then her status entails more than just diarrhea, and for the other conditions like skin rashes, colds, and frequent headaches, she has to pay the full price, which is expensive. After paying consultation fees, she still has to buy prescribed drugs from pharmacies, which she finds extremely costly. The alternative is to buy over-the-counter drugs from local shops, mainly aspirin, and these are usually ineffective.

She attributes her frequent headaches to worry, mostly over how she will feed her children. Occasionally she has to forgo tea, and this is another cause of her headaches. Tea, though addictive, becomes a luxury when she has to spend about ksh 50 (about U.S.$1.00) per week on drugs. Skin rashes are a frequent affliction for Jane, recurring almost once every two weeks. The medicine for this costs ksh 350 per tube, which, in most cases, she does not have. She has to live with the discomfort.

Jane attends AIDS counseling sessions, where she is encouraged to live on a healthy and varied diet. It is difficult advice to comply with "because of lack of money." Jane's diet, like many other Kenyans', consists of ugali and sukuma wiki. (Ugali, Kenya's main staple, is derived from maize meal. Previously associated with West Kenyans, it has now been adopted by most Kenyan communities because it is considered the cheapest food in terms of input and preparation. Sukuma wiki is similar to kale and is the most common vegetable available to both rich and poor.) Meat is a luxury Jane can rarely afford. Plenty of fruits are encouraged, "but where is the money?" she asks. The combined effect of the disease and her inability to afford the best for herself has reduced Jane's weight from eighty-six to sixty-four kilograms.

Times are hard, and Jane often must choose between buying her medicine or buying food for her children: "I cannot leave my children to starve. When I am not feeling very badly, I opt for food. This does not make things any better. As I continue to worry about what I will feed my children tomorrow, I get severe headaches and I eventually fall ill."

Jane's children are in school but she has difficulties providing school fees. "My first born is in Form I. His first-term fees were paid by a church organization, but I don't know where to get his second- and third-term fees. My last born is in Standard 1. Buying books and other requirements for him is a nightmare. My survival options are limited as I battle this disease and at the same time try to fend for my children."

Mary Adala

Mary Adala, in her early forties, believes she was infected with HIV through a blood transfusion. "I conceived a child in 1986 but later miscarried. I was operated on and had a blood transfusion in the process. It is after this that I started getting ill." Initially, however, Mary had no other suspicions about her illness beyond the fact that she had had an operation.

Mary, a mother of five between the ages of nine and twenty and a former businesswoman, takes care of her children single-handed. Her husband left home in 1990 to look for work and has never been seen again.

Until January 1993, when her health became very poor, she cooked and sold food to construction workers, sustaining her family on the little money she earned. "Then it reached a time when I could not continue doing this. I had frequent headaches, my whole body was very weak, and even walking became a problem."

She went to dispensaries for treatment and tried traditional medicine but to no avail. She became so ill that she could not continue with her business. Then her sister advised her to go for blood tests at KEMRI, where she tested HIV-positive.

Mary recalls her shock: "I went home and attempted suicide. I tied a rope around my neck and was about to take a drug overdose when my sister came in and stopped me. I was worried about my children. Who was going to feed them when I became very sick and could no longer move? I didn't want to see them dying of hunger, and I didn't want them to see me dying."

Mary cannot afford hospital treatment for her condition and has to depend on KEMRI, a research institute, whose functions enable it to give free medicine in the course of its various experiments. Severe chest pains are a common affliction, as are headaches and colds. When she can afford it, Mary buys pain relievers from the local shop. In a week she spends about ksh 60 (U.S. $0.85) on such drugs. When she is moody, the result of worrying over her children, she has more headaches and needs to buy more drugs.

Unable to bear the rigors of food vending, which she previously did, Mary has resorted to distilling chang'aa, an illegal gin, which is quite demanding but does not entail long walking distances in search of construction sites—the most lucrative areas for food vending. Also, Chang'aa tends to guarantee higher returns, especially among a well-established clientele.

Mary's pressures go beyond the care of her own children. Her second-born daughter gave birth out of wedlock, compounding her pressures. "I have to take care of her and her baby," she says.

The stress of looking after her children and her grandchild on top of nursing her AIDS is taking the toll on Mary, who feels her health quickly deteriorating.

At the counseling sessions she is encouraged to eat well. "Getting any kind of food is a struggle," she says. "My main dish is ugali and sukuma wiki. I find this expensive and I cannot even think of buying meat unless someone sympathizes with me and buys me a kilo (of meat). Most of the time we go hungry."

When it comes to choosing between buying food or drugs, Mary opts for the latter. "This is because if my health gets worse, I will not have the strength to look for money to feed my family." Only her two youngest children are still in school. The others had to drop out because of fee problems.

Jacinta Mati

Jacinta Mati's employment as a traditional birth attendant lasted just over six years. She began working in 1986 and was carrying on normally, until she agreed to join nine other TBAs for an HIV test in 1992. She tested positive. When she broke the news to her husband, he abandoned her. Jacinta is convinced that she got the virus by handling infected blood without gloves.

"When I left TBA work I started selling charcoal," she says. "My business collapsed because of heavy expenditures I had to make on medicines. I used to spend all my week's earnings on medicine. Now I just live on handouts."

Jacinta is the mother of five children between the ages of three-and-a-half to fifteen. At the time of the interview she was not working but felt that if she got capital to resume business, she would like to sell charcoal again, which she would supplement with omena, a sun-dried variety of finderling fish.

Jacinta's relationship with her husband is erratic. Recently he started coming home, and occasionally he gives her some money. When she was very sick recently, however, he did not show up at all. She mainly lives on handouts.

Jacinta is suffering from tuberculosis (TB), a disease that has had a major resurgence in the era of AIDS. She goes to KEMRI for TB drugs. Generally she does not like taking medicine. She believes that preventive medicine only makes one worse, so she normally waits until she is very ill before taking drugs.

She visits the local clinic for ailments other than TB, which include skin rashes and severe headaches. She needs ksh 120 per visit, which she does not have. At the time of the interview, she owed the clinic ksh 400.

It is not enough that Jacinta has AIDS. Three months ago she had a breast abscess, for which she was treated as an outpatient at a private hospital for a cost of ksh 800. The consultation fee was more than the actual treatment—ksh 500 of the total. She spends about ksh 50 per week on aspirin for her frequent headaches.

Most Kenyans have had to sacrifice variety in their diet, and Jacinta is no exception. She mainly lives on ugali and sukuma wiki, which she still finds extremely expensive. Occasionally when she has some money, she buys smoked fish. She has lost fifteen kilograms of her original weight.

All her five children are still in primary school. She struggles on her own to buy them books and other school necessities, relying largely on good samaritans to contribute to the cost.

Responses to the Negative Impact of SAPs

The three cases are striking in their similarity. Initially all these women faced personal stigmatization. In all but one case, they were deserted by their husband when they disclosed their HIV status. They also face economic and social hardships. As single heads of households, they are then forced to make a living in a shrinking labor market with declining social services. All three must trade off their own personal health needs with their families' overall welfare.

With the growing concern about the impact of structural adjustment, the Social Dimensions of Adjustment (SDA) initiative was begun in 1988 to address the problem of, first, protecting poor and vulnerable groups, especially women, from bearing undue hardships resulting from structural adjustment and economic reform, and, second, integrating these groups into the economic mainstream of the countries (World Bank 1990). This effort was jointly sponsored by the African Development Bank, the United Nations Development Program, and the World Bank and was supported by several bilateral and multilateral donors.

In cooperation with external agencies, African governments began to design and implement interventions such as Social Action Programs and Social Funds. Both Social Action Programs and Social Funds aim to reduce poverty and reintegrate destitute groups into the economy. A total of thirty Social Action Programs and Social Funds have been implemented by the World Bank.

Social Action Programs and Social Funds generally support two types of activities: (1) they provide support for basic social services, and (2) they create employment and improve income-generating activities. Most Social Action Programs and Social Funds are urban-based. This raises questions about their sustainability and whether they directly impact the poor and women affected by structural adjustment. The international agencies recognize that undoubtedly a period of increased poverty occurs in some communities when SAPs are introduced and that poverty resulting from SAPs is linked to the AIDS epidemic. Activists, internationally, have therefore called for an overhaul of economies so that these can lead to more favorable terms for the poor. Such economies would be driven by "community need rather than export opportunity" (Swift 1994).

Beyond SAPs, with or without "a human face," governments and donors need to implement policies that empower women to have greater control over their lives. This calls for challenging the existent sociocultural norms that keep women subservient to men. In Kenya the attorney general recently instituted a task force to review the laws relating to the status of Kenya women. The task force has seven subcommittees invested in the following: civil and legal rights, health matters, sociocultural factors, education, the economy, politics, and information and the media. The subcommittees are charged with the task of reviewing the existing status in the listed areas and proposing legal reform and new policy measures. The right of wives to refuse unprotected sex with promiscuous husbands who are likely to infect them with HIV is one issue addressed by the civil and legal subcommittee.

In Tanzania a major initiative is in place to educate people on the need to write valid wills in order to protect the interests of their survivors in the event of their death. Legal services are being given free of charge to needy clients by the Tanganyika Law Society, the Faculty of Law of the University of Dar es Salaam, SUWATA (a women's section within the Union of Workers of Tanzania), the Tanzania Legal Corporation, and the Office of the Administrator-General.

Policies enacted by these organizations must be directed toward successful implementation of programs that empower women economically and socially to avoid infection, gain access to health care, and improve the quality of their lives.

Much support has been garnered around the importance of home-based care for people with AIDS. Although the arguments for this are sound, namely, that the dying need to be close to the love and warmth of the home environment, such support needs to be backed by clear government policies that empower members of the family, especially women—the traditional caregivers—to care comfortably for their dying. For many, home care means that women are left to care for their dying at home without any support from the state.

Across Africa, community-based initiatives have been set up to combat the problem of HIV/AIDS. Such efforts, as spearheaded by the Chikankata Hospital and the Copperbelt Health Education Project in Zambia, the AIDS Support Organization of Uganda (TASO), and the Small Christian Communities of Ghana, are positive moves toward helping women and men cope with AIDS. All such initiatives need the full backing of their governments. Presently most community-based actions are left to manage, either as societies or nongovernmental organizations (NGOs), outside formal government support. Once the African governments realize the crucial role these citizens' groups play in the nations' well-being, women will be given a fairer deal in the battle against AIDS.

Strategies for the Future

Though the debate continues about SAPs and their effect on the AIDS epidemic, we need to move beyond these debates to determine practical ways of addressing the issues raised and their future implications for women. Based on the sub-Saharan experience, in particular, policy makers must take greater cognizance of the economic environment under which SAPs are introduced, if their harmful effects are to be avoided, especially on poor and vulnerable groups that include women.

Improving the gender-responsiveness of adjustment improves adjustment itself. Adjustment measures that raise women's labor requirements without corresponding actions to ease the labor constraints (through labor-saving elsewhere or through complementary investment to improve the efficiency and accessibility of infrastructure and services) are not sustainable and should not be implemented. To increase the effectiveness of adjustment programs, both men and women must participate and be heard in the design, implementation, and monitoring of these programs (World Bank 1994).

In addition, if adjustment and development programs are to achieve their intended objectives, gender analysis must be an integral part of the design of policies and programs aimed at economic growth and alleviating poverty. Such analysis must account for and seek to redress the imbalances in the gender division of labor, the diversity and asymmetry of household and intrahousehold relationships, and differentials in incentives resulting from different resources. The implications of the invisibility of women's work in the economic paradigm of choices and strategies must be confronted and women's experiences considered as new SAP programs are designed. More specifically, to diffuse the possible impact of SAPs on the AIDS epidemic and to protect women against the risk of AIDS, donor agencies and governments need to mobilize and allocate resources to benefit the entire population.

REFERENCES

Dixon, R. 1982. Women in agriculture: Counting the labor force in developing countries. *Population and Development Review* 8 (3): 558–59.
Donors to African Education. 1994. Statistical Profile of Education in Sub-Saharan Africa. Paris: DAE.
Due, J. M. 1986. Agricultural policy in tropical Africa: Is a turnaround possible? *Agriculture Economics* 1:19–34.
Elabor-Idemudia, P. 1991. The impact of structural adjustment programs on women and their households in Bendel and Ogun States, Nigeria. In Christine Gladwin, ed., *Structural Adjustment and African Women Farmers*, 128–50. Gainesville: University of Florida Press.
Elson, D. 1989. *The Impact of Structural Adjustment on Women*. Vol. 2: *Concepts and Issues, the IMF, the World Bank, and the African Debt*. Edited by Bade Onimode. London: Zed.
Gladwin, C., et al., eds. 1991. *Structural Adjustment and African Women Farmers*. Gainesville: University of Florida Press.
Gladwin, C. and D. McMillan. 1989. Is a turnaround in Africa possible without helping African women to farm? *Economic Development and Cultural Change* 37 (2): 345–69.
International Labor Organization (ILO). 1994. The Impact of Recession and Structural Adjustment on Women's Work in Developing and Developed Countries. Working Paper. IDP Women/WP-19. Geneva, December.
Lele, U. 1991. Women, structural adjustment, and transformation: Some lessons and questions from the African experience. In Gladwin, *Structural Adjustment and African Women Farmers*, 46–80.
Meena, R. 1991. The impact of structural adjustment programs on rural women in Tanzania. In Gladwin, *Structural Adjustment and African Women Farmers*, 169–90.
Munyakho, D. 1994. The Impact of Structural Adjustment Program on the Health of Kenyan women. Unpublished.

Nzomo, M. 1994. The Impact of Structural Adjustment Programmes on Women's Participation in Decision Making. Unpublished.

Odada, E. O. and L. O. Odhiambo. 1989. Report of the proceedings of the workshop on cost sharing in Kenya. Naivasha, March 29 to April 2.

Panos Institute. 1993. *The Hidden Cost of AIDS: The Challenge of HIV to Development.* London: Panos Institute.

Schoepf, B. G. 1988. Women, AIDS, and economic crisis in Central Africa. *Canadian Journal of African Studies* 22 (3): 625–44.

———. 1992. Women at risk: Case studies from Zaire. In G. Herdt and S. Linderbaum, eds., *The Time of AIDS: Social Analysis, Theory, and Method,* 75–106. Newbury Park, Calif.: Sage.

Schoepf, B. G. and E. Walu. 1991. Women's trade and contributions to household budgets in Kinshasa. In J. MacGaffey, ed., *The Real Economy in Zaire.* London: James Currey.

Swift, R. 1994. Squeezing the South: 50 years is enough. *New Internationalist* (July): 4–7.

UNESCO/UNICEF. 1993. The Education of Girls. The Ouagadougou Declaration and Framework for Action. Pan-African Conference on the Education of Girls, Burkina Faso.

United Nations Economic Commission for Africa (ECA). 1989. *African Alternative Framework to Structural Adjustment Programs for Socioeconomic Recovery and Transformation.* E/ECA/CM. 15/6/Rev 3. United Nations. New York.

Whiteside, A. 1993. AIDS, Poverty, and Structural Adjustment Towards a "Pro-Poor" Development Strategy. The AIDS in Africa Conference, Marrakesh.

World Bank. 1981. *Accelerated Development in Sub-Saharan Africa: An Agenda for Action.* Washington, D.C.

World Bank. 1990. The Social Dimensions of Adjustment in Africa. A Policy Agenda. SDA Unit. Africa Technical Note No. 9 (March).

World Bank. 1993. Statistical Indicators of Female Participation in Education in Sub-Saharan Africa. Africa Technical Human Resource Division (AFTHR) Technical Note.

World Bank. 1994. Gender and Economic Adjustment in Sub-Saharan Africa. Gender Responsive Action Development (GRADE) Team Human Resources and Poverty Division. Technical Department (February).

PART THREE

Issues and Concerns

11 | The Epidemiology of HIV and AIDS in Women

JEANINE M. BUZY AND HELENE D. GAYLE

Since the beginning of the pandemic of HIV and AIDS, more than 15 million people have been infected by HIV worldwide. By the year 1993 more than 5 million women were estimated to have been infected with HIV. The rate of new HIV infections is rising faster in women than in their male counterparts, and in some countries women, including adolescent girls, are at greater risk of acquiring HIV than any other group. In the first half of 1992, women accounted for 50 percent of all new cases of HIV infection worldwide, and in parts of Africa, women already outnumber men in new HIV infections. Conservative estimates of global infections project that by the year 2000, 30–40 million people will have been infected with HIV since the beginning of the pandemic. Given the increasing infection rates in women, in the year 2000 there will be more than 13 million HIV-infected women worldwide (WHO/GPA 1993).

Globally, HIV/AIDS is primarily a heterosexual disease affecting young people in developing countries. Among adults worldwide, an estimated 70 percent of all HIV infections have been acquired through heterosexual contact. For women, heterosexual transmission accounts for 90 percent of all HIV infections compared to 60 percent for men. The developing world has been particularly affected by the HIV/AIDS pandemic; 80 percent of people infected by HIV have been from Africa, Asia, Latin America, or the Caribbean. The average age of women with HIV infection in most regions of the world is between fifteen and twenty-five years of age, ten years younger than the average age of HIV-infected men (United Nations Development Program [UNDP] 1992; Chin 1990; Hira et al. 1990; O'Farrell, Windsor, and Becker 1991).

Regional Differences

In many regions of the world, it was initially believed that the HIV/AIDS epidemic was limited to and likely to remain confined to sectors of society practicing high-risk sexual behavior or using drugs, including prostitutes, their clients, intravenous drug users, and gay men. As the epidemic progressed, the boundaries between the risk of HIV infection for those engaged in high-risk behavior and the rest of society have blurred. Women are at increased risk of exposure to HIV infection during their lifetime for a variety of reasons related to their age, education, socioeconomic level, and marital status.

Africa

Of all the regions in the world, the heaviest burden of the world's HIV/AIDS pandemic is in Africa. Africa contains 11 percent of the world's population and over 60 percent of the world's HIV infections. Most of these infections are found in sub-Saharan Africa and over 90 percent are attributable to heterosexual transmission (WHO/GPA 1993; Mann and Chin 1988; Hira et al. 1990). It is currently estimated that more than 4 million women of childbearing age in Africa are infected with HIV (WHO/GPA 1993). In some major cities in sub-Saharan Africa, AIDS is the leading cause of death among women twenty to forty years of age (Chin 1990).

   HIV seroprevalence rates in pregnant women are often thought to reflect the level of HIV infection among the general female population with the assumption that pregnant women represent a sector of society who are sexually active but otherwise not at particularly increased risk. Data now suggest that pregnant women in some African nations, even those in stable relationships, are at high risk of acquiring HIV infection. In Kigali, Rwanda, in 1991 it was reported that at prenatal and pediatric clinics 29 percent of women attendees were HIV-seropositive (Allen et al. 1991). Of the women with HIV infection 50 percent were in either common-law unions or legal marriages (Allen et al. 1991). The most recent seroprevalence rates available in women attending antenatal clinics in urban areas of Africa are listed in table 11.1. These seroprevalence rates in urban women range from 15 percent to over 30 percent. These data suggest the possibility that one in three women are infected with HIV in some urban settings in Africa. Over the past six years the average rate of yearly increase of HIV infection in pregnant women in Malawi was 4 percent; in Uganda, 3 percent; in Côte d'Ivoire, 2 percent; and in Kenya, 2 percent (see figure 11.1). At this rate in Malawi, by the year 2000, over 50 percent of pregnant women in urban areas could be HIV-positive. It is difficult to imagine how communities will be able to handle the impact of infection of this magnitude in women and their children.

TABLE 11.1.

HIV Seroprevalence in Pregnant Women, Female STD Patients, and Prostitutes in Africa

Group	Country	Year	% HIV+	Reference
Pregnant women	Porto Novo, Benin	1991	0.06	Davo
	Seven Areas, Botswana	1993	22.5	Namboza
	Bujumbura, Brundi	1992	19.9	Buzingo
	Abidjan, Côte d'Ivoire	1992	16.0	Diallo
	Nairobi, Kenya	1992	15.0	Gichangi
	Lilongwe, Malawi	1993	32.0	U.S. Dept. of State
	Mbeya, Tanzania	1992	10.2	Riedner
	Kampala, Uganda	1992	30.0	Asiimwe
STD Patients	Bangui, CAR	1989	21.0	Gresenguet
	Addis A, Ethiopia	1989	30.0	Zewdie
	Nairobi, Kenya	1992	18.7	Ndinya-Archola
	Kigali, Rwanda	1991	69.0	Karita
	Johannesburg, S. Africa	1991	9.8	RSA, MOH
	Kampala, Uganda	1990	30.0	Hellman
	Lusaka, Zambia	1991	30.0	Hira, 1991
Prostitutes	Atlantic Pro., Benin	1990	17.0	Bigot
	Douala, Cameroon	1992	45.3	Monny-Lobe
	Abidjan, Cote d'Ivoire	1992–93	86.0	Tarore-Ettiengne
	not specified, Ghana	1991	37.5	Diaw
	Nairobi, Kenya	1992	85.5	Mungai
	Blantyre, Malawi	1986	55.9	Gurtler
	Kinshasa, Zaire	1989	38.0	Zaire, MOH

The presence of other sexually transmitted diseases (STDS) facilitates HIV transmission and is associated with high-risk sexual behavior. The presence of a single STD increases the risk of HIV infection at least three- to fivefold (Wasserheit 1992). Therefore HIV seroprevalence in female STD patients is generally higher than in pregnant women (see table 11.1). In Kampala, Uganda, 45 percent of more than four thousand female STD clinic attendees from 1989 to 1991 were HIV-positive (Grant et al. 1992). At a single health center in Kigali, Rwanda, one study demonstrated in 1991 that 69 percent of female STD patients were HIV-seropositive (Karita et al. 1993). In Lusaka, Zambia, one study found 68.7 percent of the women STD patients in 1991 were HIV-seropositive, and in Addis Adaba, Ethiopia, 36.8 percent of the women in 1989 were found to be seropositive (Hira et al. 1991; Zewdie et al. 1989). The recognition that the presence of another STD increases the risk of HIV infection is critical for women's health.

Engaging in commercial sex puts both men and women at risk of HIV infection and serves to catalyze the HIV/AIDS epidemic. In sub-Saharan Africa, prostitutes or commercial sex workers (CSWS) in urban settings have the highest rates of HIV seroprevalence in the world (table 11.1). In Abidjan, Côte d'Ivoire, a study of more than 1,200 female CSWS in 1993 found a seroprevalence rate of 86 percent (Traore-Ettiegne et al. 1993). In 1992 in Nairobi, Kenya, the sero-

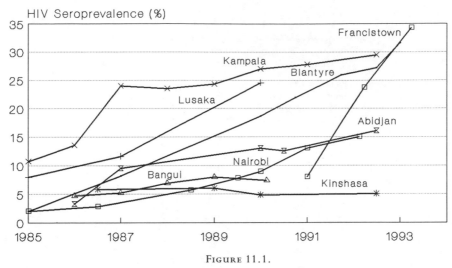

FIGURE 11.1.

HIV seroprevalence for pregnant women in selected urban areas of Africa, 1985–1993 (includes infection from HIV-1 and/or HIV-2).

prevalence rate in a study of 330 prostitutes was 85.5 percent (Mungai et al. 1992), and in Addis Ababa, Ethiopia, in 1989, 54 percent of the 1,225 prostitutes tested were HIV-positive (National AIDS Control Program/Ministry of Health [NACP/MOH] [Ethiopia] 1992).

In Africa, although 60 to 90 percent of the population live in rural settings, HIV seroprevalence is higher in urban areas than in rural. Populations initially at lower risk in rural communities are increasingly being affected by labor migration and prostitution associated with commercial trade routes (Hunt 1989). In the rural Rakai district in southwest Uganda, with a population of 350,000, the seroprevalence rates in 1991 were found to be the highest in trading centers along main roads and higher in women than in men—47 percent and 26 percent, respectively (Wawer et al. 1991). In the intermediate rural trading villages on secondary roads, 29 percent of the women compared to 22 percent of the men were HIV-seropositive, and in the rural agricultural villages 9 percent of women and 8 percent of men were HIV-seropositive. Overall, the Rakai district contained a seroprevalence rate of 12 percent (Wawer et al. 1991). In a study in rural villages in Tanzania, the village prevalence rate in employed women was 6 percent and the seroprevalence rate in women living in roadside settlements was as high as 23 percent; overall, women were 1.5 times more likely to be infected with HIV than men (Barongo et al. 1992). These and other studies show that even though the urban areas are currently the most affected by the epidemic, the rural communities in Africa, and particularly rural women, are threatened by the epidemic.

Latin America and the Caribbean

By 1993, 1.5 million people were estimated to have been infected with HIV in Latin America and the Caribbean. Of these, 470,000 were women. Initially heterosexual transmission accounted for less than 20 percent of AIDS cases. Now a rapid increase in the number of AIDS cases in Latin America and the Caribbean can be attributed to increases in heterosexual transmission that have been associated with an increase in the number of women infected with HIV (Kimball, Gonzalez, and Zacarias 1991). In Brazil 34 percent of the AIDS cases in women are attributable to heterosexual transmission, 32 percent to intravenous drug use, and 18 percent to blood transfusions (Kimball et al. 1991). Among Mexican women 66 percent of the AIDS cases have been the result of blood transfusions and 31 percent of heterosexual transmission (ibid.).

In Central and South America the HIV prevalence among pregnant women is still relatively low with a couple of exceptions (table 11.2). In Rio de Janeiro, Brazil, of 4,536 pregnant women tested in 1991, 0.8 percent were HIV-seropositive (May et al. 1993). In 1992 in Tegucigalpa, Honduras, 0.2 percent of 1,292 pregnant women were found to be HIV-positive (Menjivar 1991). However, in San Pedro Sula, 3.6 percent of 415 pregnant women tested were HIV-positive (NACP [Honduras] 1991). In 1991 in Mexico, only 0.1 percent of pregnant women were HIV-seropositive (Menjivar and Fernandez 1991; Valdespino et al. 1992). In a small sample of 145 pregnant women in Guyana, the reported seroprevalence in 1992 was 6.9 percent (Ministry of Health [MOH] [Guyana] 1993). Although these rates are lower than in other regions, the next few years will be critical if Central and South America hope to substantially slow the spread of HIV infection.

In the Caribbean, HIV seroprevalence in pregnant women is generally higher than in Latin America (see table 11.2). In Santa Domingo, Dominican Republic, 1.3 percent of 400 pregnant women tested in 1991 were HIV-positive (Goodman et al. 1992), and in the Bahamas 3.6 percent of 1,019 pregnant women in 1993 were HIV-positive (MOH [Bahamas] 1993). In a three-year study of pregnant women in Haiti it was found that seroprevalence rates increased from 8.9 percent in 1986 to 9.9 percent in 1987 and 10.3 percent in 1988 in 4,474 pregnant women tested (Boulos et al. 1990). In the study in Haiti, factors that were independently associated with HIV-1 seropositivity in pregnant women were (1) not being married, (2) being twenty to twenty-nine years of age, (3) having had more than one sex partner in the year before pregnancy, and (4) having had a positive serologic test for syphilis (Boulos et al. 1990).

The HIV seroprevalence data for women attending STD clinics in both Latin America and the Caribbean demonstrate an increased risk in this population. In

TABLE 11.2.

HIV Seroprevalence in Pregnant Women, Female STD Patients, and Prostitutes in Latin America and the Caribbean

Group	Country	Year	% HIV+	Reference
Pregnant women	Bahamas	1993	3.6	Bahamas, MOH
	Rio de Janeiro, Brazil	1991	0.8	May
	British Virgin Islands	1991	2.8	PAHO/WHO 1991a
	Santa Domingo, Dom. Rep.	1991	1.3	Goodman
	Guyana	1992	6.9	Guyana, MOH
	Haiti	1992	10.2	Liautaud
	Tegucigalpa, Honduras	1991	0.2	Menjivar
	Mexico	1991	0.1	Valdespino
	St. Kitts/Nevis	1991	2.0	PAHO/WHO 1991a
STD Patients	Buenos Aires, Argentina	1988	5.5	Boxaca
	Bogota, Colombia	1987	0.6	Boshell
	Sta. Dom., Dom.Rep.	1989	1.6	Rodriguez
	Haiti	1992	13.0	Liautaud
	Jamaica	1991	1.9	Figueroa
Prostitutes	Buenos Aires, Argentina	1991	6.3	Zapiola
	Three Urban Areas, Brazil	1990–91	24.0	Fernandez
	Dominican Republic	1992	3.4	Gomez
	San S., El Salvador	1991	2.2	PAHO/WHO Epi. Unit
	Guyana	1990	25.0	Gayle
	Port-au-Prince, Haiti	1989	41.9	Glordano
	Kingston, Jamaica	1990	14.6	White
	Mexico City, Mexico	1987–89	2.2	Uribe

Buenos Aires, Argentina, from 1987 to 1988, 5.5 percent of 109 women attending STD clinics were HIV-positive (Boxaca et al. 1989); in Bogota, Colombia, from 1985 to 1987, the number was 1.5 percent of 809 women (Boshell et al. 1989); in Santa Domingo, Dominican Republic, in 1989, 2 percent of 123 women (Rodriguez et al. 1993); in Jamaica from 1990 to 1991, 3 percent of 484 women (Figueroa et al. 1992); and in Haiti in 1992, 13 percent of 92 women attending STD clinics were HIV-seropositive (Liautaud et al. 1992). Although HIV infection in women in Latin America and the Caribbean is still relatively low (see table 11.2), the increases in heterosexual transmission rates indicate that women in this region are becoming exposed to HIV at a higher incidence than in the past.

Asia

The Asian and Pacific region of the world contains more than fifty countries and half the world's population. Early reports of HIV infection in this region began in the mid-1980s. As seen in other regions of the world, the primary mode of transmission varies, depending on the local social, cultural, and economic factors that affect the spread of the epidemic. In many Asian countries, the use and practice of the commercial sex trade and intravenous drug use have contributed to the rapid spread of the epidemic in this region of the world. Women involved in commercial sex work or intravenous drug use are at particularly high risk of HIV infection. There is growing evidence, however, that the epidemic is now spreading to women who are not engaging in classically high-risk behavior.

The geographic distribution of HIV seroprevalence rates among pregnant women are shown in table 11.3. Northern and central Thailand contained the highest HIV seroprevalence in pregnant women in 1993, at 3.1 percent and 1.9 percent, respectively (Ministry of Public Health [Thailand] 1993). Both northeast and southern Thailand contained a seroprevalence rate of approximately 1 percent in pregnant women in 1993 (ibid.). Recent reports in pregnant women in Burma showed a 2.2 percent seroprevalence rate (Frerichs et al. 1992).

Northern and central Thailand have a higher HIV seroprevalence in CSWS than southern and northeast Thailand (table 11.3) (Ministry of Public Health [Thailand] 1993). In northern Thailand, which includes the city of Chiang Mai, the seroprevalence of CSWS in 1993 was 40 percent (ibid.). A year earlier the prevalence was 27 percent (ibid.). In the city of Chiang Mai the seroprevalence of HIV infection in CSWS was 5 percent in 1990, increasing dramatically to 53 percent by 1993 (ibid.). The reasons for such dramatic increases are currently debated but include not only behavioral practices but the efficiency of some strains of HIV to be passed through heterosexual sex. In central Thailand and southern Thailand the HIV prevalence in CSWS was 30 percent and 20 percent, respectively, in 1993 (ibid.) (see figure 11.2).

TABLE 11.3.
HIV Seroprevalence in Pregnant Women and Prostitutes in Asia

Group	Country	Year	% HIV+	Reference
Pregnant women	Burma	1992	2.2	Frerichs
	Bombay, India	1992(?)	0.1–0.8	Joshi
	Thailand			
	Central	1993	1.9	Thai., MOH
	North	1993	3.1	Thai., MOH
	Northeast	1993	1.1	Thai., MOH
	Southern	1993	1.3	Thai., MOH
Prostitutes	Bombay, India	1992	41.2	Bhave
	Tel Aviv, Israel	1991	1.1	Modan
	Phillipines	1987	0.1	Dayrit
	Thailand:			
	Central	1993	39.5	Thai., MOH
	North	1993	30.4	Thai., MOH
	Northeast	1993	19.3	Thai., MOH
	Southern	1993	20.9	Thai., MOH
	Chiang Mai, Thailand	1993	53.1	Thai., MOH

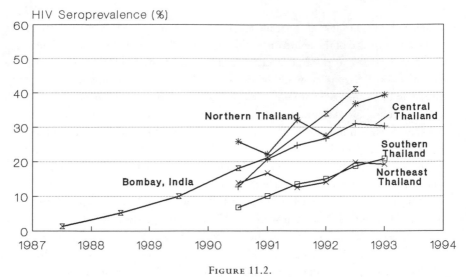

FIGURE 11.2.

HIV seroprevalence for commercial sex workers in India and Thailand, 1987–1993. (U.S. Bureau of the Census, Center for International Research.)

Some cities in India have experienced rapid increases of HIV infection among csws similar to what has been seen in Thailand. In Bombay the seroprevalence in csws was close to 1 percent between 1987 and 1988; by September 1992 seroprevalence in this group had increased to over 40 percent (Bhave et al. 1990; 1992). The average yearly rate of increase in seroprevalence in Bombay csws during this period was 8 percent. These trends do not seem to be leveling off (see figure 11.2) (Bhave et al. 1990; 1992). The pandemic in South and Southeast Asia is growing at a pace reminiscent of that in sub-Saharan Africa in the early 1980s; however, the potential for an even more devastating impact exists given that the adult population in Asia is 500 million compared to 225 million in sub-Saharan Africa.

North America

In the United States by mid-1993, according to the Centers for Disease Control (CDC 1993) 40,702 women had AIDS. This represented 12 percent of the total cases of AIDS in the United States. The incidence was higher for women than for men: in 1991–92, 6,153 women were reported to have AIDS, and in 1992–93, there were 14,792 women with AIDS, a 140 percent increase (ibid.). Women between the ages of twenty-five and forty represent over 60 percent of all women with AIDS and one-third are between the ages of thirty and thirty-four (ibid.). Women with AIDS in the United States are primarily located in urban areas in the East, although there are exceptions, including Puerto Rico, California, and Nevada (ibid.). African-American women represent 53 percent of all women with AIDS; white women, 25 percent; Hispanic women, 20 percent; and all others, less than 1 percent (ibid.).

Intravenous drug use represents the most frequent means of transmission for women in the United States. In 1992, 49 percent of all women with AIDS reported their infection to be the result of transmission through IV drug use and 37 percent said it was caused by heterosexual contact. Of those women who contracted HIV through heterosexual contact, 55 percent reported having sex with an IV drug user and 25 percent reported having sex with a person known to be HIV-infected (CDC 1993).

In a study of childbearing women conducted in forty-four states in the United States, the District of Columbia, Puerto Rico, and the Virgin Islands, the national average HIV seroprevalence was estimated at 0.17 percent in 1991–92, compared to 0.16 percent the previous year (CDC 1993). This percentage corresponds to the almost seven thousand births that occur yearly among HIV-infected women (ibid.). States along the Atlantic Coast contain the highest prevalence of HIV infection in pregnant women. New York, Florida, Maryland, and New Jersey, along with the territory of Puerto Rico, reported HIV seroprevalence ranging from 0.45 percent to 0.60 percent in pregnant women in 1991 92 (ibid.).

In women attending STD clinics who reported no IV drug use, a survey of 112 STD clinics found a 0.6 percent seroprevalence (CDC 1993). For women attending these STD clinics who reported using IV drugs, the median seroprevalence was 4.5 percent, ranging from none to 27 percent (CDC 1993).

Europe

A cumulative total of 103,552 people were reported to have AIDS in the WHO/EC (World Health Organization, European Community) as of September 1993. The proportion of women with AIDS has been increasing yearly. In 1991 in Europe, 17.3 percent of the total persons with AIDS were women; by September 1993, 19.2 percent of the total, or approximately 19,800 women, had developed AIDS (ibid.). In 1993 France, Italy, and Spain were the European countries that reported the highest cumulative total number of women with AIDS, 4,833, 4,244, and 4,275, respectively (ibid.). These countries are followed by Germany and the United Kingdom, where the cumulative totals of women with AIDS through 1993 were 1,028 and 713, respectively (ibid.). The incidence of women acquiring HIV through heterosexual contact is increasing throughout Europe. In 1991, 32.7 percent of women with AIDS acquired HIV through heterosexual contact; this increased to 49.3 percent by September 1993 (ibid.). In 1993 women represented 45.2 percent of the total number of cases of heterosexually acquired AIDS in Europe (ibid.). Intravenous drug use still represents the most frequent route of transmission of HIV for women in Europe (54 percent of the cumulative total). Although intravenous drug use is decreasing as a mode of HIV transmission for women, heterosexual transmission is increasing (ibid.).

Risk Factors for HIV Transmission in Women

There are multiple biological, behavioral, and sociocultural factors that make women particularly vulnerable to HIV infection. The behavioral and sociocultural risk factors are discussed in several other articles in this volume.

Several biological risk factors enhance the ability of HIV to infect sexually active women. This is consistent with the evidence that most sexually transmitted diseases are more easily transmitted from men to women than from women to men (Peterman et al. 1988). Additionally, considerable epidemiologic data support an association between HIV and other STDs (Plummer et al. 1991; O'Farrell, Windsor, and Becker 1991; see also Parker and Patterson in this volume). In a study of seronegative prostitutes in Nairobi, 76 percent of the women with genital ulcer diseases tested HIV-positive within two years in comparison with 44 percent of women without genital ulcer diseases (Piot et al. 1987). Another study of women attending an STD clinic in Nairobi found that women reporting a history of genital ulcers were 3.8 times as likely to be HIV-seropositive (Plourde et al. 1992). Since the same behaviors that increase the risk of HIV are associated with other STDs, it is possible that differences in risk behaviors between the two groups could contribute to the differences in the HIV and STD rates.

Although behavioral differences may in part account for the association of HIV with other STDs, it is now generally accepted that STDs other than HIV are a major biological risk factor for HIV infection in both women and men. This risk varies with the particular infection. Ulcerative STDs are associated with the greatest increased risk. For genital ulcers (mainly chancroid) the estimated increase risk of HIV infection is approximately 4 times (ranging from 3.3 to 18 times); for syphilis, 1.8 to 9.9 times; for genital herpes, 1.9 to 8.5 times; for gonorrhea, 3.8 to 8.9 times; for anogenital warts, 3.1 to 4.1 times; and for trichomoniases, 2.3 times (Wasserheit 1992). STD infections in women are often asymptomatic compared to those in men, contributing to a delay in diagnosis and care of STDs in women. This is also likely to augment women's risk of acquiring HIV (see article 12, Sexually Transmitted Diseases as Catalysts of HIV / AIDS in Women).

One mechanism by which STDs are hypothesized to facilitate the transmission of HIV is through disruption, or physical ulcerations, of the normal epithelial barriers in a woman's vagina and cervix (Alexander 1990; O'Farrell, Windsor, and Becker 1991). HIV has been shown to infect both monocyte/ macrophages and endothelial cells within the cervix (Pomerantz et al. 1988). Ulcerations caused by some STDs not only affect the integrity of the vaginal protective barrier but also cause the recruitment of the host's immune cells in a normal response to tissue damage and infection. Therefore STD infections cause ulcerations that open portals of entry for HIV infection but also increase the local pool of cells that HIV potentially infects. A few studies address the risk of HIV transmission in an individual infected with nonulcerative STDs, particularly inflammatory-discharge syndromes, where women are at greater risk of acquiring HIV than men (Plummer et al. 1989).

A small number of studies have suggested that oral contraceptive use in conjunction with the presence of some STDs increases the risk of HIV infection. When genital ulcers occurred in combination with the use of oral contraceptives, women have been found to be 25.7 times as likely to be HIV-seropositive (Plourde et al. 1992). Oral contraceptives may increase the susceptibility of HIV infection through an estrogen-produced cervical ectopy. Cervical ectopy, defined by the presence of endocervical columnar epithelium, has been inversely related to age and directly associated with pregnancy, oral contraceptive use, and *C. trachomatis* infection of the cervix (Louv et al. 1989; Gottardi et al. 1984). The presence of cervical ectopy has been associated with approximately a fivefold increased risk of HIV seropositivity among stable female partners of HIV-positive men (Moss et al. 1991). Further research is needed to address the association of a woman's choice of contraceptive use and her possible increased risk of HIV infection.

The younger the age of first pregnancy or first intercourse for women, the higher the incidence of HIV infection (UNDP 1992). This finding is attributable to the increased genital susceptibility in adolescent women (Wawer et al. 1991). There are several possible explanations for the increase in adolescent female's physiological vulnerability. The mucous membrane of the vagina and cervix in adolescence is very thin. The transition of a single layer of cells to a thick multilayer wall is not complete until the late teens or early twenties. Additionally, the vaginal mucous, which protects the vaginal and cervical walls during intercourse and contains immunoprotective capabilities, may not be produced as readily in adolescent women. These features combined may increase adolescent women's biologic vulnerability to HIV transmission.

Clinical Features

The diagnosis of AIDS in women in industrialized countries generally features opportunistic infections that are reported as AIDS-defining conditions. These include *Pneumocystis carinii* pneumonia, or PCP; cryptococcal meningitis; candida esophagitis; herpes simplex virus disease; wasting syndrome; cytomegalovirus; tuberculosis; toxoplasmosis; and lymphoma (Hankins and Handley 1992). These illnesses are more similar than they are different in men and women. In some studies in the United States the differences in rates of opportunistic infections between men and women were primarily associated with the mode of transmission of the virus rather than with gender differences. Within transmission categories, however, some gender differences in opportunistic infections have been noted. A recent study that analyzed gender differences in a large group of intravenous drug users found that esophageal candidiasis, herpes simplex virus, and cytomegalovirus disease were more common in women than toxoplasmosis, cryptococcosis, Kaposi's sarcoma, and lymphomas (Fleming et al. 1993). In developing countries, where data on natural histories are generally limited, even fewer studies have been specifically designed to define the HIV-associated illnesses that affect women more often than men.

Clearly both men and women latently infected with Mycobacterium tuberculosis are at increased risk for developing clinically active tuberculosis when infected with HIV (Selwyn et al. 1989). In women of childbearing age in Kinshasa, Zaire, HIV-seropositive women were 26 times more likely to be diagnosed with pulmonary or other clinical tuberculosis than were HIV-seronegative women (Braun et al. 1991). Women with clinical tuberculosis had a 2.7 times greater mortality rate compared to women who were only HIV-infected (Braun et al. 1991). Tuberculosis has now become a parallel public health threat in many developing and industrialized countries.

Several gynecological disorders are associated with various stages of HIV disease in women worldwide. In 1993 the U.S. Centers for Disease Control and Prevention revised the definition of AIDS to include one condition specific to women, invasive cervical carcinoma. Genital-tract infection with human papillomavirus (HPV) has been implicated in the pathogenesis of cervical and anal carcinoma (Koutsky, Galloway, and Holmes 1988). Cervical cancer is among the most common malignancies in developing countries and is by far the most common malignancy in African women (Parkin, Stjernsward, and Muir 1984).

Some studies have found that women infected with HIV are more likely to have detectable HPV than HIV-seronegative women and that HIV-induced immunosuppression may exacerbate HPV-mediated cervical cytologic abnormalities or dysplasia (Feingold, Vermund, and Burk 1990; Maiman et al. 1991). Among HIV-infected women, 50 percent of those who were symptomatic had cervical dysplasia whereas only 23 percent of the asymptomatic women had that condition (Feingold et al. 1990). Other studies have shown an association between immunosuppression and the severity of the cervical carcinoma associated with HPV infection (Maiman et al. 1991). Because medically induced immunosuppression in transplant patients has been associated with an increased risk for HPV infection and cervical neoplasia, it has been suggested that immune dysfunction may facilitate oncogenic transformation (Halpert et al. 1986; Alloub et al. 1989). There is also evidence that suggests that HIV regulatory proteins enhance HPV gene expression; therefore concomitant infection may increase the severity of the HPV infection (Steffy and Weng-Staal 1991). These studies taken together suggest an increased susceptibility of HIV-infected women to cervical carcinoma. However, in some studies in developing countries, detectable HPV infection concomitant with HIV infection has not always been associated with the development of cervical cytological abnormalities even though types 16 and 18, the most common forms associated with cervical abnormalities, are present (Kreiss et al. 1992; Meulen et al. 1992; Koutsky, Galloway, and Holmes 1988). More studies are needed that examine HIV-positive women's gynecological disorders and needs for care.

Some early studies in HIV-positive women suggested that pelvic inflammatory disease (PID) occurred more frequently and was more difficult to care for than in HIV-negative women. More recent studies have shown that HIV-positive women with PID present with greater clinical severity of the disease but have similar microbial etiologies and respond to treatments as quickly as HIV-negative women (Irwin et al. 1993; Moorman et al. 1993). For women in the developing world where treatment is either unavailable or too expensive, the clinical severity of the disease has strong implications for women's daily health.

Candida infections of mucous membranes are another frequent opportunistic infection associated with women infected with HIV around the world (Carpenter et al. 1989). The degree of immunosuppression has been associated with the location and severity of candida infection in one three-year study (Iman et al. 1990). Oral and esophageal candidiasis were often associated with decreases in CD4+ cell counts and decreased ratios of CD4 to CD8; however, vaginal candidiasis was not associated with either indicator of immunosuppression (Iman et al. 1990).

Disease Course and Rate of Progression

The rate of progression from HIV infection to the development of AIDS has been primarily studied in homosexual men and transfusion recipients in the United States and Europe. The rate of progression in this group ranges from two to more than eleven years (Moss and Bacchetti 1989; Rutherford et al. 1990). Over 50 percent of homosexual men take more than nine years to develop AIDS.

One retrospective review in the United States estimated that women develop AIDS approximately nine years after infection (Flanigan et al. 1992). Very few studies in the developing world have measured the rate of progression from HIV infection to AIDS in either sex, and fewer studies worldwide have compared gender differences. Two studies in Europe have investigated whether gender affects the rate of progression. In a Spanish study of fifty-eight male and eighteen female intravenous drug users and a Swedish study of AIDS patients infected by blood transfusions, investigators found no statistically significant differences in the progression from HIV to AIDS between the sexes (Fernandez-Cruz et al. 1990; Blaxhult et al. 1990). Larger prospective studies are needed in developing countries where heterosexual transmission is the primary mode of transmission for women.

Effect of Pregnancy on Disease Progression

Early in the HIV/AIDS epidemic there was concern about the effects of pregnancy on the progression of HIV infection in the mother because of the mild form of immunosuppression women experience during pregnancy (Biggar et al. 1989). Early studies suggested that pregnancy had a deleterious effect on disease progression (Scott et al. 1985). However, large prospective studies have shown no increase in disease progression associated with pregnancy in HIV-positive women in the United States (Deshamps et al. 1993). A study in Malawi showed similar findings. The changes in the proportion of CD4, helper, and CD8, suppressor/cytotoxic, T lymphocytes were measured in urban Malawian women between the third trimester of pregnancy and six weeks postpartum (Miotti et al. 1992). The absolute number of CD4 and CD8 lymphocytes increased from the third trimester to six weeks postpartum in both seropositive and seronegative women, and there was no significant change in CD4 and CD8 percentages or ratios (Miotti et al. 1992).

Survival

Despite the impact on mortality that HIV/AIDS has on women in developing countries, few studies allow conclusions to be drawn about either the survival of women from the time of HIV infection or that from the development of AIDS. In the United States, until recently, most studies concluded a shortened survival period for women with AIDS in comparison with men by about five months (Araneta et al. 1991). Additional studies in the United States that controlled for the use of antiviral drugs and the route of HIV transmission concluded a similar survival time for women and men of a little more than nine months from the time AIDS was diagnosed (Lemp et al. 1992). These studies and others showed that women who are infected with HIV are often diagnosed late in the course of infection and are therefore less likely to use early intervention therapies that help prolong survival.

The measurement of mortality rates in HIV-infected populations are now thought to be a more accurate measurement of the impact of HIV/AIDS in Africa, especially for women. In 1992 a study of more than four hundred seropositive women and a comparison cohort of seronegative women were recruited from prenatal and pediatric clinics in Kigali, Rwanda. The clinical signs and symptoms of HIV disease, AIDS, and mortality were measured over a period of two years. The two-year mortality among HIV-positive women was 7 percent overall; for the forty women who fulfilled the WHO case definition of AIDS at entry, the rate was 21 percent (Linden et al. 1992). Compare this to a two-year mortality rate of 0.3 percent for those women who were HIV-seronegative. Independent baseline predictors for mortality in HIV-positive women were low body mass, low income, chronic diarrhea, and a history of herpes zoster and oral candida, in that order (ibid.). HIV-related illness was the cause of death in thirty-eight of the thirty-nine HIV-positive women, but only twenty-five met the WHO definition of AIDS before death. This study concluded that HIV disease now accounts for an astounding 90 percent of all deaths among childbearing urban Rwandan women (ibid.).

Treatment Issues

Many studies have concluded that the early detection of HIV serostatus and the availability of antiretroviral therapy, treatment for opportunistic infections, and general health maintenance will affect both the survival time and the patient's condition. Confidential testing and counseling services are now widely available in most developed countries; however, this is not true for most developing countries. Both the fear of stigmatization and the fear that knowing your status increases the onset of AIDS prevent women from seeking HIV testing and counseling around the world. Proper and timely identification of HIV infection can affect women's long-term health and life choices.

In the United States available therapy may be made less readily available to women than to their male counterparts. One study in the United States showed that, despite the similarities in disease between sexes and races, white patients were 10 percent more frequently offered zidovudine (AZT) than minority patients, and men were offered AZT 17 percent more often than women even though AZT was equally efficacious in women (Stein et al. 1991).

Financial access to trained health care providers who are aware of HIV/AIDS issues for women is of utmost importance. Obstetricians and gynecological professionals must be trained in the complexities of HIV and AIDS diagnosis and care. Financial access to professional care is an issue HIV-positive women face daily worldwide (see article 15, Care and Support Systems). Additionally, women's access to knowledge about possible treatments and their involvement in clinical trials have become an emerging issue in the United States. Sexually active women of childbearing age were often excluded from clinical trials because of liability in case of pregnancy. It is hoped that legal reforms will lead to women's greater access into clinical trials for new HIV/AIDS treatments.

Women's Vulnerability

Women throughout the world are increasingly vulnerable to HIV/AIDS. An estimated 5 million women are currently infected with HIV, and by the year 2000 this number could triple. Young women around the globe are particularly vulnerable to acquiring HIV through heterosexual transmission, especially in Africa, Asia, Latin America, and the Caribbean. The low socioeconomic status of women along with several biological, cultural, and behavioral risk factors contribute to their particular vulnerability to HIV infection. The implications for prevention of the spread of HIV are multifaceted and involve social, economic, and culturally appropriate behavioral changes for women.

Most of the current research on the natural history of HIV infection and the testing of new therapeutics has been conducted in developed countries in so-called high-risk groups that have not included women or addressed the specific needs of HIV-positive women adequately. As the number of HIV-infected women grows, research into the female-specific complications of HIV infection, combined with accessible treatment with a woman's focus, should be a global priority.

REFERENCES

Alexander, N. J. 1990. Sexual transmission of human immunodeficiency virus: Virus entry into the male and female genital tract. *Fertility Sterility* 54:1–18.
Allen, S., et al. 1991. Human immunodeficiency virus and malaria in a representative sample of childbearing women in Kigali, Rwanda. *Journal of Infectious Diseases* 164:67–71.
Alloub, M. I., et al. 1989. Human papillomavirus infection and cervical intraepithelial neoplasia in women with renal allografts. *British Medical Journal* 298:153–56.

Araneta, M. R., et al. 1991. Survival trends among women with AIDS in San Francisco. International Conference on AIDS, June 16–21. *Proceedings* 7 (1): 328. Abstract M.C.3122.

Asiimwe, G., et al. 1992. *AIDS Surveillance Report: June 1992*, Ministry of Health, AIDS Control Program Surveillance Unit, Entebbe, Uganda. Unpublished report.

Barongo, L. R., et al. 1992. The epidemiology of HIV-1 infection in urban areas, road-side settlements, and rural villages in Mwanza Region, Tanzania. *AIDS* 6:1521–28.

Bhave, G. G., et al. 1990. HIV Surveillance in Promiscuous Females of Bombay India. Sixth International Conference on AIDS, San Francisco, June 20–24. Poster. F.C.612.

Bhave, G. G., et al. 1992. HIV Surveillance and Prevention. Second International Congress on AIDS in Asia and Pacific, New Delhi, India, November 8–12. Poster. C401.

Biggar, R. J., et al. 1989. Immunosuppression in pregnant women infected with human immunodeficiency virus. *American Journal of Obstetrics and Gynecology* 161:1239–44.

Bigot, A., M. Bodeus, and G. Burtongboy. 1992. Prevalence of HIV Infection among Prostitutes in Benin (West Africa). *Journal of Acquired Immune Deficiency Syndromes* 5 (3): 317–19.

Blaxhult, A., et al. 1990. The influence of age on the latency period to AIDS in people infected by HIV through blood transfusion. *AIDS* 4:125–29.

Boshell, J. S., et al. 1989. AIDS in Columbia. In *AIDS: Profile of an Epidemic, PAHO*, 37–44. Scientific Publication no. 514.

Boulos, R., et al. 1990. HIV-1 in Haitian women 1982–1988. The Cité Solcil/JHU AID Project Team. *Journal of Acquired Immune Deficiency Syndromes* 3 (7): 721–28.

Boxaca, M., et al. 1989. HIV Infection in Heterosexuals from Buenos Aires City Consulting for Venereal Disease. Fifth International Conference on AIDS, Montreal, June 4–9. Poster. W.P.G. 18.

Braun, M. M., et al. 1991. A retrospective cohort study of the risk of tuberculosis among women of childbearing age with HIV infection in Zaire. *American Review of Respiratory Diseases* 143:501–504.

British Virgin Islands Public Health Department. 1992. PAHO/WHO (Pan American Health Organization/World Health Organization) HIV Surveillance, September 15.

Buzingo, T., et al. 1993. The Epidemiology of HIV and AIDS in Brundi. Tenth International Conference on AIDS, Berlin, June 6–11. Poster. PO-C07–2750.

Carpenter, C. J., et al. 1989. Natural history of acquired immune deficiency syndrome in women in Rhode Island. *American Journal of Medicine* 86:771–75.

Chin, J. 1990. Current and future dimensions of the HIV/AIDS pandemic in women and children. *Lancet* 336:221–24.

Clemenston, D. B. A., et al. 1993. Detection of HIV DNA in cervical and vaginal secretions. *JAMA* 269:2860–64.

Colebunder, R., et al. 1987. Clinical case definition of AIDS in African adults. *Lancet* 2:972.

Comez, E., et al. 1992. Sentinel Seroprevalence Surveys for HIV-1 Infection in the Dominican Republic. Seventh International Conference on AIDS, Amsterdam, July 19–24. Poster. PoC 4066.

Dallabetta, G. A., et al. 1993. High socioeconomic status is a risk factor for human immunodeficiency virus type 1 infection but not for STD in women in Malawi. Implications for HIV-1 control. *Journal of Infectious Diseases* 167:36–42.

Davo, N., et al. 1992. Approche de l'Epidémie VIH/SIDA au Bénin. Seventh International Conference on AIDS in Africa, Yaounde, Cameroon, December 8–11. Poster. T.P.018.

Dayrit, M. M., et al. 1987. Emerging patterns of HIV infection and control in the Philippines. *Western Journal of Medicine* 147:723–25.

DeCock, K. M. 1989. Rapid emergence of AIDS in Abidjan, Ivory Coast. *Lancet* 2:408–11.

Deshamps, M. M., et al. 1993. A prospective study of HIV-seropositive asymptomatic women of childbearing age in developing countries. *Journal of Acquired Immune Deficiency Syndromes* 6:446–51.

Diallo, M. O., et al. 1992. Sexually Transmitted Diseases and HIV-1/HIV-2 Infections among Pregnant Women Attending Antenatal Clinics in Abidjan, Cote. Seventh International Conference on AIDS in Africa, Yaounde, Cameroon, December 8–11. Poster. T.P. 041.

Diaw, I., et al. 1991. Prévalence du HIV et MST Majeures chez les Prostituées Nouvellement Inscrites. Sixth International Conference on AIDS in Africa, Dakar Senegal, December 16–19. Session. W.O.128.

Dolmas, W. M. V., et al. 1989. Prevalence of HIV-1 antibody among groups of patients and healthy subjects from a rural and urban population in the Mwanza region, Tanzania. *AIDS* 3:297–99.

Feinberg, S. A. and R. Shinella. 1990. HIV infection in women: Report of 102 cases. *Modern Pathology* 3 (5): 575–80.

Feingold, A. R., et al. 1990. Cervical cytological abnormalities and papillomavirus in women infected with human immunodeficiency virus. *Journal of Acquired Immune Deficiency Syndromes* 3:896–903.

Fernandez-Cruz, E., et al. 1990. Immunological and serological markers predictive of progression to AIDS in a cohort of HIV-infected drug users. *AIDS* 4:987–94.

Fernandez, M. E., et al. 1992. HIV in Commercial Sex Workers in São Paulo, Brazil. Seventh International Conference on AIDS, Amsterdam, July 19–24. Poster. PoC4190.

Figueroa, J. P., et al. 1992. Risk Factors for HIV in Heterosexual STD Patients in Jamaica. Eighth International Conference on AIDS, Amsterdam July 19–24. Poster. PoC 4322.

Flanigan, T., et al. 1992. Fall in CD4 Count among HIV-Infected Women: A Comparison of Intravenous Drug Use and Heterosexual Transmission Groups. International Conference on AIDS, July 19–24. *Proceedings* 8 (2): C306. Abstract PoC 4367.

Fleming, P. L., et al. 1993. Gender differences in reported AIDS-indicative diagnosis. *Journal of Infectious Disease* 168 (1): 61–67.

Frerichs, R. R., et al. 1992. Comparison of saliva and serum for HIV surveillance in developing countries. *Lancet* 340 (8834/8835): 1496–99.

Gayle, C. and J. Farley. 1993. Trends in Patterns of Transmission over Ten Years of the AIDS Epidemic in the English-Speaking Caribbean and Surinam. Ninth International Conference on AIDS, Berlin. June 6–11. Poster. PO-CO6–2710.

Gichangi, P., et al. 1992. Rapid Increase in HIV-1 Infection and Syphilis between 1989 and 1991 in Pregnant Women in Nairobi, Kenya. Eighth International Conference on AIDS, Amsterdam, July 19–24. Poster. PoC 4029.

Global Program on AIDS. 1993. *The HIV/AIDS Pandemic: 1993 Overview*. Geneva: WHO.

Glodano, M., et al. 1989. The Seroprevalence of HTLV-1 and HIV-1 and Co-infection in Haiti. Fifth International Conference on AIDS, Montreal, June 4–9. Poster M.G.P.3.

Goldacre, M. J., et al. 1978. Epidemiology and clinical significance of cervical erosion in women attending a family planning clinic. *British Medical Journal* 1:748–50.

Gomez, M. P., R. Bain, and S. Reed. 1992. Seroprevalence of HIV Infection in the Commonwealth of the Bahamas. Eighth International Conference on AIDS, Amsterdam, July 19–24. Poster. PoC 4045.

Goodman, S., et al. 1992. Risk Behaviors for HIV among Women of Childbearing Age in the Urban Dominican Republic. Eighth International Conference on AIDS, Amsterdam, July 19 24. Poster. PoC 4029.

Gottardi, G., et al. 1984. Colposcopic findings in virgin and sexually active teenagers. *Obstetrics and Gynecology* 63 (5): 613.

Grant, R. M., et al. 1992. Trends of HIV Seroprevalence and Risk Behaviors in STD Patients in Uganda. Eighth International Conference on AIDS, Amsterdam July 19–24. Poster. PoC 4022.

Greenblatt, R. M., et al. 1988. Genital ulceration as a risk factor for human immunodeficiency virus infection. *AIDS* 2:47–50.

Gresenguet, G., et al. 1991. Séroprévalence de l'infection à VIH1 au sein des consultants de la clinique des maladies sexuellement transmissibles. *Bulletin de la Société de Pathologie Exotique* 84 (3): 240–46.

Gurtler, L., et al. 1987. Prevalence of HIV-1 in Selected Populations of Areas in Malawi. Second International Symposium: AIDS and Associated Cancer in Africa, Naples, Italy, October 7–9. Abstract TH-44.

Halpert, R., et al. 1986. Human papillomavirus and lower genital neoplasia in renal transplant patients. *Obstetrics and Gynecology* 68:251–58.

Hankins, C. A. and M. A. Handley. 1992. HIV disease and AIDS in women: Current knowledge and a research agenda. *Journal of Acquired Immune Deficiency Syndromes* 5:957–71.

Hayes, C., et al. 1989. Epidemiology of HIV-1 Infection among Prostitutes in the Philippines. U.S. Naval Medical Research Unit no. 2, Manila. Manuscript.

Hayes, C., et al. 1989. Prospective Studies on HIV Infections of Prostitutes in the Philippines. Fifth International Conference on AIDS, Montreal June 4–9. Poster. Th.G.O.25.

Hellman, N. S., et al. 1991. Genital Trauma During Sex Is a Risk Factor for HIV Infection in Uganda, Seventh International Conference on AIDS, Florence, Italy, June 16–21. Poster. M.C. 3079.

Hira, S. K., et al. 1990a. Clinical and epidemiological features of HIV infection at a referral clinic in Zambia. *Journal of Acquired Immune Deficiency Syndromes* 3: 87–91.

Hira, S. K., et al. 1990b. Epidemiology of human immunodeficiency virus in families in Lusaka, Zambia. *Journal of Acquired Immune Deficiency Syndromes* 3:83–86.

Hira, S. K., et al. 1991. Control Strategies in STD/HIV Clinics in Zambia: A Demonstration Project. Seventh International on AIDS, Florence, Italy, June 16–21. Poster. W.C.3082.

Hunt, W. H. 1989. Migrant labor and sexually transmitted disease: AIDS in Africa. *Journal of Health and Social Behavior* 30:353–72.

Imam, N., et al. 1990. Hierarchical pattern of mucosal candida infections in HIV-seropositive women. *American Journal of Medicine* 89:142–46.

Irwin, K., et al. 1993. The clinical presentation and course of pelvic inflammatory diseases in HIV+ and HIV- women: Preliminary results of a Multicenter study. The Multicenter HIV and PID Study Group. International Conference on AIDS, June 6–11. *Proceedings* 9 (1): 50. Abstract WS-B07–1.

Karita, E., et al. 1992. HIV Seroprevalence among STD Patients in Kigali, Rwanda, during the Four-Year Period 1988–1991. Eighth International Conference on AIDS, Amsterdam, July 19–24. Poster. PoC 4468.

Karita, E., et al. 1993. HIV infection among STD patients—Kigali, Rwanda, 1988 to 1991. *International Journal of STD and AIDS* 4:211–13.

Koutsky, L. A., D. A. Galloway, and K. K. Holmes. 1988. Epidemiology of genital papillomavirus infection. *Epidemiological Review* 10:122–63.

Kimball, A. M., R. Gonzalez, and F. Zacarias. 1991. AIDS among women in Latin America and the Caribbean. *Bulletin of PAHO* 25 (4): 367–2373.

Kreiss, J. K., et al. 1986. AIDS virus infection in Nairobi prostitutes: Spread of the epidemic to East Africa. *New England Journal of Medicine* 314:414–18.

Kreiss, J. K., et al. 1992. Human immunodeficiency virus, human papillomavirus, and cervical intraepithelial neoplasia in Nairobi prostitutes. *Sexually Transmitted Disease* 19:54–59.

Laga, M., et al. 1993. Nonulcerative sexually transmitted diseases as risk factors for HIV-1 transmission in women: Results from a cohort study. *AIDS* 7:95–102.

Lallemant, M., et al. 1992. Characteristics associated with HIV-1 infection in pregnant women in Brazzaville, Congo. *Journal of Acquired Immune Deficiency Syndromes* 5:279–85.

Lemp, G. F., et al. 1992. Survival for women and men with AIDS. *Journal of Infectious Diseases* 166 (1): 74–79.

Liautaud, B., et al. 1992. Preliminary Data on STDs in Haiti. Eighth International Conference on AIDS, Amsterdam, July 19–24. Poster. PoC 4302.

Lindan, C. P., et al. 1992. Predictors of mortality among HIV-infected women in Kigali, Rwanda, *Annals of Internal Medicine* 116:320–28.

Louv, W. C., et al. 1989. Oral contraceptive use and the risk of chlamydial and gonococcal infections. *American Journal of Obstetrics and Gynecology* 160:396–402.

Maiman, M., et al. 1991. Colposcopic evaluation of human immunodeficiency virus-seropositive women. *Obstetrics and Gynecology* 78:84–87.

Mann, J. and J. Chin. 1988. AIDS: A global perspective. *New England Journal of Medicine* 319:302–3.

May, S. B., et al. 1993. High Prevalence of HIV-1 Infection in a Representative Sample of Childbearing Women in Rio de Janeiro, Brazil. Ninth International Conference on AIDS, Berlin, July 6–11. Poster. PO-C11–2856.

Menjivar, A. and J. Fernandez. 1991. KAPs on the AIDS and HIV/AIDS Seroprevalence Studyicas Sobre VIH/SIDA Y Estudio de Seroprevalencia de VIH en mujeres. National AIDS Control Program, Ministry of Health. Unpublished report.

Mertens, T., et al. 1989. Epidemiology of HIV and hepatitis B virus (HBV) in selected African and Asian populations. *Infections* 17:4–7.

Meulen, J. ter, et al. 1992. Human papillomavirus (HPV) infection, HIV infection, and cervical cancer in Tanzania, East Africa. *International Journal of Cancer* 51:515–21.

Ministry of Health (MOH) (Bahamas). Community Health Service. 1993. PAHO/WHO HIV Surveillance, May 18, Pan American Health Organization/World Health Organization.

Ministry of Health AIDS Program (Guyana). 1993. PAHO/WHO HIV Surveillance, February 1, Pan American Health Organization/World Health Organization.

Ministry of Health and Women's Affairs (St. Kitts and Nevis). 1992. PAHO/WHO HIV Surveillance, April 13. Pan American Health Organization/World Health Organization.

Ministry of Public Health (Zaire). 1993. Serosurveillance Report of HIV Infection, Republic of Zaire, National Control Program against AIDS. *Central Coordination Bureau, BCC/SIDA.* Official Report.

Ministry of Public Health (Thailand). 1993. National Sentinel Seroprevalence. June. Unpublished tables.

Miotti, P. G., et al. 1992. A retrospective study of childhood mortality and spontaneous abortion in HIV-1 infected women in urban Malawi. *International Journal of Epidemiology* 21 (4): 792–99.

Mmiro, F., C. Ndugwa, and L. Gray. 1993. Effect of human immunodeficiency virus-1 infection on the outcome of pregnancy in Ugandan women. *Pediatric AIDS HIV Infections* 2:67–73.

Modan, B., et al. 1992. Prevalence of HIV antibodies in transsexual and female prostitutes. *American Journal of Public Health* 82 (4): 590–92.

Monny-Lobe, M., et al. 1993. A comparative HIV seroprevalence study among CSWs in Yaounde and Douala, Cameroon. Ninth International Conference on AIDS, Berlin, June 6–11. Abstract PO-C31–3300.

Moorman, A., et al. 1993. The microbiologic etiology of pelvic inflammatory disease (PID) in HIV+ and HIV- women: Preliminary findings of a multicenter study. The Multicenter HIV and PID Study Group. Ninth International Conference on AIDS, Berlin, June 6–11. *Proceedings* 9 (1): 458. Abstract PO-B23–1937.

Moss, A. R. and P. Bacchetti. 1989. Natural history of HIV infection. *AIDS* 3:55–61.

Moss, G. B., et al. 1991. Association of cervical ectopy with heterosexual transmission of human immunodeficiency virus: Results of a study of couples in Nairobi, Kenya. *Journal of Infectious Diseases* 164:588–91.

Mungai, J. N., et al. 1992. Laboratory Findings for the Prevalence of HIV, Neisseria Gonorrhoea, and Chlamydia Trachomatis Infections among Women Prostitutes. Seventh International Conference on AIDS in Africa, Yaounde, Cameroon, December 8–11. Abstract W.P.189.

NACP/MOH (Honduras). 1991. Centennial Study of the National AIDS Control Program of Prenatal Women.

Namboze, J. M. 1993. AIDS/HIV Update—Botswana. Unpublished memo.

National AIDS Control Program/Ministry of Health (NACP/MOH) (Ethiopia). 1992. Surveillance and research activities on HIV/AIDS: Activities accomplished so far in Ethiopia, 1984–1991. Ethiopia NACP/MOH Data. Unpublished report.

Ndinya-Achola, J. O., et al. 1993. Gender-Specific Sexual Behaviors among STD Patients at a Nairobi Primary Health Care Clinic. Ninth International Conference on AIDS, Berlin, June 6–11. Poster. PO-D01–3406.

O'Farrell, N., I. Windsor, and P. Becker. 1991. HIV-1 infection among heterosexual attenders at a sexually transmitted disease clinic in Durban. *South African Medical Journal* 80:17–20.

Oxtoby, M. J. 1990. Perinatally acquired human immunodeficiency virus infection. *Pediatric Infectious Diseases Journal* 9:609–19.

PAHO/WHO. 1991a. Epidemiology Unit, Centinel Site. PAHO/WHO Surveillance. Pan American Health Organization/World Health Organization.

PAHO/WHO. 1991b. Pan American Health Organization. "Health Situations and Trend Assessment Program."

Pallangyo, K. J., et al. 1987. Clinical case definition of AIDS in African adults. *Lancet* 2:972.

Parkin, D. M., J. Stjernsward, and C. S. Muir. 1984. Estimates of the worldwide frequency of twelve major cancers. *Bulletin of the World Health Organization* 62:163–82.

Peterman, T. A., et al. 1988. Risk of human immunodeficiency virus transmission from heterosexual adults with transfusion-associated infections. *JAMA* 259:55–58.

Piot, P., et al. 1987. Retrospective seroepidemiology of AIDS virus infection in Nairobi populations. *Journal of Infectious Diseases* 155:1108–12.

Plourde, P. J., et al. 1992. Human immunodeficiency virus type 1 infection in women attending a sexually transmitted disease clinic in Kenya. *The Journal of Infectious Disease* 166:86–92.

Plummer, F. A., et al. 1989. HIV-1 infection in sexually exposed women: Risk factors for prevalent and incident infections. Fifth International Conference on AIDS, Montreal, Canada. Abstract TAP 87.

Plummer, F. A., et al. 1991. Cofactors in male-female sexual transmission of human immunodeficiency virus type 1. *Journal of Infectious Disease* 163:233–39.

Pomerantz, R. T., et al. 1988. Human immunodeficiency virus (HIV) infection of the uterine cervix. *Annals of Internal Medicine* 108 (3): 321–27.

Pope, J. W., et al. 1983. Characteristics of the acquired immunodeficiency syndrome (AIDS) in Haiti. *New England Journal of Medicine* 309:945–50.

Republic of South Africa (RSA). Department of National Health and Population Development. 1991. AIDS in South Africa: Status on World AIDS Day 1991. *Epidemiological Comments* 18 (11): 229–49.

Reidner, G. Y., et al. 1993. The Use of Serologic Trends of HIV Survey of HIV and Syphilis for the Evaluation of the Mbeya Regional ACP Tanzania, 1986–1992. Ninth International Conference on AIDS, Berlin June 6–11. Poster. PO-C29–3262.

Rodriguez, E. M., et al. 1993. HIV-1 and HTLV-1 in sexually transmitted disease clinics in the Dominican Republic. *Journal of Acquired Immune Deficiency Syndromes* 6 (3): 313–18.

Rutherford, G. W., et al. 1990. Course of HIV-1 infection in a cohort of homosexual and bisexual men: An eleven-year follow-up study. 301:1183–88.

Scott, G. B., et al. 1985. Mothers of infants with acquired immunodeficiency syndrome. Evidence for both symptomatic and asymptomatic carriers. *JAMA* 253:363–66.

Selwyn, P. A., et al. 1989. A prospective study of the risk of tuberculosis among intravenous drug users with human immunodeficiency virus infection. *New England Journal of Medicine* 320:545 50.

Steffy, K. and F. Weng-Staal. 1991. Genetic regulation of human immunodeficiency virus. *Microbiology Review* 55:193–205.

Stein, M. D., et al. 1991. Differences in access to zidovudine (AZT) among symptomatic HIV-infected persons. 1991. *Journal of General Internal Medicine* 6:35 40.

Traore-Ettiegne, V., et al. 1993. High Prevalence of HIV Infections and Other STDs in Female Prostitutes in Abidjan. Ninth International Conference on AIDS, Berlin, June 6–11. Sessions. WS-CO8–3.

United Nations Development Program (UNDP). 1992. *Young Women: Silence, Susceptibility, and the HIV Epidemic.* New York: UNDP.

Uribe, P., et al. 1990. Analysis of Factors Related to HIV Infection in 961 Female Sexual Workers. Sixth International Conference on AIDS, San Francisco, June 20–24. Abstract Th.D.777.

U.S. Department of Health and Human Services, Public Health Service. 1993. U.S. AIDS cases reported through September 1993. *HIV/AIDS, Surveillance Report* 5 (3).

U.S. Department of State. 1993. AIDS/HIV in Malawi: A Status Report. Unclassified Cable 8/93, Lilongwe 03703.

Valdespino, J. L., et al. 1992. Infection in Mexico through National Sentinel Surveillance System. An Update. Eighth International Conference on AIDS, Amsterdam, July 19–24. Poster. PoC 4063.

Vanichseni, S., et al. 1990. First seroprevalence survey of Bangkok drug addicts: Determinants of HIV status. *Aids Research in Thailand, Bangkok Ministry of Health*, 68–69.

Vithayasi, V. and P. Vithayasi. 1990. An analysis of HIV infection rates in Northern Thailand. *Thai AIDS Journal* 2 (3): 99–108.

Wasserheit, J. N. 1992. Epidemiological synergy, interrelationships between human immunodeficiency virus infection and other sexually transmitted diseases. *Sexually Transmitted Diseases* 19:61–77.

Wawer, M. J., et al. 1991. Dynamics of spread of HIV-1 infection in a rural district of Uganda. *British Medical Journal* 303, no. 6813 (November 23): 1303–6.

Weinberg, E. D. 1984. Pregnancy-associated depression of cell-mediated immunity. *Reviews of Infectious Disease* 6 (6).

White, E., et al. 1990. National AIDS Control Program, Jamaica Program Director, University of California, San Francisco. Sixth International Conference on AIDS, San Francisco, June 20–24. Abstract F.C.591.

WHO/EC. 1993. European Center for the Epidemiological Monitoring of AIDS. AIDS Surveillance in Europe. *Quarterly Report*, no. 39.

WHO/GPA. 1993. 1.5 Million New HIV Infections in Africa Pushes Global Total over 15 Million. Press Release. December.

Zapiola, I., et al. 1992. HIV-1 and HTLV-I/II Among Prostitutes in Buenos Aires, Argentina. Eighth International Conference on AIDS, Amsterdam July 19–24. Poster. PoC 4661.

Zewdie, D., et al. 1989. High Prevalence of HIV-1 Antibodies in STD Patients with Genital Ulcer. Fifth International Conference on AIDS, Montreal, June 4–9. Poster. T.A.P.102.

12 | Sexually Transmitted Diseases as Catalysts of HIV / AIDS in Women

BARBARA PARKER AND DAVID W. PATTERSON

There is overwhelming evidence that sexually transmitted diseases (STDs) are both a significant health problem in their own right as well as a contributing factor in the global spread of HIV/AIDS. STDs are prevalent in both developed and developing countries. In the developing areas of the world, however, they are particularly common (see table 12.1). Among women attending antenatal services, gonorrhea rates are ten to fifteen times higher in developing than in developed countries, and syphilis rates are ten to a hundred times greater (Wasserheit and Holmes 1992). It is estimated that in high-prevalence communities sexually transmitted diseases rank third among common diseases in developing countries, after measles and malaria, in their socioeconomic impact. Using the concept of "productive healthy life years lost" (per capita per year) to compare the negative impact of various diseases, STDs are second only to measles in their burden on human health (ibid).

The consequences of untreated STDs in developing countries are of even greater concern now that the scientific community has established that infection with some STDs (particularly those that cause genital ulceration) facilitate both transmission and acquisition of the HIV virus. Because of the relative absence of curative health services in the world's poor countries, STDs go untreated for longer periods, are more likely to progress to severe forms of the disease, and may be transmitted more widely than in developed countries. Women in developing countries are the victims most likely to remain untreated for extended periods of time.

TABLE 12.1.

Prevalence of RTI/STDs* among Women in Developing Countries

STDs	High Risk (%)		Low Risk (%)	
	Median	Range	Median	Range
Chlamydia	14	2–25	8	1–29
Gonorrhoea	24	7–66	6	0.3–40
Trichomoniasis	17	4–20	12	0.01–33
Syphilis	15	4–32	8	0.4–33
Chancroid	9	3–16	Not Applicable	

SOURCE: J. N. Wasserheit and K. K. Holmes. Reproductive Tract Infections In A. Germain et al., eds., *Reproductive Tract Infections: Global Impact and Priorities for Women's Reproductive Health* (New York: Plenum, 1992).

*Reproductive tract infections, including STDs. High-risk refers to commercial sex workers and those who attended STD clinics; low-risk women are those who attended prenatal clinics.

The Role of STDs in HIV Transmission

The STDs that include genital ulcers among their symptoms are those that show the best documented associations with transmission of HIV. According to a recent review the results are mixed, but a number of studies in Zaire and Kenya have found that persons with genital ulcers were two to five times more likely to be infected with HIV (Population Reports 1993). Open lesions are a clear pathway of infection. This pathway is two-directional: for persons with genital ulcers who are HIV-negative, the lesion provides a site where skin or mucous membrane is breached and viral penetration facilitated; at the same time HIV-positive persons with lesions pose a greater risk to their uninfected partners than do those without lesions. In Nairobi the HIV virus was isolated from genital ulcers of commercial sex workers (CSWs) (Cameron et al. 1989).

Even among the nonulcerative STDs, however, links have been established. In a study of 431 initially HIV-negative commercial sex workers in Kinshasa, those who seroconverted had much higher rates of chlamydia, gonorrhea, or trichomoniasis. After controlling for sexual exposure, it was found that adjusted odds ratios for seroconversion were 4.8 for gonorrhea, 3.6 for chlamydia, and 1.9 for trichomoniasis (Laga et al. 1993). The exact mechanism of transmission in these cases is not clearly established, but it is possible that transmission takes place either through microlesions caused by inflammation, through the increased density of white blood cells, or through changes in the Ph balance of the vaginal mucosa.

If untreated STD infection does, as these studies indicate, facilitate the transmission of HIV, this may explain why HIV is spreading more rapidly among women and among the heterosexual population in the developing world than in the industrialized countries. The higher incidence of untreated STDs in developing countries, combined with women's greater vulnerability to STD infection, may be significant contributing factors in the relatively high rates of HIV infection among even low-risk women in Africa and other poor countries. Targeting these women and their partners for prevention and treatment of both ulcerative and nonulcerative STDs may therefore be critical in controlling the HIV epidemic in the developing world.

Scope of the STD Problem

STDs, although a worldwide problem, are not equally prevalent in all regions. Prevalence rates in the developing world exhibit a wide range. One or more high prevalence countries exists in almost every region of the world, but the majority of these countries are clustered in sub-Saharan Africa. Prevalence is also high in some Latin American countries, however, and it is rising in South and Southeast Asia. Southern Asia may join Africa as a high-prevalence region if further spread is not prevented.

Collection of comprehensive data on the prevalence of STDs in the developing world has been hampered by the stigma attached to these diseases, which inhibits people from seeking treatment or even reporting their illness, and by poor record keeping in many health systems. Worldwide, more than twenty infectious organisms are sexually transmitted, but the most common STDs in the developing world are gonorrhea, syphilis, chlamydia, chancroid, bacterial vaginosis, HIV, human papilloma virus (genital warts), and herpes simplex-2. During the past decade the classical "venereal diseases" (syphilis, gonorrhea, and chancroid) are beginning to be displaced by the "new generation" of diseases (chlamydia and the viral diseases including HIV) (De Schryver and Meheus 1990), particularly in the more prosperous developing countries.

Nevertheless estimates reveal unexpectedly high rates of bacterial infections among "low-risk" populations (see table 12.2). Among women attending family planning, antenatal, and gynecology clinics, infection with gonorrhea has been found to be as high as 40 percent in some African countries, 18 percent in some Latin American countries, and 12 percent in some Asian countries (Dixon-Mueller and Wasserheit 1991). "Low-risk" women are those selected by factors such as attendance at family planning and antenatal clinics, who would be expected to show rates of STDs typical of the population at large. It should be borne in mind that among "high-risk" populations, such as commercial sex workers, STD clinic attendees, intravenous drug users, and (in some countries) truck drivers and military personnel, rates are generally much higher.

Though little or no information exists from earlier periods for comparison,

TABLE 12.2.

*Countries with High STD Prevalence Rates among Pregnant Women**

Country	Gonorrhoea (%)	Chlamydia (%)	Syphilis (%)
Africa			
Botswana	14		
Cameroon	15		
Ethiopia			18
The Gambia	7	7	15
Kenya	7	29	
Malawi	5	3	12
Tanzania	6		19
Zaire		9	20
Asia			
Thailand	12	13	
Latin America/ Caribbean			
El Salvador		44	

SOURCE: Family Health International, 1992.

*Only countries for which data are available on STD rates among pregnant women have been included. It should not be inferred that the problem is absent or less severe in many countries for which no comparable data have been collected.

there is reason to believe that rates of some of the STDs are increasing in the developing countries. For example, studies of trends in Latin American countries between 1987 and 1991 revealed that, although the incidence of gonorrhea decreased in fifteen out of twenty-one countries, the incidence of primary and secondary syphilis increased in twelve countries.

Among the factors that explain the current STD-prevalence rates in developing countries is a demographic bulge in the reproductive age group (ages fifteen to forty-five). The reproductively active age group is at highest risk of contracting STDs, and individuals under the age of twenty-five are the most common STD cases. This group is now at an all-time high and still growing. In addition, the social changes brought on by the dislocations of economic and political change—including coups, interethnic warfare, and other types of political violence—have weakened traditional behavioral controls that served in the past as a restraint to extramarital sexual activity. Even conservative and relatively intact social systems are not immune, however. The practice of polygynous marriage, traditional in many countries, is thought to be a factor in the spread of STD and HIV among the heterosexual population—particularly when one of the partners involved has sexual contacts outside the primary union.

Rural poverty, which leads to urbanization and the growth of migrant labor, is another cause. Migration of poor and landless men to cities in search of temporary or long-term employment is common throughout the developing world. Often, particularly when wives have been left behind in the villages, these men patronize commercial sex workers. Those who acquire an STD through this practice may infect their wives during visits to their home villages. In both rural and urban areas, poor women are more at risk of developing STDs than are their wealthier sisters. CSWs are more likely to contract STDs if they are poor, and poor men are the most common customers of these women. Even in industrialized countries, poor men are at greater risk of acquiring STDs and transmitting them to their wives or regular partners.

A third factor in the relatively high STD rates among the general population in the developing world is the scarcity of effective control programs in poor countries. In the industrialized countries with effective services and good coverage, although there is no indication that the rate of partner change dropped significantly among the general population, bacterial STD rates nevertheless have declined in the last two decades. For example, in Sweden the rate of gonorrhea declined by 95 percent between 1970 and 1989 (Aral and Holmes 1991).

Women and STDs

Women are disproportionately affected by STDs for a number of reasons. In contacts between infected and uninfected partners, infection is more easily transmitted from male to female than the reverse. In any given act of coitus with an infected partner, the risk of acquiring gonorrhea is approximately 25 percent for men and 50 percent for women (Hatcher et al. 1990). STDs in women are particularly pernicious in that they are asymptomatic roughly half the time. Without symptoms to prompt women to seek treatment, they sometimes do not learn they have been infected until permanent damage has been done.

What is more, women in many traditional societies are at risk of infection by their own husbands, and power relations within the family may deny them the right to refuse sex with an infected spouse or to demand use of a condom. This may be particularly true in cultures in which money or material assets change hands at the time of marriage. The exchange of bride-price or dowry often gives social and financial support to the notion that a woman's reproductive potential has been formally transferred to the control of her husband and his family. In the societies of most developing country, moreover, women typically lack the economic opportunities that would allow them to escape easily from an unsatisfactory marital union. Even if the wife is aware that her husband engages in behaviors that place him at risk of acquiring STDs and HIV/AIDS, she may have no means of supporting herself and her children independently.

Women are also likely to suffer more serious consequences from STDs than do men. Data suggest that 10–20 percent of untreated gonorrheal infection of the cervix and 8–10 percent of untreated chlamydial infection of the cervix will ascend to the upper reproductive tract and cause pelvic inflammatory disease (PID) (Meheus 1992). Evidence from Papua New Guinea suggests that PID accounts for 15 percent of gynecological hospital admissions and 40 percent of women's attendance at outpatient gynecology departments (Mala 1987). Cervical cancer is also found to be associated with a history of reproductive tract infections. In addition, some common complications of childbearing have been linked to infection with STDs, including ectopic pregnancy and sepsis. Ectopic pregnancy was found to be the third leading cause of maternal death in Jamaica during the 1981–83 period (Walker et al. 1986). Many maternal deaths are also the result of postpartum infections that are associated with ongoing STD infections. One of the most common consequences for women, however, is infertility. Infertile women may find themselves abandoned by their husbands and stigmatized in their communities. Women may also have less access to curative facilities and financial resources, particularly in cultures that value female seclusion in the home.

A brief consideration of the difficulties confronting the woman seeking treatment for STDs in the developing world is enlightening. In the developed countries, a woman who experiences a persistent vaginal discharge usually visits her private doctor. If she is economically disadvantaged, she normally has access to services through government-sponsored clinics and programs. Though she may face economic constraints, there are relatively few social and cultural constraints to seeking treatment. A woman from a developing country with a similar discharge may find that she faces one or more of the following additional problems:

1. There may be no doctor or clinic available within feasible travel distance. In a country such as Nepal, for example, the physician-to-population ratio is approximately one to thirty thousand, and many people live in remote mountainous areas unreachable by road.

2. In families living largely outside the cash economy, women may have no cash income to pay for services, transport, or medication. In the poorest countries, such as Chad, annual GNP per capita is only $190 (World Bank 1992).

3. In countries that place a religious and social value on female seclusion (called *purda* in the countries of South Asia), women usually face disapproval if they attempt to travel unchaperoned by a husband or relative or, in extreme cases, if they appear in public at all. This disapproval may be expressed by harassment or even physical threat.

4. If the woman from the developing country should reach a clinic, she may be subjected to a prolonged wait and suffer discourteous treatment from

health workers who regard her as a social inferior. Clinic personnel may be poorly trained, unmotivated, and short of supplies and equipment.

5. The woman from the developing country may be reluctant to submit to examination by a strange doctor, who is often male. This is particularly true of those women who, having spent their adult lives in seclusion, may have little or no experience interacting with men who are not relatives.

6. After her examination, she may be told to return the following day for test results and treatment. If so, she may be unable to stay overnight near the clinic because of lack of safe and affordable lodging or because she would be missed at home. She is unlikely to make a second difficult and expensive trip.

7. If she tests positive for an STD, clinic staff may refer her to a second facility that is publicly recognized as an STD-treatment clinic. If so, she may be unwilling to risk visiting the facility out of fear of revealing her condition to passersby or other witnesses.

8. If she surmounts all these obstacles, secures treatment, understands the treatment regimen, and follows it correctly, she is very likely to be reinfected by her husband or regular partner if he is not treated simultaneously.

A woman in any cultural setting might find it awkward to reveal to a husband or regular partner that she is infected with an STD. Any attempt to discuss the problem with her partner exposes her to the risk that he will blame her for the infection and suspect infidelity. In some cases she might fear beating or abandonment. For this reason, the woman who suspects she is an STD victim may seek diagnosis and treatment without her partner's knowledge. In such a case, follow-up treatment of the partner is a serious ethical dilemma and a practical challenge to the health worker. Without the partner being treated, however, cure of the primary patient is likely to prove ineffective or short-lived. Careful culture-specific assessment of the costs and benefits of notifying partners is in order, and a flexible approach is recommended.

STDs and Children

STDs exert a significant negative impact on the offspring of infected women. Transmission of syphilis from mother to fetus is nearly 100 percent for mothers who have been infected for less than two years, and about half the pregnancies of women with syphilis end in miscarriage, stillbirth, perinatal death, or premature delivery (Over and Piot 1988). Various STDs (especially chlamydia) can cause neonatal pneumonia, an often fatal acute respiratory infection (ARI), in many infants born to infected mothers.

Among those who survive, the children of infected women are more likely to be mentally or physically disabled than are the children of uninfected women. Children of women infected with gonorrhea are likely to be disabled from blindness if they are not treated for ophthalmia neonatorum. Without prophylaxis at the time of birth, there is a 30–40 percent risk of transmission from the infected mother to the infant's eyes. Chlamydia in infected mothers also causes ophthalmia neonatorum, though this condition does not appear to destroy sight as commonly as gonococcal ophthalmia (Over and Piot 1988). Taken collectively, however, there is no doubt that various sequelae of STDs contribute significantly to perinatal mortality and disability.

What Can Be Done?

Each year approximately 250 million new infections are acquired through sexual transmission throughout the world. Most of these transmissions could be prevented if condoms were used in every sexual contact. Evidence indicates that spermicides, such as nonoxynol-9, also reduce the likelihood of sexual transmission of infection. Because these solutions rely on a constant supply of condoms or other barrier contraceptives, which are often costly or unavailable in developing countries, programs aimed at changing patterns of sexual interaction may be a more dependable and sustainable approach to preventing the spread of STDs.

One of the high-priority approaches to prevention involves identifying and targeting core groups of STD transmitters. They may be a subset of the larger population with behavioral characteristics, such as frequent partner change, that facilitate the high rate of transmission of one or more STDs. Their rate of sexual contact with the general population is often an important determinant of the progress of STD epidemics there.

The benefit of focusing on core groups with STDs may be high. Prevention or treatment of a case of STD in the core group can have a much greater impact in terms of cases averted than does the prevention or treatment of a case in the general population. Over and Piot (1988) found that preventing 100 cases of gonorrhea in the general population will avert 426 future cases of gonorrhea. By contrast, preventing the same number of cases of gonorrhea in the core group will avert 4,278 cases.

When aiming a communication program at an identified core group such as CSWs, however, caution should be observed. When a core group is identified and, ipso facto, treated as a danger to public health, there is the risk of creating a stigma or exacerbating an existing stigma associated with the core group in the eyes of the general public. In the worst scenario, the "public health menace" stigma could contribute to legal or informal persecution of the core group. What is more, the social stigma attached to membership in a category such as "prostitutes" may lead the at-risk woman to deny membership in that category even if she engages in practices such as trading sex for money or drugs. This denial may take two forms. On the one hand she may engage in self-deception, attempting to cling to the belief that she is not really a member of the core group and therefore she is not at risk. A woman may also fail to seek diagnosis and treatment because she fears this would reveal her to be a member of a stigmatized group.

Core groups, therefore, should not be the exclusive focus of prevention programs. As noted above, the incidence of STDs is high even among low-risk populations in many developing countries. A carefully planned information, education, and communication (IEC) program is one approach to generating changes in sexual behavior that would slow the spread of STDs. Several steps are involved in developing an appropriately targeted and successful IEC program of this type. In brief, they are the following:

1. *Identifying the target group.* Available epidemiological evidence on STD rates among subgroups within the larger population should be consulted to identify the groups at greatest risk.

2. *Determining target group characteristics, attitudes, and relevant behaviors.* Target group characteristics such as age, literacy and income levels, residential patterns, and so on, should be researched to determine how to aim messages and when and where to present them. In addition, levels of knowledge about human reproduction, disease transmission, and sexuality, as well as frequency of partner change and condom use, can be examined through surveys, rapid assessment methods, and other qualitative research techniques. Service utilization and preferences for types and locations of services can also be revealed through these methods.

3. *Identifying appropriate channels of communication.* Ascertaining women's use of and access to various media through research is a critical step in choosing the correct channels for messages about STDs and sexual behavior. Mass media is not the only or necessarily the best choice, however, particularly in very poor countries. When women in the target audience have little exposure to mass media, opinion leaders who are held in high regard can be of assistance, provided they can be motivated to cooperate in the communication program. Outreach by government health and family planning workers or by community development workers of nongovernmental organizations (NGOs) can be an effective source of information and counseling, if the target group regards these workers as trustworthy and they are trained for the task. Health education and counseling sessions are an important part of STD treatment and should be included in the pro-

grams of STD clinics and, in areas of high prevalence, in family planning and antenatal clinics as well.

4. *Developing messages.* There are several types of messages. Informational messages are appropriate when prior research reveals that the target group has a poor understanding or awareness of the problem. Messages of this kind might include the recognizable symptoms of STDs, routes of transmission, and the locations of curative services. Motivational messages are aimed at changing attitudes or at persuading the target group to take specific actions. These messages, if based on an assessment of the social, psychological, and economic costs and benefits of adopting protective behaviors, can emphasize those benefits of behavioral change that are of particular interest and concern to target group members. For example, truck drivers might be urged to protect their own families by avoiding contact with CSWs or using condoms. A third aspect of communication is skills building. Counseling sessions can be used to teach CSWs to negotiate condom use with clients through role playing—rehearsing arguments, responding to counterarguments, and taking a stand. The effectiveness of negotiation training can, however, be limited when women have no real power base from which to negotiate (see article 18, Talking about Sex: A Prerequisite for AIDS Prevention).

The specific behavioral changes that will be protective to the individual and that will help control the spread of STDs and HIV are determined by the target individual's current patterns of behavior. STD-prevention strategies should not focus exclusively on the individual, however. Social factors that support the spread of STDs must also be attacked. Female education has been found to be negatively associated with the number of CSWs in urban areas, suggesting that when women are prepared for other types of employment opportunities, they are less likely to turn to commercial sex. Men who contribute to STD spread in developing countries tend to be transients such as military servicemen, truck drivers, and migrant laborers. Social conditions, then, are factors in the existence and growth of STD transmission.

Some of these social conditions may be amenable to government action. Consistent with the Charter for Health Promotion adopted in Ottawa in 1986 by the First International Conference on Health Promotion in Industrialized Countries, health impact should be a significant consideration in policy development in all government sectors. This is no less true in the developing world. Governments can support STD control through policies that contribute to stabilizing employment conditions, improving economic opportunities in rural areas, promoting female education, and creating an environment that allows family members to accompany military personnel and other transient labor.

5. *Diagnosis.* Although common STDs such as syphilis, gonorrhea, chlamydia,

and many of the ulcerative STDs are treatable with antibiotics once they have been correctly diagnosed, health professionals are still in the process of developing diagnostic tools that are appropriate for resource-poor settings. Rapid (nonculture) diagnostic tests are preferred, since they allow the patient to be examined and treated in the same visit. Rapid diagnostic tools for gonorrhea and chlamydia currently exist, but they are too expensive for broad utilization in most developing countries. For detection of syphilis, the rapid plasma reagin (RPR) test is quick and relatively inexpensive but not always accurate or simple to utilize.

Since 1990, an international group has been working to develop quick and accurate diagnostic tools for developing countries. Called the STD Diagnostics Initiative, the group receives support from a variety of U.S. organizations, including the U.S. Agency for International Development and the Centers for Disease Control (CDC). Three working groups—the gonorrhea, syphilis, and syndromic working groups—have been tasked with developing, testing, and evaluating techniques such as the finger-stick method of diagnosing syphilis and the field culture method of screening for gonorrhea. Under the working group's direction, the Program for Appropriate Technology in Health (PATH) (1992) is now testing a method for detecting gonorrhea in men that involves applying a swab of urethral exudate to a paper strip and watching for a color change.

In some resource-poor settings, medical personnel rely on visual diagnosis of the more common STDs. A single patient may be infected with more than one STD simultaneously, however, and multiple infections can mask or distort the appearance of recognized symptoms. Recently medical personnel have begun to employ the syndromic approach, which focuses on identification of a group of indicative symptoms, and treatment of all diseases that can cause that set of symptoms (Population Reports 1993). Accuracy of the syndromic approach to diagnosis can be improved considerably by adding simple tests such as checking the pH (acidity or alkalinity) of vaginal secretions. Whenever fast and low-cost diagnostic tests are not available or appropriate, use of syndromic diagnosis and presumptive treatment are usually preferable to the use of expensive and complicated diagnostic tools that require repeat visits and consume inordinate levels of clinic funds.

6. *Treatment.* There is no effective cure for the viral STDs, including HIV. Prevention is therefore the proper focus of initiatives aimed at controlling these diseases. Most of the common bacterially caused STDs, on the other hand, are treatable with commonly available antibiotics. All these STDs are appropriate targets for treatment as well as prevention programs, from the perspective of both maternal/child health and HIV/AIDS prevention.

In developed countries ophthalmia neonatorum is routinely treated through antibiotic prophylaxis of infants at birth in the hospital. In developing countries, most babies are not born in hospitals and a majority of births are not attended by medically trained and supplied physicians or nurses. The traditional birth attendant (TBA), who usually has had no formal training, provides much of the care of women and their infants during pregnancy and delivery. During the 1980s, initiatives were launched in a wide spectrum of countries to bring formal training and basic supplies and equipment to TBAS in rural areas. TBA "safe delivery kits" have been designed and marketed to TBAS as part of some of these programs. Silver nitrate, tetracycline salve, or other prophylactic agents for the prevention of ophthalmia neonatorum can be included among the supplies in the TBA kits. Government health posts and other outreach facilities should also include neonatal ocular prophylaxis in their primary health care and health promotion packages.

Oral or injectable antibiotics are the recommended methods of treating STDs. The efficacy of many of the most commonly used antibiotics has been compromised, however, by the appearance of disease-resistant strains of STDs, particularly gonorrhea. Because of the problem of antibiotic resistance, it is currently recommended that patients may need to be given two or more complementary drugs to treat gonorrhea and that health workers follow up to be certain that treatment regimens are followed correctly.

Antibiotic resistance is thought to have been a result of overuse and inappropriate use of antibiotics over many years. Patients, in developed countries as well, commonly fail to follow treatment regimens as prescribed. In developing countries, semiliterate or illiterate patients may be unable to read or recall detailed instructions or they may be unable to afford the cost of the full course of prescribed treatment. Health practitioners are seldom trained in patient communication skills and so they may be unable to provide instructions that are clear to the layperson. The physician and patient may be separated by cultural and linguistic gaps that render communication difficult. Communication is a particular problem for women in developing countries. They are usually less educated than their male counterparts, and if they have learned to be silent and deferential in the presence of strangers, they may forbear to ask questions that could clarify their understanding of medical information. Evidence indicates that education of women, even at the early primary levels, strengthens their ability to utilize treatment services effectively (Cleland and van Ginneken 1988).

In order to be effectively delivered, antibiotics must reach the STD victim. Women, the focus of this volume, are particularly underserved by STD curative services, and intensive efforts must be launched if they are to be reached in the numbers required for control of STDs in developing countries. Women of reproductive age, the group most likely to be affected, can frequently be contacted through family planning and antenatal clinics. Since resources are limited, research on the cost-effectiveness of delivering services through these and other types of facilities should be undertaken in order to identify the most efficient use of scarce funding.

For the many women who are not aware of the common symptoms of STDs or of the existence and location of treatment sources, messages should be developed and information disseminated through the popular media. As noted above, commercial sex workers and other high-risk sub-populations should be a special target of STD communication campaigns. Peer counseling by current or former CSWS has been found to be one of the most effective means of reaching this subgroup and persuading them to seek treatment (Cohen et al. 1988). In some countries resource-intensive outreach programs in villages and homes may be necessary to reach women who are not accustomed to traveling outside their own communities and who may have scant access to messages through the media.

Integrated Services

To achieve maximal effectiveness, treatment programs for STDs in women should have a dual focus. First, they should be integrated with services that are used by women for other purposes. Services such as antenatal, gynecological, and maternal/child health programs should be equipped with supplies and expertise that will prepare the staff to screen and treat STDs. Given the higher than expected prevalence of STDs in the general populations of many countries, family planning services should screen patients routinely for STDs. This is particularly critical when invasive procedures such as IUD insertion and abortion are provided. Another virtue of the integrated approach is that women who are concerned about the stigma attached to STD patients can be treated privately and discreetly without publicly visiting a facility recognized as an STD treatment center.

There is, however, a degree of controversy over the question of integration. On the one hand, most family planning and public health professionals agree that family planning clinics should provide STD screening and treatment, for two reasons: (1) STDs represent a true medical risk, since IUD insertion or abortion could introduce STD pathogens into the upper reproductive tract, and (2) infected women may blame their disease symptoms on the contraceptive method they are using, leading them to reject the method or family planning more generally. On the other hand, some family planning professionals are uncertain as to whether all services should be integrated. Below are some potential problems they have raised.

Stigma

Family planning clinics (like antenatal and gynecological services) could be contaminated in the eyes of the public as they are associated with use by high-risk groups. If so, low-risk women might avoid visiting the facility. What is more, family planning workers may be reluctant to discuss sexuality with STD patients, and they may lack the requisite skills for doing so.

Opportunity Costs

The introduction of ancillary services in family planning clinics may divert the staff's time and financial resources from the clinic's primary purpose, particularly when no additional funding has been provided.

Despite these concerns, family planning clinics are one of the few points of contact between reproductive-aged women in developing countries and medical systems. Given the urgency of STD control, particularly in light of the clear role of STDs in facilitating the spread of the HIV virus, the balance of factors favors the integration of STD services (particularly treatment services) with family planning and antenatal facilities.

The second goal of STD treatment programs should be to develop and implement the "one-stop shop." A significant proportion of women will not return for treatment when told they will have to wait twenty-four hours or more to learn the results of a diagnostic test. Single-visit diagnosis and treatment is therefore the optimal choice. It is important that current research into quick, simple, and low-cost diagnostic tools be continued and that STD control budgets include funding for these tools. Where appropriate and easy-to-use diagnostic tools are unavailable, presumptive treatment of patients exhibiting symptoms of STDs is an option that is both cost-effective and convenient to the patient. Antibiotic treatment protocols that are clear and explicit should be developed, and health care workers should be trained to describe them in terms easily understood by women in developing countries.

REFERENCES

Aral, S. O. and Holmes, K. K. 1991. Sexually transmitted diseases in the AIDS era. *Scientific American* 264 (2): 62–68.

Cameron, W., et al. 1989. Isolation of human immunodeficiency virus from genital ulcers in Nairobi prostitutes. *Journal of Infectious Diseases* 106 (3): 380–84.

Cleland, J. and J. K. van Ginnekin. 1988. Maternal education and child survival in developing countries: The search for pathways of influence. *Social Science and Medicine* 27:1357–68.

Cohen, J. B., et al. 1988. Sexual Behavior and HIV Information Risk among 354 Sex Industry Women in a Participant Based Research and Prevention Program. In *Fourth International Conference on AIDS* (Stockholm) Book 1:272.

De Schryver, A. and A. Meheus. Epidemiology of sexually transmitted diseases: The global picture. 1990. *Bulletin of the World Health Organization* 68 (5): 639–54.

Dixon-Mueller, R. and J. Wasserheit. 1991. *The Culture of Silence: Reproductive Tract Infections among Women in the Third World*. New York: International Women's Health Coalition.

Hatcher, R. A., et al. 1990. *Contraceptive Technology*. New York: Irvington Publishers.

Laga, M., et al. 1993. Non-ulcerative sexually transmitted diseases as risk factors for HIV-1 transmission in women: Results from a cohort study. *AIDS* 7 (1): 95–102.

Mala, G. 1987. Pelvic inflammatory disease. *Papua New Guinea Medical Journal* 30:1–2.

Meheus, A. 1992. Women's health: Importance of reproductive tract infections, pelvic inflammatory disease, and cervical cancer. In A. Germain, K. K. Holmes, P. Piot, and J. N. Wasserheit, eds., *Reproductive Tract Infections: Global Priorities for Women's Reproductive Health*, 61–91. New York: Plenum Press.

Over, M. and P. Piot. 1988. HIV infection and sexually transmitted diseases. In D. T. Jamison, W. H. Mosley, A. R. Meashan, and J. L. Bobadilla, eds., *Disease Control Priorities in Developing Countries*, 455–527. New York: Oxford University Press for the World Bank.

Program for Appropriate Technology in Health (PATH). 1992. STD Diagnostics Product Information Sheet. Seattle, Washington. Population Reports. June 1993. Controlling sexually transmitted diseases. Issues in World Health. Series L, 9.

Walker, G.J.A., et al. 1986. Maternal mortality in Jamaica. *Lancet* 1:486–88.

Wasserheit, J. N. and K. K. Holmes. 1992. Reproductive Tract Infections: Challenges for International Health Policy, Programs, and Research. In A. Germain, K. K. Holmes, P. Piot, and J. N. Wasserheit, eds., *Reproductive Tract Infections: Global Impact and Priorities for Women's Reproductive Health*, 7–33. New York: Plenum.

World Bank. 1992. *Social Indicators of Development 1991–92*. Washington, D.C.

13 | HIV and Breast-feeding: Informed Choice in the Face of Medical Ambiguity

CHLOE O'GARA AND ANNA C. MARTIN

> Congratulations and may you breastfeed well.
>
> —Traditional greeting for a new mother in Kigali, Rwanda, where nearly
> 30 percent of women attending prenatal consultations test positive for HIV.

For women in many societies childbearing and rearing are key to self-esteem, social value, strategic action, economic viability, and survival. Few women are willing to forego having children. Studies from New York to Kampala show that most HIV-positive or high-risk women bear children at the same rates as their noninfected sisters (Holman 1993; Allen et al. 1993; Lindan et al. 1991). HIV is just one factor in a multifaceted, culturally specific, and complicated reproductive decision.

Breast-feeding is an integral part of mammalian reproduction. It minimizes infant morbidity and mortality, especially in situations of poverty. It is the least expensive and best infant food. It maximizes infant brain development and maternal-infant interaction. It reduces maternal fertility and risk of reproductive cancers.

Yet breast-feeding can transmit HIV. Mothers face a terrible dilemma: they do not know whether breast-feeding improves or threatens their infants' survival odds. Unfortunately, no one can estimate precisely the risk of transmission associated with breast-feeding and HIV. Suggestions in the literature range from 7 to 14 percent attributable risk for women infected before giving birth (Nicoll, forthcoming; Ziegler 1993). The risk for transmission to the infant for "women who become infected in the breast-feeding period . . . [is] substantial" (WHO/UNICEF 1992). Although there is consensus that some transmission occurs, how it happens, to which mothers and which babies, and at what rates are still unknown. Today's estimates may be revised tomorrow.

Women and caregivers must compare the potential for HIV transmission to another unknown—the potential for other infant infections which breast-feeding would prevent. Although any threat of HIV is dangerous, bottle-feeding is also dangerous to babies. In New York City, twice as many bottle-fed babies die as breast-fed babies (Lederman 1992); in developing countries the relative risk of infant death attributable to bottle-feeding versus breast-feeding may be as high as twenty (Victora 1989).

In 1992 the World Health Organization issued a statement on breast-feeding and HIV:

> The breast-feeding of babies should be promoted and supported in all populations, irrespective of HIV infection rates. . . . Breast-feeding is a crucial element of child survival. A baby's risk of dying of AIDS through breast-feeding must be balanced against its risk of dying of other causes if not breast-fed. (WHO Press 1992)

The WHO guidance recognizes that in most developing countries infants of HIV-positive mothers are at greater risk of death from other diseases that breast-feeding prevents or mitigates than they are from HIV infection itself. For the great majority of infants in developing countries, the probabilities of survival are better with breast-feeding than with bottle-feeding. The mothers' health and well-being is likely to be better as well (Dunn et al. 1992; Heymann 1990; Hu, Heyward, and Byers 1992; Kennedy et al. 1990; Lederman 1992; Nicoll, forthcoming; Nicoll, Killewo, and Mgone 1990; Ruff et al. 1992; Ryder et al. 1989).

However, the WHO statement goes on to say:

> On the other hand, in settings where the main cause of death during infancy is not infectious diseases and the infant mortality rate is low, the consultation concluded that the usual advice to pregnant women known to be infected with HIV should be to use a safe feeding alternative for their baby rather than breast-feed. (WHO Press 1992)

The statement essentially instructs poor women to breast-feed and wealthy women to bottle-feed. Health service providers have the task of assessing each woman's situation, deciding whether risks of bottle-feeding outweigh the unknown risks of breast-feeding by an HIV-positive woman, and counseling a mother accordingly.

Evidence for Transmission of HIV via Breast-feeding

Transmission of HIV from an infected mother to her infant occurs in utero, during birth, and possibly postnatally via breast milk. No other mechanisms of vertical transmission have been plausibly documented.

Current knowledge suggests that overall between 20 and 40 percent (Dunn et al. 1992) of infants of HIV-infected mothers will be infected. Reported rates of transmission among breast-feeding mother-infant dyads vary from 18 to 52 percent. Rates among bottle-fed infants in the same studies vary from 25 to 33 percent (Ruff 1992). These ranges reflect variability across populations. They also reflect diagnostic uncertainty about which infants are infected.

Currently it is estimated that more than a million children have been infected with HIV-1, most of whom have acquired the infection from their mothers (Ruff et al. 1992). Generally, infants born to seropositive mothers in impoverished circumstances are infected more frequently than infants in higher-income situations. Most infants living in poverty in the developing world are breast-fed. Many infants born in wealthy industrialized countries are not breast-fed. Poverty and breast-feeding are confounded for analytic purposes. Nevertheless, Peckham (1993) and Dunn et al. (1992) suggest that differences in transmission rates between developing and industrialized countries are a result of different rates of breast-feeding. They also cite higher transmission rates among a small cohort of breast-feeding mothers in the European Collaborative Study (1992) to support this interpretation. They estimate the additional risk of transmission attributable to breast-feeding by a mother with established infection to be approximately 15 percent.

Current diagnostic tools cannot identify with certainty which infants are infected in utero or at birth since maternal antibodies confound results. Detection of p24 antigen in newborns offers new possibilities for newborn diagnosis, but even this new approach appears to be only 80 percent accurate (Boodman 1993). We cannot expect in the near future that clinical data will solve this puzzle.

Evidence for transmission of HIV via breast milk also is derived from twenty-two (Hira, Mangrola, and Mwale 1990; Ruff et al. 1993) individual case reports in which vertical transmission followed postnatal transfusions of mothers with HIV-contaminated blood or in which other circumstances led to a plausible interpretation of breast milk as the route of transmission. Infections of nursing infants appear to be most probable when they are breast-fed by a mother who is experiencing the viremia (explosive multiplication of the virus accompanied by flu-like symptoms) common shortly after infection occurs or during late-stage AIDS (Datta, Embree, and Kreiss 1992; Dunn et al. 1992; Lepage, van de Perre, and Msellati 1991; Rubini and Passman 1992; van de Perre, 1992).

There may be other cofactors for transmission such as specific feeding practices, nutritional status of mother or baby, or infant susceptibility. Research to date offers few clues. Published reports on HIV transmission in breast-fed infants do not characterize the kind of breast-feeding (exclusive, predominant, occasional) nor the duration of breast-feeding. They also fail to examine possible related but separate means of transmission, such as cracked nipples, thrush, or other trauma (see van de Perre et al. 1991; de Martino et al. 1992; Lepage et al. 1987, 1991; Datta et al. 1991, 1992). Information on maternal and infant characteristics or behaviors would be invaluable.

Giving breast milk substitutes—water, juices, liquids, or solids (as the breast-feeders in the European cohorts did)—might contribute to the transmission of HIV. Other foods decrease breast milk's ability to prevent the binding of viruses to cells in the infant gut. Laboratory studies have shown that factors in breast milk inhibit the binding of GP120 to the CD4 receptor (Newburg et al. 1992). It has also been suggested that since HIV is an acid labile virus and the introduction of breast milk substitutes into the infant gut decreases acidity, mixed feeding may increase the chances of transmission compared to that of exclusive breast-feeding (Arnold 1993). Furthermore, bottle-feeding sharply increases the incidence and severity of infant diarrhea and other diseases. These disrupt the mucosal integrity of the infant gut. Lesions may also occur with severe diarrhea. Thus mixed feeding—combining breast-feeding with bottle-feeding—may be a pattern that results in points of opportunistic entry for the HIV virus. These considerations suggest that if an HIV-positive woman breast-feeds, she should attempt to breast-feed exclusively until her infant absolutely requires food supplements.

HIV is carried in the cellular component of milk (Ruff 1992; van de Perre et al. 1993). Colostrum, the early yellowish milk produced for several days postpartum, has a much higher cellular content than later milk. Researchers are considering whether discarding colostrum may decrease the risk of HIV transmission (van de Perre, personal communication, 1993; Ruff, personal communication, 1994). On the other hand, colostrum provides essential nutrients for the first few days of life and contains a bifidus factor that contributes to the growth of a healthy lining in the infant gut.

Conducting research on colostrum would be extremely problematic. It is difficult to define the exact moment at which colostrum changes to mature milk; the length of this process is different for every woman. Withholding colostrum from a research cohort raises the questions of what to give infants during the first several days of life and whether trauma related to mixed feeding might increase their chances of morbidity and mortality from many causes, including HIV.

Unfortunately no studies of HIV have examined the quality and quantity of breast-feeding. Information on specific infant feeding practices would be invaluable. The difficulty of extracting such information from current studies appears insurmountable. In Rwanda (van de Perre 1991, and personal communication), sixteen women who were HIV-negative at the time of their infants' births seroconverted over the following eighteen months. These women came from upper-income urban households. Many women in this cohort gave both breast milk and bottled formula to their children (O'Gara and Martin 1992), which may have increased infant susceptibility to HIV. The intensity and duration of breast-feeding, bottle-feeding, and other food and fluid supplements were not recorded, and breast exams were not conducted. Eight of the sixteen infants seroconverted, all within the same three-month period as their mothers. Five of the mothers seroconverted during the first three months postpartum, as did four of their infants. These four infants therefore could have been infected in utero or during birth. Four infants seroconverted later than three months postpartum with no other risk factor than receiving breast milk. The mother of one infant who seroconverted at eighteen months had a severe case of mastitis (inflammation of the breast).

In the European study a subsample of 36 breast-fed infants was identified among 721 infants drawn from ten collaborating centers. All HIV-positive women were discouraged from breast-feeding. The overall vertical transmission rate from mothers to infants was 14.4 percent. Among the 36 who chose to breast-feed, 11, or 31 percent, converted within eighteen months. The median duration of breast-feeding in this group was four weeks, indicating that the infants were breast-fed and bottle-fed.

Design flaws weaken the infant feeding-related conclusions of the European study. The 36 breast-feeding subjects were not a random sample of the population. Who were these women, the 5 percent of the sample who chose to breast-feed despite strong recommendations from their health advisers to the contrary? How did they differ from the women in the sample who chose to bottle-feed? What was their stage of infection? Several cohorts were identified using different criteria. Those cohorts were combined for the breast-feeding and transmission analyses. This design seems questionable in light of the very small subsample of breast-feeders and the potential importance of stage of infection for HIV transmission via breast milk.

In a recent review of published studies to date, investigators from The Johns Hopkins University who are conducting research in Haiti concluded:

> Additional data are needed to guide decision making in this complex and often emotional area of public health policy. The available epidemiologic and virologic data regarding transmission of HIV-1 through breast-feeding are incomplete. . . . Until additional data become available, it will be difficult to assess accurately the risk of HIV-1 transmission through breast-feeding, and we must continue to base our recommendations for seropositive mothers on limited information. (Ruff et al. 1992)

Why Do Women Breast-feed?

Human reproduction begins at conception and ends when the young child ceases to suckle. Breast-feeding is integral to the process of successful mammalian reproduction. It is most beneficial when not diluted with other foods or fluids until the infant needs supplementation, usually at around six months of age (WHO/CDD 1992).

There are significant advantages to breast-feeding over substitutes for both mothers and babies. For mothers breast-feeding offers:

- *Reduced risk of reproductive cancers.* Women who breast-feed reduce their risk of breast, ovarian, and other reproductive cancers (Newcomb et al. 1994; Anonymous 1993; Rosenblatt and Thomas 1993; Wolff et al. 1993).
- *Longer birth intervals in the absence of contraceptive use.* Many demographers estimate that even today in most regions of the world, more months of birth spacing are attributable to breast-feeding than to any other factor, including all modern contraceptives combined (Gray et al. 1990; Israngkura et al. 1989; Labbok and Booher 1990).
- *Economy.* In Cameroon, feeding an infant on breast milk substitutes costs 382 percent of the average family income for one year (Cameroon National Breast-feeding Policy). Commercial substitutes to feed a Ugandan three-month-old infant for twenty-four hours would cost from 217 to 900 percent of the daily wage of a low level hospital worker (Cutting 1994).
- *Convenience.* For women who are not separated from their infants for long hours, breast-feeding is easier and more efficient than bottle-feeding. This is particularly the case when water is not available in the home or must be boiled.
- *Satisfaction.* Breast-feeding mothers bond emotionally with their infants. They enjoy the experience (Cunningham et al. 1981; Baume, Coreil, and Mukanjiwe 1994).
- *Respect.* In many cultures a woman is expected to breast-feed and is respected for doing so. Some breast-feeding mothers enjoy services from their household and community that may not be offered to them at any other time during their lives (O'Gara and Martin 1992; Baume et al. 1994).

Breast-feeding has many advantages for infants as well. Benefits to infants (and thus to their mothers) include:

- *Reduced incidence and severity of diarrheal disease, upper respiratory infection, otitis media, and diabetes* (Brown et al. 1989; Chandra 1979; Cunningham, Jelliffe, and Jelliffe 1981; Duncan et al. 1993; Feachem and Koblinsky 1984; Huffman and Combest 1990; Popkin 1990; Victora et al. 1989; Wright et al. 1989).
- *Better chances of survival.* The relative risk of death as a result of diarrhea for breast-fed infants versus infants not breast-fed ranges from 1:2 (Grosse 1993) to 1:20 (Victora et al. 1989).

- *Longer intervals before the next sibling.* Longer birth intervals correlate with improved maternal and infant nutrition, health, and survival rates (Labbok and Booher 1990).
- *Improved nutrition.* Breast milk is the best food for infants (Huffman and Combest 1990; Labbok and Booher 1990).
- *Higher Intelligence Quotients (IQ).* Breast milk stimulates brain development. Recent controlled studies of cognition of premature infants showed infants fed breast milk significantly outperformed those on breast milk substitutes (Lucas et al. 1992).
- *Cognitive, tactile, and social stimulation associated with higher intelligence, social adaptability, and satisfaction* (Jelliffe and Jelliffe 1978).

The infant factors add up to significant indirect benefits to mothers—greater joy and satisfaction, community approval, logistic support, savings of time and money, as well as being spared the grief of caring for sick or dying infants.

Breast-feeding significantly improves probabilities of survival for infants in circumstances where heavy investment in pediatric health care is not possible. Bottle-fed babies in industrial societies typically survive, but they do so with more medical intervention than is available to most mothers in the world. This is an important consideration for families where AIDS has already put pressure on human and financial resources.

Breast-feeding may improve survival of infants already infected by HIV (Tozzi 1992; Ryder et al. 1991). Since breast-feeding provides excellent nutrition and protects infants against incidence and severity of many illnesses (CDD/NUT 1993; van de Perre et al. 1993) this is not surprising. Acknowledging the public health significance of breast-feeding, WHO, UNICEF, national governments, and private voluntary organizations around the world have initiated programs to protect, promote, and support breast-feeding. UNICEF and WHO have launched the "Baby Friendly Hospital Initiative" (UNICEF 1994). The Surgeon General of the United States has set the goal that, by the year 2000, 70 percent of U.S. infants will be breast-fed. Countries as diverse as Honduras, Cameroon, Mexico, the Philippines, and Indonesia have adopted national breast-feeding policies and launched ambitious programs to improve breast-feeding practices.

Is Informed Choice Possible?

Women who want to become pregnant cannot easily avoid exposure to HIV, particularly if their partner is infected. There are no prevention technologies designed to meet their needs. The most empowering option for these women—

most of the world's women—is informed choice. This is as true for infant feed-ing as it is for sexual activity.

Fully informed choice about breast-feeding requires a better understanding than we have today of HIV transmission, maternal feeding behaviors, breast milk physiology, and infant variability. These are issues that the international research community and mothers will need to explore and learn about together. Models of mothers' decision-making strategies and their understanding of disease, rel-ative risks, and probability are needed.

Women making choices about infant feeding rarely know their own serosta-tus and virtually none know the serostatus of their infant at birth. Thus most women will never have the ability to make infant feeding decisions (any more than they can make decisions about sexual activity) based on knowledge of the serostatus of the principals involved. In the absence of knowledge about serosta-tus, however, women can make more or less informed choices about breast-feeding just as they do about sex. They need to know which infant feeding prac-tices are more or less risky and under what circumstances. However, virtually no information is available to inform women's choices about how to minimize risks for themselves or their infants after birth. In addition, much of the avail-able information is frightening, incomplete, and misleading.

Inaccurate and rather sensational reports about breast-feeding and HIV have appeared in the popular press. In late July 1992, following the AIDS conference in Amsterdam, NBC news ran a story on breast-feeding and HIV that concluded with the chilling statement: "Few poor mothers can afford formula, even though for many infants, breast-feeding has become a death sentence" (NBC Nightly News, 24 July 1992). Also in July 1992, at the Democratic National Conven-tion, a well-known wife of a TV personality explained that she had acquired HIV through a blood transfusion, and reported her tragic story of transmitting the virus to her first child through breast-feeding and to her second child in utero. None of these stories presented balanced information on the benefits of breast-feeding. None described why breast milk substitutes are more dangerous for babies in most of the developing world. And none provided useful information to help women make informed choices about infant feeding.

Research Issues

Most HIV-positive women in developing countries will have no choice but to breast-feed regardless of the results of any study. It is therefore critical to find out the relative risks of different feeding patterns.

Women need information on the outcomes of specific behaviors that are under their control. A verdict on whether HIV has *ever* been transmitted via breast-feeding is not information for action. Currently, research is not being conducted that will give mothers the information they need.

Research to date on HIV and breast-feeding has not focused on the critical features of infant feeding practices; it is therefore neither conclusive nor as pro-grammatically helpful as it might be. Future research can be designed to provide more information on breast-feeding and HIV that would be useful to women. Although a fully informed choice is not possible, a *better* informed choice should be. Questions to be asked include:

- What maternal factors (e.g., viremia, nutritional status, cracked nipples) play a role in transmission?
- What infant characteristics (e.g., prematurity, illness, lesions, morbidity, nutritional status) play a role?
- Does colostrum contribute disproportionately to transmission? If so, what are other appropriate ways to manage feeding in the first days of life?
- Does transmission occur to older infants? What are the relative risks and benefits of breast-feeding at three months? Six months? Twelve months? Twenty-four months?
- Is mixed feeding especially risky? If so, when should weaning occur and how should weaning be handled when a mother is HIV-positive?
- What are the best models on which to base decisions about the relative ben-efits versus risks of breast-feeding when mothers are HIV-seropositive?
- Does breast-feeding benefit the HIV-positive infant (infected in utero or during birth)?
- Does lactation affect the health of HIV-positive women?

Research and Ethical Issues

Research protocols to compare HIV transmission between bottle- and breast-fed cohorts raise complicated ethical and design issues. On the one hand, encouraging anyone to bottle-feed can result in infant exposures to a host of contaminants, allergies, and diseases. On the other hand, if breast milk or breast-feeding can transmit HIV, one cohort of infants will be exposed to that risk. Defining behaviors in such a design is also very tricky. Should exclusive breast-feeding be contrasted with exclusive bottle-feeding, even though neither pattern is the mode? If the bottle-fed cohort is provided with clean formula the results cannot be generalized to most of the world, yet it is clearly unethical to encourage poor women to bottle-feed without providing the means to do so. Most research is conducted in developing countries where populations do not have safe access to bottle-feeding as an option. Study participants and their com-munities will not benefit from research conducted in their midst. Support for bottle-feeding may have adverse negative demonstration effects. Recommending that any sector of a population *not* breast-feed fuels worries about breast milk. Researchers and policy makers need to proceed with caution. Nicoll (forthcoming) offers a thoughtful and comprehensive review of both ethical and interpretive questions related to infant feeding trials.

Evidence already suggests that research on HIV and breast-feeding poses hazards for subject populations. In Rwanda, for example, where studies on vertical transmission have been under way for several years, a feasibility study for a protocol comparing HIV transmission rates among exclusively breast-fed and exclusively bottle-fed infants reported that most urban-educated mothers associate breast-feeding with HIV transmission. This strongly held belief among a literate and relatively well-off cohort suggests that there has been an adverse effect on breast-feeding attitudes and practices.

Public Health Response

Public health policy and clinical recommendations are not always identical and cannot always be reconciled. This is particularly true when variables of gender and class affect treatment options. Breast-feeding by HIV-positive women is a health behavior in which both gender and class play explicit and critical roles. But what is unique about the response to this issue is that recommended infant feeding practices explicitly diverge for wealthy versus poor women who may be HIV-positive. Decades of investment into infant formula research ensure a "remedy" for wealthy women but not for poor women. Yet the most current information available indicates that a decline in the quantity or quality of breast-feeding in countries where HIV is most prevalent will result in a significant net increase in infant mortality even if breast-feeding transmits HIV at the highest rates that have been suggested (Grosse 1992; Hu 1992). Decades of research neglect mean that even wealthy women do not know what they give up when they decline to breast-feed nor what the real probabilities are that they are making the best choice for themselves or their infants.

The problems with WHO's two-tiered recommendation are staggering. Beyond the obvious ethical dilemma posed by an explicit double standard for health care, implementing this policy is simply impossible. The recommended course of action is clear for only a fraction of the world's mothers. Wealthy HIV-positive mothers should bottle-feed. Very poor HIV-positive mothers without access to good hygiene should breast-feed. Most women fall somewhere in-between.

Which course of action is recommended for the woman in a middle-income country who is monogamous but suspects that her husband is not? Is she "high risk"? Are her infant's chances for good health better with breast milk or bottles? Should the household bankrupt itself to purchase breast milk substitutes? What about her own health, economic future, emotional bond with her infant? What about her infant's social and cognitive development? What will the neighbors think if she does not breast-feed? If she does not use contraceptives and does not breast-feed, what about the impact on her health and family of a premature next pregnancy? The public health establishment has little to say to such a woman either about how to minimize her risk of contracting HIV or how to minimize the risk of mortality for her infant.

Unless women and their care providers are intensively educated about the probable outcomes of infant feeding options, it is possible that in the near future women who are positive or uncertain of their HIV status will try to avoid or (perhaps worse) reduce breast-feeding. Both critics and supporters of the current WHO policy agree that we need information on which to base education (Zeigler 1993). Today there is neither adequate knowledge, political will, nor funding for health education to empower women to make informed choices about infant feeding.

Breast-feeding as Women's Choice

Which strategies for management of breast-feeding might bring more comfort, control, and security to mothers who suspect they may be HIV-positive? Given all we do not know, a guiding rule for interactions with HIV-positive women of reproductive age should be *specificity is always appropriate*. Women want to know about risk factors they can control. Information needs to be widely disseminated and understood so that individual mothers are not daunted by complex issues that are difficult to weigh when they are overwhelmed with the birth of a new baby and knowledge of their HIV-status.

Information, guidelines, and participatory training are needed in order to:

- discourage mixed feeding (combining breast and bottle). Infants should get only breast milk to the exclusion of any other food or fluid for the first six months of life. This has long been a public health objective for its beneficial effects on infant morbidity and mortality as well as its impact on fertility. But if mothers have a clearer understanding of the increased potential for transmission of HIV that may accompany mixing other liquids and foods with breast milk, they might practice exclusive breast-feeding more rigorously.
- enlist families and communities to minimize workload and stresses on HIV-positive mothers and the probability of viremia while breast-feeding.

- alert women and men to the significance for the breast-feeding baby of HIV infection of a mother during lactation. This might lead to improved vigilance regarding women's possibility of exposure. If the probability of transmission is found to be highest via colostrum (a possibility that is not widely cited), consider discarding colostrum. Alternative feeding strategies for the first days of life would need to be researched.
- reinforce women's expertise to spot cracks and fissures in the breast as well as early signs of mastitis. Teach women how to express milk from the affected breast while continuing to breast-feed from the healthy breast.
- respond promptly to minimize dangers. Research whether brief suspension of breast-feeding by HIV-positive mothers may be appropriate during bouts of infant diarrhea or when the infant shows mucosal lesions of any kind.
- delay introduction of supplements and wean quickly once supplementation is needed if transmission is found in the later months of breast-feeding. Help mothers and others in the community to understand the relationship between frequent suckling and increased milk production in order to extend exclusive breast-feeding as long as possible and ensure good infant nutrition.
- assist families and mothers who decide not to breast-feed to calculate their ability to purchase breast milk substitutes for at least a year. Also help them to assess the quality of water sources, environmental hygiene, and access to pediatric care as they weigh their options.

We lack a solid information base to support these recommendations, but they are based on the best available evidence. Breast-feeding is a necessity for most mothers and babies. Rather than discourage them, we need to explore with them how to modify practices to minimize risk.

This century we have already experienced the results of discouraging breast-feeding. The creation of breast milk substitutes, billed as scientifically superior "formulas," was adopted by the medical community and women alike as convenient and healthy food for infants. In most cases women have continued to breast-feed but unnecessarily "supplement" their breast milk with formula substitutes. Yet millions of infants have died and will die because of improper use of breast milk substitutes. This trend will be exacerbated if supplementation expands among mothers frightened of HIV. The most prevalent pattern of infant feeding—supplementation of breast milk with other milks, liquids, and foods—may be the worst infant feeding pattern of all in a world of HIV.

Work at the local level by women in communities is essential to develop feasible alternatives to mixed infant feeding practices in each sociocultural context. Mothers themselves will find solutions to this problem if they have good information and support.

REFERENCES

Allen, S., et al. 1993. Pregnancy and contraception use among urban Rwandan women after HIV testing and counseling. *American Journal of Public Health* 83 (5): 705–709.

Anonymous. 1993. Breast feeding and risk of breast cancer in young women. *BMJ* 307 (6895): 17–20.

Arnold, Lois. HIV and breast milk: What it means for milk banks. 1993. *Journal of Human Lactation* 9 (1): 47–48.

Baume, C., J. Coreil, and L. Mukanjiwe. 1994. *Qualitative Research on Breastfeeding in Kibungo and Gitarama Provinces, Rwanda*. Wellstart International's Expanded Promotion of Breastfeeding (EPB) Program, January.

Boodman, Sandra. 1993. New test identifies HIV-infected newborns. *The Washington Post*, February 9, p. G24.

Brown, K. H., et al. 1989. Infant feeding practices and their relationship with diarrheal and other diseases in Huascar (Lima), Peru. *Pediatrics* 83 (1): 31–40.

Chandra, R. K. 1979. Prospective studies of the effect of breast-feeding on incidence of infection and allergy. *Acta Paediatrica Scandanavia* 68:691–94.

Cunningham, Allan, D. Jelliffe, and P. Jelliffe. 1981. Breast-feeding and health in the 1980s: A global epidemiologic review. *Journal of Pediatrics* 118:659–66.

Cutting, William. 1994. Breastfeeding and HIV in African Countries. Letter to the editor. *Lancet* 343:362.

Datta, P., et al. 1991. Perinatal HIV transmission in Nairobi, Kenya: Five-year follow-up. Abstract MC.3, prepared for the Seventh International Conference on AIDS, Florence, Italy.

Datta P., J. E. Embree, and J. K. Kreiss. 1992. Resumption of breast-feeding in later childhood: A risk factor for mother-to-child immunodeficiency virus type 1 transmission. *Pediatric Infectious Disease Journal* 11:974–76.

De Martino, M., et al. 1992. HIV transmission through breast milk: Appraisal of risk according to duration of feeding. *AIDS* 6:991–97.

Duncan, B., et al. 1993. Exclusive breast-feeding for at least four months protects against otitis media. *Pediatrics* 91:867–72.

Dunn, D. T., et al. 1992. Risk of human immunodeficiency virus type 1 transmission through breastfeeding. *Lancet* 340:585–88.

European Collaborative Study (ECS). 1992. Risk factors for mother-to-child transmission of HIV-1. *Lancet* 339:1007–12.

Feachem, R. G. and M. A. Koblinsky. 1984. Interventions for the control of diarrheal diseases among young children: Promotion of breast-feeding. *Bulletin of the World Health Organization* 62:271–91.

Gray, R. H., et al. 1990. The risk of ovulation during lactation. *Lancet* 335 (8680): 25–29.

Grosse, Scott. 1993. *Modeling the Effects of Breastfeeding and HIV-1 on Child Survival in Rwanda*. Ann Arbor: Population Planning and International Health, School of Public Health, University of Michigan.

Heymann, S. J. 1990. Modeling the impact of breast-feeding by HIV-infected women on child survival. *American Journal of Public Health* 80:1305–09.

Hira, S. K., U. G. Mangrola, and C. Mwale. 1990. Apparent vertical transmission of human immunodeficiency virus type 1 by breast-feeding in Zambia. *Journal of Pediatrics* 117:421–24.

Holman, Susan. 1993. Special Considerations in HIV Research in Pregnant Women: Considerations from the Perinatal HIV Transmission Study at SUNY-Health Science Center, Brooklyn. Oral presentation at the National Institutes for Health meeting on "Ethical Considerations in Research on Breastfeeding and the Vertical Transmission of HIV," June.

Hu, D. J., W. L. Heyward, and R. H. Byers. 1992. HIV infection and breast-feeding: Policy implications through a decision analysis model. *AIDS* 6:1505–13.

Huffman, S. L. and C. Combest. 1990. Role of breastfeeding in the prevention and treatment of diarrhoea. *Journal of Diarrhoeal Diseases Research* 8:68–81.

Huffman, S. L., et al. 1992. *Breastfeeding: A Natural Resource for Food Security*. Washington, D.C.: Wellstart, Expanded Promotion of Breastfeeding (EPB) Program.

Israngkura, B., et al. 1989. Breastfeeding and return to ovulation in Bangkok. *International Journal of Obstetrics and Gynecology* 30 (4): 335–42.

Jelliffe, D. B. and E. F. P. Jelliffe. 1978. Mother-infant interactions. In D. B. Jelliffe and E. F. P. Jelliffe, eds., *Human Milk and the Modern World*, 142–160. Oxford: Oxford University Press.

Kennedy, Katherine, J. A. Fortney, and M. G. Bonhomme. 1990. Do the benefits of breastfeeding outweigh the risk of postnatal transmission of HIV via breastmilk? *Tropical Doctor* 20:25–29.

Labbok, M. and P. Booher. 1990. *Breastfeeding: Protecting a Natural Resource*. Washington, D.C.: The Institute for International Studies in Natural Family Planning.

Lederman, Sally A. 1992. Estimating infant mortality from human immunodeficiency virus and other causes in breast-feeding and bottle-feeding populations. *Pediatrics* 89:290–96.

Lepage, P., et al. 1987. Postnatal transmission of HIV from mother to child. Letter. *Lancet* 2 (8555): 400.

Lepage P., C. Munyanakazi, and P. Hennart. 1981. Breastfeeding and hospital mortality in children in rural Rwanda. Letter. *Lancet* 1 (8268): 403.

Lepage, P., P. van de Perre, and P. Msellati. 1991. Natural history of HIV-1 infection in children in Rwanda: A prospective cohort study. International Conference on AIDS, Florence.

Lindan, Christina, et al. 1991. Knowledge, attitudes, and perceived risk of AIDS among urban Rwandan women: Relationship to HIV infection and behavior change. *AIDS* 5:993–1002.

Lucas, A., et al. 1992. Breast milk and subsequent intelligence quotient in children born preterm. *Lancet* 339:261–64.

Newburg, David S., et al. 1992. A human milk factor inhibits binding of human immunodeficiency virus to the CD4 receptor. *Pediatric Research* 31 (1): 22–28.

Newcomb, P., et al. 1994. Lactation and a reduced risk of premenopausal breast cancer. *New England Journal of Medicine* 330 (2): 81–87.

Nicoll, Angus. Forthcoming. International Research on Transmission of HIV-1 in Relation to Breastfeeding: Notes from a Public Health Perspective. Distributed at the National Institutes for Health meeting on "Ethical Considerations in Research on Breastfeeding and the Vertical Transmission of HIV," June 1993.

Nicoll, A., J. Z. Killewo, and C. Mgone. 1990. HIV and infant feeding practices: Epidemiological implications for sub-Saharan African countries. *AIDS* 4:661–65.

O'Gara, C. and A. Martin. 1992. *Breastfeeding Assessment for Rwanda*. Wellstart International Expanded Promotion of Breastfeeding (EPB) Program, May.

Peckham, C. S. 1993. Mother-to-Child Transmission of HIV: Risk Factors and Timing. International Conference on AIDS, Amsterdam. Abstract PS-04–2.

Popkin, B. 1990. Breastfeeding and diarrheal morbidity. *Pediatrics* 86:874–82.

Rosenblatt, K. and D. B. Thomas. 1993. Lactation and the risk of epithelial ovarian cancer. *International Journal of Epidemiology* 22:192–97.

Rubini, N. and L. J. Passman. 1992. Transmission of human immunodeficiency virus infection from a newly infected mother to her two-year-old child by breastfeeding. *Pediatric Infectious Disease Journal* 11:682–83.

Ruff, A., et al. 1992. Breastfeeding and maternal-infant transmission of human immunodeficiency virus type 1. *Journal of Pediatrics* 121:325–29.

Ryder, R. W., et al. 1989. Perinatal transmission of the human immunodeficiency virus type 1 to infants of seropositive women in Zaire. *New England Journal of Medicine* 320:1637–42.

Ryder, R. W., et al. 1991. Evidence from Zaire that breast-feeding by HIV-1 seropositive mothers is not a major route for perinatal HIV-1 transmission but does decrease morbidity. *AIDS* 5:709–14.

UNICEF. 1994. *The Progress of Nations*. New York: UNICEF.

Van de Perre, Philippe. 1992. *Preventable Patterns of HIV-1 Transmission in Rwanda*. Brussels: School of Medicine of the Free University of Brussels.

Van de Perre, Phillippe, et al. 1991. Postnatal transmission of human immunodeficiency virus type 1 from mother to infant. *New England Journal of Medicine* 325 (August): 593–98.

Van de Perre, Philippe, et al. 1993. Infective and anti-infective properties of breast milk from HIV-1 infected women. *Lancet* 341 (April): 914–18.

Victora, Cesar G., et al. 1989. Infant feeding and deaths due to diarrhea: A case control study. *American Journal of Epidemiology* 129:1032–41.

WHO Press. 1992. HIV and Breastfeeding. Press Release WHO/30, May 4.

WHO/UNICEF. 1992. Consultative Meeting of April 30—May 1. Statement on breast-feeding and HIV. *Weekly Epidemiological Record*, 177–84.

Wolff, M., et al. 1993. Blood levels of organochlorine residues and risk of breast cancer. *Journal of the National Cancer Institute* 85:648–52.

Wright, A. L., et al. 1989. Breastfeeding and lower respiratory tract illness in the first year of life. *BMJ* 299:946–49.

Zeigler, John B. 1993. Commentary: Breastfeeding and HIV. *Lancet* 342:1435–36.

14 | Women, Children, and HIV/AIDS

CARRIE AUER

Shirley waits in the clinic exam room quietly watching her two young children, Kendra (four years old) and Orlando (three years old), running and playing around the clinic with the other children. They laugh as they tumble over a giant teddy bear and engage in a game of "tickling tag" with a volunteer. Shirley cracks a slight smile and tears form in her eyes. "I just cannot believe this is happening, no sir, just cannot. It is like a nightmare you are never going to wake up from." Shirley shakes her head as tears roll down her cheeks. She looks more tired and depressed than usual. Eighteen months ago Shirley was hospitalized for an unknown respiratory illness. Doctors tested her for HIV, and she was found to be positive. Shock and disbelief were her reactions. She has not been promiscuous nor engaged in drug use. She has been married for the past five years and never strayed. Her husband refuses to be tested. On the advice of the health care workers, Shirley had Kendra and Orlando tested. Both are HIV-positive and in the early stages of AIDS. They are referred to a pediatric infectious diseases clinic at a major medical center where their care is now being coordinated. What once had been a simple, carefree life has now turned into unending medical appointments, medications, and fear.[1]

Situations like that of Shirley and her children are becoming increasingly common as HIV/AIDS affects more women and children worldwide. HIV and AIDS continue to rise among the world population at an alarming rate, especially among women of child-bearing age. For example, more than 60 percent of infected persons in Uganda are women (World Development Report 1993), and this pattern is becoming more common in other countries as well. Because mother-to-infant transmission represents the most frequent cause of pediatric

HIV infection, the distribution of HIV/AIDS in children will be shaped largely by patterns of HIV infection in women.

Families affected by HIV disease and AIDS often face unique social stress and an absence of community support that is usually available to individuals with life-threatening illnesses. HIV/AIDS can evoke such reactions as discrimination, isolation, social ostracism, public fear and ignorance regarding the nature and transmission of HIV, and stigma and fear of physical and mental disability (Wierner and Septimus 1994). In addition to these types of social stress, many families must deal with the additional burdens of poverty, limited housing services, inadequate health care, and in some instances problems associated with illicit drug use. In the United States over 80 percent of families of HIV-infected children are from minority backgrounds (Rogers et al. 1987), most are from families with little or no economic resources (Arno and Lee 1987), and most women become infected through intravenous (IV) drug use or by having sex with men who are IV drug users. In addition, generally more than one adult member in the family is either infected or ill, further limiting the family's ability to care for their children.

Children in families with HIV/AIDS face many risk factors (such as poverty, prenatal drug exposure, etc.) and are at multiple risk for poor developmental outcome whether or not they themselves are found to be HIV-positive. Intervention approaches must address the range of child and family needs, both biological and environmental. The effects of HIV disease on child development and treatment of affected children are mediated by the complex family lives and needs associated with the disease. An HIV-infected baby most often means an infected mother, which has profound implications for the children's quality of life: a sick parent(s), the death of a parent(s), isolation from extended family and lack of supportive care from the extended family, community fear, and possible placement outside the home. HIV/AIDS not only affects those within the immediate family, but also affects the extended family and the community. To understand fully how HIV/AIDS affects children, women, families, and communities, I discuss the scope of the problem, discuss mother-to-child transmission, and treat the characteristics and treatment of pediatric HIV/AIDS as context for a discussion of the psychosocial impact of HIV/AIDS on infected and noninfected children, women, families, and communities.

Transmission and Prevalence of Pediatric HIV/AIDS

Wanjiku, a young mother from a rural village, sits waiting in the health clinic for the local health care worker to see her young baby. This is the fifth visit she has had to make to the clinic in the last few months. Her small baby suffers from continual

diarrhea and a persistent fever. He has been sick for the past several weeks. Noth-
ing she does seems to help her infant get any better. Now her baby has developed
oral thrush and has difficulty nursing.Wanjiku is greatly concerned about his small
size and inability to keep food down. Surely there must be something they can do
to help her.Wanjiku has heard about the awful illness that has caused the death of
so many people she knows. She cannot believe that her infant could possibly have
this same illness. How could he have contracted it? She has heard that some chil-
dren can get if from their mothers. But she feels fine.What can she do? Her husband
and family are so proud of her son. She looks at him and wonders what kind of
future he will have. She imagines that he will go to school and have a good job some
day.Things starting out this way is surely a bad omen. She hopes the health worker
will be able to help her baby.

Transmission

Pediatric HIV infection occurs in three ways: (1) vertical transmission from
mother to infant (prenatally, perinatally, or postnatally); (2) transmission from
contaminated blood or blood products, especially in countries where the blood
supply is not routinely screened; and (3) sexual transmission through sexual
abuse or sexual activity. It is believed that most infection occurs late in pregnancy or during labor and delivery, when the likelihood of the infant coming
into contact with contaminated blood is higher. However, evidence is growing
that infection occurs during the prenatal period, though at this time the mechanisms are unclear (Oxtoby 1994).

Postnatally, HIV transmission from mother to child has been linked to breast-
feeding (see article 13 in this volume, "HIV and Breast-feeding," by O'Gara and
Martin, and see Oxtoby 1988). There have been case reports of HIV transmission to nursing infants. It is believed that when transmission occurred through
breast milk, the women had their primary infection after the child's birth or the
infants were nursed by wet nurses unrelated to them (Oxtoby 1988). As
O'Gara and Martin observe, it has been very difficult to determine the rate of
transmission from the chronically infected woman to her nursing newborn
because of difficulties in diagnosing infection at birth and in separating prenatal
from postnatal transmission.

The possibility of HIV transmission through breast milk is of great concern,
especially in Africa, Asia, Latin America, and the Caribbean where breast-feeding is the preferred choice of infant feeding (see article 13 for further discussion
of breast-feeding). The mortality rates of nonbreast-fed infants in developing
countries are two to five times higher than those of breast-fed infants (Quinn,
Ruff, and Halsey 1994). The World Health Organization (WHO) recommends

that in areas where infectious diseases are the predominant causes of infant mortality, women continue to breast-feed their infants regardless of their HIV status. However, in areas where infectious diseases are not the predominant cause of infant mortality, women with HIV infection are advised not to breast-feed their infants.

The concern of infection from contaminated blood or blood products has decreased in most industrialized Western countries. Fewer cases of transfusion-related AIDS occur in adults and children in these countries because of the use of serologic tests for HIV that are used to screen blood and blood products routinely. In areas where blood is not routinely screened, such as sub-Saharan Africa, transmission from blood and blood products continues. As many as 10 percent of cases of HIV infection in both adults and children are estimated to be the result of exposure to blood given for medical indications. Other blood-related exposures, such as circumcision, scarification, and contaminated or reused needles and syringes are believed to account for less than 1 percent of cases (Goldfarb 1993).

Prevalence

Perinatal HIV transmission rates appear to vary between populations. Several African studies suggest that up to 40–50 percent of infants born to HIV-infected women may become infected (Goldfarb 1993). Transmission rates from a European collaborative study (1991) were estimated to be under 20 percent, and U.S. rates have been estimated to be about 30 percent. It is still unknown which specific factors predispose a child to transmission of HIV infection from the mother, and the factors are thought to be complex. Several working theories suggest that the severity of illness in the mother may be a factor, as well as the genetic makeup of the child and the strain of the virus.

Pediatric AIDS accounts for as much as 15–20 percent of all AIDS cases in developing countries, whereas in developed countries, pediatric AIDS accounts for 2 percent of all reported AIDS cases (Quinn, Ruff, and Halsey 1994). This is partly because a greater proportion of women of reproductive age have been infected with HIV in developing countries. The number of children who are HIV-infected and die each year of HIV disease and AIDS is increasing. In 1990, 58,000 deaths in children from birth to age four were caused by HIV; in persons five and older, 233,000 deaths were caused by HIV (World Development Report 1993). The majority of these deaths occurred in sub-Saharan Africa. By 1992, 450,000 AIDS cases were reported to the World Health Organization but about 1.5 million AIDS cases are thought to have occurred, including 500,000 in children (WHO 1992).

Maternal mortality directly affects infant survival. Infants whose mothers die have a 95 percent chance of dying within the first year of life. Projections have recently been made regarding the substantial impact of mother-to-infant transmission of HIV on the mortality of children under five years of age. For example, in a population where 10 percent of the women are infected with HIV, and given a 25 percent perinatal transmission rate, the under-five mortality rate will be increased by 18 percent. This increase will reach 36 percent in a population where 20 percent of women are HIV-infected; thus, if the under-five mortality rate is 100 per 1,000 live births without HIV infection, an additional 36 deaths per 1,000 will be because of HIV, giving a rate of 136/1,000 (Guidotti and Mann 1990).

Diagnosis

Perinatal risk of HIV transmission is hard to estimate because of the difficulty in diagnosing infection in the newborn period. Advances in technological developments in HIV research have increased the ability to correctly diagnose HIV infection in infants. However, many of these are highly specialized, costly, and available only at major medical centers.

Several new technologies are being developed that will likely improve the precision of early diagnosis in perinatal transmission: the polymerase chain reaction (PCR) and viral cultures. Studies evaluating the use of PCR for early diagnosis of HIV infection in infants have shown that approximately 30–50 percent of HIV-infected infants will test positive around the time of birth. This percentage increases to nearly 100 percent by one to three months of age (Rogers, Schochetman, and Hoff 1994). PCR is more widely available, can be done at most hospitals, and is less expensive than viral cultures. However, PCR does result in more false-positives. Viral cultures used for diagnosis of infection are costly, technically difficult, and may be negative early in infection (Goldfarb 1993).

The most common method used for detecting the presence of HIV in the blood is serologic tests such as the Elisa or Western blot, which look for the presence of HIV antibodies. When used with adults, these two tests are highly reliable. However, serologic tests are unreliable with children under eighteen months of age because passively transferred maternal antibodies may still be present in their blood. After eighteen months, children tend to slough off maternal antibodies and develop their own. For children under eighteen months of age, the use of PCR or viral cultures is better for early diagnosis.

Parents who do not have access to one of the more advanced diagnostic technologies must often wait eighteen months to find out if their child is truly HIV-positive. If HIV infection is suspected and a child is frequently ill, it can be very stressful to cope with illnesses not knowing whether they are HIV-related (van de Perre et al. 1991). Uncertainty is present all the time and continuing support is needed. Health care staff and support organizations are crucial at this time. There may be many misunderstandings about HIV disease, how infection occurs, and what this means to women in caring for their children. Women need to be educated about HIV/AIDS, how transmission occurs, what tools are being used to diagnose infection status, and what this means for caretaking.

Women and Issues of Choice

A woman's reproductive choices may not be readily influenced by the knowledge of her own HIV status and the possibility that she may pass the infection on to her child. Other factors that have greater influence over a woman's decision to carry a pregnancy to term are (1) life demands, and (2) the desire to have children. In many countries, having children is fundamental to a woman's role in society (Lamptey and Finger 1990). In many societies adults depend on their children to provide for them in their old age, and having many children is seen as a necessity and holds high value within the society. Because children with HIV infection are more likely to die within the first year of life, some women with HIV express the determination to have even more children than they might otherwise have had to ensure that some survive (Temmerman et al. 1990). In communities where the infant mortality rate is 10–30 percent, this is not an uncommon perspective. The greater the perception of infant mortality, the more a woman may feel she has to take her chances to ensure that a child will survive (Williams 1990). Reports from UNICEF (1994) indicate that a one-in-three risk of having a child with HIV/AIDS may not seem high when compared to a one-in-four chance of a child dying before the age of five from other health problems. In Haiti, for example, pregnancy was found to be as common in women with AIDS as those who did not have HIV/AIDS or who knew they were HIV-positive (UNICEF 1994).

Should a woman's choice to have a child be limited by the fear of passing HIV onto her child? Women need options that will allow them freedom of choice when it comes to having children. Advancements in the treatment of HIV/AIDS may provide alternatives for women, as illustrated in the following vignette.

> *With husky voices and teary eyes, Denise and her husband Jim explain: "Faith, we're calling her Faith. We thought it was an appropriate name and it's how we feel." They are at the pediatric infectious diseases clinic for the first time since Faith was born. Denise was identified as being HIV-positive early in her pregnancy. The health*

clinic she attended offered anonymous screening for all pregnant women, and she decided to be screened. She had no reason to believe she would be positive. She had had a couple of sexual relationships before her marriage and did not use drugs. Denise simply wanted to put her mind at ease. When Denise learned the results she was devastated. She and Jim struggled with the decision to carry her pregnancy to term, knowing that their child could be infected with HIV. When the doctors offered them an opportunity to participate in a new study for pregnant women with HIV that would provide treatment to reduce the chance of transmitting the virus to their child, they jumped at the chance. They were willing to try anything that would reduce the risk of their child becoming infected. Denise and Jim were both thankful that Jim's test results were negative. "Who would be there for Faith if we both were HIV-positive? It gives me some peace of mind knowing he will be around but I regret knowing I won't be able to see her grow up!" Denise said, sobbing in her husband's arms. Faith will be followed for two years. They may know as early as six months if Faith is infected with HIV; until then all they can do is wait and have faith that all will turn out well.

Until recently, Denise and her husband Jim would not have been given any additional hope that their daughter might not be among the 30 percent of children who become infected from their mothers. It was thought to be impossible to prevent the transmission of HIV from an infected woman to her child. However, a study conducted by the AIDS Clinical Trials Group (ACTG) (Connor et al. 1994) in the United States shows that when antiretroviral therapy is given during pregnancy to an infected woman and then given to her child for the first six weeks of life, infection rates are significantly reduced. The infection rate in the group that received antiretroviral therapy was 8 percent, and in the control group the infection rate was 25 percent (Connor et al. 1994). This translates into a relative reduction of 67.5 percent in the risk of HIV transmission. Although this new finding provides hope and may increase the options available to women who have HIV/AIDS, prohibitive costs of antiretroviral drugs and medical care in general are but two of the factors that will create barriers for women and their unborn children in receiving treatment.

HIV/AIDS in Children

Thomas struggled to his feet with the help of his walker, smiling and laughing as everyone looked on and cheered. He was now almost two years old and able to stand on his own for the first time. It had been a long haul for his mother and grandmother. Thomas was very sick his first fourteen months of life. His physical development was slow, and he showed delays of up to eight months on developmental evaluations. Thomas was often cranky and would cry if anyone tried to hold him except his mother or grandmother. He was a difficult child to examine. Within the first few months of his life, doctors had diagnosed AIDS. He was hospitalized shortly after birth for respiratory infections. At that time it was thought he would not survive very long. He was given antiretroviral medication and other prophylaxis treatment for infections. He showed some improvement initially but over time did not improve very much. The medical team then decided to change his medication, and since that time he has made great progress. His developmental evaluations now show only delays in his motor skills. He is talking and seems to be much happier. He likes to play with other children and will let others hold him. His mother is very proud of his accomplishments and says he is much easier to handle at home. She says he tries to run away from her now that he can walk with his walker. His grandmother is simply exasperated by him. "He thinks he's so smart. He sticks his tongue out and teases me so! I could just squeeze him to death! We love him so much!" She knows that someday she may have to care for him herself. Her daughter does not always take good care of herself. Instead she fusses after Thomas. For now, they know that they have overcome great difficulties and Thomas is doing better. It has been difficult at times, and it may be difficult again. For now they just want to enjoy Thomas and the wonderful child he has become.

Symptomatology

Thomas is among the growing number of children identified as having HIV/AIDS since pediatric AIDS was first reported in 1982. Since then, as more has been learned about perinatal transmission of HIV, the importance of the AIDS pandemic to maternal and child health workers has become obvious. Diagnosing pediatric AIDS in both industrialized and poor countries has met with the same difficulties as for adults in poor countries where the availability of diagnostic tools is limited.

The World Health Organization established a clinical case definition for pediatric AIDS. A child is diagnosed with AIDS who has both of the following major signs:

- Weight loss or failure to thrive;
- Chronic diarrhea or fever (each must be present for more than one month);

and these major signs are associated with at least two of the following minor signs:

- Generalized lymphadenopathy;
- Repeated common infections (e.g., otitis media);
- Generalized dermatitis;
- Persistent cough;
- Confirmed maternal HIV infection;

and these signs appear in the absence of any known immunosuppression such as cancer or severe malnutrition of other recognized etiology (Pizzo and Wilfert 1991).

There is still difficulty in identifying infected children without the use of laboratory tests because many symptoms resemble common childhood illnesses. It is only after efforts to treat a repeatedly sick child fail that medical practitioners may conclude that the child has HIV/AIDS.

Disease Progression

HIV/AIDS progresses at varying rates among children. In some children with HIV/AIDS the disease may progress quickly: the children are beset by severe illnesses and live only a short time. Other children may be healthy for years and deteriorate slowly, experiencing milder illnesses (Sokal-Gutierrez, Vaughn-Edmonds, and Villarreal 1993). In general, perinatal HIV infection is asymptomatic at birth, although the newborn may demonstrate symptoms of other problems such as prenatal drug exposure or prematurity (Brouwers et al. 1991).

Symptoms may begin to develop over the first few months of life. A recent prospective study showed that 50 percent of HIV-infected babies experienced symptoms by twelve months of age, 78 percent were diagnosed with AIDS by two years of age, and 50 percent died by three years of age. Although the prognosis for many children with HIV is poor, some perinatally infected children have lived to twelve years of age (Scott et al. 1989). The life expectancy of some infants with HIV/AIDS has been prolonged with advances in early treatment such as antiretroviral therapy and the use of prophylaxis drugs for opportunistic infections, which are a major cause of mortality for some infants with HIV/AIDS.

For children in nonindustrialized countries, treatment of recurrent infections and diarrhea is difficult to obtain and these diseases can be life-threatening. HIV-infected children are two to seven times more likely to contract diarrhea than noninfected children, and oral rehydration is not as effective when the child is HIV-infected (World Development Report 1993). The prognosis for children with HIV/AIDS in developing countries is worse than the prognosis for children in developed countries where access to appropriate medical care is more likely.

Caretaking

Children with HIV/AIDS present many caretaking challenges to their families. The course of HIV/AIDS is variable between children and within the same child over time. Children can have healthy periods in which they can be cared for at home and express mild effects. At other times, children can be sick, have disabling complications requiring intensive care, usually hospitalization.

The care of children with HIV/AIDS is further complicated by developmental delay or regression as they become more medically fragile. Reports suggest that 60–90 percent of children infected with HIV will have manifestations of developmental delay (Belman et al. 1988; Spiegel and Mayers 1991). Malnutrition and general malaise owing to illness also can affect children's development. These problems can occur in addition to the effects of perinatal drug exposure and caretaking dysfunction in families where caretakers are using illicit drugs.

> *Arnella lay on the exam table screaming, her arms and legs flailing. It is difficult for her to return to a calm state. "Once she gets going, she's out of here," her foster mother reports. "I really need some help in calming her down." The developmental specialist talks with Arnella's foster mother and shows her ways to help Arnella calm down. Arnella's foster mother learns how to swaddle her and to respond in nonintrusive ways, using one intervention at a time so she does not overstimulate her. Not only is Arnella HIV-positive, she also was exposed to drugs prenatally. Her biological mother used crack cocaine and drank heavily. Arnella displays common signs of prenatal drug exposure. She is either "screaming her head off" or "out like a light," as her foster mother describes it. She is beginning to have longer periods of quiet, alert states where she smiles and is easier to handle. Her foster mother is frustrated by Arnella's ups and downs and it makes caretaking more difficult. She never knows what may upset her.*

When prenatal drug exposure is involved, as in Arnella's case, caretaking can become very challenging. Caregivers not only have to deal with the factors related to HIV/AIDS, but they also must take on the additional challenges presented by some children exposed to drugs prenatally. This can range from mild effects to more severe ones such as premature birth, low birth weight, developmental delays, and wide-ranging behaviors. Some infants prenatally exposed to drugs can manifest disorganized behaviors that are difficult for caretakers to understand (Johnson and Rosen 1990). For example, some infants, like Arnella, have difficulty maintaining an alert state and may "shut down" during interaction. Infants also may be irritable or lethargic.

Young children depend on their caregivers to meet their daily and developmental needs. However, if the caregiving environment is compromised, for example, by the caretaker's use of illicit drugs, the child's development is challenged as well. In cases like Arnella's, children may be removed from the biological mother and placed in foster care. Drug use by the mother does not automatically mean she will be incapable of providing appropriate care for her children. However, in most instances, the chaotic life-style that goes with drug use can place children in compromising environments. For children with HIV/AIDS, this can be especially detrimental if appropriate medical care is jeopardized.

The physiological effects of HIV/AIDS on children, as well as the psychological effects, make caretaking an extra challenge drawing on already scarce family resources. In addition to their medical needs, children with HIV/AIDS may have other developmental needs. For instance, Thomas not only has extensive medical appointments, he also receives developmental services from an early-intervention team. His mother and grandmother must juggle their schedules to make sure Thomas receives all the services he needs. They do this because it is important for them to see Thomas making progress. Like other women, Thomas's mother puts her son's needs before her own and often neglects her own care. When a mother herself is in the advanced stages of disease progression, caring for a sick child can be difficult and place additional burdens on her and the family. Ensuring that both mother and child have support and care for all their needs is critical.

Children and families affected by HIV/AIDS are best served by programs that provide family-focused, community-based care. Services for children are most effective when they are provided within the context of the caregiving environment, which is usually the child's family. The health of the child and the family's well-being have a profound impact on each other and the strengths and needs of each must be addressed when providing services.

Women's Issues with Pediatric HIV/AIDS

Taneika sits in the exam room with the door closed; her daughter is with her. She is always nervous when she comes to the clinic and slithers back to an exam room as soon as she arrives. Often she goes unnoticed until one of the clinic staff discovers her in the exam room. She does not interact with the other families and likes to come in and leave quickly. Taneika is withdrawn and talks little. She always comes by herself and never mentions family or friends. Keeping her diagnosis secret is very important to her. She does not feel she can tell anyone about it, not even her mother or sister. No one knows except her, and the strain is beginning to show. Taneika is from a small rural town in the South. She works at a local factory and is afraid that if her employers discovered she is HIV-positive they will fire her. She schedules her appointments on her days off and doesn't allow anyone from the clinic to call her at home or at work. When her daughter has an earache, cold, or other illness, she does not want the doctors from the clinic calling her local pediatrician. She takes care of it herself. Taneika shows no interest in participating in the support group. She is very isolated. She often wonders what she will do if her daughter turns out to be HIV-positive as well. After one year of coming to the pediatric clinic, her daughter's test results have all been negative. This is a relief to Taneika, but she is beginning to wonder what she will do when she begins to get ill. Taneika is afraid no one will take care of her daughter if they know she herself is HIV-positive. Some day she will have to tell someone, most likely her mother, but she hopes to put that off as long as possible.

Taneika's concerns and feelings are not uncommon among women living with HIV/AIDS. Even though she is relieved her daughter is not HIV-positive, Taneika still worries about what will happen to her daughter if people find out that Taneika herself is HIV-positive. She also worries about having to confide in someone and what their reactions might be. Taneika does not know if she is ready to deal with all the questions and the silent wonderings of those she tells—"How did she get it?" "Is she using drugs?" "Has she been sleeping around?" "Does her man have it, too?" Also, she is concerned about what will happen to her daughter when she becomes too ill to take care of her and after she dies. Will her daughter be branded for life?

Women as Mothers

As a woman enters motherhood with HIV infection, she faces many obstacles in dealing with issues ranging from her own disease and treatment to the planning for the care of her children after her death. A woman may become aware of her HIV status during her pregnancy or directly after the birth of a child. Many women learn of their own HIV status when they hear about their child's. Shock and disbelief are common reactions as most women never considered themselves to be at risk (Weedy 1993). Common reactions to the diagnosis include denial, anger, depression, guilt, blame, and shame (Weedy 1993). A woman needs an understanding health care professional to respond supportively as she works through these issues, a person who is sensitive to the psychological issues surrounding diagnosis and the impact on the child's care.

Once a woman finds out she has HIV/AIDS she will face many decisions, and the support of family, friends, and professionals will be imperative to her ability to cope with her HIV infection. If her infection status is known and health care is available, frequent clinical checkups for the woman, and after delivery, for the child, are constant reminders of the disease. Fear of isolation and discrimination make it difficult for an HIV-positive woman to tell others that she has HIV/AIDS and that her child may also be infected. Many women keep this knowledge to themselves, unable to draw on others for support. Women also may live with self-imposed isolation, further reducing the social network from which they can draw on for support (Cooper et al. 1988).

A woman may be faced with a mirror image of her own fate as she watches the advancement of HIV/AIDS in her child. A sense of guilt and hopelessness may cause a woman to let her own health care needs be neglected as she focuses her energy on caring for her sick child. Support for a woman with HIV infection should not stop at the time of her child's death but should be continued for the duration of her life.

Another common scenario involves the woman who is in the advanced stages of HIV disease at the time of her child's birth. She will need to face the fact that her child will survive her, and she will need to make arrangements for his or her care. The woman may live through the final stages of her illness knowing her child is HIV-positive and faces a similar fate. Her child may have to go through this ordeal without the comfort of her being there. Many women in this situation must make difficult decisions. For example, a woman may need to make arrangements with other family members to care for her child after she dies. This may mean that her infection status and that of her child will have to be disclosed to people from whom she had previously withheld this information. If she has uninfected children, she may have to decide whether to tell them of her HIV infection and make arrangements for their care after she has died. The father may or may not be infected himself, and uninfected siblings may be the only survivors of the affected family.

Disclosure

Many women will struggle with how and when to reveal the diagnosis of HIV infection to their infected and noninfected children. Some mothers prefer to handle this alone whereas others want assistance or want a health care professional to reveal the diagnosis. As children get older they often ask questions about what is happening to them or their parents and why they have to see the doctors so much. This can be very stressful for the mother and family. For an infected child, if vertical transmission of infection occurred, women may be overcome with feelings of guilt and be unable to let their children know that they may be responsible for their illness. There is no single, simple answer to the questions asked. Honest information at a level the child can understand is the most reassuring, rather than denial or half-truths which may have to be retracted later (Weedy 1993; Berer 1993).

Women as Caregivers

More often than not, the burden of care for those with HIV/AIDS falls on women's shoulders. They provide care during illness and death, usually with little or no support from extended family members or the community. Women are involved in the care of children, adult children, partners, other family members, or friends who have HIV/AIDS. Many times they are expected to take responsibility for the care of any children when the other adult members of the family are no longer able to provide appropriate care.

The burden of care for orphaned children, noninfected and infected, usually falls to a grandmother, aunt, or other female family member. In developed as well as developing countries many women take on the responsibility of caring for those left behind. Many women must deal with the realization of the loss of adult children and that they will no longer be able to spend their "golden years" simply as grandparents. As one grandmother put it, "I thought I was done with all this potty training, homework, and day-to-day care of young children. I was looking forward to just being grandma. Now I'm mama all over again" (P., personal communication).

In a study conducted in Mexico, psychologists found that women have great difficulty leaving a child or a partner who has HIV or AIDS. Women will care for their ill child and partner even at the cost of their own health; however, in contrast, men more frequently abandon their families if the woman has HIV (Liguori 1993). Thus more often women with HIV are single parents and left on their own to cope because (1) they may not be able to turn to their families for help owing to ostracism or physical separation from their families; (2) they do not want to disclose their HIV status; (3) they do not want to reveal their life-style choices (e.g., being a commercial sex worker, abusing drugs, etc.); (4) they may have become alienated from their families through their own or their partner's drug use; and (5) their partners may become ill and die of AIDS (Berer 1993).

As their health fails, women will become less and less capable of being sole caretakers. Support services will need to be in place that can assist women, as needed, in the care of themselves and their families. Social services, self-help groups, and support from voluntary organizations can be utilized by women to help them in planning for their own and their families futures. Assistance should not wait until a woman is ill. Once a woman knows her HIV status, assistance should be made available to help her cope with her own and possibly her children's diagnosis. Knowing that help is available when she feels she needs it can reduce some of the stress a woman may experience.

Support Services

Women affected by HIV/AIDS will need a variety of support services to meet their individual needs. In an effort to improve support services for mothers with HIV, twenty-eight HIV-positive mothers in Scotland were asked to indicate persons they felt they could talk to about HIV. Health care professionals, including doctors, nurses, social workers, researchers, or voluntary sector workers, were reported by 82 percent of the women, 68 percent said a parent or sibling, 64 percent said their partner, 46 percent said a friend, and 7 percent said they could not talk to anyone (Cosgrove 1990, as cited in Berer 1993).

When asked if they knew other mothers who were HIV-positive, 82 percent said they did. Of this group, 29 percent discussed HIV with other mothers. Eighty-eight percent of the women who discussed HIV with other mothers found this useful. When asked if they would like to meet other parents who were HIV-positive, 32 percent said yes, several said not at this time, and the rest said no.

The main conclusions drawn from this group were (1) HIV remains a closely guarded secret and women are selective about where they draw their support; (2) most of the women preferred not to meet others for support; and (3) the type of support offered should be tailored to each family's needs if it is to be of any value. Some women will require practical and financial help; others will require emotional support because of relationship complications or their own psychological difficulty in coping with HIV infection (Cosgrove 1990, as cited in Berer 1993).

Drug Use

In the United States the use of illicit drugs is implicated in 71 percent of HIV/AIDS cases among women (Centers for Disease Control 1990). Either women themselves are IV drug users or they have unprotected sex with men who are IV drug users. In addition to medical care needed for HIV/AIDS, many women also may need help with their drug addiction.

Continued use of illicit drugs not only jeopardizes a woman's health, but it also can impact her ability to care for herself and her children. Lack of a supportive or adequate caregiving environment can hinder the development of a child at biological risk (e.g., HIV/AIDS, prenatal drug exposure, etc.). Abuse of illicit substances can be complicated by other environmental risk factors such as polydrug use, poverty, poor nutrition, dysfunctional families, and poor medical care, all of which can influence the developmental outcome of infants.

As soon as she enters the clinic, Janell hands her newborn son over to one of the clinic staff and runs outside for a cigarette. This is her first visit to the clinic, and she appears very fidgity and agitated. She nervously paces the waiting room and, once in an exam room, can't sit still. She talks to clinic staff about her need to be finished by 4:30 so she can make it to the rehab clinic for her methadone. Janell found out she was HIV-positive late in her pregnancy when she entered a methadone treatment program for heroine addiction. Janell is comfortable with the staff and talks freely about her addiction. She describes how "using" was the focal point of her existence—and the hell she now lives through trying to give it up. "You know, the greatest high is when, after you put the needle in and draw back, and the first sight of blood, . . . well that's it for me. That's the greatest feeling in the world, when I see that first drop of blood. I know what comes next. That's what's the hardest for me to give up. I dream about that moment and want it so bad I could die." Janell leaves her baby at the clinic and disappears. It is the end of the day, and nobody knows what to do with the baby. The social worker calls the methadone clinic to see if Janell is there. She has not arrived yet but they expect her. Two hours go by and no sign of Janell. There is no choice but to call social services and find a temporary place for the baby.

Janell's needs, like those of many women with HIV, do not just focus around medical care for HIV/AIDS. She needs services that will help her cope with her drug addiction, meet her HIV/AIDS needs, and support her in her role as a new mother. Like the other women described in this article, Janell did not actively seek to become infected with HIV. Often women who use illicit drugs and are HIV-positive are thought of as less-than-innocent victims and blamed for their own infection and that of their child's. Women who use illicit drugs during pregnancy and who are HIV-positive not only have to deal with the guilt and shame associated with HIV but have the added burden of guilt associated with exposing their children to drugs. Many women may want to stop using drugs but don't have access to support services that can help them do so. Services must address a range of child and family needs, both biological and environmental.

Impact on Children

Josh stands on the sidewalk and watches as the paramedics attend to his sister Christina. She collapsed as they were walking out of the local restaurant with their grandmother. Christina was just released from the hospital after spending two months there. He is so glad to have her home again. It was lonely without her. He is now seven and Christina is eight. They have been living with their grandmother most of their lives, at least since Josh could remember. He does not remem-

ber much about his mom or dad. One day he overheard his aunts talking about his mom and how she had been so sick when he was a baby. He wished he could remember what she looked like. Everyone always helped their grandmother take care of Christina and him. She was getting old and couldn't get after them as well as she used to. Now she is standing next to him crying. Christina is in the ambulance with its lights and sirens going. Josh and his grandmother follow in their car. As they arrive at the hospital, the doctors tell them that Christina died. His grandmother continues to cry and says she has to call his aunts. Josh is scared—his best friend in the whole world is not going to be around anymore! How can this be? He is not sure why Christina died. All he knows is that he and Christina always go to the big hospital far away together to see the doctors and to get their medicine that their grandmother is always after them to take. He does not really like to take it; it tastes funny. Josh also does not like having all those tests done on his heart and pictures of his head taken. They listen to his heart and his lungs; they make him run and jump and answer questions, some of them are really hard. Now what is he going to do. One day will he be sick like Christina and die? Josh is not sure. He will ask his grandmother or one of his friends at the clinic. He loves Christina very much. She always makes him laugh and gives him hugs when he cries. He will miss her!

Like other children in families affected by HIV/AIDS, Josh and his sister Christina experience the suffering and loss that result from the disease. They lost both parents to HIV/AIDS and were left orphaned to be cared for by family members willing to take them in. Josh will succumb to the same fate as Christina and his parents. Children feel the impact of HIV/AIDS when they contract the disease themselves, when they live with ill parents or siblings, or when they are left orphans.

Orphans

As more adults are infected with HIV, especially women of childbearing age, more children will be left without the care of their parents. It is estimated that an average of two children will be left by a woman dying of HIV/AIDS. Countries predicted to have the highest numbers of children orphaned because of HIV/AIDS are those in Central Africa, with a minimum of three to five million children without parents (UNICEF 1994).

The fate of many of the children orphaned by the death of their parents to HIV/AIDS is often uncertain. There is a tradition of extended families taking in orphans in developing countries. However, because of declining economic resources and the loss of able-bodied men and women to HIV/AIDS, this is becoming increasingly difficult. Other factors that influence the ability of extended families to take in orphaned children are a misunderstanding of how HIV/AIDS is spread, the social stigma associated with the disease, and the lack of physical ability because of age (Colletta 1992).

The number of children who will lose their primary caregiver because of HIV/AIDS in New York City alone is estimated to be ten thousand to twenty thousand by mid-decade (Landesman 1989). Many children who test positive for HIV are being abandoned and left as "border babies" in hospitals. Myers and Weitzman (1991) indicate a number of reasons why babies and children are abandoned:

1. They have just been left by their mothers.
2. Mothers are not able to care for them because they are too sick.
3. Mothers may have died from HIV/AIDS.
4. Fathers are unknown or choose not to be involved.
5. Fathers are unaware that they have a child or that the child has been abandoned.
6. Extended family members are unaware of the situation or are unwilling or unable to help because of limited resources.
7. Communities lack the resources to provide alternative caregiving situations.

In developed countries the standard alternative is to place abandoned children with foster families, in the hope that the families will eventually adopt them. For those children who are HIV-positive and who have AIDS, finding appropriate homes for them can be a difficult task. Training programs for potential foster families need to be developed that address the special health care needs of children with HIV/AIDS (Guidotti and Mann 1990).

In Germany the "AIDS and Children" program offers supportive services to people affected with HIV/AIDS and their families. Those who are affected with HIV/AIDS are encouraged to enroll in the program early on in their disease progression so that appropriate planning for and the transition of their children to foster care, if needed, can be achieved. The program goal is to keep families together as long as possible. As parents become ill, it may become necessary to move children into a foster home for care. Finding families able and willing to cope with these children is hard because the children may have special needs and because of the stigma of AIDS. Training and support are needed (Schwartz 1991).

Some nonindustrialized countries also are investigating the use of foster care as an alternative solution to institutions and to a life on the streets, especially where the number of orphans is high and increasing (Berer 1993). Usually there are no formal government-run social services for foster care programs, and often community-based groups or nongovernmental organizations arrange placements for children.

Children on Their Own

Other solutions must be sought to handle the growing number of orphans. In Uganda, for example, where the number of orphans is among the highest, many children whose parents have died of HIV/AIDS are living on their own, as no family member or community services are available to take care of them. Children who are left on their own have a better chance of surviving if they are left with a plot of land, a house, and have among them at least one girl, preferably the eldest child. Because girls take on household responsibilities at an early age, they are more likely to know how to cook, grow food, and participate in income-generating activities in order to provide basic subsistence and even school fees. Once the amount of help from community sources (e.g., neighbors) is reduced, families with boys only or boys as the elder children usually resort to begging and a life on the streets. It is critical for children living on their own to be near relatives if possible because of the social and psychological support they may offer by including the children in social celebrations (Berer 1993).

In other countries, such as Zambia, extended families and communities are seeking and trying alternatives. One example is kibbutz-style homes. The use of this model involves help from extended families and communities. In Israel, where the kibbutz model originates, the parents and the community share responsibility for the children. Children live in children's houses staffed by houseparents and spend certain times each day and week with their parents (Berer 1993).

Both orphaned children and adult members of their extended families have been involved in designing ways to adopt the kibbutz-style homes in Zambia. One possible permutation of the kibbutz model would be to have all siblings from one or more families live together in group houses situated near helping family members. Extended family members would act as parents on the kibbutz, supervising and providing emotional support for the children by spending a specified amount of time with them each week (Berer 1993).

For some children a gradual move to the group house is possible and preferable. The children begin by attending school and recreational facilities in the community with other children. A child is able to make a gradual move, for example, when one parent has died and the other is still alive but ill. The children begin to have meals or attend a play group after school at the group house. The success of such programs in communities depends on the involvement of community leaders and extended families in the planning and supervision of the group homes. Church groups and women's clubs and organizations have said that they are quite willing to be involved in such programs (Berer 1993).

The loss of parents to HIV/AIDS affects adolescents as well as young children. Because adolescents are often more aware of the association of HIV/AIDS with immoral sexual behavior, substance abuse, and alternative life-styles, they may think that their parents were immoral and transfer the shame and stigma to themselves. This burden can have a substantial impact on their self-esteem and sense of self-worth. In order to cope, these children may engage in high-risk behaviors, placing themselves at risk of being infected with HIV. Health workers and other social service providers need to be sensitive to the emotional needs of children and adolescents who have had to watch their parents die from HIV/AIDS. Many social stigmas are still attached to the disease and children may be especially sensitive to them.

Families Affected by HIV

Matthew had been born prematurely and required a long stay in the hospital and several operations on his heart. During the operations he received several transfusions, which later his family found out had been infected with HIV. Matthew is now eight years old and relatively healthy. He still sees a heart specialist and is treated for AIDS by a medical team who specializes in infectious diseases. Matthew's parents own their own business and have insurance. They have never used their insurance to pay for his medical care and have told only a few close family members and friends of their son's condition. They are afraid they will lose customers and be isolated in their community if people knew that Matthew has AIDS. They have decided not to tell Matthew of his diagnosis until he is older. Matthew asks a lot of questions and knows that something is really wrong with him. Matthew's older sister, Rebecca, who is eleven, knows of his diagnosis. She confronted her parents about it and thought it was best they told Matthew. Her parents forbid her to tell her brother about his diagnosis. Rebecca has learned about HIV/AIDS in school and from other sources. She and her friends talk about it sometimes, but she never tells them that her brother has AIDS. Matthew has told his sister that he thinks he has AIDS. Rebecca told him never to tell his parents what he thought, at least not yet. Matthew and Rebecca talk about it sometimes, only when their parents are not around. Matthew is often sad that he cannot talk to his parents about his illness. They keep telling him that he will get better as long as he takes his medicine and does what the doctors say. Matthew attends school; when he has to miss school because of medical appointments, he tells his friends and his teacher that it is because of his heart problem, even though he knows that is not always the case. Sometimes Matthew stays awake at night and wonders if he really has AIDS, *will he die soon. He would really like to ask his parents these questions. Maybe tomorrow he will.*

Families are essential to children's well-being. The presence of HIV/AIDS in the family, whether or not a child is infected, can have a direct impact on the well-being of the child. Like Matthew and Rebecca, children and other family members can feel isolated within their families without open and honest communication about HIV/AIDS. Responses to HIV/AIDS by family members vary, but all members are affected and this can affect relationships within the family as well—between husband and wife, between parents and children, and between siblings. Adults and children may respond to HIV/AIDS differently. Many parents feel sadness, frustration, anger, and guilt. They may feel injustice over the child's fate and their own. Parents are often burdened with the care of their child and with providing both the physical and emotional support they need. Because they wish to be strong for their children, parents often neglect their own physical and emotional health. Families should be provided services that take into account the stress that occurs in caregivers and family members of persons with HIV/AIDS.

Psychosocial Impact

The social stigma associated with HIV/AIDS (e.g., homosexuality, drug abuse, etc.) can arouse fear in families affected by HIV/AIDS and lead to family shame and a tendency to hide the disease. When HIV/AIDS is introduced into a family it is typically through one parent. Eventually the disease may affect the health of the other parent and of children born later, if the diagnosis is unknown or unprotected sexual intercourse continues. HIV/AIDS not only affects the physical health of family members but also the psychosocial and economic well-being of the family. Psychosocial effects on the family are described by Colletta (1992:135) as follows:

1. *Isolation.* With many misconceptions about how it is transmitted, AIDS has become a disease that causes great fear. People suspected of having AIDS are often shunned by their neighbors, friends or family. The truth is that AIDS is not caught by living in a household with someone who has the disease. . . .
2. *Shame.* AIDS is also seen as a disease of shame because of its association with sex outside of marriage as well as with homosexuality. Depression and suicide are not uncommon among people who know they have AIDS.
3. *Fear of the future.* Parents worry about not being able to feed their families when they fall ill. They fear losing their jobs and housing. One of their

greatest fears is of leaving their children as orphans who will not be cared for.

4. *Stress from the daily care of ill family members.* Both adults and children who have AIDS are also sick with persistent diarrhea, weight loss, recurrence of illnesses (tuberculosis, some cancers, some parasitic diseases, pneumonia). Their families must spend countless hours caring for them, assuming their responsibilities, and mourning their certain death.

5. *Poor functioning from AIDS-related mental problems.* Parents with AIDS may suffer from forgetfulness, confusion, poor concentration and dementia. Depression over the bleak situation is not uncommon. All of these mental disabilities make it impossible for parents to respond to their children's needs. Parental responsibilities frequently have to be assumed by older children when they are too young to manage them (Colletta 1992:135).

Service Needs

Services for children and families affected by HIV/AIDS should be family-focused and community-based identifying family strengths and needs. Intervention programs should target activities that educate communities in order to further an understanding of HIV/AIDS. Such programs would provide information on the transmission of HIV/AIDS in order to prevent its spread and, in themselves, would decrease the isolation and shame associated with HIV/AIDS. According to Colletta (1992) the approach must have a multilevel focus:

1. early identification of HIV-infected adults and infants
2. education about HIV/AIDS transmission
3. family-focused, community-based services
4. provision of support services for children orphaned as a result of HIV/AIDS-related deaths.

Families affected by HIV/AIDS are confronted with many potential problems. They may be faced with less economic support because of the loss of able-bodied adults in the work force. Many children will be left orphaned to fend for themselves or will be taken in by relatives. Grandparents will be faced with having to care for their dying children and then take responsibility for their grandchildren at a time in their lives when they thought they would be less burdened with child care. Families may face isolation, shame, and fear in the community and thus be less likely to ask for assistance. As members of a family become progressively debilitated by HIV/AIDS, their families will have to cope with mental and physical deterioration. It is crucial for the survival of families during this difficult time to have community support.

Societal Impact

There is a need to focus on the broader social and economic implications of HIV/AIDS in women and their children. Women are having to cope with the effects of HIV/AIDS on their households and communities. More elderly women are having to take care of their adult children and then their grandchildren orphaned by HIV/AIDS, and young women afflicted with the disease are struggling to care for themselves and their children.

Economic Impact

In areas where the prevalence of HIV/AIDS is especially high, the disease will have a great economic impact. It will affect the work force, economic development, and investments in children. Two-thirds of those infected with HIV are under twenty-five years of age. This means that during the most productive years of their lives, these young adults will be limited by long-term illness and their productive cycle will be cut short. This will result in income loss to their families, communities, and the nation. For example, income lost because of HIV/AIDS exceeds 7 percent of the nation's gross domestic product in Malawi. This trend is expected to continue with income loss doubling and perhaps tripling by the year 2000. Malawi has the world's highest incidence of AIDS and the government already spends one-fifth of the health budget on AIDS treatment (UNICEF 1994).

Families and children will also feel the economic impact. Children in families where HIV/AIDS is present will be at greater risk for developmental challenges because of the economic, social, and physical stress the disease places on their families. Because of illness adults will produce less, bringing fewer resources into the family. Fewer investments in their children will be able to be made, and this may mean lower school attendance and lower health status because families will not be able to pay school fees or pay for standard health care. Children orphaned because of HIV/AIDS will face additional difficulties. These children are likely to have lost aunts and uncles as well. They will have fewer extended family members to take them in or to turn to for support (Ainsworth 1992).

HIV/AIDS is usually concentrated in communities, which results in concentrated numbers of children orphaned by HIV/AIDS. The care for these children will fall to these communities, placing a greater burden on them. Children are not only affected by the loss of their parents, but many face substantial emotional trauma from caring for their parents throughout a long and painful illness and finally death. Even after their parents' death, children may be subjected to social stigma that accompanies HIV/AIDS. They may be isolated and ostracized by their communities because their parents died of HIV/AIDS (Ainsworth 1992).

Children and families affected by HIV/AIDS have multifaceted needs, and the support services necessary to provide appropriate care must address these varied needs. This will cost money. Many communities are already struggling to provide care for their youngest members. With fewer able-bodied adults to help contribute to the economic base, many communities will need to search for alternative ways to care for the families and children affected by HIV/AIDS.

Intervention Responses for Women, Children, and Communities

Prevention is the best hope for reducing the number of adults and children infected with HIV. Countries' primary prevention efforts should be placed on public health education. In almost all countries, prevention programs for HIV/AIDS are increasingly mobilizing every possible resource for reaching the public. In Uganda a recent Ministry of Health survey found that over 60 percent of Ugandans now know how HIV/AIDS is spread (UNICEF 1994). This is primarily the result of Uganda's program of sex education and self-esteem for primary school children and their parents. This program has been continued into secondary schools and colleges. A combination of school programs and mass media—including television, radio, popular music, and theater—is being used in most countries (UNICEF 1994).

Information and education on how to prevent the spread of HIV/AIDS continue to be scarce in many regions. Some countries have taken steps toward providing information on protection against HIV/AIDS. African countries have been led by Uganda in developing and revising school programs to include information on the prevention of HIV/AIDS. Through mass media such as television, radio, and posters, many popular campaigns have been launched throughout the world (Boyden 1993).

Campaigns focusing on the prevention of HIV/AIDS have had mixed results. There are signs of hope that differences have been made. Condom use has increased wherever social marketing programs have been in place. For example, the government of Thailand made a decision to support a prevention program and, as a result, the use of condoms has increased from 10 million to 120 million in a year. Another area where change is beginning to be seen is with the youth in countries that have actively focused on sex education. Safer sex practices, including the reduction of sexual partners, have been adopted by those participating in the programs (UNICEF 1994).

Women's and Children's Experiences

For Shirley and her two children Kendra and Orlando; Wanjiku and her son; Faith and her parents Denise and Jim; Thomas, his mother, and grandmother; Arnella and her foster mother, Taneika; Janell; Josh; and Matthew and his sister Rebecca, HIV/AIDS has profoundly affected their life histories and relationships. Illustrated in their stories are the many issues with which women, children, families, and communities struggle when facing the HIV/AIDS epidemic. As the epidemic spreads, many more women and children will be affected by it. Our global response to this epidemic must include intervention strategies that provide support not only to those who have HIV/AIDS but also to those who provide care for them and those left behind.

In many instances it is women who are left to care for the sick and dying, and then for the children who are left orphaned by HIV/AIDS. These women often have no choice. As one grandmother described her situation:

> *I just have to do it. No one else is going to take care of her and her children. I watched my baby die. She laid in her bed . . . looked at me . . . and took her last breath. I was with her when she had her first and I was the only one there when she had her last. Now I have to take care of her children. The older one, she is going to be all right, but the little one, she is going to die just like her momma. Sometimes I ask myself how I could do it, but then I just tell myself, I have to because no one else is going to do it. (P., personal communication)*

For every infant who falls victim to HIV during the mother's pregnancy, there is a woman with HIV infection. Mother and child are a unit whose best interests are served by preventing HIV infection in women to begin with. Although prevention is the first line of defense, intervention strategies for those already affected by HIV/AIDS should be broadly defined and address families' needs. These needs may be emotional, physical, social, financial, religious, and/or spiritual. Families may have many requirements or only a few at any given time. Care should be family-focused and community-based. Programs that provide services should be flexible and let families dictate their participation.

Pediatric HIV/AIDS brings women face to face with many issues that are in direct conflict with their cultural roles. Women will be forced to make decisions that can have a direct effect on their ability to fulfill what is seen as their cultural responsibilities. A woman may be forced to cope with issues that range from deciding to have a baby to telling her child that she is dying.

Intervention strategies should also focus on advocating for the advancement of women's and children's rights. The HIV/AIDS epidemic has highlighted the need to promote these rights in order to prevent the spread of the disease and to deal with the millions of children who will be left orphaned in its wake. Women and children should have equal access to educational and economic opportunities that may mitigate the circumstances that place them at risk for HIV infection.

REFERENCES

Ainsworth, Martha. 1992. The Economic Impact of AIDS on Orphaned Children: What Does the Evidence Show? Briefing paper prepared for the Expert Meeting on Family and Development, sponsored by the Committee on Population, National Academy of Sciences/National Research Council, July 16–17.

Ammann, A. J. 1988. Immunopathogenesis of pediatric acquired immunodeficiency syndrome. *Journal of Perinatology* 8:154–59.

Arno, P. S. and P. R. Lee. 1987. Economic costs of AIDS. In V. Gong and N. Rudnick, eds., *AIDS: Facts and Issues*, 157–78. New Brunswick, N.J.: Rutgers University Press.

Barth, Richard, Jeanne Pietrzak, and Malia Ramler. 1993. *Families Living with Drugs and HIV: Intervention and Treatment Strategies*. New York: Guilford.

Belman, A., et al. 1988. Pediatric acquired immunodeficiency syndrome: Neurologic syndromes. *American Journal of Diseases in Childhood* 142:29.

Berer, Marge. 1993. *Women and HIV/AIDS: An International Resource Book*. London: Pandora.

Boyden, Jo. 1993. *Families: Celebration and Hope in a World of Change*. New York: Facts on File.

Brouwers, Pim, Anita Belman, and Leon Epstein. 1991. Central nervous system involvement. In Philip Pizzo and Catherine Wilfert, eds., *Pediatric AIDS: The Challenge of HIV Infection in Infants, Children, and Adolescents*, 318–35. Baltimore: Williams and Wilkins.

Chicago Tribune, 1 December 1990, section 1, p. 19.

Colletta, Nancy D. 1992. *Understanding Cross-Cultural Child Development and Designing Programs for Children*. Richmond, Va.: Christian Children's Fund.

Conner, Edward M., et al. 1994. Reeducation of maternal-infant transmission of human immunodeficiency virus type 1 with Zidovudine treatment. *New England Journal of Medicine* 331 (18): 1173–80.

Cooper, Ellen, Stephen Pelton, and Mireille LeMay. 1988. Acquired immunodeficiency syndrome: A new population of children at risk. *The Pediatric Clinics of North America* 35 (6): 1365–88.

Cosgrove, John. 1990. *Children Affected by HIV*. Proceedings of the Third National Conference, Women and HIV/AIDS network, Crieff, Scotland, November 29–30, pp. 27–28.

European Collaborative Study. 1991. Risk factors for mother-to-child transmission of HIV-1. *Lancet* 339:1007–12.

Goldfarb, Johana. 1993. The acquired immunodeficiency syndrome (AIDS) in African children. *Advances in Pediatric Infectious Diseases* 8:145–58.

Guidotti, Richard and Jonathan Mann. 1990. AIDS in Mothers and Children in Developing Countries. In Helen Wallace and Kanti Giri, eds., *Health Care of Women and Children in Developing Countries*, 68–79. Oakland, Calif.: Third Party.

Johnson, H. L. and Teva S. Rosen. 1990. Mother-infant interaction in a multirisk population. *American Journal of Orthopsychiatrists* 60 (2): 281–88.

Myers, Alan and Michael Weitzman. 1991. Pediatric HIV disease: The newest chronic illness of childhood. *Pediatric Clinics of North America* 38 (1): 169–94.

Novello, A. C., et al. 1989. Final report of the United States Department of Health and Human Services Secretary's Work Group on Pediatric Human Immunodeficiency Virus Infection and Disease: Content and implications. *Pediatrics* 84:547.

Oxtoby, Margaret. 1988. Human immunodeficiency virus and other viruses in human milk: Placing the issues in broader perspective. *Pediatric Infectious Diseases Journal* 7:825–35.

———. 1994. Vertically acquired HIV infection in the United States. In Philip A. Pizzo and Catherine M. Wilfert, eds., *Pediatric AIDS: The Challenge of HIV Infection in Infants, Children, and Adolescents*, 2d ed., 3–20. Baltimore: Williams and Wilkins.

Pizzo, Philip and Catherine Wilfert. 1991. *Pediatric AIDS: The Challenge of HIV Infection in Infants, Children, and Adolescents*. Baltimore: Williams and Wilkins.

Quinn, Thomas, Andrea Ruff, and Neal Halsey. 1994. Special considerations for developing nations. In Pizzo and Wilfert, *Pediatric AIDS*, 31–50.

Rogers, M., et al. 1987. Acquired immunodeficiency syndrome in children: Report of the Centers for Disease Control national surveillance, 1982–1985. *Pediatrics* 79:1008–14.

Schwartz, Gabriele. 1991. Problems in Caring for Children with HIV-Infected Parents. Seventh International Conference on AIDS, Florence, Italy. Abstract No. W.C. 3273.

Scott, G., et al. 1989. Survival in children with human immunodeficiency virus type-1 infection. *New England Journal of Medicine* 321 (26): 1791–95.

Sokal-Gutierrez, Karen, Holly Vaughn-Edmonds, and Sylvia Villarreal. 1993. Health care services for children and families. In Richard Barth, Jeanne Pietrzak, and Malia Rambler, eds., *Families Living with Drugs and HIV: Intervention and Treatment Strategies*, 119–43. New York: Guilford.

Spiegel, Ladd and Aviva Myers. 1991. Neuropsychiatric aspects of HIV in children and adolescents. *Pediatric Clinics of North America* 38 (1): 153–67.

Temmerman, M., et al. 1990. Infection with HIV as a risk factor for adverse obstetrical outcome. *AIDS* 4:1087–93.

UNICEF. 1994. *The State of the World's Children*. New York: Oxford University Press.

Van de Perre, Phillippe, et al. 1991. Postnatal transmission of HIV-1 from mother to infant: A prospective cohort study in Kigali, Rwanda. *New England Journal of Medicine* 325 (9): 593–98.

Weedy, Chris. 1993. Psychosocial issues in pediatric AIDS. *NCMJ* 54 (1): 18–23.

Wierner, L. and A. Septimus. 1994. Psychosocial support for child and family. In Pizzo and Wilfert, *Pediatric AIDS*, 809–28.

Williams, Ann. 1990. Reproductive concerns of women at risk for HIV infection. *Journal of Nurse-Midwifery* 35 (5): 292–98.

World Development Report. 1993. *Investing in Health: World Development Indicators*. New York: Oxford University Press.

World Health Organization. 1992. Current and Future Dimensions of the HIV/AIDS Epidemic: A Capsule Summary. Global Program on AIDS. Popline abstract.

15 | Care and Support Systems

E. MAXINE ANKRAH, MARTIN SCHWARTZ, AND
JACLYN MILLER

The continuing spread of the AIDS epidemic and its impact on health care and support systems for women are factors of global significance to women. The reasons for concern are multifaceted; the first relates to current shifts in the epidemiology of the disease. Women, who are the majority of caregivers, will themselves make increasingly heavy demands on health care and social support systems in the years ahead.

The second reason for concern is that in the face of a looming epidemic of heterosexually transmitted HIV infection, women are confronted by existing models of AIDS care and support that were not originally conceived to address the status, roles, relative power, or natural history of HIV/AIDS in women. An alternative is needed that is shaped by women's experience, defined here as the totality of a woman's situation that conditions her perception of and responses to the disease. This model rests on two premises: first, that the care and support systems function synergistically to meet the needs of women, and, second, that women-sensitive care and support systems derive from cooperation or "solidarity" between HIV-positive and -negative women. This presupposes that women in need of AIDS care and those acting to avoid the disease or on behalf of others will together determine the women's AIDS agenda, which services are prioritized, how these are provided, and by whom.

In this article we first define care and support systems and then identify current paradigms to argue the need for the woman-centered alternatives proposed. We use the experiences of women in nonindustrial and industrial countries to illustrate how HIV-infected and -uninfected women come together through the two systems to deal with the epidemic of AIDS in women. Finally, we recommend policies that could transform prevailing paradigms and usher in caring systems for women.

Who Cares and with What Support?

Nearly 30 percent of women attending antenatal clinics in Rwanda and Uganda, and an equally high proportion of women in commercial sex work in Bombay, India, are already HIV-infected or AIDS sufferers. With no affordable vaccine or cure in sight, the provision of care and support to women is one of the most pressing problems that AIDS policy makers, service providers, governments, and donors confront in the 1990s. Scientists at the Eighth International Conference at Amsterdam (Boom and Gostin 1992) noted that a lack of early diagnosis and access to care were critical variables in differences seen between men's and women's disease progression. The AIDS literature has only recently turned its attention to these two issues, with no major research reported that examines care and support systems together as these affect women. Assessing either system separately obscures the full dimension of the problem of AIDS care and the design of appropriate systems for women.

Defining Care and Support

To create systems that meet women's needs, care must be conceptualized broadly, and from two perspectives: as a response and as a structure. In 1989 the World Health Organization (WHO) defined care broadly as "a comprehensive, integrated process which recognizes the range of needs for well-being; it includes services and activities providing counseling and psychosocial support, nursing and medical care, legal, financial and practical services" (Mann, Tarantola, and Netter 1992:452). The concept of care used here is less far-ranging. We look at processes focused on services and activities designed primarily to deliver clinical management of the disease and to ensure health maintenance. Such care must also address prevention (O'Neill et al. 1991).

HIV-positive and -negative women are frustrated in having their needs met through formal care institutions. The term *health care systems* is used in this discussion to encompass the formal structures of medical management and service delivery. Support as a response denotes the various forms of social assistance provided to mediate the effects of the various stresses attendant to HIV/AIDS (Lynch 1992:59). Lynch points out that tangible aid (material goods and services), psychological aid (verbal communication), emotional support (esteem and concern), appraisal support (feedback), and information support are included among concepts of support (62).

We view support systems as interacting structures of social relations designed to access the assistance women need to cope with the multifaceted demands of HIV/AIDS. Although our major emphasis in this article is on care and support as systems, and the way these do and could respond to HIV-infected and -affected women, we also consider care and support as responses where relevant.

Health care and support systems may show similar features and provide the same services. We highlight those facets that most distinguish the two: the major focus of activities, characteristic formalization, the nature of membership, and decision-making and control mechanisms. These differences are shown in table 15.1.

TABLE 15.1.
Health Care and Support Systems in Industrial and Developing Countries

Health Care Systems	Support Systems
Major types of care	
clinical management	psychosocial support
pyschosocial support	spiritual support
counseling	counseling
referral services	education, information
	alternative therapies
	traditional healing
	specialized support to categories of AIDS
	sufferers (women, orphans, drug users)
Facets of structure	
public facilities	informal groups (family, communities)
private facilities	nonformal small networks
eligibility requirements	AIDS service organizations (ASOs, NGOs)
(fees, insurance, etc.)	need
paid staff	unpaid/paid services
regulated, coordinated	non- or loosely linked to other systems
	material assistances
	housing
	financial aid
	food
	clothing
	transportations
Locations of care	
hospital (inpatient	community-based activities
hospital (out-patient)	within households and homes
clinics	outreach services
primary care facilities	home care
outreach services	
health centers	
hospices	
Regulated conditions of work	
work time regulated	less or no regulation of hours of caregiving
protective measure for prevention	risk in caregiving
of infection to workers	few. limits to demands for support
backup and support to workers	
Membership	
professional health care providers	infected and affected persons
health paraprofessionals	nonprofessional caregivers
specialists	professional/paraprofessional health
	service providers
	volunteers

Other important differences in the structures and delivery of care between the developing and industrial regions are not presented in table 15.1. In North America and in Western European countries, health care systems provide the latest in diagnostic and treatment regimes, drugs, and alternative therapies to patients with AIDS. By contrast, in Asia, Africa, Latin America, and parts of the former Soviet Union, resources for formal and informal health care delivery systems were declining before AIDS. This decline negatively affects the quality of care (Panos Institute 1992). Many public health care agencies, in particular, can no longer deliver needed medical care at a satisfactory level because of the pressure AIDS patients put on existing systems (Mann, Tarantola, and Netter 1992).

Whether in resource-poor or wealthy nations, women with HIV/AIDS confront care systems that are not structured to give priority to the health of women per se. Several researchers note that during most of the first decade of AIDS, women were the "invisible" dimension—ignored, marginalized, or shut out from the prevailing systems (Reid 1990; Rosser 1991; Noor, Tlou, and Noor 1993; Patton 1993). Their presence was recognized only to the extent that they functioned in roles as mothers or prostitutes, respectively. In either case their health was considered mainly as it affected HIV transmission to the man and the child. With recognition of the scale of HIV/AIDS in women and the inroads it is making among women in monogamous relationships and among young women (United Nations Development Program [UNDP] 1992; Heterosexual Contact Displaces Drug Abuse 1993; Washington Post, 1993), attention is turning to the health of women and their need for care in their own right (Patton 1993). The definition of "women at risk" is broadening to include other categories of sexually active women, especially those who are in situations of risk such as war, poverty, and high HIV-prevalent contexts. Increased numbers of women of the general population will ultimately require health care.

Women Confronting Health Care Systems

Women's recognition of the health care system's failure to meet their particular needs and to reach them within the situations of their lives spurred the women's health movement worldwide (Wetzel 1993). Over the past three decades women have used a variety of opportunities to influence the system toward increased sensitivity to their concerns with their own health. At the Eighth International Conference on AIDS in Amsterdam, women identified several existing models that may block their access to care. The problem is exacerbated as the epidemic evolves and shifts to populations of women in need who are not so easily targeted as prostitutes and pregnant women. The general population of HIV-infected women often has class and racial as well as gender characteristics that further challenge existing care models.

Several studies (Williams 1992a; Williams 1992b; Berlin Conference 1993) report that women of both resource-poor and wealthy nations who most need responsive health care systems are usually those least able to obtain the care. The disease is spreading fastest where women's status is low (Merson 1993; Gould 1993). The AIDS epidemic is increasingly driven by heterosexual transmission and affects more lower-income populations than affluent ones. At the Ninth International Conference on AIDS in Berlin (Berlin Conference 1993) it was reported in the *Conference News* that the rate and pattern of the spread of AIDS cases in the United States strongly correlates with three variables associated with poverty: percentage of families on Medicaid, percentage of families in multifamily housing units, and percentage of the population that is African-American. At the same conference, Greco et al. (1993) reported that in Belo Horizonte, Brazil, HIV infection most affects women and low-income persons, and Roongpisuthipong et al. (1993) noted that the spread of HIV in Thailand has moved from intravenous drug users and female prostitutes to other women. Among the latter population, poor women are overrepresented. Puentes-Markides (1993) observes that in Latin American countries women constitute the largest proportion of the population within or below the poverty line. Their situation has further deteriorated with the economic crisis that has plagued the region over the past decade. Women are forced to work in the informal sectors for lower wages and longer hours with fewer social and health benefits. Such conditions make it harder for them to maintain their own health. These same economic conditions contribute to the growing number of women who enter commercial sex work in Africa (Schoepf 1988; Ulin 1992). In their research in the United States, Stein and Mor (1993) find that among symptomatic HIV-positive persons, individuals who report that they usually obtain care from private physicians are most likely to be white with private insurance. Individuals who usually attend HIV clinics are more likely to be females without insurance.

Beyond gender and class, race constitutes another fundamental variable that conditions the experience of HIV-positive women with health care systems. In the United States, African-American and Hispanic women are disproportionately infected. By 1987 minority women made up more than 70 percent of the cases of AIDS and were ten times more likely than white women to contract the disease (AIDS and Women, *Time* magazine 1987:66). By 1990 in New York City, 52 percent of all women with AIDS were African-American and 32 percent were Hispanic (Watstein and Laurich 1991). A study done in Maryland shows that women living in Baltimore have the highest rate of infection in the state, and that nonwhite women comprise almost 90 percent of the HIV-positive persons surveyed (Dambita 1993). In the nonurban areas in the southern United States, with many communities underserved by the health system, HIV rates of infection are also high. Whether in urban or nonurban areas of the United States, infection rates were between three and thirty-five times higher in African-American women than in white women (Wasser, Gwinn, and Flemming 1993). Among the reasons given by Richardson (1988) for this steady rise among minorities is their poor access to health education and care as well as problems of racial discrimination (William 1992). Gostin (1990) likewise argues that minorities have long been alienated from the predominantly Caucasian health care establishment, which over the years has progressively decreased the proportion of health care targeted to people of color.

Although Caucasian women constitute 77 percent of the female population in the United States, they comprise only 12 percent of the AIDS cases (Watstein and Laurich 1991). Impoverished white women may confront many of the same problems within the health care system that are faced by poor African-American and Hispanic women (Robb, Rodriguez, and Wickins 1992). However, they often do not encounter the same discrimination experienced by minority women who must negotiate a system designed without regard for their cultural or ethnic differences. Some women will not even attempt to access health care services that they perceive to be unaccepting of them as persons (Robb, Rodriguez, and Wickins 1992). Robb, Rodriguez, and Wickins (1992:2) contend: "Although it is understandable, it is unacceptable that women die before they reach full-blown AIDS because of the obstacles to health care."

The influence of women's ethnic background on their experiences with health care is obscure. Ethnicity may be conflated with class/income differences in resource-poor countries. Its relevance, though, seems obvious, as indicated by the present ethnic-based atrocities committed against women in Bosnia and Rwanda. The impact of ethnic differences on institutions of health care warrants research, especially because the demand for care will be highest in countries where cost-sharing may more adversely affect women's than men's utilization of services (Moses et al. 1992). Sexual identification or orientation as an obstacle to care may also affect women in industrialized countries, where women have been more willing to declare that they are lesbians (Denenberg 1992).

In the industrialized countries, the concern is less about the ability of the health care system to deliver appropriate care. The problem rests primarily with the experiences of discrimination faced by the population in need—predominantly marginalized, minority, or poor women. In less industrialized and resource-poor countries, socioeconomic factors add to the forces that constrain the delivery of health care to a new majority—the low-status, female population seeking help with a disease for which the system, materially and ideationally, is poorly equipped to provide. Programs and policies of AIDS care are needed that are population-specific as well as appropriate in the contexts of the women seeking care. Quinn (1993), who refers to this phenomenon as a triple burden of gender, class, and race, argues that health educators must overcome fears, prejudices, and racial biases to form an interracial coalition to stop the spread of AIDS among such women. Getting the attention of health care systems to groups of the most vulnerable women poses a special difficulty. Stryker et al. (1993) observe:

> Where an epidemic is concentrated among marginalized groups, its presence will have minimal influence on the key institutions of American life. . . . Targeted approaches in areas high in HIV infection should be combined with more global efforts . . . to avoid giving the impression that unless they are among the poor and homeless and ill, they no longer need to be concerned about AIDS. . . . [T]he disease will evaporate into the socially marginalized groups for whom some do not care, anyway.

The immediate need is for a care model for women that addresses the health needs of all women and overcomes gender, class, and racial barriers to ensure that the health care system is truly woman-sensitive in its response.

Androcentrism in Health Care

Rosser (1991) observes the prevailing androcentric dominance of clinical research and medical practice. A male bias was carried into AIDS when the disease was first identified with specific groups and as a gay male disease (Rosser 1991; UNDP 1992). Consequently, women's experience with the disease was largely ignored by the health care system for an entire decade. The focus on the disease in men also accounts for the neglect of symptoms of AIDS in women and their exclusion as research subjects (Williams 1992a, 1992b). The bias in the system toward men who set priorities has implications for change in perspectives in health care.

Access

Lack of "access" best identifies what vulnerable women themselves perceive as the major predicament. Puentes-Markides (1992) defines access as it applies to and affects women in Latin America. She argues that access is a consequence of the interaction of many other factors that relate to the structure of the health care system, the behavior of health care professionals, and the characteristics of populations seeking care. These are further influenced by macro-level variables—the country's political orientation, its macroeconomic policies, and its health policies. She points out that although "access," a difficult concept to operationalize, is often related to utilization, the two are quite distinct. "Utilization" indicates the actual transaction that has occurred between the clients and the system, "the point in time where demand and supply meet" (ibid., 621). Demand explains a set of behaviors. Reviewing the literature, Puentes-Markides notes that access is implicit in such other concepts as availability and acceptability. Others (cited in Puentes-Markides 1993) include in their definition such factors as affordability, the "degree of fit" between client and the health care system, and the relationship resulting from equal use for equal need. According to Puentes-Markides, the major determinants of access are socioeconomic factors, distance, belief in the type of services being offered, and cultural factors associated with the status of women.

Women's access to care is compromised in nonindustrialized countries as well. The androcentric bias in African countries, for example, is accentuated by economic factors such as fees. Men, by virtue of earning incomes and controlling resources, can command preference in treatment and care. Moses et al. (1992) find that with the cost-sharing imposed by the Kenyan government for medical care in Nairobi, the percentage of men who use the health care system is greater than that of women.

Women are also constrained by a lack of infrastructure (Koblinsky et al. 1993). When located outside one's community, or in the urban areas, formal health care is out of rural women's reach in many nonindustrialized countries because of inadequately developed communication and transportation systems (McNamara 1992). In Mexico, for example, the existence of a "good road" is associated with a 30 percent increase in prenatal care utilization (Koblinsky et al. 1993:221). Lack of money to cover treatment costs, religious or other cultural norms restricting care, or the perception that the care received is inappropriate all serve as powerful influences against women's willingness to use the health care system. Similarly, poor and minorities in the United States, because of a lack of insurance or lack of adequate medical coverage, depend on medical clinics and emergency rooms instead of the care of a familiar family doctor (Robb, Rodriguez, and Wickins 1992).

Exclusions

Several barriers related to service delivery result in women's rejection (Donnan 1991) or alienation (Gostin 1990) from the health care system. Among these barriers is the difficulty women face in being diagnosed. The Centers for Disease Control (CDC) in the United States recognized the gender-distinct medical problems of HIV-seropositive women only after a decade had passed in the AIDS epidemic (Reese and Thomas 1993; 1993 Revised Classification 1992). Although clinical studies in Africa from the early 1980s had diagnosed virtually as many women as men with HIV (UNDP 1992), the diagnostic criteria of the CDC continued to characterize the disease by the male gender, male symptoms and syndromes, and male sexual orientation (UNDP 1992). This contributed to a global pattern of late diagnosis and inappropriate and inadequate care and also weakened the physical and emotional capacity of women who, unaware of their own serostatus, had to care for themselves and attend to the needs of other, often ill family members.

When the health care system finally acknowledged that women were being infected, it was initially argued that women acquired HIV/AIDS mainly through intravenous drug use or through sexual intercourse with a seropositive partner who used drugs. By 1993, however, practitioners recognized that heterosexual HIV transmission had displaced drug use as the prime factor in the infection of women with AIDS in the United States (Heterosexual Contact Displaces Drug Abuse 1993). Still few drug treatment programs are open to women and only a small number of these admit seropositive women (Wells and Jackson 1992; Reed 1991). Women and minorities are less likely than white males to be enrolled in the protocols of AIDS Clinical Trial Groups. (D'Eramo et al. 1991). Medicaid data indicate that seropositive women also have significantly lower utilization rates of AZT than men (Solomon, Merwin, and Jogan 1990, Dennon 1991).

Arrangement of Care

Health care designed for infected women is often poorly arranged. Given the stigma associated with HIV/AIDS and STD diagnosis, women's perceptions of the way care is arranged are critical. The lack of integration of related services can deter their use by women in need. Little attention has been given to channeling HIV/AIDS services through maternal and child health facilities or family planning programs that reach most childbearing women. HIV-positive women could be attracted to settings that provide help for a wide range of women-specific problems, including sexually transmitted diseases (STDs). Asymptomatic women go undiagnosed and untreated where the health care system neither integrates the STD service into other programs that reach women nor provides a stand-alone facility.

Such separation of services exposes women to public scrutiny, shame, and stigmatization. With STD treatment in much of Africa, for example, specialty services are used mainly by men who can afford to pay (Fransen and Emmerman 1993), whereas women must use general public health services (Manji et al. 1992). These general services are less costly but often inadequate because of lack of appropriate treatment service regimes and appropriately trained staff for STD services (Fransen and Emmerman 1993). In the United States seropositive women increasingly receive services through the Health Resources and Services Administration (HRSA) (Gordon et al. 1993). During the two-year period of 1991–92, more women were served than diagnosed as new AIDS cases. By 1992, 21 percent of the 119,000 recipients served through Title II programs were women. Forty percent of 158,000 clients assisted by Title IIIb were women. These percentages, nevertheless, leave many seropositive women unserved who may not come to the attention of HRSA. For women already alienated from formal care structures by poverty, race, location, society, and age, the required provision of a continuum of services has yet to become the norm in the health care system (Levine 1990a). HIV-positive women must look elsewhere if the gap is to be bridged between themselves and the medical and social care that they need.

Although public health agencies continue to be the major access points for HIV/AIDS services for women, neither in industrial nor nonindustrialized countries do they provide counseling and testing facilities for assessing the women's prevention or medical needs (Valdiserri et al. 1992). Traditional healers, who in Africa provide care to 70–80 percent of the population, could channel information and education on AIDS, identify AIDS sufferers and make referrals, and supply a culturally relevant context for discussion of sexuality and behavioral change. But traditional practitioners are largely left out of the programs aimed at the care of HIV-infected women (Manci 1993).

Research

Research models focusing on HIV and AIDS conditions in men (Rosser 1991) have only slowly turned to women's experiences with the disease (Miller, Turner, and Moses 1990; Sturdevant, Powers, and Clarke 1992). Research on microbicides and barrier methods has not been treated as a priority by pharmaceutical companies (Elias and Heise 1993 [see also article 19 in this volume, "The Development of Female-Controlled Vaginal Microbicides, by Elias and Heise]; Fransen and Emmerman 1993; Stein and Mor 1993). The lack of commitment accounts for the failure of the research establishment to produce safe protective measures that women can control (Stein 1992; Stein and Mor 1993). WHO (Merson 1993) urges that the development of virucides be stepped up and made available to women who are unable to negotiate consistent condom use with their partners. The health care system will need to ensure that such products are distributed at affordable prices to women who are vulnerable principally because of their partner's behavior.

Training

The prevailing medical training paradigm largely omits a gender analysis, assumes a male model of the disease, and is biased toward technological solutions to health problems and "mechanical" care versus integrated medical and psychosocial approaches required by vulnerable populations. However, an increased number of women are joining the health care system as doctors; in 1993 the Mt. Sinai School of Medicine in New York graduated more women than men. Moreover, 18 of the 126 medical schools in the United States enrolled more women than men in the first-year classes during that year (Boodman 1993).

As women continue on to higher education and training worldwide, the pattern emerging in the United States is expected to be reflected in health systems in other regions as well. Training must increase knowledge and skills in making an appropriate diagnosis and carrying out treatment of HIV/AIDS and STDs. But it should also inculcate attitudes and values to remove the perception of "distance" between care providers and HIV-positive women who are often of lower socioeconomic class or of different ethnic background and cultural traditions (Allen and Mitchell 1993). The reluctance of health care staff to serve HIV/AIDS patients remains a persistent problem (Rosser 1993, Allen and Mitchell 1993; Brenner and Kauffman 1993; Rushton and Hogue 1993; Samaranyake and Sully 1993). Some health care providers are reluctant to perform certain procedures, including surgery, for fear of contracting HIV (Brenner and Kauffman 1993; Rushton and Hogue 1993; Samaranyake and Sully 1993). In hospitals serving HIV-positive women in many nonindustrialized countries, poor relations between health care professionals and women seeking care are evidenced in long waiting periods, administrative "red tape," withholding or providing partial information, and ignoring or showing benign neglect (Wintersteen and Young 1988). Suspicious practices, such as uniform but unexplained blood screening, also contribute to HIV-positive women's dissatisfaction with care and the health system (Rossner 1991).

Reforming the System

The existing health care system that responds best to acute care through "high tech solutions and interventionist strategies" (Gostin 1990:46) is not the most appropriate model for AIDS (Levine 1990a). A decentralized and integrated approach to HIV-infected persons and those who live with them is needed (Gostin 1990). With the increase in numbers, overcommitted health care specialists and institutions cannot provide quality care. Care based in the community, within the home, with use of specialized services only as necessary, is becoming the norm.

Some advocates (Mansfield and Singh 1993; O'Neill 1991; Haines 1993; Noor, Tlou, and Noor 1993) believe that the primary health care model is most suited to women's needs, especially in nonindustrialized countries. A program in Côte d'Ivoire integrates AIDS prevention with its primary health care mobile teams serving rural villages (Noor, Tlou, and Noor 1993). Likewise, mobile vans are used in the United States. This model is being used in Brazil to reduce the disparity in health care provision between the poor and the rich, between urban well-served populations and slum dwellers or rural Brazilians (Haines 1993). An increasing number of women in high-incidence and underserved areas served by national programs under the Ryan White Care Act in the United States are gaining access to a range of family-centered care systems (Gordon et al. 1993). The positive outcome for women when the health care system moves out into the community is demonstrated by Kloser et al.'s (1990) research which showed that HIV-infected women in underserved inner city clinics live longer when followed in outpatient settings.

The primary care model is not without important limitations. Gostin (1990:96) notes a "lack of coordination of the vast array of services required by persons with HIV/AIDS." Mansfield and Singh (1993) suggest that a perception of a lack of confidentiality among primary care providers keeps many persons away from such facilities, although they potentially provide appropriate and comprehensive care. Levine (1990:57) argues that only if outpatient settings offer a funded "continuum of care" are these likely to be better for patients. An array of alternative approaches to hospitals within the health care system, for short- and long-term care, include outpatient clinic care, home care, day care, respite care, and support housing (Levine 1990). Making the "unwieldy" health care system more flexible and more coordinated would, according to Levine (1990:61) require "patience, persistence and unprecedented collaboration among all those whose interests are at stake."

Changing Paradigms

An appropriate response for a complex mix of models requires patience, persistence, and collaboration. No population of "interested" persons is more likely to take on the challenge than women themselves, that is, those who are in the health care system and recipients of services. Women health care providers have taken the lead as nurses, doctors, family planners, and health educators to introduce services for women with AIDS. Minkoff and DeHovitz (1991) believe it is the responsibility of health care providers to identify women at risk, to educate them, and to steer them through the programs required by their diagnosis.

In Africa, Asia, and Latin America—regions where many of the sexually active women within and outside the health care system are equally vulnerable, yet few have been tested and know their HIV status—the imperative for HIV-positive and -negative women to collaborate is critical. Worldwide, women who are HIV-seronegative in both community and health care systems have an increasing chance of being infected or affected by the epidemic. By way of their status and influence in the community, professionally trained women may gain control over resources and also participate in policy and decision making and program implementation. However limited their power, HIV-negative women are working to help HIV-infected women in an attempt to make the health care system more responsive to all women's needs.

Quite disparate groups of women can bury differences to fight for a common cause in which all women have a stake, as shown in India (Moore 1993). There, to ensure that their husbands reduced the level of alcoholism and contributed the money saved to the family welfare, Brahmin and lower-caste women united to confront the state authorities. The consequence of their collective effort was legal reform governing the use of cheap alcohol to raise state revenue. AIDS calls for similar efforts of women whose common interest is health care reform.

Women's Support

As a strategy to combat the AIDS pandemic, governments and the major donors have placed patient care low on the list of priorities compared to AIDS prevention, diagnostic and epidemiological research, and vaccine and drug development (Panos Institute 1992). This neglect has negative implications for resources channeled for care in health systems, and for the impetus for change within the health care system. Increasingly, the burden of AIDS care is shifted to the nonformal/informal support systems: interested groups, community-based organizations, and the family unit. These groups are critical to improving the quality of care to HIV-infected women who globally must fill gaps in services (Berer and Ray 1993; Lynch 1992; Keogh et al. 1989; Leserman, Perkins, and Evans 1992; Kalibala and Kaleeba 1989; UNICEF 1993). As table 15.1 indicates, these groups provide for commonly identified needs of HIV-infected and affected women: counseling, emotional support, assistance with funeral services, skills building for sexual negotiations, financial support, child care, housing, protection of rights, meetings and conferences to address broad issues related to AIDS in women, and linkages to resources—including those of the health care systems.

Organizing Care

Some support systems are established as project components of international, large North American and European private voluntary organizations (PVOS) and nongovernmental organizations (NGOS). Most, however, are initiatives started by concerned local communities with sufficiently high HIV prevalence rates to spur people to action. These groups bring together persons from the religious, business, academic, political, and health establishment who take on an advocacy role. Many support systems draw on traditional patterns of treatment and care, and use indigenous systems to effect normative and behavioral change. Quite frequently the wide range of emphasis of support systems such as "empowerment" results in their giving less attention to the more narrowly focused conventional AIDS prevention goals of safer sex or condom use (UNICEF 1993).

Several support organizations have been established that offer services to women. In Africa, groups that have attained international recognition include The AIDS Support Organization (TASO) and the AIDS Information Center (AIC) for counseling and testing in Uganda, the Chikankata Hospital's rural program for counseling and support in Zambia, and Waliokatika Na AIDS Tanzania (WAMATA). WAMATA, for example, concentrates on developing quality care to Tanzanians through hospital and home-based counseling services and collaborates with other local organizations.

Other support groups and organizations specifically target women. These groups are often linked through networks to provide advocacy and services to HIV-infected women and to design strategies to protect uninfected women from the epidemic. One such network is the Society for Women and AIDS in Africa (SWAA) with branches in twenty-six African nations. Such groups now guide much of the support activity directed to women in Africa (Berer and Ray 1993). SWAA works with governments, NGOS, and other groups from international to grass-roots levels to advocate for (1) changes in economic and sociocultural conditions that increase women's vulnerability to HIV/AIDS; (2) care and support services to HIV-infected women, their children, and families; and (3) training and research on AIDS in women (Williams et al. 1991).

At the national level in Zimbabwe, the Women and AIDS Support Network (WASN) encourages women in their various organizations to support HIV-positive women and one another in protecting themselves against HIV infection. WASN has also focused attention on women caregivers and health care providers. They provide information and practical assistance to women in handling patients to ensure their personal safety.

The Progressive Primary Health Care Network in South Africa focuses on community-based initiatives, assists with the start-up of local activities, supports community care of HIV-infected individuals, and provides for training, employment, and support to regional community AIDS workers (CAWS). A major target group for CAWS is women (Berer 1993).

Several organizations in Asia provide support to women in areas of STD treatment, reproductive health, and sex and health education. The Indian Health Organization, which emphasizes care, uses a mobile clinic to offer STD treatment and clinical services to commercial sex workers in Bombay's red-light districts. The Gabriela Commission on Women's Health and Reproductive Rights of the Philippines responds to needs for consultation and management related to gynecology/obstetrics and pediatric care. The Bacolod Center, in its outreach to bar workers in Olongapo City, Philippines, arranges for night care for the women's children.

The Casa Pensamiento de Mujer del Centro in Aibonito, Puerto Rico, and Central America includes counseling on domestic violence, rape, and sexual assault among the assistance it renders to women. In São Paulo, Brazil, the Grupo de Apoio a Prevencao a AIDS lists home care as one of its primary provisions.

In Europe, the Women and AIDS Bureau of the Netherlands monitors and encourages projects offering quality care for women and children with HIV. The Community Family Planning Council in New York is one of a large number of organizations that have incorporated AIDS into their agenda. Health care, HIV testing, practical support, and counseling are offered in the context of a health care program mainly for African-American and Hispanic women. The Council also provides clinical services, family planning, antenatal care, and primary health care. The Native American Women's Health Education Resource Center in South Dakota organizes self-help through its support initiatives and provides tutoring for pregnant teens.

In addition to the international network that has been established by SWAA in Africa, HIV-infected women have created global linkages through the International Community of Women Living with AIDS (ICW). The Latin American and Caribbean Women's Health Network has been created to mobilize women in that region of the world as well.

This is by no means an exhaustive list of women's collective actions (Berer and Ray 1993). Nevertheless, it indicates the extent to which women perceive that AIDS is a major threat to womankind and are addressing critical care and support issues.

The "self-help," implicit in the support systems, however, can become a double bind for women. As the support groups and organizations fill the vacuum of unattended needs of women, the inadequacies and obstacles—especially as they appear in public-funded services and in research—may go unnoticed and thus unremedied by the health care system for reasons discussed earlier. Pizurki et al. (1987) point out that almost every program developed to improve primary health care in the world assumes that women will be the providers. Their warning should be heeded, especially by women developing programs of care and support in the AIDS epidemic, which Denenberg (1993:258) observes are "too often underfunded and understaffed."

Families

Research has paid little attention to the role the family plays as a provider of AIDS care and support. Several studies (Ankrah 1993; Caldwell et al. 1993; Ankrah 1991) suggest that the family is an indispensable support to persons suffering with HIV/AIDS in Africa. Although variously defined, the family here refers to individuals having differing types of relationships, but with some degree of obligation to assist one another. Noerine Kaleeba, founder of TASO, who defines AIDS as a "family disease," observes that when HIV-infected women or men have their own mothers to care for them, their chances of receiving "quality care" are greatly enhanced (Panos Institute 1990: 61).

Home-based Care

The African extended family has traditionally shared in the treatment of its members, including directly securing the herbs and other remedies needed or collaborating with traditional healers for the care of the sick (Jaensen 1988; Brokenshaw et al. 1987; Kalibala and Kaleeba 1989; Ankrah 1993). For the lesbian HIV-infected woman, the family of lovers or friends secure care for the person with AIDS who may be estranged from biological parents or other relatives. Ankrah et al. (1993), in a study of forty-six families in Uganda, found no difference between rural and urban families in their willingness to give care within the home. Such care was often given at considerable sacrifice by other members of the unit. Some went without health care for themselves. Others sold land or other property in order to meet the treatment costs of patients. Seeley et al. (1992) studied families in Masaka District, Uganda, among which seventeen women and thirteen men were HIV-infected and in need of care. The individuals received home-based care through bimonthly visits and material support from a counselor and medical officer. Of these, a large number said that they had been abandoned by their families. Other families could cope with caregiving only if they themselves were being assisted.

Although informal social networks of neighbors and community members offer emotional support through home visits and contributions of food and money at the time of funerals, they are usually unable to sustain material assistance over a long period (The World Council of Churches [WCC] 1993; Ankrah et al. 1992). In Tanzania, Uganda, and Kenya (WCC 1993) the break with the tradition of caring for the sick is seen as a consequence of the overall declining economies of the region rather than as a reluctance to honor traditional obligations. Neighbors who assist with giving physical care often feel the pressure of caring for their own family members, frequently also sick with AIDS (Ankrah et al. 1992). The reliability of the extended family network as a support system is influenced by other factors such as mobility and perceptions of persons with AIDS (McGrath et al. 1993). The sick need to remain near the relatives who assist them and to avoid withdrawing from family and community social networks of support because of perceived stigma or rejection.

Home-based care will become an inevitable alternative in other parts of the world, as it has become in Africa (Rutuyuga 1993). Its increased use is not explained solely by the inadequacies of the health care system. There is recognition that the family as a support system potentially provides psychosocial comfort to the AIDS patient and the opportunity to die with dignity among kinsmen and friends.

Women as Caregivers

Although laudable as a trend, the family as a primary support system nevertheless can have negative consequences for women. Most health care given in the home becomes the responsibility of women: mothers, wives, sisters, aunts, and/or girlfriends (Panos Institute 1990; McArthur 1990; Puentes-Markides 1993; Crystal et al. 1989; Seeley et al. 1992; Ankrah et al. 1993; Ankrah, Nkumbi, and Lubega 1989a). Most caregiving is unremunerated labor, imposed on the women by cultural traditions or circumstance. Although the women's role is indispensable, paradoxically it is valued little as a component of AIDS care. Although 329 abstracts reported studies at the Berlin Conference (1993) on the risks of infection, burnout or stress, support needs, and other aspects of professional care providers, only a single abstract focuses on women as caregivers. Ssemukasa and Brehony (1993) describe rural women in Rakai District, Uganda, who are used outside their families to give care to any person in the village who is sick with AIDS. But rather than project a collaborative and esteem-enhancing role for women, an exploitative traditional pattern is apparently being institutionalized by an AIDS service organization. Although trained to provide herbal treatment for symptomatic AIDS, these same women must also gather firewood, collect water, and cultivate the land.

The second important consequence to women of a shift to a family-centered system of care and support relates to the health care needs of the women themselves. Before AIDS, it could be assumed that the women caregivers were healthy. HIV-positive women must now attend to the needs of others—especially sick husbands—while they themselves are ill (Ankrah 1993; Ankrah, Nkumbi, and Lubega 1989a, 1989b; Ankrah et al. 1993; Ankrah et al. 1992; Kreyenbroek et al. 1992). Keogh et al. (1989) find that the fifty-five HIV-infected women enrolled in a cohort study in Kigali, Rwanda, have no programs to meet their survival needs apart from the counseling services supplied through a research project. Kerering (1992) reports the predicament of HIV-infected women heads of households in the Netherlands who have no close family members with whom to plan for the surviving children or to help with their own care. Ankrah (1989b) and Olowo-Freers (1992) find that among families in Uganda, when women become ill with AIDS before their husbands do, they may be sent back to their parents or kin. If husbands needed care first, the women are usually obligated to attend to them. HIV-positive women may also be sent away by the family because of the assumption that they brought the disease into the family to be passed on to other males of the household through levirate (the practice of marrying one's deceased husband's brother). Bertozzi, Ankrah, and Ngaiza (1990), in assessing support for survivors in Kagera, Tanzania, observe that when women are household heads, but without traditional or religious sanction for the marriage, the HIV-positive woman cannot claim an inheritance of property for the children of the deceased husband. For many who have weakened ties with their own rural-based families, viable support systems are lacking and prostitution becomes an alternative to starvation. Similar family and home care scenarios could develop in Asia and Latin America, especially as HIV-infection and AIDS increase among female factory workers and among commercial sex workers, who migrate to urban cities (Cash 1993).

Living Without Support

Social isolation may be the greatest impediment faced by HIV-infected women and others at high risk in forming and utilizing social networks and support systems. Isolated rural women of nonindustrialized countries, as well as the marginalized poor women of the inner cities of industrial North America and Europe, may lack the information, communication, and often the self-esteem to initiate collective action for self-protection or to reach out to others for help.

Hammel and Jaeger (1992) find that economically secure European women with child care responsibilities commonly have only parents and children available with whom to talk. As the disease worsens, and with a lack of close friends, they are forced to turn to the professional network of care providers for support. Researchers suggest that apart from medical care, emphasis must be placed on the social function of transmitting information, including its value in putting HIV-infected women in contact with other women to break down their social isolation. Erik et al. (1992), who studied a peer support and family therapy program for HIV-infected former drug users in the Women's Center in the Bronx, New York, observe that these women also face considerable social isolation. Of seventy subjects (thirty-five women and thirty-five men), 83 percent live alone and 50 percent have no telephone. They conclude that because of "social alienation and difficulties in accessing health care and effecting reunions with families, peer support groups filled an important need and should be included in all health care" (Erik et al. 1992). Bertozzi, Ankrah, and Ngaiza (1990) find that HIV-infected and uninfected women in Kagera, Tanzania, have the same dread of being infected, have lost spouses, and have to care for orphans. But women have never made any attempt to come together to share their perceptions and needs.

The assumption should not be made that nonformal and informal systems of social networks, community-based organizations, and families are assured alternatives when and where the health care system inadequately addresses the needs of HIV-infected women or uninfected women in high prevalence countries. Such services that exist may not be perceived as socially welcoming, or they may be physically out of reach. Women may be constrained by caregiving to other family members or even forbidden to participate in collective actions by husbands in cultures where women's movements and contacts with others are circumscribed or at the discretion of men.

Women Working with Women

Transforming the health care system and utilizing support systems more effectively must start with women's perceptions, perspectives, and experiences of AIDS. That is, a change in the models described above will necessitate a change in the way women perceive the challenge that the disease poses for them and the way they realign their forces to cope with it. This is not a revolutionary idea. Women have traditionally solved problems by coming together around some common issues (Ameda 1992). March and Taqqu (1982) say that "women's associations promote confidence, organize leadership and resources, and thereby create leverage for women. Although they may not invert the overall structural authority of men over women, they do redistribute power and resources in some important ways." Ulin adds that the solidarity of women in rural African communities may be their greatest source of strength for coping with the AIDS epidemic.

We propose model care and support systems that highlight the collaborative efforts of the HIV-positive and the HIV-negative women in meeting women's needs. Women have clearly moved toward one another via their groups, organizations, and networks. But they have not yet substantially moved *together* as women who are HIV-infected and uninfected to challenge the crippling effects AIDS will have on millions of women by the end of this decade (Merson 1993; Preble 1990).

Part of the problem lies in the continued perception of uninfected women that AIDS is something that happens to some "other" woman. This view allows such women to feel that their homes, their children, their lives cannot be touched by the "pain" of the infected women (Ruzek 1978:215). Although this perception characterizes a vast majority of women questioned in KAP surveys, others have decided to get involved in combating the disease. "Women Positive" networks have been established, for example, in Argentina, Canada, Kenya, Australia, England, and the Netherlands. The initiative for structuring care and support for HIV-positive women, however, has frequently come from HIV-negative women. Much of this leadership has come from women professionals in the health care system (Berer and Ray 1993).

Women have only recently begun to move, collectively, within or against health care structures to remove constraints that block care to women. The change in the CDC diagnosis of AIDS to include women-defined criteria (1993 Revised Classification 1992) is an example of a major effort that has opened up the prospects of care to all women at risk because of the advocacy and activism of a few. The power to transform both care and support systems is within the capacity of women collectively, but that power must be activated by a conception that scrutinizes what HIV-positive and HIV-negative women have done and what they have learned thus far in managing the epidemic through their individual, separate capacities as health care providers, scientists, researchers, caregivers, and women infected with or affected by HIV/AIDS.

This pooling of experience should lead women to evolve strategies that engage the health care system in the process of gender-sensitive change. Raikes (1989) argues that the system has a responsibility to help women overcome the obstacles to accessing health care that have been created. The collective effort of both HIV-positive and -negative women should enhance the capacity of support systems to be a sustainable resource, actively securing for the HIV-infected women the care they need and proactively targeting other, uninfected women for AIDS prevention.

In the model described here, the woman remains a decisive figure in the provision of care and support. However, the central task is to transform both systems to work synergistically for women. Such transformation is a possibility.

Rofes and Paras (1991), for example, describe the actions taken because of the sociodemographic change in the epidemic, to make a shift from monocultural groups, where mainly homosexual white males were served, to multicultural groups. A transformation was made in the training of volunteers and health care providers, in the service delivery system and community outreach strategies, and in program design and organizational structure to respond to new populations affected by AIDS.

In essence, the health care and support systems must be brought into a continuous process of interaction through linkages and mechanisms that women devise to consider issues and provide feedback on the systems' response to women. To be effective, HIV-negative and HIV-positive women, working through both systems, must use the leverage of their solidarity—which will be greater than when HIV-positive women sought to work alone.

Women continue to be gatekeepers (Alpern 1987) to health care in the context of both nonindustrial and industrial countries. Women's visibility as power brokers can be enhanced by pivotal leaders (e.g., Hillary Rodham Clinton's efforts to transform the health care system in the United States). Women everywhere in strategic places and with high profiles should push to the limit those situations that permit high levels of involvement in restructuring health care policy.

Hillary Rodham Clinton's role at the forefront of a reform effort is significant for another reason. It illustrates how women, who may be personally unaffected by the systems' barriers to care, use their influence to ensure that marginalized, infected women who have few if any possibility of challenging the dominant powers of the system are nevertheless covered.

A good model in which HIV-negative and -positive women join hands against AIDS is seen in WAMATA's program in Tanzania. Although not exclusively targeting women, WAMATA has attracted a female HIV-positive and HIV-negative membership. It has created an environment in which women with HIV infection can share freely with uninfected women, and thus find the support denied them in the family context where they may often be accused by their husbands and relatives of causing the infection and therefore rejected by them. Through such support, they are able to accept their HIV status.

Hickert (Berer and Ray 1993; Denenberg 1993) gives several examples of how, in several low-prevalence countries in the South Pacific, a single woman, or a small group of women in their professional roles, have advanced care and support to HIV-positive women or have successfully promoted AIDS-prevention activities. In Western Samoa, the minister of education, a woman and the *Metai* or local chief, advocates the inclusion of AIDS education and family life in the school curriculum in face of opposition from the political and religious establishments. In French Polynesia, a lone community social worker at an STD clinic has established a social network of men and women who come for services at the clinics she serves. Another woman who directs the nursing school offers specialized courses in STD/AIDS prevention and has incorporated AIDS materials into nursing training. Nursing staff in the Cook Islands are spearheading AIDS-prevention activities, with the director of nursing and the head of the Health Education Unit becoming personally involved—the latter working closely with local NGOs. Other women who operate within the framework of nonmedical NGOs have developed outreach efforts with women in commercial sex work in Fiji. The Women's Crisis Center there has incorporated STD/AIDS awareness and counseling training into their national and local training programs.

Training can be designed to support women who may be or may have become HIV-positive as a result of rape or abuse. The Fiji Red Cross, with a large network of volunteer community health workers (VCHWs), most of whom are women, has given training in HIV prevention and has developed a training workbook, a flip-chart, and a script for use in their work with village populations. Similar illustrations can be found in Africa, Asia, and Latin America, as well as in the industrial countries.

Women must reassess the role they play in bringing their scientific skills to bear, for example, in tracking the natural history of the AIDS disease in women. If STDs are a major cofactor of HIV transmission and if women are underserved by STD facilities because they are asymptomatic or because of stigma or inappropriate procedures for diagnosing the disease in women, women scientists must persevere until solutions are found. The research questions and behavioral change strategies pertinent to women will be most relevant when they are posed or found by women who bring this knowledge to bear on policies and programs in their communities. At the level of caregiving and support, as long as women, through their collective efforts, do not insist on a restructuring of gender responsibilities in the management of patients in home-based care, for example, they will be left with the burden of care. Instilling a practical model of sharing needs to begin with a more ideological and activist stance spearheaded by women themselves.

AIDS Prevention

Women must use care and support systems in a way that transcends the "moment," the immediate period of dealing with a sufferer. These systems can be the vehicles for launching activities for prevention. This is obvious, for example, when health practitioners contact HIV-positive women to educate them about AIDS, when antenatal women are informed about risks, or when adolescents are provided with STD and health care along with messages on safe sex. These activities have now become conventional AIDS-prevention strategies. But the virus has shown its near-human capacity not to conform to conventional pathways. Innovative ways must be continually pursued to confront the new problems that HIV/AIDS creates for women. The use of care and support systems as a means to innovative measures for prevention is ably illustrated by the Association for Women, Orphans, and Families (AWOF), founded by St. Francis Hospital, Nsambya, a missionary facility in Kampala, Uganda. This association has devised an ingenious way to address the issue of child survivors after their parents' death. They focus on helping mothers write a will. These women have been left to care for their children after the death of the father, even when they themselves are HIV-infected or have AIDS. Considering that such mothers are often illiterate, AWOF has co-opted the services of FIDA, Uganda's association of women lawyers, to assist families with drafting a will. Many come from poor families with little if any property, since women are barred by tradition from inheriting land. Therefore, they are given a small grant to purchase a sewing machine, set up a small business, and acquire land or other transferable goods. The children, the heirs at the death of the mother, are brought into the process; they are included in formulating the will. Where necessary, the children are given school fees, training, or help in finding a job. Throughout this process the infected family member is provided the care that she sought through the hospital but that brought her to the attention of the association.

Women Working with Men

Men can assist in making this model work. Clearly transforming the response of caregiving systems is not an effort that women can tackle alone and succeed in without involving the men as health professionals, researchers, and policy makers. At the family level, men as spouses or sexual partners have a vested interest in women's posterity as well as their personal survival. In many parts of Asia and Africa, for example, considerable emphasis is placed on having sons to ensure the perpetuation of the lineage or family, the inheritance of property, and the fulfillment of obligations to ancestors. HIV-positive and -negative women collectively must show men that their self-interest is served by sharing responsibility with women to stop AIDS (Panos Institute 1992). SWAA contends that in undertaking the tasks of organizing and mobilizing themselves to provide health care and social support, they "look forward to the active participation of men, governments, and agencies" (Mahmoud, de Zalduondo, and Zewdie 1990).

The Way Ahead

This article has proposed a model of care and support built around HIV-negative and HIV-positive women who combine forces to make systems both sensitive and effective in meeting women's needs. The AIDS pandemic is gradually being acknowledged as the disease of "everywoman" and "everyman," as no nation or population is spared. Unfortunately women are being infected and affected as HIV and AIDS spread. Yet formal systems are slow to respond to this new reality. Women, who have much at stake—and are at great risk if they adopt a posture of denial and indifference—can make a difference in how quickly this model becomes a dominant pattern in strategies to deal with AIDS. Because of a recognized capacity of women to organize, communicate, and share experiences of their lives with one another, a model that capitalizes on this strength has enormous potential. Women have already seized the initiative to use their social networks to create support systems. Although the obstacles imposed by the formal health care system have not been removed, they have been identified. Reforms for improving the support system and getting health care systems to give a high priority to creating women-centered models are possible. Such reforms require that concerned HIV-negative and HIV-positive women seize the initiative to produce models in which all women in their various situations and contexts fit and in which women can play a role in combating AIDS.

REFERENCES

AIDS and women: Nonwhites face the biggest risk. 1987. *Time* 129 (27 April): 66.

Allen, Machelle H. and Janet Mitchell. 1993. Bridging the gap between people of color and their physicians: How to build a partnership. *Positively Aware* (Spring).

Alpern, Barbara A. 1987. *Reaching Women: The Way to Go in Marketing Health Care Services*. Chicago: Pluribus.

Ameda, Regina. 1992. Forging Effective Networks: Forgotten Lessons from Traditional African Women. Mayatech Corporation. Unpublished.

Ankrah, E. Maxine. 1991. The impact of AIDS on the social, economic, health and welfare systems: Preserving the family of mankind. In G. Gaetano, ed., *Science Challenging AIDS*. Basil: Karger.

———. 1993. The impact of HIV / AIDS on the family and other significant relationships: The African clan revisited. *AIDS CARE* 5 (1): 5–22.

Ankrah, E. Maxine, et al. 1992. Stress and Coping Among Rural Families in Uganda. International Conference on AIDS, Amsterdam, July 19–24. Abstract Th.G.P.19.

———. 1993. Family Provision of Care to Persons with AIDS in Urban and Rural Uganda. International Conference on AIDS, June 6–11. Abstract PO-D22–4086.

Ankrah, E. Maxine, Stephen Nkumbi, and Monica Lubega. 1989a. AIDS and African Women. Fifth International Conference on AIDS, Montreal, June 4–9. Abstract Th.G.P.19.

———. 1989b. The Family and Caregiving in Uganda. Fifth International Conference on AIDS, Montreal, June 4–9. Abstract WGP 32.

Berer, Marge and Sunanda Ray. 1993. *Women and HIV/AIDS: An International Resource Book*. London: Pandora.

Berlin Conference. 1993. Ninth International Conference on AIDS. Summary.

Bertozzi, Stephen, E. Maxine Ankrah, and Magdalene Ngaiza. 1990. Tanzania—Assistance to Survivors of the AIDS Epidemic: A Review of the Policy Options. *World Bank*. Unpublished. June.

Boodman, Sandra G. 1993. Medical school grads: More women than men. *The Washington Post*, July 6, p. 5.

Boom, Frans van den and Larry Gostin. 1992. The Social Construction of AIDS. *Conference Summary Report*. Amsterdam. International Conference on AIDS, 33–43.

Brenner, B. E. and J. Kauffman. 1993. Reluctance by internists and medical nurses to perform mouth-to-mouth resuscitation. *Archives of Internal Medicine* 153 (9 August): 176–69.

Brokenshaw, David, ed. 1998. Anthropological Perspectives on AIDS in Africa: Priorities for Intervention and Research. *Executive Summary*. Workshop. Family Health International. Washington, D.C., January.

Caldwell, John, et al. 1994. African Families and AIDS: Context, Reactions, and Potential Interventions. Canberra: Health Transition Series No. 4: *Sexual Networking and AIDS in Sub-Saharan Africa: Behavioral Research and the Social Context*, ed. I. O. Orubuluye et al., 235–41. Canberra: Australian National University.

Cash, Kathy. 1993. Experimental Educational Interventions for the Prevention of AIDS among Northern Thai Single Female Migratory Adolescents. International Center for Research on Women. Unpublished.

Crystal, S., et al. 1989. Female Family Members as Mediators of Utilization of Health and Social Services. International Conference on AIDS, Montreal, June 4–9. Abstract Th.D.P. 15.

Dambita, C. 1993. AIDS spreads fastest among young women. *The Washington Post*, July 29, A1.

Denenberg, Risa. 1992. Invisible women: Lesbians and health care. *Health PAC Bulletin* 22 (1): 14–21.

———. 1993. The community: Mobilizing and accessing resources. In Felissa L. Cohen and Jerry D. Durham, eds., *Women, Children, and HIV/AIDS*. New York: Springer.

D'Eramo, J. E., D. Z. Kirshenbaum, M. McCarthy, and T. Davis. 1991. Women and

Minorities Have Less Access to AID Drug Trials. Seventh International Conference on AIDS, June 16–21. Abstract W.D. 4291.

Donnan, K. 1991. The Rejection/Denial Syndrome Re Heterosexual Women with AIDS. International Conference on AIDS, Florence, June 16–21. Abstract W.D. 4292.

Elias, Christopher J. and Lori Heise. 1993. The Development of Microbicides: A New Method of HIV prevention for Women. Working Paper No. 6. New York: The Population Council, Program Division.

Erik, K., et al. 1992. The Women's Center: A Peer Support and Family Therapy Program for HIV-Infected Ex-Drug Users in the Bronx. International Conference on AIDS, Amsterdam, July 19–24. Abstract POB 3412.

Esu-Williams, Eka. 1992. The Worldwide Epidemic, 1992. Keynote Address. Eighth International Conference on AIDS, Amsterdam, July 19.

Fransen, Lieve and M. Emmerman. 1993. Major Shortcomings in Programmes to Control STD/HIV among Women in Developing Countries. European Economic Community. Belgium. Mimeo.

Fraser, Howze D. and M. L. Lopez. 1989. AIDS and minorities: Strategies for prevention. International Conference on AIDS, Montreal, June 4–9; *Proceedings* 9 (5): 818. Abstract M.E.O. 23.

Gordon, Shelley B., et al. 1993. Analysis of HIV/AIDS Services Delivery for Women across National Programs. Ninth International Conference on AIDS, Berlin. June 7–11. Abstract PO-DO3–3520.

Gostin, Lawrence, ed. 1990. *AIDS and the Health Care System*. New Haven: Yale University Press.

Gould, Peter. 1993. *The Slow Plague: A Geography of the AIDS Epidemic*. Oxford: Blackwell.

Greco, D. B., et al. 1993. Changes in epidemiological characteristics of a population with risk behavior for HIV infection in Belo Horizonte, Brazil (1986–1992). *Conference News*. International Conference on AIDS, Berlin, June 10, Abstract WS-C04–3.

Greif, G. L. 1993. A support group for nurses working with AIDS patients in a hospice. *AIDS Patient Care* 7 (4): 210–12.

Haines, Andy. 1993. Education and debate: Health care in Brazil. *British Medical Journal* 306 (6876): 503–6.

Hammel, G. and H. Jaeger. 1992. Heterosexually HIV-infected Women: Their Special Needs, Social Networks, and Support Systems. International Conference on AIDS, Amsterdam, July 19–24. Abstract PoB 3414.

Heterosexual contact displaces drug abuse as main source of AIDS in women. 1993. *American Journal of Hospital Pharmacy* 50 (10): 2011–12.

Hu, D. J., et al. 1993. AIDS Rates and Socioeconomic Variables in the Newark, New Jersey, Metropolitan Area. Ninth International Conference on AIDS and the Fourth STD World Congress, Berlin, June 6–11. Abstract WS-C04–2.

Jaensen. 1988. Workshop. Family Health International. In David Brokenshaw, ed., *Anthropological Perspectives on AIDS in Africa: Priorities for Intervention and Research. Executive Summary*. Washington, D.C., January.

Kablinsky, Marge, Judith Timyan, and Jill Gay. 1993. *The Health of Women*. Boulder: Westview.

Kajura, Ellen, et al. 1993. Building Community Capacity to Cope with Adversity: The Role of a Traditional Support Network. Marrakech. Eighth International Conference on AIDS in Africa; Eighth African Conference on Sexually Transmitted Disease, December 12–16. Abstract M.R.T. 024.

Kalibala, S. and Noerine Kaleeba. 1989. AIDS and community-based care in Uganda: The AIDS Support Organization, TASO. *AIDS Care* 1 (2): 173–75.

Keogh, P., et al. 1989. Evaluation of the Social Services Needs of HIV+ Women Enrolled in a Cohort Study in Kigali, Rwanda. International Conference on AIDS, Montreal, June 4–9. Abstract T.E.O.3.

Kloser, P., et al. 1990. Women's Clinic: A Full Service Clinic for Women with HIV Disease. International Conference on AIDS, San Francisco, June 20–23. Abstract S.D. 816.

Kreyenbroek, Marion, et al. 1992. Need for Comprehensive Care in HIV-Infected Families. Eighth International Conference on AIDS, Amsterdam, July 19–24. Abstract MoD 0067.

Leserman, Jane, Diana O. Perkins, and Dwight L. Evans. 1992. Coping with the threat of AIDS: The role of social support. *American Journal of Psychiatry* 149:1514–20.

Levine, Carol. 1990. In and out of hospital. In Lawrence Gostin, ed., *AIDS and the Health Care System*, 45–61. New Haven: Yale University Press.

Lewin, Ellen and Virginia Ilesen, eds. 1985. *Women Health and Healing: Toward a New Perspective*. New York: Tavistock.

Lynch, Maureen F. 1992. Social support in men and women with AIDS. In M. Ross Seligson and Karen E. Peterson, eds., *AIDS Prevention and Treatment*, 59–73. New York: Hemisphere.

Manci, Merci. 1993. Traditional Medicine, Practice in HIV/AIDS and Sexually Transmitted Disease Prevention in South Africa. Eighth International Conference on AIDS in Africa; Eighth African Conference on Sexually Transmitted Diseases, December 12–16. Abstract Th. R T 029.

Mann, Jonathan. 1990. AIDS and Health Workers from a Global Perspective. Afterword. In Lawrence O. Gostin, eds., *AIDS and the Health Care System*, 233–38. New Haven: Yale University Press.

Mann, Jonathan, Daniel J. M. Tarantola, and Thomas W. Netter, eds. 1992. *AIDs in the World*. Cambridge: Harvard University Press.

Mansfield, S. and S. Singh. 1993. Who should fill the care gap in HIV disease? *Lancet* 4342 (8873): 726–28.

March, K. S. and R. Taqqu. 1982. *Women's Informal Associations and the Organizational Capacity for Development*. Monograph Series No. 5. Rural Development Committee. Center for International Studies. Ithaca, N.Y.: Cornell University.

McArthur, L. C. 1990. *Report of the Public Hearing on AIDS: Its Impact on Women*. New York State Division for Women, p. 63.

McGrath, Janet, et al. 1993. AIDS and the urban family: Its impact in Kampala, Uganda. *AIDS Care* 5 (1): 55–70.

McNamara, Regina. 1992. Female Genital Health and the Risk of HIV Transmission. HIV and the Development Programme. New York: UNDP. Unpublished.

Merson, Michael H. 1993. Slowing the spread of HIV: Agenda for the 1990s. *Science* 260 (May): 1260–68.

Miller, Heather G., C. F. Turner, and L. E. Moses, eds. 1990. *AIDS: The Second Decade.* Washington, D.C.: National Academy.

Minkoff, H. L. and J. A. DeHovitz. 1991. Care of Women Infected with the Human Immunodeficiency Virus. *JAMA* 266 (16): 2253–58.

Moore, Molly. 1993. Indian village women fight state, husbands to ban liquor. *The Washington Post*, December 19, A33, 38.

Moses, Stephen, et al. 1992. Impact of user fees on attendance at a referral centre for sexually transmitted diseases. *Lancet* 340 (August 22).

1993 Revised Classification System for HIV Infection and Expanded Surveillance Case Definition for AIDS among Adolescents and Adults. 1992. *Morbidity and Mortality Weekly Report* 41 (December): 1–19.

Noor, Kathleen, Sheila Tlou, and James Noor. 1993. The threat of AIDS for women in developing countries. In Felissa L. Cohen and Jerry D. Durham, eds., *Women, Children, and HIV/AIDS.* New York: Springer.

Olowo-Freers, Bernadette. 1992. *Cultural and Social Aspects of Sexual Behavioral Practices That Contribute to the Transmission of HIV/AIDS in Uganda.* Proceedings of the Workshop, February 19–21, Kampala, Uganda. Unpublished.

O'Neill, J., et al. 1991. Increasing Capacities of Community-based Primary Care Health Systems to Provide HIV Services. International Conference on AIDS, Florence, June 16–21. Abstract W.D. 114.

Panos Institute. 1990. Panos Dossier. Who cares, who pays? *Triple Jeopardy—Women and AIDS.* London: Panos Institute.

———. 1992. Panos Dossier. A development issue. *The Hidden Cost of AIDS—The Challenge of HIV to Development.* London: Panos.

Patton, Cindy. 1993. With champagne and roses: Women at risk from/in AIDS discourse. In Corinne Squire, ed., *Women and AIDS: Psychological Perspectives*, 165–87. Newbury Park, Calif.: Sage.

Pizurki, Helena, et al. 1987. *Women as Providers of Health Care.* Geneva: WHO.

Quinn, S. Crouse. 1993. AIDS and the African-American woman: The triple burden of race, class, and gender. *Health Education Quarterly* 20 (3): 305–20.

Raikes, A. 1989. Women's health in East Africa. *Social Science Medicine* 28:447–59.

Reese, J. and D. Thomas. 1993. HIV manifestations in women. *Positively Aware* 21 (Spring).

Reid, Elizabeth. 1990. Placing Women at the Centre of the Analyses. Paper presented to CIDA, Ottawa, December 6.

Richardson, Diane. 1988. *Women and AIDS.* New York: Methuen.

Robb, Linda, C. Rodriguez, and C. Wickins. 1992. Designing Service Delivery Plans for HIV Positive Women and Their Children. Mimeo.

Rofes, E. and M. Paras. 1991. Transforming AIDS Groups from Monocultural to Multicultural. Seventh International Conference on AIDS, Florence, June 16–21. Abstract W.D. 57.

Roongpisuthipong, Anuvat, et al. 1993. Siriraj Hospital, Bangkok, Thailand. HIV/AIDS Collaboration, Bangkok. Centers for Disease Control, Atlanta. Rapid Rise in Maternal HIV-1 Seroprevalence, Siriraj Hospital, Bangkok, Thailand. Ninth International Conference on AIDS and Fourth STD World Congress, Berlin, June 6–11. Abstract WS-C04–4.

Rosser, Sue V. 1991. Perspectives, AIDS, and women. *AIDS Education and Prevention* 3 (3): 230–40.

Rushton, C. H. and E. E. Hogue. 1993. Balancing personal risk and professional responsibility: The case of AIDS. *Pediatric Nursing* 19 (4): 418–20.

Rutuyuga, John B. K. 1993. AIDS Home-Based Care in Africa. International Conference on AIDS, Berlin, June 6–11. Abstract PO. B-34–2303.

Ruzek, Sheryl B. 1978. *The Women's Health Movement: Feminist Alternatives to Medical Control*. New York: Praeger.

Samaranyake, L. P. and C. Sully. 1993. Revised guidelines for HIV-infected health care workers. *British Dental Journal* 175 (1): 2.

Schoepf, Brooke G. 1988. Women, AIDS, and economic crises in Central Africa. *Canadian Journal of Africa Studies* 22:625–44.

Schoepf, Brooke G., et al. 1991. Gender, power, and the risk of AIDS in Zaire. In Meredeth Turshen, ed., *Women and Health in Africa*, 187–203. Trenton, N.J.: Africa World Press.

Seeley, Janet, et al. 1992. Family support for AIDS patients in a rural population in Southwest Uganda: How much a myth? International Conference on AIDS, Amsterdam, July 19–24. Abstract MoD 071.

Solomon, D. J., S. D. Merwin, and A. J. Jogan. 1990. Analysis of the Cost of Treatment for HIV Infection through the Michigan Medical Program. Paper 117. Annual Meeting of the American Public Health Association, October.

Ssemukasa, M. and E. Brehony. 1993. Women: The Key to Caring for the Sick at Home. Ninth International Conference on AIDS, June 6–11. Abstract WS-B33–5.

Stein, M. and V. Mor. 1993. The use of multiple physicians among symptomatic HIV-positive persons. *Medical Care* 31 (10): 968–74.

Stein, Zena. 1992. The double bind in science policy and the protection of women from HIV infection. Editorial. *American Journal of Public Health* 82 (11): 1471–72.

Stryker, Jeff, et al. 1993. AIDS–Policy: Two divisive issues. *JAMA* 270 (2): 2436.

Sturdevant, Nancie, N. Powers, and P. Clarke. 1992. Promoting Research and Health Care Delivery to HIV Women. Eighth International Conference on AIDS, Amsterdam, July 17–21. Abstract PoD 5744.

Ulin, Priscilla R. 1992. African women and AIDS: Negotiating behavioral change. *Social Science Medicine* 34 (1): 63–73.

UNDP (United Nations Development Program). 1992. *Young Women: Silence, Susceptibility, and the HIV Epidemic.* New York: UNDP.

UNICEF. 1993. Family and Community Core. Technical Support Group Meeting. *Report,* June 15–18. New York: UNICEF.

Valdiserri, Ronald, et al. 1992. Structuring HIV prevention service delivery systems on the basis of social science theory. *Journal of Community Health* 17 (5): 259–69.

Wasser, S. C., M. Gwinn, and P. Flemming. 1993. Urban-nonurban distribution of HIV infection in childbearing women in the United States. *AIDS* 6 (9): 1035–42.

Watstein, Sarah B. and R. A. Laurich. 1991. Other Women of Color and AIDS. *AIDS and Women: A Source Book.* New York: Oryx.

Wells, Deborah V. B. and J. F. Jackson. 1992. HIV and chemically dependent women: Recommendations for appropriate health care and drug treatment services. *International Journal of the Addictions* 27 (5): 571–85.

Wetzel, Janice W. 1993. *The World of Women: In Pursuit of Human Rights.* London: Macmillan.

Williams, A. B. 1992a. The epidemiology, clinical manifestations, and health maintenance needs of women infected with HIV. *Nurse Practitioner* 5 (May 17): 31–34, 37–38.

———. 1992b. Women and the AIDS epidemic: No longer hidden. *Today's OR Nurse* 7 (July 14): 23–27.

Williams, Eka, F. Mahmoud, D. Zewdie, N. Luo, M. Kabeya, C. Banura, and H. Isaack. 1991. Coping with AIDS: The Challenges Facing Women in Africa. Fifth International Conference on AIDS in Africa, Kinshasa, October 10–12. Abstract W.O.C. 1.

Wintersteen, Richard T. and L. Young. 1988. Effective professional collaboration with family support groups. *Psychosocial Rehabilitation Journal* 1 (July 12): 19–31.

Women and Poor Bear the Brunt. 1993. *Conference News.* International Conference on AIDS, Berlin. June 10, p. 7.

World Council of Churches. 1993. *Participating Action Research on AIDS and the Community as a Source of Care and Healing.* Kampala: WCC.

World Health Organization (WHO). 1993. *The Global AIDS Strategy.* AIDS Series 11. Geneva: WHO.

Young women are more susceptible to AIDS, UN study reveals. 1993. *American Journal of Hospital Pharmacy* 50 (10): 2012.

PART FOUR

Promising Directions

16 | Dilemmas for Women in the Second Decade

ELIZABETH A. PREBLE AND GALIA D. SIEGEL

Never before has sexual activity created such risks and resulted in such devastating consequences for women worldwide. Before the onset of the AIDS epidemic, women's sexual activity all too often resulted in painful emotional and physical repercussions: sexually transmitted diseases (STDs), unplanned pregnancy, and unsafe abortion. Sexually transmitted diseases and infections, while associated with varying levels of morbidity and infertility, are rarely fatal. In contrast, HIV infection in women frequently results in severe social stigma and family dissolution, and inevitably in prolonged periods of morbidity and early death.

The natural course of HIV/AIDS in women shows similar patterns throughout the world. Nevertheless, women living in developing countries face the disease in considerably different contexts than their developed country counterparts. Perhaps the most critical distinction between the epidemic in developing and developed countries is that women's HIV prevalence rates are dramatically higher in the poorest regions of the world (see article 11 in this volume, "The Epidemiology of HIV/AIDS in Women," by Buzy and Gayle). The second important difference is one of resources. Despite the contributions of foreign donors and modest allocations of funds from developing country budgets, the financial and human resources available to address HIV/AIDS in the poorest countries represent a small percentage of that spent on AIDS prevention in developed countries. Third, the structural factors maintaining women's subordinate status in many developing countries—illiteracy, lack of education, exclusion from the formal workplace—often isolate women from receiving HIV prevention messages. It is important to note that although women from developed countries tend to be less isolated from prevention messages, social marginalization and poverty increasingly correlate with women's HIV infection throughout the world (Ankrah, Schwartz, and Miller, this volume; Seeley et al. 1994; Sweat and Denison 1994).

In this article we explore a number of critical dilemmas that women, and AIDS policies and programs designed to serve women, are encountering in the second decade of the epidemic. We begin with an overview of "Women and AIDS" issues identified in the first decade, the 1980s, to establish a context for the dilemmas that have emerged in the 1990s. In addition, the similarities and distinctions between epidemics in developing and developed countries provide an informative background to the current challenges being faced by HIV-positive women, advocates, and program staff attempting to be gender-sensitive.

AIDS and Women in the 1980s

The first decade of the epidemic (the 1980s) in developing countries focused on Africa. Early studies in Zaire, Rwanda, and Uganda revealed large numbers of adults becoming HIV-infected through heterosexual transmission (Piot 1984; Van de Perre 1984; Serwadda 1985). In contrast, the initial preoccupation in the United States and Europe during this period was the rapid spread of the virus among homosexual men through sexual transmission. Globally, fear of both the illness and death caused by the disease escalated.

In the West, tensions emerged early on between those advocating a traditional public health approach to prevention of the disease—vigorous promotion of voluntary testing and counseling, public health reporting, and contact tracing—and those arguing that protection of human rights (privacy, confidentiality, etc.) conflicted with, and took precedence over, the public health approach (Joseph 1992). Fear of increased discrimination against homosexual men was central to this debate. The first decade included the initial identification of HIV/AIDS and a rapidly growing epidemiological and clinical understanding of the nature and course of this new disease. Knowledge of blood-borne transmission of HIV led to the development of a blood test for antibodies to the virus, and steps were put into place to protect blood supplies.

Behavioral researchers, health educators, and other communication experts in both developing and developed countries attacked the problem of promoting behavior change for AIDS prevention but often with the unspoken assumption that these were only temporary measures, as a vaccine would be developed in the near to medium-term future. This proved, unfortunately, to be a false hope, as the prospect of a safe, effective, and affordable vaccine continues to be elusive (Bolognesi 1994). Meanwhile, no proven models of influencing sexual behavior at the level necessary to curb the epidemic existed. The family planning field, from which one might have expected relevant experience, had taken more than two decades and significant levels of funding to demonstrate increases in the use of modern contraceptive methods and concomitant falling birth rates. Even then, this success is limited to selected countries in the developing world.

During the 1980s in both developing and developed countries, issues of HIV infection among women played little or no part in the unfolding, dramatic dialogue. Most of the women initially found to be infected in the United States and Europe (outside the blood transfusion route) were intravenous drug users or sexual partners of intravenous drug users. These women did not have a voice in the emerging AIDS movement. This movement was led by economically advantaged, well-educated, white homosexual men. In high prevalence countries in Africa, despite the fact that women constituted 50 percent of those infected, women's concerns and ideas were similarly absent from the AIDS prevention debate led by governments, international donors, and nongovernmental organizations. For the most part, the growing women's health and "Safe Motherhood" movement also ignored AIDS; the epidemic was not viewed as a serious threat to female mortality.

Since the beginning of the epidemic in Africa, female morbidity and mortality caused by HIV/AIDS have been significant. AIDS-related deaths in women now rival deaths related to pregnancy and childbirth in most developing countries. In a number of high-prevalence urban areas in Africa, one in three to four women are infected with HIV, whereas estimates of a woman's lifetime risk of dying from pregnancy-related causes in Africa approximate one in twenty (WHO 1991a). Further, HIV/AIDS was not embraced as a priority health problem by child survival programs in the 1980s despite early data from Africa documenting high rates of HIV infection among women in their reproductive years, and an increasing understanding of perinatal transmission rates.

As the epidemic unfolds, however, it becomes increasingly clear that HIV/AIDS interacts with, and has profound effects on, a wide range of health and development efforts. In a 1990 study of ten AIDS-affected African countries, AIDS was projected to cause a 12 percent to 25 percent increase over the number of under-five deaths projected by the United Nations in the 1990s, an additional 1.4 to 2.7 million under-five deaths in these countries (Preble 1990). The successes of many infant and child mortality interventions are reversing as a result of the epidemic, largely due to rates and patterns of HIV infection in women (Valleroy, Harris, and Way 1990; WHO 1991b).

Dilemmas for Women in the 1990s

In the 1990s, the areas of most rapid HIV spread are clearly in developing countries. Up to 30 percent of pregnant women have been found to be infected in several sub-Saharan African urban centers, including such as Kigali, Rwanda; Kampala, Uganda; Francistown, Botswana, and Blantyre, Malawi (U.S. Bureau of the Census 1995). Data from the second decade of the epidemic in the United States and Western Europe show signs that HIV transmission rates among the male homosexual population have slowed, whereas incidence is increasing among sexually active women and intravenous drug users and their sexual partners (see article 11 in this volume).

More than a decade into the epidemic, the social and economic consequences of HIV/AIDS are becoming increasingly well understood. The effects of the epidemic are not confined to the health sector but pose broad-based economic development problems. Programs designed to promote women's development, however, through improving literacy, income-generation, or child care practices, are ill-equipped to deal with more fundamental and socially sensitive problems of sexuality, gender relations, death, and dying. A better understanding of the magnitude of the problem has promoted a keener vision of the actual range of needs of AIDS-affected women and families. Despite dramatic increases in female morbidity and mortality because of AIDS, for example, the burden of care and support still falls disproportionately on women, the traditional caretakers of families. Taking on additional responsibilities in the home further isolates women from the public sphere, reinforcing and preserving gender inequality (du Guerny and Sjöberg 1993).

As inadequate as critics may feel AIDS *prevention* efforts have been, efforts in the area of *care and family support* in developing countries have been virtually untouched. Despite gains in the HIV/AIDS field, a number of fundamental dilemmas, both in the prevention and care domains, remain to be addressed in the second decade in order to develop effective and appropriate policy and program strategies for women.

Status of Women

One of the often-debated dilemmas of AIDS prevention for women mirrors an ongoing discussion in the overall field of women's development: whether it is more effective to develop vertical AIDS prevention efforts targeted to women or to focus on broader efforts to improve women's status. Some argue that the former is ineffective without first improving women's empowerment, literacy, economic and social status, and the fundamental sociocultural environment, and that AIDS prevention programs must attack structural and environmental determinants of HIV infection.

A variety of programs have been developed over the years (before the AIDS epidemic) to improve the status of women. These approaches are described by

Rathgeber (1990) as WID, WAD, and GAD. The WID (women in development) approach from the early 1970s involves the "integration of women into global processes of economic, political, and social growth and change." WID was based on the modernization paradigm and focused on "minimizing the disadvantages of women in the productive sector and ending discrimination against them," ignoring or minimizing women's reproductive lives. The WAD (women and development) approach followed in the latter 1970s, focusing on the relationship between women and the development process, in which "women's condition is seen primarily within the structure of international and class inequalities." Under the WAD approach, women's income-generating activities flourished. The GAD (gender and development) approach, which was developed in the 1980s, is based on socialist feminism, and identifies the root of women's oppression in the social construction of production and reproduction. Women are seen as "agents of change rather than passive recipients of development assistance."

Regardless of which philosophical approach is adopted, the benefits of any major women's development activity or policy will likely arrive too late to prevent millions of women from becoming HIV-infected and dying of AIDS. Both efforts to improve women's status and specific approaches to help women avoid HIV transmission, are needed simultaneously. With limited resources, however, determining the optimal balance between the two is not always clear. Increasingly, HIV/AIDS programs working with women address the structural factors that subordinate women, while simultaneously providing prevention services. For example, in Nigeria and Thailand, groups of brothel- or hotel-based sex workers, with the support of the establishments' management, have organized and gained the power to, as a group, refuse to service those clients who reject condom use. In Nigeria, one year after this intervention began, enhanced confidence and assertiveness were noted among the sex workers, and 94 percent of the women had increased their fees (de Bruyn 1992).

Targeting Women or Men with AIDS Prevention Interventions

In the area of behavioral interventions for AIDS prevention, debate centers around whether to offer women-centered HIV prevention interventions or to target men, who hold the decision-making power about sexual activity in many societies. Targeting women assumes, perhaps inaccurately, that women have the power or can attain the power to change the outcomes of sexual encounters. This approach can also result in a stigmatization of women as major transmitters of the virus. In addition, targeting women may miss the opportunity to challenge masculine cultural and sexual norms that promote HIV transmission, and may support the perception that men need not take responsibility for the outcomes of their sexual pursuits. Targeting men, in contrast, can be criticized for failing to bring women into the mainstream of HIV/AIDS prevention efforts, for relying on men's dubious compliance or reliability, and for missing opportunities to empower women. The targeting debate is further complicated by the absence of studies that analyze negotiation and decision making between sexual partners.

Models of Behavioral Change

Most AIDS prevention intervention designs were initially based on strategies that were expedient and intuitively appropriate, but not necessarily proven effective. Early AIDS prevention campaigns in the United States were generic and emphasized fear-arousing messages ("AIDS kills"), and avoidance of risk behaviors—abstinence from sex and injection drug use—as the only means of preventing HIV infection. Since then it has been documented that positive, constructive AIDS prevention messages lessen the likelihood that an individual will "deny the validity of a message, dismiss its applicability to themselves, or adopt a fatalistic attitude if they are not presented with concrete steps they can take on their own behalf" (Solomon and DeJong 1986). In addition, prevention messages are most effective when tailored to a target population, indicating the need for specificity according to gender, culture, ethnicity, and religion (Mays 1988). In the early years of the epidemic, however, no proven prevention models existed, and few studies from the behavioral change intervention literature were appropriate for HIV/AIDS work.

In sites where KAP (knowledge, attitudes, and practices) studies were undertaken at baseline and some months or years after AIDS prevention and educational projects were initiated, great strides have been documented in increasing "K" and "A," with disappointing findings concerning the "P." There remain insufficient levels of change in high-risk practices to alter the alarming course of the epidemic. A KAP study among urban Rwandan women found that although 96–98 percent of women accurately identified routes of transmission, only 16 percent reported taking action to avoid HIV transmission. Only 7 percent of the women had tried condoms and 68 percent thought condom use may be dangerous. KAP studies in Zimbabwe, Uganda, and Botswana report similar findings (Lindan et al. 1991). Behavioral change programs informed by behavioral research can better identify and address such issues as the status of women and whether to target women or men in interventions.

In cases where behavior does appear to have changed, it is often difficult to attribute the change to any single intervention, as behavior change is driven and maintained by a complex and mutually reinforcing array of individual and social forces. Even where change is present, the millions of previously HIV-infected individuals continue to progress to AIDS. Some program critics fail to understand that the epidemic's course will be slow to change and difficult to document, no matter how effective the interventions (Philipson, Posner, and Wright 1994). Lack of proven effectiveness, however, makes it difficult to raise and maintain funding for programs addressing HIV/AIDS prevention.

In the family planning arena, changes in family size norms and corresponding fertility rates took many years to achieve, even with accompanying improvements in socioeconomic status and the availability of the family planning field's "magic bullets" of modern contraception and sterilization. The technological equivalent to contraception in the AIDS field, such as HIV vaccines and effective female-controlled methods, are many years away (Curran 1994; The Population Council 1994). Successful models of behavioral change that can reduce the spread of HIV on the population, as well as on the level of the individual, need to be identified, documented, shared, and replicated.

Vertical versus Integrated Programming

A debate strangely absent in the AIDS prevention field is one so often argued in health and other development circles: the relative effectiveness of vertical versus integrated programming. Because of the perceived immediacy of the AIDS epidemic and the enormity of its consequences, vertical national AIDS control programs have been developed in health ministries with the impetus and funding mainly from international donors. This "verticalization" of AIDS results in missed opportunities to piggyback onto other developmental efforts, particularly within the health sector itself. Many potential developmental allies regard AIDS as a new funding competitor rather than a broad-based development problem that affects, and is affected, by other sectors. The selective integration of HIV/AIDS programs with the maternal and child health (MCH) and family planning (FP) sectors could strengthen prevention efforts, and potentially mitigate the impact of HIV/AIDS on MCH and FP programs (Preble, Elias, and Winikoff 1994).

One of the strongest arguments for integration is the fact that AIDS has major repercussions on all phases of women's reproductive lives. AIDS is altering many standard approaches to the management of MCH services related to fertility regulation, pregnancy, delivery, and the postpartum period. For example, the most effective methods for fertility regulation—IUDs, oral contraceptives, and other hormonal methods—provide no protection against HIV infection. This poses a dilemma for health workers counseling women who desire both effective contraception and protection from HIV. Providing HIV prevention for women who desire pregnancy presents an even more complex question to MCH programmers, as condoms are then contraindicated. In addition, increased AIDS-related caseloads, AIDS-related deaths among health workers owing to both occupational and sexual transmission, and reduced resources could significantly compromise MCH services. MCH program managers and service providers can minimize this impact by understanding the nature of both technical and service-related issues that intersect the MCH and AIDS fields, and by seeking opportunities for program integration where appropriate (Preble, Elias, and Winikoff 1994).

Some potentially exciting and effective examples of integration of HIV/AIDS with nonhealth sector development programs are emerging. The use of an AIDS prevention curriculum for Peace Corps English language training in Africa and World Relief's Gateway Project linking women's microenterprise development to health promotion and education, including HIV prevention, are two innovative examples of integration. In New York City, HIV/AIDS prevention and care services are being integrated into programs providing combined foster care prevention and drug treatment services to women and their families. Although the obstacles to integration of services are formidable, a comprehensive understanding of the impact of HIV/AIDS on women, as well as on families and the community more broadly, signals the need for integrated approaches.

Lack of Attention to HIV/AIDS Care and Treatment

In the early years of the epidemic, developing country governments were advised by the World Health Organization's Global Programme on AIDS and others to concentrate scarce financial resources on prevention rather than care efforts. The concept of care was too often simplistically equated with the administration of AZT and other complex and expensive pharmaceutical regimens and lengthy inpatient hospital care, and hence deemed unrealistic. More fundamental, and ultimately more easily addressed needs were largely overlooked: general family care and social support, palliative treatment for opportunistic infections to relieve suffering and improve quality of life, and home (versus hospital) care for AIDS patients.

Within governments, social sector ministries in developing countries, on which such support depends, are usually the weakest and most poorly funded. According to the 1994 World Development Report, the percentage of total central government expenditures spent on social services such as housing, social security, and welfare ranged between 2 and 6 percent in Malawi, Kenya, India, Indonesia, the Philippines, El Salvador, and the Dominican Republic. These same services accounted for between thirty-one and thirty-eight percent of total central government expenditures in the United States, the United Kingdom and Brazil (The World Bank 1994).[1] In the present economic crisis befalling most African countries, the social service sector receives the first cuts and is ill-equipped to address an ongoing crises such as AIDS. The burden of care and the development of a social service infrastructure in poorer countries, therefore, is likely to remain with nongovernmental organizations (NGOs).[2] In the United States, providers of HIV/AIDS-related care and support are struggling to access private funding, as the pool of both government and private dollars is increasingly sparse.

Expatriate private voluntary organizations (PVOs)[3] and national or indigenous NGOs are traditionally best placed to address social-sector problems, yet few have developed appropriate AIDS care and support programs. Emergency relief projects, which care for women and families in times of short-term crises, often do not provide adequate models. Most refugee programs assume an intact family unit for placement and support. Furthermore, women with AIDS often do not come forward for support because of the stigma of the illness. Such women can be difficult to identify without intensive outreach efforts, which are often neither affordable nor available.

The policies of some major NGOs that support local child fostering or placement, or fund local group homes, often inadvertently preclude these organizations from working with AIDS-affected families. One NGO that supports sponsorship of African children in local group homes discovered that its by-laws limited support to needy children who resided in intact, biological families. Another "children's village" was prohibited from accepting children with serious illnesses, hence prohibiting the admission of AIDS orphans who may be HIV-infected and subsequently develop serious health problems. The alternative of foreign adoption of AIDS orphans from developing countries is unlikely on a large scale.

Many NGOs and PVOs find the development of HIV/AIDS prevention and/or care programs too overwhelming, as the epidemic challenges some basic tenets of program design. Organizations seek programs that are ultimately sustainable with indigenous resources, as well as those that are clearly time-limited, such as natural disaster relief. AIDS care programs tend to require in-kind materials and cash grants, making financial accountability particularly challenging. Moreover, both prevention and care programs may be socially and politically contentious because of the stigma of AIDS, specifically the association of the disease with sexuality and drug use. This stigma requires the development of sensitive and culturally appropriate means of addressing sexuality and sexual norms. Particularly for HIV/AIDS care and support, few models exist, and in the absence of credible models, many groups fail to know where to begin.

The development of home-based care services for persons with AIDS represents an essential shift from frequently inadequate inpatient, hospital-based care. Home-based care may, however, further burden women who are the providers.

Donor Engagement

All the fundamental elements that international donors typically avoid are inherent in providing care for patients with AIDS. First, it is difficult to make the recipients self-sufficient. AIDS patients will die soon after diagnosis, and their orphans will require care until adolescence. Second, it is difficult to ensure programmatic accountability. Funds channeled to the community level for food, clothing, and other in-kind donations are traditionally difficult to account for and are prime targets for corruption. Third, AIDS is a problem of long duration and broad scope. Unlike natural disasters, the epidemic is not confined to one well-defined disaster area and will be with us well into the next generation. Major donors, therefore, have largely avoided the challenge of HIV/AIDS care for women and families. Donor reticence to become involved in care and treatment is particularly problematic for women. On the one hand, women with AIDS are less likely than men to access what little hospital-based medical care is available. Second, as the primary caregivers in both hospital and family settings, women will continue to provide support to the ill, while receiving inadequate financial and social support services for themselves.

Biomedical Interventions

In both developed and developing countries, in the absence of a vaccine against HIV, there is an urgent need to develop female-controlled chemical and physical barrier methods, such as vaginal microbicides, that can be made available, acceptable, affordable, reliable, and confidential (see article 19 in this volume; Potts 1994; Stein 1990). However, if women's health advocates and female users of the technology are not involved in the research dialogue usually conducted with scientists, those funding the research, and policy makers, such technologies may be greeted with the same skepticism with which some feminists have come to regard modern contraceptive methods.

The force with which some feminists have spoken out against population programs has led some demographers and population experts to claim that feminists are blocking the introduction of important technologies and that "new rhetoric and political correctness may collide with effective approaches to the population problem" (Westoff 1994). Some 1990s feminists respond that they object not to family planning itself, but to "cavalier bureaucrats, misguided strategies and poor services that have harmed women's health, wasted money, and undermined the reputation of even the most well-intentioned providers" (Chesler 1994). Collaborative work to establish an ongoing dialogue between women's health advocates, program planners, and scientists on vaginal microbicide research and development is promising (The Population Council 1994), and may offer useful lessons to the AIDS field.

Debates on microbicide research and other female-controlled barrier methods address only one of the many ethical dilemmas and challenges regarding HIV/AIDS-related technologies that affect women. Until July 1993, 1977 Food and Drug Administration Guidelines excluded women "with child-bearing potential" from participating in U.S. drug manufacturers' antiviral therapeutic trials because of the fear of possible teratogenic effects on the fetus (Center for Women Policy Studies 1994). Although the federal AIDS Clinical Trial Group (ACTG) program has no such explicit regulations excluding women, the absence of women from clinical trials has been extensively documented (Long, Kirschenbaum, and McCarthy 1989; D'Eramo et al. 1991; Pearl et al. 1992). Subsequently, when the administration of AZT to pregnant women was found to help block vertical transmission of HIV, the CDC recommended its use with pregnant women who meet the initial study's eligibility criteria (Centers for Disease Control 1994). Currently, many public health groups in the United States are recommending routine voluntary HIV testing and counseling for pregnant women in light of these study results. Feminists fear the results of the AZT trial will be used to demand mandatory HIV testing of pregnant women and mandatory zidovudine treatment for HIV-positive women during pregnancy, despite concerns about the effects of AZT treatment on both pregnant women and their offspring (Bayer 1994; Kolata 1994). Throughout these debates on women's inclusion in clinical trials and the more current discussions about HIV testing and treatment regimens for pregnant women, some worry that concern for the fetus will overshadow efforts to protect pregnant women.

The Future

The AIDS prevention community—advocates, policy makers, program designers, project staff and clients—is only beginning to understand the multiple dimensions of the HIV/AIDS epidemic that concern women: the determinants of the rapid spread of HIV infection in women, the consequences of the epidemic for women and their families, and the complexity of preventing transmission of HIV to women. Initial efforts to develop AIDS prevention and care programs for women in the second decade of the epidemic have revealed immense challenges.

Policy makers and program designers concerned about women and AIDS must address various structural dilemmas. First is the question of how to balance the urgency of providing prevention options for women with the simultaneous need to address women's subordination and lack of power. A second critical decision, with both political and programmatic implications, is how to target both women and men appropriately with AIDS prevention interventions. Third, programs must decide whether to establish vertical or integrated interventions, an area in which the experiences of the family planning field can offer guidance.

Even as questions about how to best structure AIDS prevention interventions to serve women remain unanswered, there are also few models of successful behavior change for program designers to adopt. Those that have been proven effective need to be disseminated expeditiously. In addition, models for cost-effective and self-sustaining AIDS treatment and care are sorely lacking. As models are developed, it is critical that persons involved in the design and implementation be sensitized to concerns about burdening women as caregivers. Finally, decision making on the design and testing of female-controlled chemical and physical barrier methods for the prevention of HIV transmission and on the development of treatment strategies involving women must include women's health advocates and women users of the products.

Inclusion of women in prevention and care debates will promote greater insight into the multifaceted dilemmas facing women in the second decade of the AIDS epidemic and will help ensure that AIDS prevention programs are effective in protecting women.

REFERENCES

Bayer, R. 1994. Ethical challenges posed by Zidovudine treatment to reduce vertical transmission of HIV. *New England Journal of Medicine* 331 (18): 1223–25.
Bolognesi, D. P. 1994. The Dilemma of Developing a Vaccine Against HIV. Paper presented at the Tenth International Conference on AIDS, Yokohama. Abstract PS4.
de Bruyn, M. 1992. Women and AIDS in developing countries. *Social Science and Medicine* 34 (3): 249–62.
Center for Women Policy Studies. 1994. *Women and HIV/AIDS Fact Sheet.* Washington, D.C.: Center for Women Policy Studies.
Centers for Disease Control. 1994. Zidovudine for the prevention of HIV transmission from mother to infant. *Morbidity and Mortality Weekly Report* 43 (16): 285–87.
Chesler, E. 1994. Stop coercing women. *The New York Times Magazine*. February 6.

Curran, J. 1994. Personal communication. November 29.

D'Eramo, J. E., et al. 1991. Women and Minorities Have Less Access to AIDS Drug Trials. Paper presented at the Seventh International Conference on AIDS, Florence. Abstract WD4291.

du Guerny, J. and E. Sjöberg. 1993. Inter-relationship between gender relations and the HIV/AIDS epidemic: Some possible considerations for policies and programmes. *AIDS* 7: 1027–34.

Joseph, S. C. 1992. *Dragon Within the Gates: The Once and Future AIDS Epidemic.* New York: Carroll and Graf.

Kolata, G. 1994. Discovery that AIDS can be prevented in babies raises debate on mandatory testing. *New York Times.* November 3.

Lindan, C., et al. 1991. Knowledge, attitudes, and perceived risk of AIDS among urban Rwandan women: Relationship to HIV infection and behavior change. *AIDS* 5:993–1002.

Long, I., D. Kirschenbaum, and M. McCarthy. 1989. Women Underrepresented in AIDS Clinical Trials. Paper presented at the Fifth International Conference on AIDS, Montreal. Abstract C590.

Mays, V. M. 1988. Education and Prevention—Special Issues. Section Introduction. *American Psychologist* 43 (11): 948.

Pearl, M., et al. 1992. Women in U.S. Government Clinical Trials. Paper presented at the Eighth International Conference in AIDS, Amsterdam. Abstract PoB3866.

Philipson, T. J., R. A. Posner, and J. H. Wright. 1994. Why AIDS prevention programs don't work. *Issues in Science and Technology* (Spring).

Piot, P., et al. 1984. Acquired Immunodeficiency Syndrome in a heterosexual population in Zaire. *Lancet* 2 (8394): 65–69.

The Population Council. 1994. Partnership for prevention: A report of a meeting between women's health advocates, program planners and scientists. *Critical Issues in Reproductive Health and Population.* New York: The Population Council.

Potts, M. 1994. The urgent need for a vaginal microbicide in the prevention of HIV transmission. *American Journal of Public Health* 84:890–91.

Preble, E. A. 1990. Impact of HIV/AIDS on African children. *Social Science and Medicine* 31:671–80.

Preble, E. A., C. Elias, and B. Winikoff. 1994. Maternal health in the age of AIDS: Implications for health services in developing countries. *AIDS Care* 6 (5): 499–516.

Rathgeber, E. M. 1990. WID, WAD, GAD: Trends in research and practice. *The Journal of Developing Areas* 24:489–502.

Seeley, J. A., et al. 1994. Socioeconomic status, gender, and risk of HIV-1 infection in a rural community in south west Uganda. *Medical Anthropology Quarterly* 8 (1): 78–89.

Serwadda, D., et al. 1985. Slim disease: A new disease in Uganda and its association with HTLV-III infection. *Lancet* 2 (8460): 849–52.

Solomon, M. Z. and W. DeJong. 1986. Recent sexually transmitted disease prevention efforts and their implications for AIDS health education. *Health Education Quarterly* 13 (4): 301–16.

Stein, Z. A. 1990. HIV prevention: The need for methods women can use. *American Journal of Public Health* 80:460–62.

Sweat, M. D. and J. A. Denison. 1995. Reducing HIV incidence in developing countries with structural and environmental interventions. *AIDS* 9 (supplement A): S251–57.

U.S. Bureau of the Census. 1995. *HIV/AIDS in Africa*. Research Note 20. Washington, D.C.

Valleroy, L. A., R. J. Harris, and P. O. Way. 1990. The impact of HIV-1 infection on child survival in the developing world. *AIDS* 4:667–72.

Van de Perre, P., et al. 1984. Acquired immunodeficiency syndrome in Rwanda. *Lancet* 2 (8394): 62–65.

Westoff, C. F. 1994. Finally, control population. *New York Times Magazine*. February 6.

The World Bank. 1994. *The World Development Report 1994*. New York: Oxford University Press.

World Health Organization. 1991a. *Maternal Mortality Ratios and Rates: A Tabulation of Available Information*. 3d ed. WHO/MCH/MSM/91.6. Geneva: World Health Organization.

———. 1991b. *Projecting the Demographic Impact of the HIV/AIDS Pandemic*. Sixth Meeting of the Management Committee. Provisional agenda item 8, GPA/GMC(1)91.8. Geneva: World Health Organization.

17 | Women Educating Women for HIV / AIDS Prevention

KATHLEEN CASH

Northern Thailand

It is 11:00 P.M. at a garment factory in Thailand. The streetlights around the gates of the factory silhouette young female workers leaving the factory one by one or in clusters. Beyond the gate, waiting for them on motorcycles, are young men. Some couples drive off, others linger to talk. Inside the factory the door to the young men's dorm room opens and closes as women enter and leave. One young man sits under a tree within the gates, strumming his guitar, singing a love song to a fellow worker whose boyfriend has gone off with another woman. Her old boyfriend is sleeping with his new girlfriend in the men's dormitory. The guitarist tries to comfort her. Another young man tells us candidly, "I have slept with about eight women in the factory. I usually take them to the mountain or to a motel. No, I do not use a condom. I tell them I am a good boy." The truth is that he visits prostitutes so often that his mother advised him to get a blood test for AIDS. "Some young women do not even know what's happening when they have sex," one of the peer leaders tells us. They do not even know whether the boy has a condom on or not." Most of the young women tell me they don't know what to say. As I walk past the guard's post, a couple embraces in the shadows. I ask the guard about the love life of these young women. Without a trace of doubt in his voice, he vouches for their virtue. "They are all good girls. Nothing to worry about." His concern is maintaining friendly relations with them, so he minds his own business and, as a result, they trust him. "How would you compare these girls to the young girls you knew when you were growing up," I ask him. He answers that these girls are nothing like those he knew. "Girls today have boyfriends. They are free. Their parents do not know what they are doing." Aware of having contradicted himself, he looks embarrassed. "Do not worry," I assure him. But I know that all of us have a lot to worry about.

Urban America

It is 1972 in an urban classroom in the United States. I am teaching a group of mostly female adolescents about reproductive health. Despite their youth (their ages range from thirteen to seventeen) many have already had sexual experiences. In this safe environment they can talk freely, admitting their fears and vulnerabilities, why they "do it," and why they do not. One young woman, known for her promiscuity, admits she doesn't even like sex. "I just do it because I want someone to care about me. I want to be loved by somebody." Some of her classmates already have young children; a few have had abortions. Many said they did not even know what was happening the first time. "We cannot really talk to boys about stuff like this. They do not understand and we do not know what to say." That reproductive health course was an education to teachers and students alike; it opened lots of eyes. As teachers we were thinking of the need to improve women's health by educating them about reproductive health. But most important to these young women was their need for love and intimacy. AIDS was not a threat at the time, and though awful things could happen to young women, no one connected sexual activity with death.

Common Concerns

The factory workers in Thailand and teenagers in the United States have something unfortunate in common. Worldwide, the AIDS epidemic is spreading most rapidly among young women (UNDP 1992).

Much of the literature on AIDS advocates the need for new directions, claiming that current preventive efforts show signs of failure and that the initial momentum for behavioral change has stalled. But no such thing can be said of educational strategies to prevent AIDS in women—for the simple reason that few exist. Current strategies aimed at preventing AIDS and sexually transmitted diseases (STDs) neither target women nor propose behaviors that are appropriate to most women's lives. An effective educational strategy geared to women must focus on human interactions and relationships. A woman's vulnerability to HIV infection and her ability to protect herself do not depend on her actions or preferences as a socially isolated individual but rather on her social options. Her identity, and even survival, depend on her ability to meet the social expectations of others and to maneuver within often narrow sociocultural interpretations and rigid moral precepts of appropriate female behavior.

In this article I advocate targeted, highly focused interventions because, for many groups of women, these are the most needed (Parker 1992). Three questions are addressed:

1. Why has STDS/AIDS education not reached women?
2. Which STDS/AIDS educational strategies will reach women?
3. Will these strategies make a difference?

Reaching Women

Education is indisputably a powerful means of preventing the spread of the disease but more in question is what kind of education and for whom. Most money for AIDS education, whether public or private, has been spent on reaching a mass audience. Educational messages are heard on the radio and seen on television. They appear in the pages of newspapers and magazines and are distributed at health facilities or hung on bulletin boards. Most of them have the same purpose: warn and inform. But the effectiveness of mass campaigns and educational programs in changing sexual behavior is as yet unproven (Mann, Tarantola, and Netter 1992).

Though many citizens in countries where AIDS education has been promoted on a mass scale now have a basic (though sometimes confused) understanding of AIDS and its transmission, AIDS workers concur that knowledge of the disease does not automatically change risk behavior (Sepulveda, Fineberg, and Mann 1992).

The challenge is daunting. Unlike no-smoking campaigns, which try to change observable social behavior, STDS/AIDS prevention education ultimately aims at influencing people's most intimate, secret, sensitive behavior—their sexual behavior. Superficial approaches, such as materials only, short lectures, and quick workshops can have little if any effect on behavior as personal and as charged with moral ambiguity as sexual activity and are, in any case, no substitute for ongoing education based on person-to-person communication.

The effectiveness of warn/inform educational strategies is even more questionable when the general public they are aimed at is a mythical one. Often the target audience consists of those who have limited access to health services—people living in poverty and the disenfranchised, the illiterate, the migrants, teenagers, and children. More than half of this target population is female. Yet little has been done to educate women in ways that account for their particular situations.

Two handicaps prevent HIV/AIDS education from reaching women. The first is that a model of disease and prevention, though inappropriate for women, has nonetheless been imposed on the design of most programs, regardless of their audience. This model ignores formidable gender and social issues facing women who confront AIDS. It is predicated on the assumption that AIDS transmission is the consequence of actions by an individual who can change his or her behavior without social approval and without the cooperation or support of a partner. The educational messages that emanate from this model can be summarized as a series of dos and don'ts:

• Refrain from multiple sex partners
• Use condoms
• Treat and control STDS

The first message has no bearing on most women's lives as they either have one partner for a lifetime or serial partners (Brasil, Ferraz, and Ney 1992). But this inappropriate message is more than just symptomatic of the failure to account for the conditions in women's lives; it is counterproductive in that it conveys the idea that only promiscuous women get AIDS. In conveying that message it misinforms, stigmatizes, and impedes access to the facts of AIDS transmission. This message does not tell women in serial or monogamous relationships that they too are at risk. Among young female factory workers in northern Thailand, for example, AIDS was associated with promiscuity (having multiple partners). "Good" girlfriends with "good" boyfriends, did not perceive themselves as being at risk (Cash, Anasuchatkul, and Busayawong 1995). Such misconceptions promote the illusion that marriage or a conjugal relationship is an automatic immunization card (Lundgren et al. 1992). For most women, then, the message—"Refrain from multiple sex partners"—means that as long as they have only one partner they are not at risk and need do nothing more to protect themselves. Moreover, women who actively seek out information about the disease risk being perceived by others as promiscuous or believe themselves to be promiscuous for doing so.

The second message—"Use condoms"—is equally unsuitable for women. Although knowing how to use a condom and where to buy them is important, such knowledge becomes superfluous when women cannot request that their partners use them (Stein 1990). Although no one is prepared to question the efficacy of condom use at this point, the act of requesting such use is tacit acknowledgment that a risk is involved. Most important, insistence on the use of a condom challenges not only notions of trust, fidelity, and intimacy but the very character of the woman making the request, as well as her partner's character and the integrity of the relationship itself. In some countries a woman's value to her husband and the possibility of divorce or desertion depend on her ability to bear him children (Ulin 1992). Under such risks few women will advocate condom use.

Prostitutes who generally use condoms with clients forego their use with "trusted regular clients," regular partners, and lovers (Bwayo et al. 1992; Goldsmith 1993). Where prostitutes have low rates of HIV infection and use condoms routinely, nonclients present their greatest risk for infection (Kapila and Pye 1992).

The impersonality of the "Use condoms" message ignores the possibility that sexual relationships exchanged for money might involve emotional attachments as well (Ford and Koetsawang 1991). The possibility of a steady partner, a lover, or a high-paying client is not even considered. The prostitute must balance client refusal to wear a condom against her own survival. Moreover, every woman— whatever her occupation—must weigh the possibility of rejection, personal and social criticism, and even violence, if she insists on using a condom. "If a Latin woman says to a man 'Baby, you wear that condom or you're not going to have anything,' the man says, 'Well, tough luck. I'm not going to have anything with you.' He goes off with another woman, or simply smacks her" (Frieden 1989:5).

The third message—"Treat STDs and control their spread"—is unlikely to reach women for the very reason that STD control has had little impact on the general population. Even if facilities for the treatment and control of STDs are available, they are inaccessible to many women. In Thailand, for example, though there are walk-in STD clinics for the general public in the larger cities, merely entering such a clinic stigmatizes a woman as promiscuous. This is something few women are willing to risk. Education about STDs is sometimes provided to prostitutes at their place of work to obviate the stigma of entering a clinic. The existence of education and treatment centers is therefore not enough to assure their use, especially by women.

In maternal-child health (MCH), well-baby clinics, and family planning facilities geared to women's reproductive health needs, little or no information is available about STDs, including AIDS (Reid 1991). On a recent visit to the largest public Obstetrics/Gynecology facility in northern West Virginia, I found only one pamphlet on STDs (about genital warts) among the educational materials in the waiting room. When I asked why more information on the subject was not available to the public, I was told that patients "can get this information from behind the counter. Or, if she has an STD, we will give her this information."

The burden of shame, and to some extent proof, is left up to the client. When those who know little about STDs in general must ask for information about a particular STD, it is highly unlikely they will, especially when showing interest in such a sensitive subject invites speculation as to their motives and character.

Even though the messages that derive from this model are short-sighted in their approach to educating women around the world, could they nonetheless have achieved some measure of success in educating men? The answer—at least for men in the developing world—is not encouraging. These messages are unrealistic for the millions of men living in communities where customary values, expectations, and behavior are at odds with these messages. More tragically impractical are the millions of communities where the message "Use condoms" is advocated to men who have little or no access to any prevention resources, including condoms. Though these messages may have succeeded initially in galvanizing male homosexuals in the United States to change their behavior, the old admonitions and warnings have proven insufficient to the task of sustaining ongoing educational efforts as the demographic profile of HIV infection has changed. Does a message like "Refrain from multiple partners" have validity once the AIDS epidemic has gained a foothold within a community (Pollak 1992)? Unfortunately, this association of "promiscuity" and AIDS has reinforced what many societies already regard as a source of disease: social decay and immoral behavior.

A second handicap is the moral and interpersonal conflicts that AIDS prevention presents to women. Change can create conflict, not only within individuals but between those individuals and others, and most unsettling is change that questions one's moral self. According to Jean Miller (1976:83), "women stay with, build on, and develop in a context of attachment and affiliation with others," and "women's sense of self becomes very much organized around being able to make, and then to maintain, affiliations and relationships." She observes further that "eventually, for many women, the threat of disruption of an affiliation is perceived not just as a loss of a relationship but as something closer to a total loss of self." Carol Gilligan (1982) extends this interpretation of women's psychology to include the development of a moral self: "A morality of responsibility and care begins with a self who is enmeshed in a network of relations to others, and whose moral deliberation aims to maintain these relations."

If women's morality is a function of their ability to maintain and nurture these relations, and if in fact women's moral goodness is based on their social responsibility to enhance and maintain connections and attachments, then what social and moral conflicts and potential losses could the application of AIDS prevention strategies create for women? The overall issue may be one of sexual control or dominance, but the risks inherent in asserting themselves for their own protection in a relationship that makes no allowances for such assertive behavior are great indeed when one considers the potential consequences: disapproval, rejection, separation, isolation, and stigmatization.

The "double standard" that establishes different sexual norms for females and males condemns behavior in one sex that it condones in the other. Inherent in these sexual expectations are social expectations of the "good" and "bad" female: too experienced is bad, inexperienced is good; impolite is bad, respectful is good; assertive is bad, unassertive (passive) is good; too knowledgeable about sex is bad, naive and innocent is good. Consequently an active interest in AIDS prevention on the part of women (particularly during the initial stages of a sexual relationship or in the early years of marriage) requires relinquishing deeply held cultural values regarding what constitutes "goodness" in women.

As Miller points out, women have traditionally been defined and have defined themselves in relation to others. Most cultures define women as sisters, daughters, wives, mothers, and mothers-in-law (Chodorow 1974). What has surfaced during the AIDS epidemic is that these relationships are highly value-laden: women are expected to be "good" daughters, "good" wives, "good" mothers. Can a "good" girlfriend—a potential wife—risk talking about AIDS to the man she hopes to marry? Can she ask him to wear a condom? Can a wife risk questioning her husband about visiting other women when her family's stability depends on her ability to maintain family harmony? Who will be blamed or possibly deserted if the mother's questioning leads to family disharmony?

Social and familial pressures to be a "good" daughter can even threaten women's sexual and reproductive health. Whole communities in northern Thailand may be labeled by outsiders as "bad" because their young daughters are sold into prostitution. But to the families whose material as well as social survival is dependent on the sale of their daughters, the girls are "good," having fulfilled their obligation to provide a steady income for those who depend on them. So strong is the sense of obligation toward one's family that it effectively can counter efforts to promote self-preservation as a reason for preventing AIDS.

The personal conflicts faced by young women in northern Thailand became apparent during a program aimed at preventing the spread of STDs/AIDS, which was given in a garment factory by specially trained peer facilitators selected by fellow workers. Young women in this program were asked to read *Lamyai*, a novel about a young garment worker who contracts AIDS from her fiancé. When Lamyai learns that she is HIV-positive, she tells her sister that she will go on working in the factory to support her family until she is too sick to go on.

During the discussion that followed, young women in the group were asked what impressed them most about Lamyai. A frequent response was "She was like us; she was too naive." But the customary answer was "She was a good daughter." Being a good daughter was more significant than the fatal consequences of HIV infection.

Inconsistent answers can also be indicative of conflicting values, as evidenced by the results of a survey conducted among 240 unmarried female factory workers. Most of the respondents said they had a boyfriend though none admitted being sexually active.

On the other hand, male workers at the factory had few qualms about discussing their sexual behavior, whether in groups or individually. Behavior that was hidden and secret for the women was for the men a source of pride.

These contradictory results could indicate inadequacies in the survey instrument or possibly conflicts between long-standing values about the presentation of female propriety and changing values exemplified by these young women's actual behavior. Moreover, in group meetings, particularly when an outsider was present, the young women spoke as though they were sexually inexperienced. Although this denial may in fact help young women adapt to changing personal circumstances, their inability to acknowledge their real behavior can impair their ability to control its consequences and, in so doing, increase their risk of HIV infection (Cash, Anasuchatkul, and Busayawong 1995).

Finally, moral conflicts can be fueled or ignored by those responsible for making decisions and policies in the health field. Many "experts" on sexual behavior have no credentials other than their own experience and personal judgment—hardly solid qualifications for research or the elaboration of theory into practice. If the strategies and methods of those entrusted with spearheading the assault on AIDS are flawed by moralistic concepts of how women "should" behave instead of how they do in fact behave, the intended beneficiaries will suffer the consequences of these prejudices. Preconceived notions (e.g., "Women are too passive to talk about STDs and AIDS," "Sex education and AIDS education will promote sexual experimentation among young people," "We don't have to worry about these girls; they are all good girls") increase the risk factor by frustrating educational efforts and by supporting alarming beliefs. For example, a morally inspired belief—that the absence of premarital sex and ultimately marriage will protect a woman from HIV infection, a justification given for the lack of information available to girls on sex and STDs/AIDS—is simply untrue.

The gender dichotomy is nowhere more pervasive than in the belief that what is considered biologically "natural" (though culturally defined) justifies the moral order. Many cultures equate women's health with reproductive health. Women's sexuality is often silenced, feared, sublimated, or ignored. I recently critiqued a supposedly enlightened sex education curriculum for preteens. When this program talked about girls it described their reproductive system but made no mention of female sexuality, but when talking about boys it described only male sexuality. Maria Mies analyzed female oppression where men dress and act as though they lived according to seemingly contemporary values partaking in modern movies and the like but expect (and demand that) their women follow traditional norms, dress traditionally, and act traditionally, sometimes secluding them from public view (Mies 1982). In such cases the neglect of female sexuality or the use of "culture" to obstruct and control women's sexuality only furthers denial and closeted behavior.

> The moral institution of life cannot be understood by looking at moral expla-
> nations and by ignoring silences and secrets. The moral superiority of the
> respectable higher classes owes less to money than to the wealth of secrecy
> they control and use to cover their moral mistakes. (Addelson 1987:106)

Such contradictions—when translated into programs that frequently fail—only
accelerate the spread of AIDS among women and men.

Educational Strategies

In this section I address the question of which educational strategies will reach
women. I will focus on three aspects of an educational program and how these
relate to women's STDs/AIDS prevention needs. Each of these three aspects
should ideally be integrated into a program design.

The first issue is content, that is, what to teach. The content of an educational
program covers the information to be imparted, including the attitudes, values,
and behavior to be changed. The content areas that should be included in an
STDs/AIDS program for women are given below.

- *AIDS and its transmission.* Many AIDS workers have concluded that knowledge
  of AIDS does not necessarily lead to behavioral change. Some of the biggest
  obstacles to AIDS prevention in women are their ignorance about the disease
  and their illiteracy. Information about AIDS prevention should be adapted to
  what women already know and what they need to know. Access to such life-
  saving information should be the right of every citizen.
- *STDs and their transmission.* Many STDs go undiagnosed and untreated in
  developing countries in part because their symptoms are attributed to
  other causes. White discharge, for example, is said to be caused by seasonal
  changes, witchcraft, or sexual behavior (Bang and Bang 1989). Women's
  ignorance of STDs condemns victims to continual discomfort and often
  debilitating sickness, which can also bring unfortunate social consequences.
- *Acquiring and using condoms.* Women should have the chance to see, touch,
  and practice using a condom on an object that replicates a penis. In one peer
  education program young women practiced putting condoms on eggplants.
  The young women said that the activity was fun, "It taught us how a condom is worn, and if our boyfriends want to have sex with us, we can dare
  to talk to them about condoms." Women should also know where they can
  buy condoms or obtain them from different sources. Telling women to insist
  that their partners wear condoms does not necessarily enable them to do
  so, but familiarity with condoms demystifies them. Depending on the cultural context and one's personal situation, women have different opportu-

nities for self-assertion in a sexual relationship. For some this may mean being able to talk about condoms with their partner. For others it may mean insisting that their partner wear one. Whatever their circumstances, access to condoms and an understanding of their use are critical to the prevention of HIV in women.

* *Sexuality and women's sexual health.* Sex education is a controversial issue in many countries regardless of their level of economic development. There are no studies that prove or disprove the most common opposition to sex education, that it leads to early sexual experimentation. Certainly lack of knowledge has not helped prevent the spread of HIV. Culture defines, influences, and restricts women's experiences of sexuality. Information on sexuality and sexual health should include discussions on the physical aspects and variations of sexuality, distortions of sexuality, and violence against women. My own experiences in diverse settings in Asia, Africa, and the United States confirm that women want to know and share more information among themselves about sexuality and sexual health.

* *Reproductive health and family planning.* Both men and women need education that integrates reproductive health, family planning, and disease prevention. Though contraception is usually the woman's responsibility, the use of condoms is generally overlooked at family planning clinics. Having accomplished so much, family planning clinics fear stigmatization and the loss of clients if they introduce STDs/AIDS education. But unless they introduce this as a regular part of their program, not only does this fear become magnified but with the spread of AIDS some of their accomplishments may be lost. STDs/AIDS education and condom use could be integrated into family planning programs without the distinction of reproductive and sexual health but as a unified concept of family and individual health.

* *Communication and information sharing.* The most lasting sexual behavioral changes will be the outcome of person-to-person communication and contact. Learning to communicate knowledge and concerns to a partner, friends, and family is critical to AIDS prevention. Women have to be taught what to say and how to say it; they should learn how to talk to their partner about his sexual history; and within the confines of their culture they must learn how to talk to their children about AIDS and STDs. Educational materials, in combination with practice, can help them learn these skills. For example, a video entitled "Human Roulette," which tells the story of two Jamaican women, was used to generate discussion and practice in communication strategies that women might use with men (Wyatt et al. 1993).

* *Partner negotiation.* Giving women the opportunity to practice different kinds of negotiations by acting them out with a hypothetical partner is very

useful in gauging the results, as it enables women to talk about postponement, condoms, and abstinence. Women may not be able to replicate in reality the conversations they practice in an educational setting, but what they gain is communication skills and the ability to adapt their learning to an actual situation. During one such program, young women commented that although they were unable to do or say exactly what they had practiced doing and saying, the experience nonetheless gave them ideas for applying what they had learned.

- *Identifying risk behavior.* Acquiring a technical understanding of how AIDS and other STDs are transmitted does not necessarily enable a woman to apply that knowledge to her own situation and to identify personal risk behavior. An example of such selective oversight was provided by a seropositive woman who contracted AIDS from her husband. "I should have known [about the risk] because everyone said he was promiscuous," she said. But this same woman later intervened to break off a relationship between her sister and a man who had refused to have a blood test. Thus identifying risk behavior wherever it exists is an important skill, but women must also be able to communicate what they know to others and learn when and how to intercede to help them.

- *One's health and the health of others.* Enabling women to act or to assert themselves means providing them with the information and tools they need to reach a decision and to understand the consequences of that decision. Women are the primary caregivers in any family health crisis, with or without health resources, and certainly the AIDS epidemic is no exception. Women need to learn how to make decisions about protecting themselves and others from STDs/AIDS and about caring for those already afflicted.

- *Right to health education.* Women need to know where they can get information, treatment, and support in their battle against AIDS. But for the great majority of them, these sources of assistance are often inaccessible or nonexistent. Even where they do exist, women may lack the confidence to advocate for themselves or others. Learning how to do so requires that women devise strategies for improving their own sexual and reproductive health and that of their children. Their lives may depend on it. Women need to define and demand fundamental health rights that include access to information on STDs/AIDS prevention.

How realistic is it to expect that women can act on the knowledge provided above, given the social constraints placed on so many of them? Such action is possible only if communication is open and direct between the educators or the program planners and the women whose behavior they are trying to influence.

Private interviews and focus group discussions will encourage the development of effective communication. Inhibitions can block the free exchange of information, preventing some women from saying what others need to hear, forcing others to conform to what they think they should say.

Consistent attendance and honest participation in education are the best guarantees that participants' needs are being met. In Thailand, during an STDS/AIDS educational program, after peer leaders (selected by fellow female factory workers) were trained, the young women in the program felt comfortable enough to express what they wanted: information about sexuality, sex, and reproductive health.

The kind of materials most suitable for women is another important consideration. The range is enormous, and the selection depends on budget, program goals, and the participants' education and age. Generally, materials should be used to stimulate discussion and to focus thinking, but they also can be used to develop credibility for the participants and the program; for example, those who complete the program might be presented with a diploma or certificate. On the completion of a peer education project for female factory workers, participants received a diploma that also certified them as AIDS educators. Some of the young women decided, on their own, that they were henceforth responsible for teaching their families and friends what they had learned. To this end they photocopied educational materials to take to their villages. Others felt empowered by their diplomas and wanted to show them to their boyfriends, feeling themselves capable for the first time of initiating a discussion about AIDS and STDS. In Kenya a comic book was designed to educate prostitutes, which the prostitutes found useful because they could show it to clients to raise the subject of condoms more easily than if they had to broach the subject themselves (Ngugi et al. 1992). Materials can be used to initiate and focus discussion during educational programs, but the need for materials to promote the discussion of AIDS once the program is finished is often overlooked.

A second important aspect of educational strategies is the process: How is information conveyed and which teaching methods are chosen to make learning possible? In this article I will first consider process from an organizational perspective and then from a learning process perspective.

Organizational Perspective

From an organizational perspective, Project Saheli in Bombay, India, may serve as an example. This project involved a three-tier system of peer leaders, consisting of a *Saheli* (friend) for twenty girls, a *Tai* (sister) from the managerial cadre, and a *Bai* (mother) for eight *Tais* from the brothel owners' cadre. The organizational structure facilitated an interactive educational process. The project resulted in a substantial reduction of STDs (Kadam 1992).

Another example comes from sub-Saharan Africa, where informal support groups for women are common, especially in rural areas. What follows is taken from my fieldnotes in Malawi:

> I sit under the hot sun watching the rites of passage of a young girl being initiated into the rituals and knowledge of childbirth. The men of the village have been sent away. The older married women performed a highly seductive dance mimicking the sex act, their skirts lifted to their thighs. The younger married women in the audience sang and clapped and threw coins at the older women in appreciation. Finally it was time to reveal the secrets, but first the young initiate was placed on a rug in the middle of the throng, naked, exposed, and chastised for her failings. Grace (who speaks English) whispered, "The old women are telling her all the terrible things she's done."
>
> "What has she done?" I asked.
>
> "She's a gossip. Tells bad things to people and has caused lots of trouble in her family between her aunts. She's already had the baby. Not married."
>
> "Why tell her the secrets then?"
>
> "She has to be initiated. Most of these older women have been saving money for this; it's very important to them—their participation, the meal, the fun."
>
> Everyone ate beans and rice, and then I was invited into a thatched house to participate in the secrets of childbirth (promising I would never tell anyone what I had learned). The older women inside the hut dramatized the secrets of childbirth for the young initiate. I was moved by their performance and by the feelings of solidarity, competence, concern, and support that surrounded this young woman's initiation.

Many such informal groups already play a role in sex education and marriage counseling. These groups could play a significant role in STDs/AIDS prevention education in addition to that played by some nationally supported women's associations. Some promising organizations already exist, such as the Society for Women and AIDS (SWAA), with branches in twenty-six countries throughout Africa; the Neighborhood Mother Project in Zambia; the Society for Women and AIDS in Sierra Leone; TASO, the AIDS support organization in Uganda; and St. Martin's Clinic in Ghana (Panos Institute 1990; Hampton 1990).

An organization of HIV-positive and HIV-negative women in Ciudad Netzahualcoyotal, Mexico, has organized self-support groups promoting HIV prevention, education about sexuality, and human rights. The organization, SOLVIDA (Solidarity and Life), has used a process of community organization that crosses different sectors—schools, prostitutes, church groups, and housewives—to bring together women with different life experiences (Berner and Hernandez 1992).

At the Brazilian Center for Children and Adolescents, young women are trained as "multiplier agents for the defence of health." Thirty girls were selected to work in their communities as health agents, providing education about health, sexuality, and STDs/AIDS prevention. These health agents have organized meetings, held seminars, and given talks at universities and hospitals (Vasconcelos 1992).

Nonformal educational programs that provide health information, such as family planning, child survival, and maternal-child health programs (MCH), could incorporate education about STDs/AIDS into their programs. STDs/AIDS education could also be included in programs involved with economic development and women's productivity, for example, credit unions, cooperatives, self-help groups, and women's skill-training programs.

The formal educational system should incorporate STDs/AIDS prevention education at all levels of their curriculum. Countries with a high drop-out rate need to educate all children—male and female—before they leave school. School authorities must integrate STDs/AIDS education into the primary school curriculum, as that might be the only opportunity to reach young people before they engage in sexual experimentation.

Learning Process Perspective

From the perspective of a learning process, my own experience suggests that the most valuable programs have involved communication between women and between women and men. Some of the most encouraging examples of STDs/AIDS education for women have followed group process models that call for a member of the target group to be trained as a facilitator to educate her peers. Methods should be used that encourage participation and foster an atmosphere of welcome, sharing, respect, and understanding of others' problems and perspectives. Participants should be encouraged to reflect on ways that changes can be made. The most common means of fostering a participatory, supportive, and reflective process are narratives (stories), discussions, role playing, dramatizations, games, simulations, and other group process techniques that rely on the popular culture.

In Thailand young women in a garment workers' educational program played a board game that encouraged conversation and problem solving. The game challenged players to find solutions and to answer problems. Successful players were rewarded with play money. Since the young women helped one another decide which answer was correct, the game encouraged them to discuss problems associated with STDS/AIDS and fostered a spirit of cooperation among them (Cash. Anasuchatkul, and Busayawong 1995).

A successful learning process for an STDS/AIDS educational program should do the following:

- Appeal to the emotions, giving participants a personal stake in the outcome;
- Build skills and enable participants to practice new or unfamiliar behaviors;
- Enable participants to share experiences that give rise to new solutions.

Practitioners find it difficult to translate sexual behavior and AIDS research into pragmatic educational programs partly because traditional research vocabulary excludes words and nonverbal expressions that "real" women use. Without an understanding of female sexual expression—how women communicate with one another and with men about sex—educational interventions cannot connect with women's life experiences. Human beings' capacity for emotions is most fully expressed in the humor, tragedy or sadness, compassion, pity, and fear they experience in sexual relations. Women in developing countries are often depicted as living in abject misery. As a friend from Tanzania once commented, "One would think by the portrayal of African women in development literature that we would all have committed suicide by now." In my own experience I have observed women share stories about sex and sexual relations with a rich mix of emotions, especially humor.

In a peer education group among northern Thai, we produced a comic book with an invisible flying condom that talks to young women, telling them what to say to a young man about condoms. One of the writer's objectives was to provide peer leaders with material that would stimulate discussion about possible dialogues between men and women in different situations. Another objective was to use humor to facilitate conversation about subjects that young women might find embarrassing. The women admitted that although they could never talk like the flying condom, it nevertheless helped them find ways to express the same thoughts.

Lamyai, the Thai novel mentioned earlier, proved invaluable as a communication aid. Peer leaders in the factory were trained in ways to use the novel to begin discussions. The young women in the factory discussed what the heroine could have done before and after she had sex with her boyfriend to protect herself from HIV. But critical to these conversations was the learning process used to engage these young women in emotional, thought-provoking discussions and exchanges:

"I feel like I know Lamyai."

"I cried when I read this book."

"Why did Lamyai have to die?"

"Can you tell us where Lamyai lived?"

"I liked *Lamyai* because it was just like the real life of workers."

The novel's impact was evident in the degree to which the participants felt involved with and connected to the heroine's fate. They saw a possibility of their own future in what happened to her (Cash, Anasuchatkul, and Busayawong 1995).

A *Jatra* (cultural fair or carnival) was organized in Gadchiroli District, India, that focused on women's awakening and health. This intensive educational and cultural program involved a picture exhibition explained by local women that illustrated gynecological and social issues. There were also slide shows on STDs, AIDS, and reproductive health; songs about women's lives; a play entitled "When the Husband Gets Pregnant"; and a demonstration of the scientific principles behind so-called miracles performed by local magicians who often cheated women. The Jatra gave rise to a series of three-day camps for village women and youth. Men collectively signed a petition demanding a study of STDs in males as a result of the increased awareness on the subject. Village women participated in action groups to improve their reproductive health. All of this was a result of educational activities that involved the entire community in a highly participatory learning process (Bang and Bang 1992).

Second, learning how to negotiate with a partner or learning a new or unfamiliar behavior requires practice. Women need to be able to practice new behaviors, to develop skills in how to talk and communicate with a partner, friends, or family about STDs/AIDS prevention. Role playing is often advocated in nonformal educational programs as a means to assess behavior and to understand communication and conflict. This is certainly an effective technique. Role playing in some cultural contexts and without well-trained leadership can be too unfamiliar and misguided. I have frequently heard young women say, "We do not know what to say to a boyfriend." While practicing role plays or discussing various possibilities, young women revealed that they could not say what they said in the role play or what the materials suggested. On the other hand, these young women also said, "The practice gives us ideas and helps us think about things we do and say."

Finally, sharing, listening, and conversing with other women is an important means of education. A recent study suggests that women are most influenced by testimonials and focus group discussions (Wong-Rieger and Lindee 1992). As a child I once overheard an aunt being criticized for being a gossip. Her response was "How else do women learn except from talking and listening to one another?" Women's lives are not immutable nor is their behavior uniform.

In any context there is a range of behaviors, from women who say no to others who more willingly accept their situation. The solutions to the prevention of STDs/AIDS for women often lie within the target group itself. One of the best means for STDs/AIDS prevention is for women to learn from one another. That interaction should be the cornerstone of any educational program aimed at women.

The third important aspect of educational strategies is *context*, which involves creating an environment and circumstances that are most appropriate and supportive to women. The decision must be made as to when, in a woman's life, STDs/AIDS education should be provided, who should provide it, and where.

Environment is most significant for effective STDs/AIDS education as the venue must be private, safe, and familiar, ideally a place or space for women. Furthermore, the time set aside for meetings is a critical consideration. Times that conflict with women's work or familial obligations undermine program goals. Ideally education should reduce rather than increase daily stress. Priority should be given to young women before their first sexual experience or in the initial stages of sexual involvement or to unmarried, single women. Educators should preferably be respected members of their community or women with whom the participants can identify.

Imperative to women is that they meet where they can talk. Some programs have chosen places where women meet every day as part of their regular activities. In the factory mentioned previously, the leaders chose a dormitory room. In another program educators have created a space defined as an open educational area for young women (Vasconcelos 1992). The ideal place would be one that the women perceive as their own space dedicated to open discussion and the free exchange of information. In some countries women have access to Maternal-Child Health Clinics where a fifteen-minute educational message is often given before immunization sessions begin. Clinics such as these could also be used for STDs/AIDS education for women.

Educational programs must not conflict with women's work schedules or unnecessary demands on their time (Bhende 1993). If given the opportunity, participants should define where, when, and for how long they can meet. In one garment factory where health promoters from the public health department were the educators, worker attendance was poor because the promoters did not choose convenient times for their meetings. At another factory where meeting times were chosen by peer educators who also worked there, attendance was much higher because the workers were able to communicate to them when and for how long they could meet. Choosing a convenient time and length of session is therefore an important factor in determining success.

To maximize educational opportunities for the most vulnerable women, priority should be given to those who are most likely to change their behavior and who face the greatest risk. In countries where reproductive health and STDs education for women are low priorities and health budgets are already stretched, some groups should be given priority over others. Women not yet sexually active and young preadolescent or adolescent women deserve priority. One reason for this order of priorities is that the prevalence of HIV infection is highest in young women between the ages of fifteen to twenty-five (UNDP 1992). Another reason is that the potential is greater for changing and for influencing sexual behavior in young, never married women, particularly if STDs/AIDS education is sustained over time. Designing programs that meet the developmental needs and experiences of women between the ages of ten and twenty-five is critical to HIV/AIDS prevention. But what is most important is to reach young people before sexual habits are formed.

Finally, the frontline educator is crucial to an effective educational environment. Professional credentials have authoritative value but mere expertise is no guarantee of learning, nor does it promote the kind of long-term commitment to education required to change attitudes and behavioral norms or to provide enabling experiences for women. The best educators are often women in the community itself who are knowledgeable about health (particularly women's health) or peers who can be trained. TBAs (traditional birth attendants) and village health workers are well known health practitioners in many countries and often provide women with reproductive health information and services. These birth attendants can be trained to provide information and to educate other women about STDs/AIDS. A frontline educator should represent those with whom she is working. She must know women's roles, attitudes, and behavior and speak the local as well as generational and sexual language of women.

Peer leaders, when compared to outsiders, are likely to be more motivated to participate in an STDs/AIDS educational program, better able to acquire the skills needed by a facilitator, and more committed to the success of such programs. In one STDs/AIDS program, success depended on the leaders' ability to motivate their groups to participate in educational sessions. The peer leaders were more sensitive to the evaluation of their friends than were outsiders. In this same program, peer educators—less conditioned by pedantic methods of formal schooling—were more capable of facilitating group discussion and participatory learning activities than the more highly educated health promoters from the public health department. Some peer groups devised their own educational strategies. In a group, for example, where the peer leader was sometimes shy about initiating discussion, her friends took turns leading group discussions in her place. In another group one young woman took the role of a dunce—the one who answers all the questions incorrectly—while the others tried to find the right answers for her. Peer educators as well as participants took pride in "their" program because they felt they had made it what it was (Cash, Anasuchatkul, and Busayawong 1995).

Making a Difference

In this section, I address the final question—whether educating women will make a difference. The education of women alone might result in the same situation that is propelling the current spread of AIDS. Priority has been given to the education of men. But exhorting men to wear a condom has not been any more useful and successful than it would be to exhort women to say no. Both men and women need STDs/AIDS education.

Sexual vulnerability to STDs/AIDS has always involved a relationship between two people whether it be monetary, romantic, a relationship by choice or by arrangement, a thirty-year marriage, a five-month flirtation, or some mixture of the above. Prostitutes have children as well as steady partners, boyfriends, and sometimes husbands. Other women sometimes barter sex for economic stability and survival. STDs/AIDS prevention education for women must be developed in light of women's needs, wants, constraints, possibilities, and relationships.

The consequences of HIV infection and AIDS for women are shattering not only for the women themselves but also for women in relation to their attachments and obligations. In many societies women are regarded for their fertility, for their mothering and nurturing skills, and for their goodness as daughters, sisters, mothers, and wives. For these women HIV infection and AIDS bring stigmatization, isolation, rejection, and a dissolution of the relationships that provide identity and self-esteem. The physical suffering of many women with AIDS pales against their social ordeal as people with AIDS or as caregivers and mothers of those afflicted with AIDS.

It seems reasonable, if not obvious, that women should be enlisted in STDs/AIDS prevention educational programs in the most effective manner possible. Is the absence of programs designed for women the result of misinformed policies? Or is it indicative of an absence of political will?

A number of questions should be asked of policy makers to clarify their views on the subject of STDs/AIDS education for women. What if each country, urban center, or community supported the development of women and AIDS societies? What if these societies developed an activist, interventionist role throughout the country or region? What if these societies were made up of educators, women activists, and health practitioners whose purpose was to keep track of current educational interventions to prevent STDs, to support women, and to advocate the dissemination and implementation of interventions? What if these societies provided training opportunities for educators, women's organizations, TBAS, and village health workers to train potential educators in how to integrate and use STDS/AIDS prevention activities in their various programs? What if these societies served as clearinghouses for STDS/AIDS education within their country or region?

Similar questions should be asked of practitioners: What if all educators, health professionals, and media specialists who have contact with or influence women (particularly young women) were encouraged to think about ways they can integrate education about STDS/AIDS into their work? What if all teachers or trainers who work with women included STDS/AIDS education in their curricula?

And, finally, questions should be asked of parents, family, and community members: What if parents, families, and communities were encouraged and taught to communicate with their children to help prevent the spread of STDS/AIDS?

STDs/AIDS education for women involves both will and belief. Sometimes it involves discarding deeply entrenched, parochial, and self-seeking notions about women and replacing them with health-seeking, enabling, and empowering experiences. Turning the tide of the AIDS epidemic is inseparable from our belief and commitment to reach and educate both women and men—all its potential victims.

REFERENCES

Addelson, Kathryn Pyne. 1987. Moral passages. In Eva Kittay and Diana Meyers, *Women and Moral Theory*. Totowa, N.J.: Rowman and Littlefield.
Bang, R. and A. Bang. 1992. Why women hide them: Rural women's viewpoints on reproductive tract infections. *Manushi—A Journal about Women and Society* 69 (March–April): 27–30. New Delhi.
——. 1989. Commentary on a community-based approach to reproductive health care. *International Journal of Gynecology and Obstetrics* 3:125–29.
Berner, B. and A. Hernandez. 1992. The Formation of Women as Grassroots AIDS Education Promoters in Ciudad Netzahualcoyotl. POD 5886. Eighth International Conference on AIDS, Amsterdam.
Bhende, A. 1993. Evolving a Model for AIDS Prevention Education among Low-Income Adolescent Girls in Urban India. International Center for Research on Women, Washington, D.C.
Brasil, W., E. A. Ferraz, and C. P. Ney. 1992. Giving Subsidy to Encourage Women to Talk about Condoms. POD 5451. Eighth International Conference on AIDS, Amsterdam.

Bwayo, J. J., et al. 1992. Regular Clients of Female Sex Workers; Condom Use and Risk of HIV-1 Infection. POC 4182. Eighth International Conference on AIDS, Amsterdam.

Cash, K., B. Anasuchatkul, and W. Busayawong. 1995. Experimental Educational Interventions for AIDS Prevention among Northern Thai Single Migratory Female Factory Workers. International Center for Research on Women, Washington, D.C.

Chodorow, Nancy. 1974. Family structure and feminine personality. In M. Z. Rosaldo and L. Lamphere, eds., *Women, Culture, and Society*, 43–66. Stanford, Calif.: Stanford University Press.

Ford, N. and S. Koetsawang. 1991. The sociocultural context of the transmission of HIV in Thailand. *Social Science and Medicine* 33 (4): 405–14.

Frieden, T. 1989. Brazil: There are still people who say AIDS doesn't exist. *Links: Health and Development Report*. Brooklyn, New York.

Gilligan, Carol. 1982. *In a Different Voice: Psychological Theory and Women's Development*. Cambridge: Harvard University Press.

Goldsmith, Barbara. 1993. Women on the edge. *The New Yorker*, April 26, pp. 64–81.

Hampton, J. 1990. *Strategies for Hope*. Vols. 1–4. London: ActionAid, AMREF, and World in Need.

Kadam, M. 1992. Project Saheli: A Peer Education Model. D410. Second International Congress on AIDS in Asia and the Pacific, New Delhi.

Kapila, M. and M. Pye. 1992. The European Response to AIDS. In J. Sepulveda, H. Fineberg, and J. Mann, eds., *AIDS Prevention Through Education: A World View*, 199–236. New York: Oxford University Press.

Lundgren, R., et al. 1992. Guatemala City Women: Empowering a Vulnerable Group to Prevent HIV Transmission. POD 5445. Eighth International Conference on AIDS, Amsterdam.

Mann, J., D. Tarantola, and T. Netter. 1992. *AIDS in the World: A Global Report*. Cambridge: Harvard University Press.

Mics, Maria. 1982. *The Lacemakers of Narsapur: Indian Housewives Produce for the World Market*. London: Zed.

Miller, J. 1976. *Toward a New Psychology of Women*. Boston: Beacon Press.

Ngugi, E. N., et al. 1992. Development of an Educational Booklet for STD / AIDS Control among Female Commercial Sex Workers in Kenya. POD 5644. Eighth International Conference on AIDS, Amsterdam.

Panos Institute. 1990. *Triple Jeopardy—Women and AIDS*. London.

Parker, Richard. 1992. AIDS education and health promotion in Brazil: Lessons from the past and prospects for the future. In *AIDS Prevention Through Education: A World View*, 109–26. New York: Oxford University Press.

Pollak, Michael. 1992. *AIDS: A Problem for Sociological Research*. Newbury Park, Calif.: Sage.

Reid, Elizabeth. 1991. Placing women at the centre of the analyses. In *Women and AIDS: Strategies for the Future*. Canadian International Development Agency.

Sepulveda, J., H. Fineberg, and Jonathan Mann. 1992. *AIDS Prevention Through Education: A World View*. New York: Oxford University Press.

Stein, Zena A. 1990. HIV prevention: The need for methods women can use. *American Journal of Public Health* 80:460–62.

Ulin, P. 1992. African women and AIDS: Negotiating behavioral change. *Social Science and Medicine* 34:63–73.

UNDP. 1992. *Young Women: Silence, Susceptibility, and the HIV Epidemic*. HIV and Development Program Series, New York.

Vasconcelos, Ana. 1992. *Programme of Multiplier Agents for the Defence of Health*. Casa De Passagem, Recife, Brazil.

Wong-Rieger, D. and D. Lindee. 1992. Evaluation of Support Group Development for Men and Women with HIV/AIDS. POB 3817. Eighth International Conference on AIDS, Amsterdam.

Wyatt, G., et al. 1993. Female Low-Income Workers and AIDS. International Center for Research on Women. Washington, D.C.

18 | Talking about Sex: A Prerequisite for AIDS Prevention

GEETA RAO GUPTA, ELLEN WEISS, AND
PURNIMA MANE

With no immediate prospect of a vaccine or cure for HIV infection, existing programs to control the sexual transmission of the virus focus primarily on sexual behavior and its modification. Abstinence, partner reduction, mutual monogamy, condom use, and the avoidance of high-risk sexual practices (such as anal sex) are the behavioral recommendations promoted by such programs (WHO/GPA 1992). Although abstinence and partner reduction can be adopted by an individual, partner cooperation is essential for ensuring mutual monogamy, condom use, and the avoidance of high-risk sexual practices. A prerequisite for partner cooperation is effective communication.

Defining Effective Communication

AIDS prevention efforts depend, in large measure, on communication strategies to educate people about the risks of HIV infection and to motivate the adoption of risk reduction behaviors. At the interpersonal level as well, communication is a vital means by which an individual can influence another's behavior. For the purposes of this article we define effective communication as the ability to bring about behavioral change successfully through the transfer of information, which includes the transfer of facts, opinions, feelings, and experiences.

When faced with resistance, however, a mere transfer of information often is not sufficient to bring about behavioral change. Under such circumstances, negotiation, a special form of communication, is required. Negotiation is a form of communication designed to reach an agreement through a compromise

(Fisher and Ury 1981); it is the term most often used within the context of AIDS prevention to describe the kind of communication necessary to bring about changes in established patterns of sexual behavior.

Implicit in the term *negotiation* is the pragmatic acceptance that the behavior to be adopted is, for whatever reason, unacceptable, and therefore the partner who is concerned about risk has to convince the other partner of the value of the protective behavior. The process of negotiation may be facilitated either by offering a special asset or favor in exchange for the protective behavior or by threatening the loss of some valuable asset if the behavior is not adopted. Negotiation implies that each of those involved in the interaction have some special asset with which to bargain or something valuable to withhold.

In this article we examine the extent to which effective communication and negotiation by women for HIV prevention occur in heterosexual relationships, given the unequal power balance typical of gender relations in many societies worldwide. By drawing on findings from sexual behavior and family planning research, as well as evidence from recent studies supported by the Women and AIDS Research Program,[1] we also analyze the economic and sociocultural factors that influence a woman's ability to communicate about sexual matters, particularly with reference to condom use and mutual monogamy. We conclude with recommendations for actions to facilitate effective communication between partners for risk reduction.

Patterns of Communication on Sex

To negotiate condom use or mutual monogamy, women must be able to talk about sex and sexual matters with their partners. Given cultural norms in many societies, however, verbal communication about sex is difficult not only between sexual partners but also between parents and their children. Two studies conducted in Harare, Zimbabwe, reveal that the vast majority of adolescent girls and boys attending school do not discuss sexual matters with their parents, nor with aunts and uncles who traditionally have been responsible for the sex education of youth (Bassett and Sherman 1995; Wilson et al. 1995).

A study conducted in Mexico City among ninety-nine school-based adolescents found that approximately one-fourth of girls and boys reported never communicating with their mothers about sexuality (Givaudan et al. 1995). Reportedly, communication on sexual topics with the father was even more infrequent than with the mother. In addition, far fewer boys spoke with their fathers about sexual topics than girls. Mothers and fathers of these boys and girls interviewed in the Mexico City study reported similar patterns of communication. In general, parents who discussed sexual matters were more likely to focus on puberty and AIDS, rather than sexual relations, contraceptives, or sexually transmitted diseases (STDs) (Givaudan et al. 1995). Likewise, a national survey conducted recently in Mexico on a representative sample of 2,595 adults shows that only 35 percent feel equipped to discuss topics related to sexuality with their children (Pick de Weiss, Givaudan, and Cohen 1993). Notably, Mexican parents surveyed in both studies expressed a desire to improve their ability to communicate with their children about sexual matters.

Although little research is available on patterns of sexual communication between men and women, the evidence that exists suggests that the taboo associated with communication about sex continues into adulthood. Worldwide, many men and women do not talk to each other about sexual topics. This is equally true of societies that project diverse images of sexuality such as Brazil, which is perceived to be a highly sensual and erotic society (Goldstein 1995; Parker 1991), and India, where sex and reproductive life are more often viewed as private and secret matters (Bang and Bang 1992). In an analysis of sexual relationships in Ghana, Ankomah (1992) reports that personalized information of any sort is rarely exchanged between partners. To demonstrate the level of distrust between the sexes in Ghana, he cites a popular saying in that society, "If you receive any good news, never disclose it to your wife." Evidence suggests that open communication between partners about sex may be uncommon in other parts of sub-Saharan Africa as well (Caldwell, Caldwell, and Quiggin 1989). Similarly, a study of communication between spouses in Asian countries finds that approximately one-third of the women interviewed in the Philippines never talked to their husbands about sexual matters; the same was true of 47 percent of women in Singapore and 53 percent of women in Iran (UNESCAP 1974). In a study conducted in Guatemala, in-depth interviews conducted with twenty-two women attending prenatal and STD clinics show that half the women never spoke with their husbands about sex. In the same study Guatemalan men report that they speak more freely with commercial sex workers about sex than with their steady partners (Bezmalinovic et al. 1995).

Although it is more common to discuss contraception than sex within a steady relationship, some studies report that this topic can be a source of conflict. In Brazil, interviews with forty female factory workers, and group discussions conducted with more than a hundred participants from *favelas* in Rio de Janeiro and São Paulo, reveal that sterilization is the most common form of contraception (Goldstein 1995). This finding, coupled with data from a Jamaican study of women who work as informal commercial importers and factory workers, suggests that women's contraceptive choices reflect their desire to avoid communication with their partners on the subject (Wyatt et al. 1995).

If, as the above data suggest, strong cultural restrictions exist against communication on sex and contraception between partners, we need to know more about the ways in which women and men make decisions about when and how sex takes place and with whom. Typically men are more likely than women to initiate, dominate, and control sexual interactions and reproductive decision making. Specifically, decision making vis-à-vis the use of contraceptives often lies in the hands of men, although the responsibility of using contraceptives is often borne by women (Boulos, Boulos, and Nichols 1991; Boye et al. 1991). Several studies show that women are frequently denied the right to decide when to have sex and with whom (cited in Elias and Heise 1993). Elias and Heise (1993) also reveal the extent to which forced sex, sexual assault, and physical violence are realities in the women's lives, both within and outside consensual unions. Other evidence, however, shows that women are sometimes able to use mitigating circumstances to refuse sex. Studies conducted in India, Papua New Guinea, and Guatemala find that women use illness or that they are breast-feeding, menstruating, or pregnant to refuse sex (George and Jaswal 1995; Jenkins et al. 1995; Bezmalinovic et al. 1995). Nevertheless, such periods of refusal are temporary and may anger the man. For example, one Guatemalan woman at a prenatal clinic reported her experience of communicating the need for post-partum abstinence to her husband: "My husband is really closed. He doesn't like to talk about these things. When I came here [to the clinic] and the doctor put me on 'la dieta' (postpartum abstinence), [my husband] got angry because he thought I was lying to him because there is another man."

Preventing disease by refusing sex may be difficult and actually may increase a woman's risk if her partner seeks out other sexual partners during her period of abstinence (Ulin, Cayemittes, and Metellus 1993). In Papua New Guinea, for example, 58 percent of eighty-four rural men report having extramarital sexual relations when their wives are pregnant or breast-feeding (Jenkins et al. 1995).

In addition to sociocultural restrictions against talking about sex and contraception, women's silence is often reinforced by the unequal power balance in gender roles and relationships. The social construction of male and female sexual roles and identities reflect inequalities that are characteristic of gender relations in the social and economic spheres of life, with women relegated to a lower and more disadvantaged position than men (du Guerny and Sjoberg 1993; Schoepf 1993a; Vance 1984; McGrath et al. 1993; Ulin 1992).

Gender Inequality

In most societies, women have less access than men to education, credit, and formal employment. Although in recent years considerable progress has been made worldwide in improving women's literacy and education, significant deficiencies in poor regions and neighborhoods persist. In 1985 just half of all adult women in Asia, Africa, and Latin America were literate (Buvinić and Yudelman 1989). Women experience great difficulties in obtaining access to institutional credit, a key constraint being the lack of title to land, which is often required as collateral (Lycette 1984). Studies also show that female farmers receive a far smaller percentage of the credit available through banks and agricultural cooperatives than male farmers (Fortman 1982; Staudt 1982; Knudson and Yates 1981). With regard to formal employment, only 30 percent of women in Africa are employed in salaried or wage-earning jobs; for some African countries, this figure represents less than 10 percent of all economically active women (United Nations 1991). Economic crises and adjustment programs currently threaten women's wage employment, even in Latin America where women's participation in the formal labor force has been higher than in Africa (United Nations 1991).

Throughout the world more women than men are poor, and their numbers are growing, reflecting an increasing feminization of poverty (Sivard 1985). A significant factor explaining poverty is the increase in the number of women-headed households. Estimates indicate that women are now the sole economic providers in up to a third of the households in Africa, Asia, Latin America, and the Caribbean and that these households are disproportionately poor (Buvinić and Yudelman 1989). Given women's limited access to productive resources and their lower economic status as compared to that of men, women are at a disadvantage in the adoption of HIV prevention behaviors that require a partner's cooperation, such as mutual monogamy and condom use.

Negotiating Prevention

For many of the world's women who are already monogamous, their partners' sexual behavior puts them at risk. Studies from around the world indicate that men, both single and married, have higher reported rates of partner change than women (Jenkins et al. 1995; Orubuloye et al. 1992; Sittitrai et al. 1991). In a six-country study in Africa, more than twice as many men as women report extramarital affairs during a one-year period. Men also report having a significantly higher number of lifetime sexual partners than women (Carael et al. 1990). Thus, to protect themselves, most women have to convince their partners of the value of fidelity and negotiate mutual monogamy.

A significant number of women who are not monogamous have multiple partners to gain access to resources that are otherwise outside their reach (Carael et al. 1990). Given limited opportunities for women in education, formal sector employment, credit, and training, reliance on sexual networking for economic gain or survival becomes a survival strategy for many women world-wide. There is tremendous variation in the level of control that women exercise in paid sexual relationships and the benefits they gain through sexual favors—from cash, clothes, and food to job security, tuition fees, and physical protection. In Bombay, India, for example, interviews with poor widowed, divorced, and abandoned women show that they have sex with slum lords to guarantee their physical safety and access to community resources (George and Jaswal 1995). In Zaire women seek occasional sexual partners known as *pneus de rechange* (spare tires) to meet their immediate economic needs (Schoepf et al. 1991), and in Uganda girls from low-income families are particularly vulnerable to the enticements of older men or "sugar daddies" who offer money or gifts in exchange for sex (Panos Institute 1989). In a Zimbabwe high school girls also acknowledge the "sugar daddy" phenomenon in their communities. When shown a picture of an apparently affluent man suggestively eyeing a young girl, one young girl said, "These days there is ESAP [the Zimbabwean structural adjustment program], so maybe this girl is not getting enough money from home, so she is hoping to get a lot of money from a sugar daddy" (Bassett and Sherman 1995). When exchanging sex for money or goods is a survival strategy, mutual monogamy messages are unrealistic without alternative income-generating opportunities. Negotiating condom use with each partner is often the only way that women can protect themselves from infection.

The condom, currently the only available preventive technology in most of the developing world, requires the "full and dedicated participation" of the male partner (Elias and Heise 1993). However, the condom is not a preferred method of either contraception or HIV-prevention. According to survey results, only 4 percent of married couples in nonindustrialized countries use condoms for family planning (Lisken, Wharton, and Blackburn 1990). Extensive evidence shows that both men and women are adverse to condoms because they are thought to be unnatural and decrease sexual pleasure (Elias and Heise 1993; deBruyn 1992; Taylor 1990). Condoms may also signify a lack of trust and intimacy, making it unlikely that they will be used in primary partnerships (Handwerker 1991). Studies conducted in Brazil and Guatemala reveal that the condom is thought to be "of the street, not the home" (Goldstein 1995; Bezmalinovic et al. 1995); in Jamaica, for "outside, not inside relationships" (Wyatt et al. 1995); and in South Africa, for "back-pocket partners" (Abdool Karim and Morar 1995). Given these perceptions, it is not surprising that commercial sex workers who regularly use condoms with their clients are reluctant to use them with their steady partners (Lisken et al. 1989; Worth 1989). Condoms also raise suspicions of infidelity which can lead to violence, thus making women fearful of introducing condoms into a relationship (Goldstein 1995; Wyatt et al. 1995; deBruyn 1992). Addressing the health needs of women vulnerable to HIV/AIDS infection is complex. First, they must be convinced themselves of the need to use condoms, and second, they must overcome their partner's negative beliefs and attitudes through successful negotiation.

Sexual Communication and Negotiation

For women, sexual communication and negotiation with male partners is essential to safeguarding their own health. However, several economic and sociocultural factors influence women's ability to succeed in negotiating the adoption of safer sexual behaviors. As a prerequisite to behavioral change, designing effective and culturally appropriate programs to foster communication between partners requires an understanding of these factors.

Economic Factors

Women's disadvantaged position in terms of access to critical resources often makes them dependent on men for their own and their children's economic survival. Under such circumstances women lack the leverage to resort to persuasive or coercive negotiation to convince men of the need for protection against HIV infection. Economic dependency also makes it difficult for women to leave men whose behavior places them at risk.

Data from research projects conducted in South Africa, Brazil, Guatemala, Papua New Guinea, and India show that many women who are aware of their partner's infidelity feel helpless about their inability to change their partner's sexual behavior because raising the issue of infidelity can disrupt the partnership and even jeopardize the physical safety of the woman (Abdool Karim and Morar 1995; Goldstein 1995; Bezmalinovic et al. 1995; Jenkins et al. 1995; George and Jaswal 1995). In Papua New Guinea, for example, a fifty-three-year old woman from a rural area reports, "I don't get angry or even fight with my husband if he goes out with other ladies because he used to belt me like pigs and dogs" (Jenkins et al. 1995). Likewise, an Indian woman participating in a focus group discussion in Bombay told the group, "When I asked my husband why he had married again, he beat me very badly that night" (George and Jaswal 1995).

Raising the issue of condom use can also lead to conflict, loss of support, and violent repercussions because it often casts suspicion on the woman's motivations (Schoepf et al. 1991; Richardson 1988). In Rio de Janeiro and São Paulo, Brazil, women from low-income communities perceive they will implicate themselves as unfaithful and have to bear the repercussions of anger and violence if they ask their partners to use a condom (Goldstein 1995). When Guatemalan women attending a prenatal clinic are asked to predict their husband's reaction if they suggest using a condom, one woman replies, "First he would say, 'Who knows whom she has been with and maybe she has brought me the leftovers' " (Bezmalinovic et al. 1995).

Many women feel that risks to their physical safety and the economic consequences of separating from their partners pose greater threats than the health consequences of a disease that might affect them at some point in the future (Ulin 1992; Elias and Heise 1993). A low-income, nonworking, married woman living in Bombay, explains, "A woman needs some support. How long will her parents support her. A single woman just can't stay alone, isn't it? So, a woman like me will say, if I've got to have clothes to wear and food to eat, then you do whatever you want (with my body) but keep me as a wife" (George and Jaswal 1995). Her statement vividly illustrates that many women who are poor have little or no economic leverage for negotiating preventive behavior, which puts them at a distinct disadvantage to men in protecting themselves against HIV.

Another economic factor influencing women's ability to negotiate sexual interactions is that sex often takes place in conditions of poverty and overcrowded homes. The lack of privacy characteristic of such conditions makes it difficult for women to communicate freely with their partners, let alone negotiate (George and Jaswal 1995).

Not all women are economically dependent on a man and therefore powerless in sexual relations. A study of minority women in New Jersey, all financially independent (Elias and Heise 1993), shows that they are able to exert considerable power by withholding sex if the partner refuses to use a condom (Kline, Kline, and Oken 1992). Similarly, a study of Yoruba women from southwest Nigeria, also financially independent, shows that they are able to refuse sex without violent consequences when their partner has a sexually transmitted infection (Orubuloye, Caldwell, and Caldwell 1993).

Experts argue that commercial sex workers are in a better position to negotiate protective behaviors because of the commercial nature of their relationships with their clients (Elias and Heise 1993). The balance of power is more equal between buyer and seller, and bargaining is already a part of the sexual interaction, making it easier for the woman to negotiate condom use. That condom promotion programs targeted at commercial sex workers have succeeded in increasing condom use with clients provides support for the view that negotiation is more possible in commercial sexual exchanges than in intimate, long-term relationships (deBruyn 1992). Important to the success of such programs, however, is collective action and the creation of a supportive environment. One study demonstrates that between one-third to two-thirds of clients refuse condoms and are willing to go elsewhere or pay higher fees for unprotected sex, if available (Schoepf 1993a). An individual sex worker's negotiation is more likely to be successful if all the sex workers in a particular brothel or neighborhood collectively adhere to a "condom-only" policy. In Calabar, Nigeria, for example, sex workers, together with support from their hotel managers, collectively decided to refuse clients who would not use condoms, and thereby were successful in becoming more selective in accepting clients (Esu-Williams, Lamson, and Lamptey 1991).

Sociocultural Factors

Sociocultural beliefs and norms regarding sexual behavior and gender relations define men and women's place in society and the ways in which they interact. To understand the factors that influence women's ability to communicate about sex and negotiate HIV prevention behaviors, we examine the sociocultural context within which sexual behavior takes place.

Societies in many parts of the world consider female ignorance of sexual matters a sign of purity and, conversely, knowledge of sexual matters and reproductive systems a sign of easy virtue (Ankomah 1992; Caldwell et al. 1989; Carovano 1992). Young women's ability to seek information or talk about sex is greatly constrained by strong cultural norms that emphasize virginity and innocence. They may fear that seeking information about HIV/AIDS or sex, as well as talking about these subjects, will label them as sexually active, regardless of the true extent of their sexual activity. Talking about sex is clearly not congruent with the need to preserve the outward appearance of virginity (Schensul et al. 1995). In Brazil, Mauritius, and Thailand, studies demonstrate that many young women rarely discuss sex with their partners, and despite being sexually active, they know little about their bodies, pregnancy, contraception, and sexually transmitted diseases (Vasconcelos 1995; Schensul et al. 1995; Cash and Anasuchatkul 1995).

Lack of information about reproductive anatomy and physiology contributes to women's fears about condom use and their reluctance to negotiate its use with a partner. In Brazil, India, Jamaica, and South Africa, women report not liking condoms because they fear that if the condom falls off inside the vagina, it can get lost inside the body and cause harm to the woman (Goldstein 1995; George and Jaswal 1995; Wyatt et al. 1995; Abdool Karim and Morar 1995).

Other sociocultural norms constraining women's ability to negotiate mutual monogamy are tolerance of multiple partnerships for men (McGrath et al. 1993; Orubuloye et al. 1992; Mane and Maitra 1992) and the emphasis on male pleasure and control in sexual relations (Cash and Anasuchatkul 1995). A Guatemalan male patient at an STD clinic remarked, "A man can't be like a woodpecker, always pecking at the same hole" (Bezmalinovic et al. 1995). Haitian women participating in focus group discussions indicate that men have the right to more than one partner but not women (Ulin et al. 1993). The belief that variety in sexual partners is essential to men's nature as men but is not acceptable for women often begins during adolescence, as illustrated by this remark made by a male Zimbabwean high school student during a focus group discussion: "It feels okay about boys having more than one partner, but girls should be faithful to one boy" (Bassett and Sherman 1995). In South Africa, men from rural and peri-urban communities report needing to maintain the tradition of their fathers and grandfathers by having more than one sexual partner. Particularly for young men, having many relationships was equated with being popular and important in the community (Abdool Karim and Morar 1995). In many cultures, expecting women to negotiate mutual monogamy directly challenges the very definition of masculinity.

The emphasis on male sexual pleasure also acts as a barrier for women to negotiate safe sex. In cultures where women are socialized to please men and defer to male authority, particularly in sexual interactions, it is unrealistic to expect women to refuse to engage in high-risk sexual behavior that they believe is pleasurable for their male partners. In parts of west, central, and southern Africa, for example, many women insert external agents into the vagina to dry their vaginal passages because of the belief that the increased friction is sexually more satisfying for men. The external agents used include herbs and roots, as well as scouring powders which may cause inflammation, lacerations, and abrasions that could significantly increase the efficiency of HIV transmission (Abdool Karim and Morar 1995; Niang 1995; Brown, Brown, and Ayowa 1992; Runganga, Pitts, and McMaster 1992).

Many women engage in anal sex, and this practice often increases their risk of infection. Survey data indicate that anal sex is practiced in varying degrees by women around the world (deBruyn 1992). Some women, however, engage in anal sex not for their own pleasure but to satisfy their husbands. In individual interviews with factory workers in Rio de Janeiro and São Paulo, women report that their partners pressured them to engage in anal sex despite their reluctance. According to one married female factory worker, "My husband wants to have anal sex with me . . . he thinks it is pleasurable, but I don't. He says that I am his woman and I have to accept these things. . . . I think that my husband possibly looks outside for this" (Goldstein 1995). For some Brazilian men interviewed in the same study, anal sex implies the conquering of a second virginity and symbolizes power and control over women. In the words of a twenty-four-year-old male factory worker, "Anal sex is a conquest because women never want to give there . . . when you do it there, he did her over again like a virgin. . . . anal sex is the ultimate, the final barrier" (Goldstein 1995). Expecting women to refuse anal sex in order to protect themselves from HIV is particularly unrealistic given that such a refusal would constitute a direct challenge to male dominance in the relationship.

The above-discussion highlights the many economic and sociocultural constraints that women face in communicating about sex and in convincing their male partners to adopt HIV-preventive behaviors. Many women are at risk of infection because of their partner's sexual behavior. Thus they must attempt to communicate and negotiate with their male partners to protect themselves from infection.

Learning to Communicate and Negotiate

Providing women with opportunities to develop the skills they need to increase their ability to communicate on sexual matters is a necessary and vital prerequisite in protecting women from HIV. However, programs that focus on developing communication skills alone are not sufficient. Without a commitment to increase women's access to critical resources, all short-term interventions to strengthen women's ability to protect themselves from HIV will continue to be handicapped by women's economic vulnerability and the unequal power balance in heterosexual relationships. Communication skill-building strategies must go hand-in-hand with the implementation of broader policies and programs aimed at improving women's economic status through such measures as access to credit, skills training, employment, and education.

Furthermore, women need strategies in communication and risk-reduction negotiation that are culturally acceptable and feasible. Some programs teach women to use eroticism to gain male cooperation in condom use, and this strategy has enjoyed some success with certain populations of sex workers. In a study conducted in Haiti, both men and women used terms such as *teaching*, *explaining*, and *reasoning* to describe ways in which women should appeal to their male partners to accept disease prevention. Men also expect women to use gentle words and caresses to convince men to use condoms or to be faithful (Ulin et al. 1993).

Nevertheless, such programs are deficient in recognizing that in some societies, sex for women often takes place outside the context of and separate from eroticism and intimacy. Low-income women interviewed in Bombay, for example, report that sex within marriage often occurs quickly and furtively in the middle of the night, with no time for foreplay and often in the presence of other family members (George and Jaswal 1995). Women in Bombay, Guatemala City, and the highlands of Papua New Guinea point out that men often demand sex under the influence of alcohol, making condom use negotiation an unrealistic option (George and Jaswal 1995; Bezmalinovic et al. 1995; Jenkins et al. 1995). Although these circumstances are certainly not true for all women, it is important to recognize that the conditions under which sex takes place are not always conducive to using eroticism or reasoning to enlist male cooperation.

An appropriate first step toward identifying suitable and culturally acceptable communication and negotiation strategies for women is to provide them with opportunities for group interactions, at which time they can share personal experiences. During these group sessions women can discuss their sexual lives and the consequences of adopting or negotiating risk-reduction options, recognize that they are not alone with regard to their fears and worries, brainstorm together on feasible ways to convince their partners, and, finally, try out new behaviors in a nonthreatening environment. Opportunities to talk, even if only in the presence of other women, are also critical in helping women overcome the social norms that define a "good" woman as one who is ignorant about sex and passive in sexual interactions, as well as those that prohibit interpartner communication on sex. At these sessions women and girls can also be provided a basic education about their own bodies and human sexuality, as well as specific information about HIV and other sexually transmitted infections. Such knowledge is critical because educating women on these topics is often an important step for successful communication.

Experiences from conducting research on, and programs for, women underscore the potential for the utilization of group interactions in providing women with a safe environment to learn about their bodies, discuss their sexual concerns, and identify strategies for communicating and negotiating risk reduction with their partners. Our own findings from the Women and AIDS Research Program, for example, reveal that women in a variety of countries and settings who participated in focus group discussions or group educational sessions were relieved that they could finally talk to someone about their sexual concerns. Once they started talking, they demanded more information and additional opportunities to talk (Rao Gupta and Weiss 1993). Likewise, research that assessed women's reactions to a series of group discussions on condoms and HIV prevention in Rio de Janeiro indicates that the women find the sessions very useful. Particularly valuable about the discussions, according to the participants, is that women share strategies which they themselves have used for initiating condom use and discussions on HIV prevention with their partners (Brasil et al. 1992).

Some successes were also reported from an assessment of community-based workshops in Zaire that engaged women residents of a low-income community in problem-solving approaches to risk reduction (Schoepf 1993b). The workshop design utilizes active learning methods, including role playing and small group discussions, to encourage critical reflection of the causes of the pandemic and the opportunities women have for fostering behavioral change. Follow-up of the sixty participants reveal that two-thirds of the women said they had been successful in beginning a dialogue with their partners.

It is important to highlight, however, that the partners of the remaining one-third of the women in the Zaire workshops refused to discuss HIV risk or condom use. Moreover, over 50 percent of the women who report success in initiating communication with their partners said that their husbands believe there is no need for condoms because they are not at risk of HIV. Such findings underscore the importance of targeting men and boys in programs that promote sexual and family responsibility.

Because women's ability to negotiate condom use or ensure fidelity in partnerships is largely dependent on men, it is essential that interventions to strengthen women's sexual negotiation skills be conducted concurrently with educational programs designed for boys and men. Such programs must go beyond teaching condom skills by promoting men's participation as equal partners in safer sex planning. Because of the value most societies place on children, and the possibility of vertical transmission of HIV, the health and safety of children may be one effective way that men can be convinced of the need to adopt HIV-preventive behaviors. Pregnant women in Guatemala and Mothers' Club members in Zaire report that family-centered scenarios highlighting the impact of AIDS on parents and children are appropriate for men's groups (Bezmalinovic et al. 1995; Schoepf 1993b).

Parents also need to learn ways to communicate with their children about sex for two important reasons. First, evidence suggests that adolescent girls who openly communicate about sexual matters with their parents, particularly their mothers, are less likely to be sexually active or become pregnant before marriage (Pick de Weiss et al. 1991; Fisher 1987; Fox 1981; Shah and Zelnick 1981). Second, parents who initiate discussions about sex can become role models for young people who ultimately will have to address issues of inter-partner communication in their own lives.

To strengthen women's ability to talk about sex and negotiate risk reduction with their male partners, a multifaceted approach that reflects the complexity which gender roles and relations represent in the HIV/AIDS pandemic is paramount. Such an approach must include a focus on improving women's economic status, providing them with information about sex and HIV prevention, creating opportunities for skill-building and shared problem-solving with regard to sexual communication and negotiation, and including men and parents in the educational process.

ACKNOWLEDGMENT

The authors would like to thank Daniel Whelan of the International Center for Research on Women for research and editorial support.

REFERENCES

Abdool, Karim Q. and N. Morar. 1995. Determinants of a Woman's Ability to Adopt HIV Protective Behaviour in Natal/Kwazulu, South Africa: A Community Based Approach. Women and AIDS Program Research Report Series. Washington, D.C.: International Center for Research on Women.

Ankomah, A. 1992. Premarital sexual relationships in Ghana in the era of AIDS. *Health Policy and Planning* 7:135–43.

Bang, R. and A. Bang. 1992. Why women hide them: Rural women's viewpoints on reproductive tract infections. *Manushi*, Issue No. 69.

Bassett, M. and J. Sherman. 1995. Adolescent Sexual Behavior and HIV Prevention. Women and AIDS Program Research Report Series. Washington D.C.: International Center for Research on Women.

Bezmalinovic, B., et al. 1995. Guatemala City Women: Empowering a Hidden Risk Group to Prevent HIV Transmission. Women and AIDS Program Research Report Series. Washington D.C.: International Center for Research on Women.

Boulos, M. L., R. Boulos, and D. J. Nichols. 1991. Perceptions and practices relating to condom use among urban men in Haiti. *Studies in Family Planning* 22:318–25.

Boye, A. K., et al. 1991. Marriage law and practice in the Sahel. *Studies in Family Planning* 22:343–49.

Brasil, V. V., et al. 1992. *Creaçao do programa de apoio visando o incentivo al uso do condon.* Rio de Janeiro: BEMFAM.

Brown, R. C., J. E. Brown, and O. B. Ayowa. 1992. Study of vaginal drying practices in Zaire. *AIDSTECH Final Research Report.* Research Triangle Park, N.C.: Family Health International.

Buvinic´ , M. and S. W. Yudelman. 1989. Women, Poverty, and Progress in the Third World. In *Headline Series.* Washington, D.C.: Foreign Policy Association.

Caldwell, J. C., P. Caldwell, and P. Quiggin. 1989. The social context of AIDS in sub-Saharan Africa. *Population and Development Review* 15:185–234.

Carael, M., et al. 1990. Research on sexual behavior that transmits HIV: The GPA/WHO collaborative survey—preliminary findings. In *Sexual Behavior and Networking: Anthropological and Sociocultural Studies in the Transmission of HIV.* Liège: Editions Derovaux-Ordina.

Carovano, K. 1992. More than mothers and whores: Redefining the AIDS prevention needs of women. *International Journal of Health Services* 21:131–42.

Cash, K. and B. Anasuchatkul. 1995. Experimental Educational Interventions for AIDS Prevention among Northern Thai Single Migratory Female Factory Workers. Women and AIDS Program Research Report Series. Washington, D.C.: International Center for Research on Women.

deBruyn, M. 1992. Women and AIDS in developing countries. *Social Science and Medicine* 34:249–62.

du Guerny, J. and E. Sjoberg. 1993. Interrelationship between gender relations and the HIV/AIDS epidemic: Some possible considerations for policies and programmes. *AIDS* 7:1027–34.

Elias, C. J. and L. Heise. 1993. The development of microbicides: A new method of HIV prevention for women. *Working Paper No. 6*. New York: The Population Council.

Esu-Williams, E., N. Lamson, and P. Lamptey. 1991. Nigeria: Empowering commercial sex workers for HIV prevention (Poster WD4041). Seventh International Conference on AIDS, Florence.

Fisher, R. and W. Ury. 1981. *Getting to Yes: Negotiating Agreement Without Giving In*. New York: Penguin.

Fisher, T. D. 1987. Family communication and the sexual behavior and attitudes of college students. *Journal of Youth and Adolescence* 16:481–95.

Fortman, L. 1982. Women's work in a communal setting: The Tanzanian policy of Ujamaa. In E. G. Bay, ed., *Women and Work in Africa*, 191–205. Boulder, Colo.: Westview.

George, A. and S. Jaswal. 1995. Understanding Sexuality: Ethnographic Study of Poor Women in Bombay. Women and AIDS Program Research Report Series. Washington, D.C.: International Center for Research on Women.

Givaudan, M., et al. 1995. Strengthening Intergenerational Communication Within the Family: An STD/AIDS Prevention Strategy for Adolescents. Women and AIDS Program Research Report Series. Washington, D.C.: International Center for Research on Women.

Goldstein, D. 1995. The Culture, Class, and Gender Politics of a Modern Disease: Women and AIDS in Brazil. Women and AIDS Program Research Report Series. Washington, D.C.: International Center for Research on Women.

Handwerker, P. 1991. Gender power difference may be STD risk factor for next generation. Paper presented at the Ninetieth Annual Meeting of the American Anthropological Association, Chicago.

Jenkins, C., et al. 1995. Women and the Risk of AIDS: Study of Sexual and Reproductive Knowledge and Behavior in Papua New Guinea. Women and AIDS Program Research Report Series. Washington, D.C.: International Center for Research on Women.

Kline, A., E. Kline, and E. Oken. 1992. Minority women and sexual choice in the age of AIDS. *Social Science and Medicine* 34:447–57.

Knudson, B. and B. A. Yates. 1981. *The Economic Role of Women in Small-Scale Agriculture in the Eastern Caribbean—St. Lucia*. Barbados: University of the West Indies.

Lisken, L., C. Wharton, and R. Blackburn. 1989. AIDS education: A beginning. *Population Reports*. Baltimore: Population Information Program, The Johns Hopkins University School of Hygiene and Public Health.

———. 1990. Condoms—now more than ever. *Population Reports*. Baltimore: Population Information Program, The Johns Hopkins University School of Hygiene and Public Health.

Lycette, M. 1984. *Improving Women's Access to Credit in the Third World: Policy and Program Recommendations*. Washington, D.C.: International Center for Research on Women.

Mane, P. and S. A. Maitra. 1992. *AIDS Prevention: The Sociocultural Context in India*. Bombay: Tata Institute of Social Sciences.

McGrath, J. W., et al. 1993. Anthropology and AIDS: The cultural context of sexual risk behavior among urban Baganda women in Kampala, Uganda. *Social Science and Medicine* 36:429—39.

Niang, C. I. 1995. Sociocultural Factors Favoring HIV Infection, and Integration of Traditional Women's Associations in AIDS Prevention Strategies in Kolda, Senegal. Women and AIDS Program Research Report Series. Washington, D.C.: International Center for Research on Women.

Orubuloye, I. O., J. C. Caldwell, and P. Caldwell. 1992. Diffusion and focus in sexual networking: Identifying partners and partners' partners. *Studies in Family Planning* 23:343–51.

———. 1993. African women's control over their sexuality in an era of AIDS: A study of the Yoruba of Nigeria. *Social Science and Medicine* 37:859–72.

Panos Institute. 1990. *Triple Jeopardy: Women and AIDS*. London.

Parker, R. G. 1991. *Bodies, Pleasures, and Passions: Sexual Culture in Contemporary Brazil*. Boston: Beacon Press.

Pick de Weiss, S., et al. 1991. Sex, contraception, and pregnancy among adolescents in Mexico City. *Studies in Family Planning* 22:74–82.

Pick de Weiss, S., M. Givaudan, and S. Cohen. 1993. Development of Support for National Sex Education in Mexico (Concept Proposal). Mexico City: Instituto Mexicano de Investigación de Familia y Población (IMIFAP).

Rao Gupta, G. and E. Weiss. 1993. Women and AIDS: Developing a New Health Strategy. *ICRW Policy Series*, no. 1. Washington, D.C.: International Center for Research on Women.

Richardson, D. 1988. *Women and AIDS*. New York: Methuen.

Runganga, A., M. Pitts, and J. McMaster. 1992. The use of herbal and other agents to enhance sexual experience. *Social Science and Medicine* 35:1037–42.

Schensul, S. L., et al. 1995. Young Women, Work, and AIDS-Related Risk Behavior in Mauritius. Women and AIDS Program Research Report Series. Washington, D.C.: International Center for Research on Women.

Schoepf, B. G. 1993a. Gender, development, and AIDS: A political economy and culture framework. In R. S. Gallin, A. Ferguson, and J. Harper, eds., *The Women and International Development Annual*, 53–85. Boulder, Colo.: Westview.

———. 1993b. AIDS action research with women in Kinshasa, Zaire. *Social Science and Medicine* 37:1401–13.

Schoepf, B. G., et al. 1988. AIDS and society in central Africa: A view from Zaire. In D. Koch-Weser and H. Vanderschmidt, eds., *The Heterosexual Transmission of AIDS in Africa*, 265–80. Cambridge, Mass.: Abt Books.

———. 1991. Gender, power, and risk of AIDS in Zaire. In M. Turshen, ed., *Women and Health in Africa*, 187–203. Trenton, N.J.: Africa World Press.

Shah, F. and M. Zelnick. 1981. Parent and peer influence on sexual behavior, contraceptive use, and pregnancy experience of young women. *Journal of Marriage and the Family* (May): 339–48.

Sittitrai, W., et al. 1991. The survey of partner relations and risk of HIV infection in Thailand. Abstract MD 4113. Presented at the Seventh International Conference on AIDS, Florence.

Sivard, R. L. 1985. *Women . . . A World Survey*. Washington, D.C.: World Priorities.

Staudt, K. 1982. Bureaucratic resistance to women's programs: The case of women in development. In E. Bonepart, ed., *Women, Power and Politics*. New York: Pergamon.

Taylor, C. C. 1990. Condoms and cosmology: The "fractal" person and sexual risk in Rwanda. *Social Science and Medicine* 31:1023–28.

United Nations. 1991. The world's women, 1970–1990: Trends and statistics. *Social Statistics and Indicators*, series K, no. 8. New York.

Ulin, P. R. 1992. African women and AIDS: Negotiating behavioral change. *Social Science and Medicine* 34:63–73.

Ulin, P. R., M. Cayemittes, and E. Metellus. 1993. *Haitian Women's Role in Sexual Decision-Making: The Gap between AIDS Knowledge and Behavior Change*. Durham: Family Health International (AIDSTECH).

United Nations Economic and Social Commission for Asia and the Pacific (UNESCAP). 1974. Husband-wife communication and practice of family planning. *Asia Population Studies Series* 16:26–27.

Vance, C. S. 1984. Pleasure and danger: Towards a politics of sexuality. In Carol Vance, ed., *Pleasure and Danger: Exploring Female Sexuality*. New York: Routledge and Kegan Paul.

Vasconcelos, A., et al. 1995. AIDS and Sexuality among Low-Income Adolescent Women in Recife, Brazil. Women and AIDS Program Research Report Series. Washington, D.C.: International Center for Research on Women.

WHO/GPA (World Health Organization/Global Program on AIDS). 1992. The Global AIDS Strategy. *AIDS Series 1992*. Geneva: World Health Organization.

Wilson, D., et al. 1995. Strengthening Intergenerational Communication Within the Family: An STD/AIDS Prevention Strategy for Adolescents. Women and AIDS Program Research Report Series. Washington, D.C.: International Center for Research on Women.

Worth, D. 1989. Sexual decision-making and AIDS: Why condom promotion among vulnerable women is likely to fail. *Studies in Family Planning* 20:297–307.

Wyatt, G. E., et al. 1995. Female Low-Income Workers and AIDS in Jamaica. Women and AIDS Program Research Report Series. Washington, D.C.: International Center for Research on Women.

19 | Challenges for the Development of Female-Controlled Vaginal Microbicides

CHRISTOPHER J. ELIAS AND LORI L. HEISE

Several authors present a strong case for developing an HIV prevention technology personally controlled by women (Stein 1990; Elias 1991; Germain 1992; Cates and Stone 1992). Proponents of such technology acknowledge the significant and growing risk of HIV infection faced by women throughout the world and, simultaneously, recognize the serious limitations of current AIDS prevention strategies. Existing efforts to limit the spread of HIV infection primarily through encouraging a reduced number of sexual partners, widespread condom promotion, and the control of other sexually transmitted infections (STIS) have proven inadequate for many of the world's women (Stein 1990; Worth 1989; Ulin 1992). Underlying gender power inequities severely limit the ability of many women to protect themselves from HIV infection, especially in the absence of a prevention technology they can use, when necessary, without their partner's consent. The development of new prevention methods controllable by women would fill an important gap in the global response to the AIDS pandemic. In this article we outline the challenges faced in developing microbicides—pharmaceutical products that would reduce a woman's risk of acquiring HIV and, potentially, other sexually transmitted infections when applied intravaginally.

This paper was prepared as part of the Robert H. Ebert Program on Critical Issues in Reproductive Health and Population and supported by grants from the John D. and Catherine T. MacArthur Foundation and the Rockefeller Foundation. Heise's work on this paper was supported, in part, by a grant from the Ford Foundation. The views expressed represent those of the authors and not necessarily those of the funding institutions.

The Principal Challenge

Globally, most women are at greatest risk of acquiring HIV infection through heterosexual vaginal intercourse with an infected man. To avoid infection via this route a prevention method must establish an effective barrier between the infectious elements in the male genital secretions/ejaculate and those cells of the female reproductive tract susceptible to infection. Such a barrier might be physical (such as that provided by condoms), chemical (such as that provided by an intravaginal microbicide), or immunological (such as the mucosal immunity that could result from an effective vaccine). Ideally, such a barrier would be selective, providing effective protection against HIV and other sexually transmitted infections without impairing a woman's ability to conceive. Such an ideal barrier could be combined with a spermicide (or another method of birth control) for use when contraception was explicitly desired. Given our limited knowledge regarding several critical questions of reproductive biology, the feasibility of developing noncontraceptive microbicides is unresolved. Compared to contraceptive microbicides, the pursuit of noncontraceptive products presents a number of additional challenges and will most certainly take a longer time to be realized, but it is an essential goal when viewed from the perspective of women who desire conception yet still require protection against HIV. Ultimately, vaginal microbicides could be made available in a range of product formulations—including gels, foams, suppositories, films, and so on—to match women's preferences for acceptable and optimal use.

Biological Issues

Developing a new microbicidal compound for preventing the sexual transmission of HIV depends on resolving a number of outstanding scientific issues. These range from defining more precisely the chemical and physical properties of potential microbicides and product formulations to elucidating the exact biological mechanism of HIV transmission. Despite a considerable amount of research effort, much remains to be learned about the basic biology of sexual transmission of HIV (Alexander 1990; Alexander, Gabelnick, and Spieler 1990).

Evidence suggests that HIV-infected lymphocytes and macrophages are primary infectious elements in semen (Alexander 1990; Anderson 1992). These immune cells are abundant in normal semen and have been shown to increase in the presence of genital tract inflammation (such as that resulting from common STIs) and HIV infection (Wolff and Anderson 1988). Significant amounts of cell-free virus have also been found in semen (Borzy, Connell, and Kiessling 1988; Krieger et al. 1991; Anderson et al. 1992). Discerning whether HIV transmission involves cell-associated virus or cell-free virus or both is a critical question for microbicide development. For example, if it were convincingly demonstrated that only a virus associated with immunologically competent cells, such as lymphocytes and macrophages, was capable of infecting the female reproductive tract, this would have significant implications for the types of microbicidal compounds one would pursue. In such a scenario the virucidal action could target the infected host cells instead of the virus itself.

Some recent evidence suggests that cell-associated virus is a principal means of HIV transmission. Phillips and coworkers have developed an in vitro model of viral transmission using a confluent epithelial cell culture (Bourinbaiar and Phillips 1991; Phillips and Bourinbaiar 1992; Phillips and Tan 1992). When HIV-infected CD4 lymphocytes were added to this culture system, lymphocytes were soon observed in close association with the epithelial surface. Subsequent observation by electron microscopy demonstrated the directional release of mature viral particles into the space between the lymphocyte and epithelium, as well as the rapid uptake of virus by the epithelial cells. It is also well established that Langerhans cells are present in the vagina and cervix and could be recipients of cell-free or cell-associated HIV (Hussain, Kelly, and Fellowes 1992; Edwards and Morris 1985). One possible scenario is that cell-associated virus is primarily responsible for transmission across intact epithelial surfaces but that cell-free virus can infect mucosa when present in high concentration or when epithelial surfaces are disrupted. Studies of discordant couples, for example, have demonstrated that older/postmenopausal women are at increased risk of HIV seroconversion (Peterman et al. 1988; European Study Group 1992), a finding attributed to their increased risk of epithelial disruption during sex owing to low estrogen levels and atrophic vaginal mucosa. This may also partially explain why HIV transmission is augmented in the presence of genital ulcerative diseases that result in mucosal disruption.

This scenario might also help explain the conflicting data regarding the safety and efficacy of currently available vaginal spermicides in preventing HIV infection (Bird 1991; Rosenberg and Gollub 1992). Two recent observational studies in sub-Saharan Africa (one among sex workers and another among discordant couples) have suggested that consistent use of vaginal spermicides containing Nonoxynol-9 may provide partial protection against HIV infection (Zekeng et al. 1993; Feldblum 1992). These studies contradict a randomized controlled trial among female sex workers in Nairobi which found that daily use of the Nonoxynol-9-impregnated "Today" sponge appeared to be associated with increased risk of HIV seroconversion (Kreiss et al. 1992). These conflicting data have prompted a variety of interpretations and recommendations regarding the relative safety and efficacy of existing vaginal spermicides as methods of

HIV prevention (Bird 1991; Rosenberg and Gollub 1992; Voeller 1992a; Rekart 1992; Centers for Disease Control 1988).

More recent studies have suggested that the toxicity of Nonoxynol-9 may be related to the dose or frequency of application (Zekeng et al. 1993; Niruthis-ard, Roddy, Chutivongse 1991a, 1991b; Roddy et al. 1992). These results suggest that to the extent Nonoxynol-9 does cause mucosal inflammation, micro-ulcerations, or sores, the effects may be limited to situations of high-dose or high-frequency use or both. It remains to be established whether Nonoxynol-9 offers women measurable protection from HIV in typical use and at what point the negative consequences of potentially disrupting the epithelium outweigh the positive benefits of killing the virus. Given the nonselective detergent properties of compounds such as Nonoxynol-9 and other available spermicides, there may be a narrow range between "enough" and "too much" microbicidal spermicide.

This line of reasoning suggests the need to develop more specific intravaginal compounds that prevent the attachment of HIV-infected lymphocytes to epithelial surfaces, the secretion of virus from these cells, or the uptake of virus by the mucosal epithelium, without indiscriminately disrupting cell membranes. One such class of compounds may be polyanionic polysaccharides, such as dextran sulfate. Dextran sulfate has been demonstrated to inhibit HIV replication in vitro (Bagasra and Lischner 1988; Bagasra et al. 1988). A broad range of polysulphated polysaccharides have also been shown to inhibit the cell-associated transmission of HIV using the in vitro epithelial cell culture model described above (Pearce-Pratt and Phillips 1993). This activity has been demonstrated at concentrations a hundred to a thousand times lower than those associated with significant cytotoxicity. The hypothesized mechanism of action of these polyanionic compounds is that, by coating the epithelial surface with a highly charged macromolecular film, they may physically repel HIV and HIV-infected cells from the epithelium and thereby prevent the directional release of HIV that occurs when these infected lymphocytes attach to mucosal cells. Many polyanionic polysaccharides are currently used as food additives, and, as non-detergent compounds, they could have considerably less local toxicity than existing vaginal spermicides.

Another basic issue related to the biology of HIV transmission is our incomplete understanding of the precise cells and tissues within the female reproductive tract that are infected in the course of transmission. Disruptions of epithelial surfaces probably augment susceptibility to infection, but data from animal models, as well as case reports of infections acquired during artificial insemination, indicate that such disruption is not required in order for transmission to occur (Miller 1989; Stewart, Cunningham, and Driscoll 1985). Phillips and

Bourinbaiar (1991) suggest that cell-associated virus may infect typical mucosal cells. But does this happen throughout the vagina? Is the cervix a more or less susceptible site? What is the role of the upper genital tract structures, if any? Recent studies of HIV transmission in macaque monkeys that have had hysterectomies suggest that the presence of a cervix is not required for transmission (Alexander 1991). Given the limitations of simian animal models, however, this finding may not easily generalize to humans and, even if applicable, does not exclude an additional (and potentially more important) route of infection via the cervix or upper genital tract. Answers to such questions of basic biology are essential to understand fully the interactions of various contraceptive methods with HIV infection, as well as the possibility of identifying a noncontraceptive microbicide (Alexander 1990; Cates and Stone 1992).

Another important issue that bears directly on the feasibility of developing a noncontraceptive microbicide is the question of whether HIV infects or attaches to sperm. Several authors have suggested that HIV may become associated with sperm, either by attaching to the surface or crossing the cell membrane (Bagasra et al. 1988; Scofield 1992). Others have refuted these findings after failing to find a physical association between HIV and sperm in careful assays used to separate motile sperm from other elements of semen, as well as failure to identify HIV DNA using genetic amplification techniques on the sperm fractions of semen from more than two hundred seropositive men (Anderson 1992). Current opinion favors the lack of a significant relationship between HIV and viable sperm; the data are by no means complete, however, leaving open the possibility of an uncommon, but perhaps biologically relevant association (Anderson 1991). Obviously, a significant association of virus with sperm would make the development of a noncontraceptive microbicide extremely problematic.

Emerging data further suggest that the complex chemical, microbiological, and immunological environment of the male and female reproductive tracts may play a major role in determining the likelihood of HIV transmission. Understanding the ecology of the vaginal environment is essential for future microbicide development, because any compound introduced intravaginally has the potential to disrupt the balance of vaginal flora, pH, or immune function. For example, recent evidence has shown that the normally low pH of the vagina may be virucidal in its own right (Voeller and Anderson 1992a, 1992b). Voeller and Anderson have shown that at pH levels below 5.5 both HIV and HIV-infected host cells are rapidly inactivated. Semen typically neutralizes the acidic pH of the vagina. This finding suggests that a microbicidal preparation should be formulated to include a strong acidic buffer if feasible. It also raises the possibility of developing a prevention strategy based on keeping the pH of the vagina low.

The disturbance of vaginal pH may also partially explain why nonulcerative genital tract infections have been shown to augment the transmission of HIV to women (Wasserheit 1991). Vaginal infections, such as trichomoniasis and bacterial vaginosis are very common and often remain unrecognized or untreated in many women (Wasserheit 1989). These infections are commonly associated with an alkaline change in pH (Hillier and Holmes 1989; Rein and Muller 1989). This suggests that the routine screening and treatment of women for these common reproductive tract infections may help reduce HIV transmission, especially in areas where heterosexual transmission predominates.

Another mechanism by which reproductive tract infections augment women's susceptibility to HIV infection is by attracting large numbers of potential "host cells" into the genital tract mucosa through the inflammatory process. Data indicate that, unlike semen, healthy female vaginal secretions contain relatively few CD4+ lymphocytes and macrophages, except during menstruation (Anderson and Hill 1991). Future preparations of vaginal compounds for use as microbicides must take into account effects on the vaginal flora. Disruption of the vaginal flora might result in subclinical inflammation or pH alteration that could potentially impair the natural defenses of the reproductive tract. The potential for such effects, for example, has recently been reported for Nonoxynol-9 (McGroarty et al. 1990a, 1990b).

A final set of issues crucial to microbicide development relates to the mucosal immunity of the male and female reproductive tracts. In addition to the systemic immune defenses of the body, most mucosal surfaces exhibit immune protection against potential pathogens through the local activity of immunologically competent cells and the secretion of antibody that prevents primary infection of epithelial surfaces. Currently very little is known about the local immunity of the reproductive tract (Forrest 1991; Anderson and Pudney 1992). The data that do exist on women suggest that the mucosal secretory immune system of the endocervix provides a primary immune defense against lower reproductive tract pathogens, primarily through the local production of Immunoglobulin A (IGA) (Anderson and Hill 1991; Rebello, Green, and Fox 1975; Underdown and Schiff 1986).

The majority of people acquiring HIV today are infected by mucosal exposure to cell-free or cell-associated virus through heterosexual contact. It is not clear that the current candidate HIV vaccines, many of which are primarily targeted to stimulate systemic immunity, will provide an adequate immunological barrier at the mucosal surfaces of the reproductive tract and thereby prevent primary mucosal infection. This uncertainty provides an important reason to pursue microbicide development even in the face of possible advances in vaccine research. Women may still need a microbicide even after the first generation of vaccines becomes available.

Clinical Testing

Many concerns have been expressed regarding the feasibility of designing clinical trials of microbicides that are both scientifically valid and ethically sound. Although clearly a complex and costly endeavor, the task of testing a candidate microbicide is both feasible and considerably less problematic than testing a vaccine. Since a microbicide would be applied with each act of coitus, one does not need to determine how many days, months, or years protection lasts, as in the case of vaccines. Below we explore some of the more salient issues regarding the design of clinical trials for a female-controlled microbicide.

Before entering human testing, a candidate compound would go through standard testing for toxicity in at least two species of laboratory animals. With minor modification, the typical product-development sequence for a new contraceptive could be applied to the pursuit of new microbicidal compounds (Zatuchni et al. 1979). The sequence of preclinical, animal testing required for evaluation of new intravaginal compounds, as well as the simian models for retrovirus transmission, are discussed elsewhere and will not be reviewed here (Chvapil et al. 1980; Miller et al. 1992). The preclinical evaluation of potential compounds will obviously require significant attention to the possible mutagenicity of vaginal compounds, especially those that are potentially noncontraceptive. Following successful testing in vitro and in animal models, a carefully selected group of promising microbicidal compounds would be brought to human trials. Human trials involve three phases: Phase I trials evaluate the safety, toxicity, and acceptability of a compound in a limited number of women; Phase II trials generally involve fifty to two hundred women and are designed to establish some evidence of effectiveness; and Phase III trials expand the safety and efficacy testing to a thousand or more women. For a typical compound, completion of all three phases of human clinical trials can take at least five years but may take longer for microbicide evaluation, given the sample size requirements and special characteristics of study populations described below.

One important question concerns the appropriate study populations for Phase I safety testing. Because studies on safety, tolerance, and absorption can be done in populations not at significant risk of HIV infection, there is little need to conduct initial Phase I research among vulnerable populations. In particular, special caution should be applied in the recruitment of sex workers for Phase I trials. Given the economic, political, and violent realities of many of these women's lives, it is impossible to ensure (even through cash payments) that they will not "work" during the trial, thereby being exposed to HIV while using an intravaginal compound whose safety in humans has yet to be demonstrated. There are, however, compelling reasons to *repeat* Phase I safety and toxicity testing in developing countries and among high-risk women following initial testing in the country of origin and the accumulation of adequate safety data in low-risk populations.

The major challenge with respect to microbicide development is to design a Phase III efficacy trial that is both scientifically rigorous and ethically defensible. From a scientific standpoint, the most rigorous, and therefore the most desirable, design is a randomized controlled trial (RCT), where trial participants are randomly assigned to receive either the compound under investigation or a placebo (or an "active control" if a compound with previously demonstrated effectiveness exists). Because it would be unethical to withhold a form of HIV prevention known to be protective, participants in a microbicide trial would also receive free supplies of condoms and be counseled to use both the vaginal product *and* a condom during each act of intercourse. Statistical analysis would determine any incremental benefit offered by the experimental compound over condom use alone. Many of the practical issues of clinical trial design for evaluating the effectiveness of spermicides in preventing more common STIs (including a discussion of study population, site selection, and follow-up procedures) have recently been reviewed (Foldesy et al. 1990).

This type of trial design raises important ethical issues (Levine, Dubler, and Levine 1991; United States Public Health Service 1991; Council for International Organizations of Medical Sciences 1991). An unfortunate reality to be faced in conducting an RCT is that, at best, some members of the comparison group will become infected with HIV while participating in the study. The critical ethical question, however, is whether all study participants will benefit from participation in the trial. Researchers have an obligation to minimize harm and to maximize the benefits to all trial participants. In the optimal design, therefore, all participants, including those in the control group, would benefit from receiving condoms, reproductive health care, and intensive HIV counseling. If the trial were performed properly, the women in the control group should have a lower HIV seroconversion rate than women not participating in the study. Historical controls could be used to document improved use of condoms by all participants as a direct measure of the benefit of participating in the trial.

To illustrate this point, consider the hypothetical results presented in table 19.1. In this example, researchers randomly assign a group of women with a seroincidence rate of 4 percent per year to receive either the test compound or a placebo. In addition, both groups receive extensive counseling and free condoms, which raise their condom use from 10 percent before the trial to 50 percent after. In the control group, the women's seroincidence declines from 4 to 3 percent, a 25 percent drop, whereas in the experimental group, the rate declines to 1.5 percent, a 62.5 percent drop. This design would confirm a 50

TABLE 19.1.

Hypothetical Results for a Study Population Comprising Commercial Sex Workers with a 4% Annual HIV Seroincidence

Random Assignment	Initial		Postintervention	
	Seroincidence	Condom Use	Seroincidence	Condom Use
Experimental Group	4%	10%	1.5%	50%
Control Group	4%	10%	3%	50%

percent protective effect of the test substance while at the same time reducing the rate of seroconversion in the control group.

Researchers would have to undertake a variety of other safeguards to guarantee the ethics of microbicide trials. Among them is the need to ensure informed consent. This requires both the absence of direct or structural coercion and full disclosure of trial procedures, including the randomization process and the use of a placebo if applicable. With respect to microbicide testing, this would require that counseling, condoms, and reproductive health care be made available to women asked to participate who choose not to be in the trials (as well as to participants), so that women would not feel obliged to enroll in the trial just to gain access to these often scarce resources. Also, researchers would have to take special care to ensure that women understood the contraceptive activity of both the test substance and the control. Some women may wish to protect themselves further from pregnancy during the trial, whereas others may choose not to participate if doing so might prevent them from conceiving. Discussing the issue of contraceptive activity is especially important in settings where access to abortion is restricted by law or lack of services.

Perhaps the most vexing ethical issue, however, derives from the principle of justice, which mandates that the burdens and benefits of research be equitably distributed (Levine, Dubler, and Levine 1991). A particularly gross example of injustice would be the case where a new prevention technology was extensively tested in sub-Saharan Africa but, once proven to be effective, was unavailable to Africans because of its high cost (Freedman 1992; Ndinya-Achola 1991). This precise example has been the focus of much debate in regard to HIV vaccines, given the high cost of vaccine development, the prominence of private-sector interest, and the long-term investment that would be required to make vaccines available in many developing countries.

A variety of scientific exigencies exist which make it almost certain that Phase III testing of a microbicide (as opposed to Phase I safety testing) would take place primarily in the Third World. Two conditions are required to measure a significant decrease in HIV seroconversion attributable to an effective microbicide: a study population of women with a high seroincidence rate attributable primarily, if not exclusively, to the sexual transmission of HIV and a sufficiently large study population to achieve statistical significance. It is important to avoid any confounding that may result from "contamination" with other routes of transmission, such as intravenous drug use. Compared to sexual transmission, it is relatively easy to become infected through parenteral exposure; such contamination would obscure the effects of the product under study and greatly increase the required sample size. As table 19.2 illustrates, the number of trial participants required to achieve statistical significance quickly becomes unmanageable in populations with annual HIV seroincidence rates of less than 2 to 4 percent. For example, the number of participants required in each arm of a clinical trial seeking to establish 50 percent efficacy of a test compound in three years drops from 3,039 women to 743 women as the seroincidence of the study population increases from 1 to 4 percent (table 19.2). Note that even at a high annual seroincidence rate of 4 percent, however, it is likely that data from multiple sites would have to be pooled for analysis. As with vaccine evaluations, the greatest chance for success lies in the design of multicenter, multicountry studies that include both developed and developing country populations of women.

Study populations that fit the criteria outlined above are found more commonly in developing countries and often involve vulnerable women, such as sex workers, who are subject to economic and physical exploitation. Although there are populations of women with annual seroincidence rates in the range of 2 to 3 percent in the United States (e.g., in the major urban centers of New York and New Jersey), a large proportion of these women are intravenous drug users, making them less appropriate for microbicide testing because of their risk of

TABLE 19.2.

Number of Participants Required for Microbicide Trials

Effectiveness	Annual HIV Seroincidence			
%	1%	2%	3%	4%
25	29,008	14,376	9,499	7,061
30	19,521	9,677	6,396	4,755
50	6,078	3,016	1,996	1,486
70	2,552	1,268	840	626
90	1,118	556	369	276
99	646	322	214	160

Assumptions: Alpha = 0.05, 1 - Beta = 0.90, 2-tailed test, N = total sample size, two-armed study, three-year trial (participants enrolled for two years and followed for one year each); no loss to follow-up. For formula, see Cohen 1977.

NOTE: Sample size calculations should be based on estimates of the seroincidence that can be expected in a given study population *after* the anticipated effect of alternative intervention strategies has been taken into account.

acquiring infection through nonsexual means. Clearly the political and ethical questions raised by this reality must be addressed before initiating Phase III testing. If the developing world is to bear the major burden of clinical research related to microbicides, women in developing countries *must* realize the benefits of such compounds once proven.

Similar concerns have been raised regarding the distributive justice of vaccine testing. The issues of North/South equity raised by microbicide testing may be slightly less charged, however, because the distribution of an effective microbicide, although requiring attention to manufacturing, storage, and transportation logistics, would not necessarily depend on extensive health system support. There is good reason to expect that these compounds, once proven, would be available as nonprescription drugs and therefore could be incorporated into existing condom procurement and distribution systems, as well as social marketing campaigns. Even though microbicide development will most likely depend on a research and development effort supported by the public sector, efficient manufacture and distribution will require some degree of profitability. Therefore the major challenge (as with condom supplies today) will be identifying resources to finance the recurrent costs of commodity procurement and distribution. In many places this will require substantial infrastructure development, as well as the political will to provide public subsidy for the purchase and distribution of microbicidal products for individual use in the public good.

Programmatic Issues

A number of important programmatic issues must be considered in relation to microbicide development. Perhaps most important is a commitment to seeking women's input at each stage of the research and development effort. Soliciting women's needs and preferences at the outset will help ensure that the product, once developed, will be used and accepted. The importance of this type of consultation for contraceptive development has recently been summarized by the International Women's Health Coalition and the World Health Organization's Special Program of Research on Human Reproduction (International Women's Health Coalition 1991).

Women's input is especially critical with respect to the initial formulation criteria for a new microbicidal product. Table 19.3 lists some of the dimensions along which a new product might vary. In all likelihood, a broad range of product formulations will ultimately be necessary. The ideal formulation for an adolescent in the United States, for example, might be quite different from that required by a married woman in rural India. An important step in product

TABLE 19.3.
Some Dimensions of Microbicide Product Specification

Contraceptive activity
Interaction with existing contraceptive use
Capacity for covert use ("detectability")
Method of application (e.g., jelly, film, etc.)
Coital dependence
Postcoital effectiveness
Onset and duration of action
Spectrum of microbicidal activity
Disposability
Affordability
Smell/taste
Messiness
Shelf life
Stability at room temperature
Ease of insertion
Appropriateness for anal/oral sex

development will be to conduct field research to establish women's needs and preferences in different geographic and cultural settings.

Experience from testing the acceptability of various contraceptives suggests that one of the more critical design features for microbicide development will be its method of application (Scrimshaw 1979; Ehrhardt et al. 1992:37–67). A microbicidal compound could be manufactured in a number of ways, each with unique implications for its acceptability among users. Cultural factors, for example, might affect whether women would prefer a vaginal cream applied with an applicator or a vaginal sponge inserted by hand. In parts of Africa, for example, women use a variety of astringent substances to dry and tighten the walls of the vagina before sex (Dallabeta et al. 1990). Where this form of "dry sex" is common and preferred, a moist vaginal creme would probably receive little use.

Contraceptive research also suggests that the timing of insertion will be another factor critical to the acceptability of new microbicidal products. Couples tend to prefer methods that do not interrupt the spontaneity of intercourse, a property determined in part by the product's onset and duration of action.

Microbicidal products that become effective quickly or that can be inserted long before intercourse are likely to be preferred. A great need also exists for a product that could be used postcoitally to protect women subject to nonconsensual sex. The need for such a product is evidenced by emerging data concerning the widespread prevalence of nonconsensual and coercive sex in women's lives, even within married and consensual unions (Heise 1993). A postcoital method might also have some utility for women, especially adolescents, in communities where "planning" to have sex is unacceptable (Pick de Weiss et al. 1991).

Another set of programmatic issues revolves around the introduction, distribution, and postmarketing surveillance of any new microbicidal product. The development of appropriate information, public education, and counseling materials must complement the development of any new biotechnology to ensure that women realize the maximum benefit of such new products and that providers supply proper guidance regarding correct usage.

In contrast to vaccines, which often require delicate handling, constant refrigeration, and clinical personnel, the programmatic challenge of microbicides will be to adapt and apply the lessons learned from condom promotion to a new product targeted to women. In many cases, microbicides could potentially be incorporated into the same procurement, storage, and distribution systems presently used for condoms. Moreover, many of the same social marketing techniques used to create demand for condoms could also be used to promote microbicides. Even in very poor countries like Zaire, social marketing campaigns have been able to increase greatly the sale of condoms using a skillful mix of media, packaging, pretested slogans and advertisements, and aggressive, widespread distribution through multiple outlets (Population Services International 1992). Also promising are opportunities to distribute and promote microbicides through family planning programs, mothers' clubs, and other women's organizations. Indeed, for this type of product, word-of-mouth, woman-to-woman promotion may be the most effective.

The Need for Public Sector Leadership

There is an urgent need for public sector organizations to provide leadership in coordinating research and development of HIV prevention technologies—including both microbicides and vaccines. This will require not only support for basic and clinical research needed to answer the outstanding questions of reproductive biology and provide efficacy testing infrastructure; more specifically, it will require the organization of this research into a product development path that will result in safe and effective vaginal products eligible for registration with drug regulatory agencies and available for global distribution. A constellation of concerns regarding inadequate liability insurance, cumbersome regulatory requirements, high costs of clinical testing infrastructure, political caution, and anticipated low returns on investment have prevented the private sector from taking the lead in this area. This has long been the case in the area of contraceptive development (Bardin 1987; Mastroianni, Donaldson, and Kane 1990; Harr and Johnson 1991:31–45, 395–442.).

Although public sector leadership is needed, this sector should avoid, if possible, taking on the entire responsibility for product research and development. The most efficient motors of invention, product design, and technological advancement are in the private sector. The relatively small scale of public sector laboratories, erratic patterns of donor support and budget allocations, and the inefficiencies of multiple contracted research agreements lead to slow product development. Coordinated public-private sector collaboration is most urgently needed to increase the investment and effort of the private sector in this important area of technological development. A partnership between the public and private sectors could range from joint needs assessments, to collaboration in laboratory, clinical, and field testing, to risk sharing through public sector underwriting of research or liability insurance costs (Free 1992; World Health Organization/Global Program on AIDS 1993).

In all these partnerships both sides must have a clear understanding of each other's motivations and expectations. It is important for public sector organizations to recognize the commercial interests of industry and understand that "profit" at times has many dimensions. For example, industry will sometimes pursue "less profitable" technologies for public relations purposes in order to establish corporate goodwill or to complement other products within sales and distribution networks. The commercial sector will not pursue technologies that are frankly unprofitable. Simultaneously, the mechanisms for protecting public sector investments must be clear and specified in advance. Insuring the public sector's investment goal—the availability of affordable technology for resource-poor environments—is facilitated by establishing clear title to intellectual property and by the pursuit of licensing strategies that discourage monopolies, encourage dual pricing, and exploit economies of scale within the commercial sector (Free 1992).

The absence of monopolies encourages price competition, and public-sector pricing agreements help guarantee the affordability of technology for use in resource-poor environments. In such agreements, industry acquires technology, intellectual property, or the facility for clinical evaluation in return for assurances that the product will be sold to public sector organizations at a price that is a small, fixed percentage above manufacturing and distribution costs. Meanwhile industry enjoys freedom from price regulation in commercial sales. One reason companies agree to such public-sector pricing arrangements is that large-volume production for public sector markets provides a significant economy of scale in manufacturing and distribution, thereby increasing the profit margins of commercial sector sales.

The development and testing of microbicidal compounds will require advancing our basic understanding of human reproductive biology. It will rely on careful attention to the ethics of clinical trial design and require a genuine, lasting dialogue between scientists and advocates. It will also require the collaboration of professionals from many academic disciplines, as well as the coordination of efforts among commercial industry and various governmental, nongovernmental, and intergovernmental organizations in both developed and developing countries. Most important, it will require a renewed commitment within public sector organizations to provide the requisite leadership to champion the development of safe, effective, and affordable microbicidal products that will be accessible to all women at risk of HIV infection.

It must be stressed, however, that the complexities of AIDS will not be met adequately with a "technological fix." Efforts to develop female-controlled prevention options *must* be complemented by more concerted attempts to address the underlying gender power imbalances that shape women's risk of sexually transmitted infection, as well as their ability to protect themselves using the currently existing range of prevention strategies. Until women share power more equally with men—in both the public and the private sphere—they will remain at heightened risk of HIV/AIDS.

REFERENCES

Alexander, N. J. 1990. Sexual transmission of human immunodeficiency virus: Virus entry into the male and female genital tract. *Fertility and Sterility* 54 (1): 1–18.
———. 1991. Comments at the Biology of Heterosexual Transmission of HIV Workshop. National Institute of Allergy and Infectious Diseases. Bethesda, Maryland, May.
Alexander, N. J., H. L. Gabelnick, and J. M. Spieler. 1990. *Heterosexual Transmission of AIDS.* New York: Alan R. Liss.
Anderson, D. J. 1992. Mechanisms of HIV-1 transmission via semen. *Journal of NIH Research* 4:104–108.
Anderson, D. J., et al. 1992. Effects of disease stage and zidovudine therapy on the detection of human immunodeficiency virus type 1 in semen. *Journal of the American Medical Association* 267 (20): 2769–74.
Anderson, D. J. and J. A. Hill. 1991. Cellular and soluble factors in semen and the vaginal environment that may influence the heterosexual transmission of HIV type 1. In *Vaginitis and Vaginosis,* 69–76. New York: Wiley-Liss.
Anderson, D. J. and J. Pudney. 1992. Mucosal immune defense against HIV-1 in the male urogenital tract. *Vaccine Research* 1 (3): 143–50.
Bagasra, O. and H. W. Lischner. 1988. Activity of dextran sulfate and other polyanionic polysaccharides against human immunodeficiency virus. *Journal of Infectious Diseases* 158:1084.

Bagasra, O., et al. 1988. Interaction of human immunodeficiency virus with human sperm in vitro. *Journal of AIDS* 1:431–35.

Bardin, C. W. 1987. Public sector contraceptive development: History, problems, and prospects for the future. *Technology in Society* 9:289–305.

Bird, K. D. 1991. The use of spermicide containing Nonoxynol-9 in the prevention of HIV infection. *AIDS* 5:791–96.

Borzy, M. S., R. S. Connell, and A. A. Kiessling. 1988. Detection of human immunodeficiency virus in cell-free seminal fluid. *Journal of AIDS* 1:419–24.

Bourinbaiar, A. S. and D. M. Phillips. 1991. Transmission of human immunodeficiency virus from monocytes to epithelia. *Journal of AIDS* 4:56–63.

Cates, W. and K. Stone. 1992. Family planning: The responsibility to prevent both pregnancy and reproductive tract infections. In A. Germain et al., eds., *Reproductive Tract Infections: Global Impact and Priorities for Women's Reproductive Health*, 93–129. New York: Plenum.

Centers for Disease Control. 1988. Update: Barrier protection against HIV infection and other sexually transmitted diseases. *MMWR* 42:30.

Chvapil, M., et al. 1980. Studies of Nonoxynol-9. I. The effect on the vaginas of rabbits and rats. *Fertility and Sterility*. 33 (4): 445–50.

Cohen, J. 1977. *Statistical Power Analysis for the Behavioural Sciences*. New York: Academic Press.

Council for International Organizations of Medical Sciences. 1991. *Law, Medicine, and Health Care* 19: Appendix I.

Dallabeta, G., et al. 1990. Vaginal tightening agents as risk factors for acquisition of HIV. Abstract TH.C574. Sixth International Conference on AIDS, San Francisco, California.

Edwards, J. N. and H. B. Morris. 1985. Langerhans cells and lymphoid subsets in the female genital tract. *British Journal of Obstetrics and Gynecology* 92:974–82.

Ehrhardt, A. A., et al. 1992. *Prevention of Heterosexual Transmission of HIV: Barriers for Women*. New York: Hayworth.

Elias, C. J. 1991. Sexually transmitted diseases and the reproductive health of women in developing countries. Programs Division Working Paper No. 5. New York: The Population Council.

European Study Group on Heterosexual Transmission of HIV. 1992. Comparison of female to male and male to female transmission of HIV in 563 stable couples. *British Medical Journal* 304:809–13.

Feldblum, P. 1992. Efficacy of spermicide use and condom use by HIV-discordant couples in Zambia. Abstract No. WeC 1085. Eighth International Conference on AIDS, Amsterdam, The Netherlands.

Foldesy, R. G., et al. 1990. Design of clinical studies of spermicides for prophylaxis against sexually transmitted diseases. In N. J. Alexander, H. L. Gabelnick, and J. M. Spieler, *Heterosexual Transmission of AIDS*, 291–301. New York: Alan R. Liss.

Forrest, B. D. 1991. Women, HIV, and mucosal immunity. *Lancet* 337:835–36.

Free, M. 1992. Health technologies for the developing world: Addressing the unmet needs. *International Journal of Technology Assessment Health Care* 8: 623–34.

Freedman, B. 1992. AIDS and the ethics of clinical trials: Learning the right lessons. *Controlled Clinical Trials* 13:1–5.

Germain, A. 1992. Introduction. In A. Germain et al., eds., *Reproductive Tract Infections: Global Impact and Priorities for Women's Reproductive Health*, 1–6. New York: Plenum.

Harr, J. E. and P. J. Johnson. 1991. *The Rockefeller Conscience*. New York: Scribners.

Heise, L. 1993. Violence against women: The missing agenda. In M. Koblinsky, J. Timyan, and J. Gay, eds., *Women's Health: A Global Perspective*, 171–95. Boulder, Colo.: Westview.

Hillier, S. and K. K. Holmes. 1989. Bacterial vaginosis. In K. K. Holmes et al., eds., *Sexually Transmitted Diseases*, 547–59. New York: McGraw-Hill.

Hussain, L. A., C. G. Kelly, and R. Fellowes. 1992. Expression and gene transcript of Fc receptors for IgG, HLA Class II antigens and Langerhans cells in human cervicovaginal epithelium. *Clinical and Experimental Immunology* 90:530–38.

International Women's Health Coalition. 1991. Creating common ground: Women's perceptions on the selection and introduction of fertility regulation technologies. WHO/HRP/ITT.

Kreiss, J., et al. 1992. Efficacy of Nonoxynol-9 contraceptive sponge use in preventing heterosexual acquisition of HIV in Nairobi prostitutes. *Journal of the American Medical Association* 268:477–82.

Krieger, J. N., et al. 1991. Recovery of human immunodeficiency virus type 1 from semen: Minimal impact of stage of infection and current antiviral chemotherapy. *Journal of Infectious Disease* 163:386–91.

Levine, C., N. N. Dubler, and R. J. Levine. 1991. Building a new consensus: Ethical principles and policies for clinical research on HIV/AIDS. *Institutional Review Board* 13:194–210.

Mastroianni L., P. J. Donaldson, and T. T. Kane. 1990. Special report: Development of contraceptives—obstacles and opportunities. *New England Journal of Medicine* 322:482–84.

McGroarty, J. A., et al. 1990a. Influence of the spermicidal compound Nonoxynol-9 on the growth and adhesion of urogenital bacteria in vitro. *Current Microbiology* 21:219–23.

——. 1990b. The spermicidal compound Nonoxynol-9 increases adhesion of candida species to human epithelial cells in vitro. *Infection and Immunity* 58 (6): 2005–7.

Miller, C. J., et al. 1989. Genital mucosal transmission of simian immunodeficiency virus: Animal model for heterosexual transmission of the human immunodeficiency virus. *Journal of Virology* 63:4277–84.

——. 1992. The effect of contraceptives containing Nonoxynol-9 on the genital transmission of simian immunodeficiency virus in rhesus macaques. *Fertility and Sterility* 57 (5): 1126–28.

Ndinya-Achola, J. O. 1991. A review of ethical issues in AIDS research. *East African Medical Journal* 68 (9): 735–40.

Niruthisard, S., R. E. Roddy, and S. Chutivongse. 1991a. A randomized trial of Nonoxynol-9 and placebo for the prevention of gonococcal and chlamydial cervicitis. Abstract C-22–028]. International Society for Sexually Transmitted Disease Research, October, Banff.

———. 1991b. The effects of frequent Nonoxynol-9 use on the vaginal and cervical mucosa. *Sexually Transmitted Diseases* 18:176-79.

Pearce-Pratt, R. and D. M. Phillips. 1993. Studies on adhesion of lymphocytic cells: Implications for sexual transmission of HIV. *Biology of Reproduction* 48:1–15.

Peterman, T. A., et al. 1988. Risk of human immunodeficiency virus transmission from heterosexual adults with transfusion-associated infections. *Journal of the American Medical Association* 259 (1): 55–58.

Phillips, D. M. and A. S. Bourinbaiar. 1992. Mechanism of HIV spread from lymphocytes to epithelia. *Virology* 186:261–73.

Phillips, D. M. and X. Tan. 1992. HIV-1 infection of the trophoblast cell line BeWo: A study of virus uptake. *AIDS Research and Human Retroviruses* 8:1683–91.

Pick de Weiss, S., et al. 1991. Sex, contraception, and pregnancy among adolescents in Mexico City. *Studies in Family Planning* 22 (2): 74–82.

Population Services International. 1992. The Zaire mass media project: A model AIDS prevention and motivation project. Report No. 1/1991. Washington, D.C.

Rebello, R., F.H.Y. Green, and H. Fox. 1975. A study of the secretory immune system of the female genital tract. *British Journal of Obstetrics and Gynecology* 82:812–16.

Rein, M. F. and M. Muller. 1989. Trichomonas vaginalis and trichomoniasis. In K. K. Holmes et al., eds., *Sexually Transmitted Diseases*, 481–92. New York: McGraw-Hill.

Rekart, M. L. 1992. The toxicity and local effects of the spermicide Nonoxynol-9. *Journal of AIDS* 5:425–26.

Roddy, R., et al. 1992. Dosing study of Nonoxynol-9 and genital irritation. Abstract PoB. Eighth International Conference on AIDS/Third STD World Congress, Amsterdam, The Netherlands, July.

Rosenberg, M. and E. Gollub. 1992. Methods women can use that may prevent sexually transmitted disease, including HIV. *American Journal of Public Health* 82 (11): 1473–78.

Scofield, V. L. 1992. Sperm as vectors and co-factors for HIV-1 transmission. *Journal of NIH Research* 4:105–11.

Scrimshaw, S. C. M. 1979. The cultural acceptability of vaginal contraceptives. In G. I. Zatuchni et al., *Vaginal Contraception: New Developments*, 282–93. New York: Harper & Row.

Stein, Z. A. 1990. HIV prevention: The need for methods women can use. *American Journal of Public Health* 80:460–62.

Stewart, G. J., A. L. Cunningham, and G. L. Driscoll. 1985. Transmission of human T-cell lymphotropic virus type III (HTLV-III) by artificial insemination by donor. *Lancet* 2:581–84.

Ulin, P. R. 1992. African women and AIDS: Negotiating behavioral change. *Social Science and Medicine 1992* 34 (1): 63–73.

Underdown, B. J. and J. M. Schiff. 1986. Immunoglobulin A: Strategic defense initiative at the mucosal surface. *Ann Rev Immunol* 4:389–417.

United Nations Children's Fund (UNICEF). 1992. *State of the World's Children Report.*

United States Public Health Service. 1991. Consultation on international collaborative human immunodeficiency virus (HIV) research. *Law, Medicine, and Health Care* 19:259–63.

Voeller, B. 1992. Spermicides for controlling the spread of HIV [letter]. *AIDS* 6:341–42.

Voeller, B. and D. J. Anderson. 1992a. Heterosexual transmission of HIV. *JAMA* 267, (1): 917–1918.

———. 1992b. pH and related factors in the urogenital tract and rectum that affect HIV-1 transmission. Mariposa Occasional Paper No. 16. Topanga, Calif.: The Mariposa Education and Research Foundation.

Wasserheit, J. N. 1989. The significance and scope of reproductive tract infections among Third World women. *International Journal of Obstetrics and Gynecology*, Supplement 3: 145–68.

———. 1991. Epidemiological synergy: Interrelationships between HIV infection and other STDs. In L. Chen, J. Sepulveda, and S. Segal, eds., *AIDS and Women's Reproductive Health: Science for Policy and Action*, 47–72. New York: Plenum.

Wolff, H. and D. J. Anderson. 1988. Male genital tract inflammation associated with increased numbers of potential human immunodeficiency virus host cells in semen. *Andrologia* 20 (5): 297–307.

World Health Organization/Global Program on AIDS. 1993. *Potential for WHO-Industry Collaboration on Drug and Vaccine Development for HIV/AIDS.* Geneva: WHO.

Worth, D. 1989. Sexual decision-making and AIDS: Why condom promotion among vulnerable women is likely to fail. *Studies in Family Planning* 10 (6): 297–307.

Zatuchni, G. I., et al. 1979. *Vaginal Contraception: New Developments.* New York: Harper & Row.

Zekeng, L., et al. 1993. Barrier contraceptive use and HIV infection among high-risk women in Cameroon. *AIDS* 7:725–31.

20 | The Ethics of Social and Behavioral Research on Women and AIDS

CARL KENDALL

The AIDS epidemic has brought not only devastating consequences, but also dilemmas for policy and action. Issues
such as mandatory HIV testing, partner notification, other
civil rights of HIV-infected persons, and so on, create ethical dilemmas for both
policy makers and practitioners. Ethical research issues have included achieving
informed consent, justifying anonymous seroprevalence studies, notifying partners, and using drugs in trials whose effectiveness has not been fully demonstrated (Levine 1991). Ethical issues related to women and AIDS have focused on
issues of participation in trials (Levine 1991; Christakis 1988). In addition,
there has been a growing chorus of concern about the paucity of funding of
research on women and the ways in which women have been narrowly categorized in studies. For example, researchers have tended to identify particular
roles for women in their studies, such as prostitute or mother (Carovano 1991;
Herdt and Boxer 1991), rather than deal with the complex interaction of roles
which women assume. Researchers have also tended to adopt rational models
of sexual decision making that ignore the structure of gender relations in most
societies (Holland et al. 1994:223).

Simple solutions to these dilemmas are not provided in the literature on the
ethics of AIDS research. Rather, these dilemmas appear to call for greater participation on the part of research subjects and their communities in the design,
planning, and implementation of research (Merton 1990), as well as the application of new research methods that are sensitive to the subjective experiences
of research, sexual roles, and other ethical concerns involved. In this article, I
briefly review elements of the ethical debates concerning research before
exploring implications of various research methods and approaches.

Ethics in the Conduct of Research

The standard international ethical guidelines for biomedical research with humans is the World Medical Association's Declaration of Helsinki, Recommendations Guiding Physicians in Biomedical Research Involving Human Subjects, originally adopted by the World Medical Assembly in 1964 and amended and endorsed by World Medical Assemblies in 1975, 1983, and 1989. The Declaration of Helsinki enshrines three ethical principles: autonomy, beneficence, and justice (Gostin 1991; WHO/CIOMS 1982; Bankowski, Bryant, and Last 1991; DHHS 1981; U.S. National Commission for the Protection of Human Subjects of Biomedical and Behavioral Research 1979; World Medical Association 1978; American Psychological Association 1986).

Autonomy refers to the research subject's freedom from coercion to participate and is meant to be guaranteed through voluntary and informed consent, which the research subject provides to the researcher (Ekunkwe and Kessel 1984; Faden and Beauchamp 1986; Kaufert and O'Neil 1990; Levine 1979), and by the researcher's provision of confidentiality and privacy (Mason 1989). Beneficence means that participation in the research activity will not harm the participant or the community. The reference to justice means that the goals of the research will benefit the participant, the community, and the larger society, and that appropriate legal and moral codes will be respected.

Even simple description reveals the dilemmas presented in the conduct of research from the perspective of AIDS and from the perspective of gender. Discourse on ethics is conducted within a framework that focuses on the rights of individuals (for an example of population-based ethics, see Dickens, Gostin, and Levine 1991, and Gostin 1991). Groups and group affinity, especially among groups of women, are given short shrift. For example, the need to understand progression to disease in women is paramount, yet how can autonomy be guaranteed? Is nonparticipation in a trial or descriptive study really an option for poor women with inadequate health care coverage? Does the signing of an informed-consent form demonstrate that autonomy?

Ethical research, in order to preserve autonomy, must provide privacy for the research subject. Privacy became a preoccupation even before AIDS was identified as a disease when gay men, intravenous (IV) drug users, and recent Haitian emigrants began to become ill with strange new symptoms. As Bayer puts it:

> These socially vulnerable victims could not be expected to speak with candor or to cooperate with investigators unless they were given ironclad assurances that their revelations about themselves would be kept in confidence and that none of the information would be shared with law enforcement officials,

immigration authorities, employers, or insurers. (Bayer, quoted in Fuenzalida-Puelma et al. 1992:145)

Women, too, may be added to the list of socially vulnerable. But the epidemic has changed, and now women who have only a single partner are being
infected by that partner (Bertrand et al. 1991). In many cases physicians and
health workers would like to inform women that their husbands are seropositive so that women could protect themselves. Here, the husband's right of privacy clashes with justice for the wife and with the social and epidemiological
need for notification.

Because some of the issues discussed in AIDS prevention research may be tied
to women's often unsanctioned behavior, such as drug use or the exchange of
sex for money, the consequences of this invasion of privacy may be higher for
women than for men. If a rumor circulates that a married male participant in a
behavioral risk factor study is having sexual intercourse with women other than
his wife, the public response is likely to be "boys will be boys." If, on the other
hand, a married woman is known to have multiple partners, her status in the
community may be seriously jeopardized. Many ethical considerations have different consequences for women, both because of their lower status and their
conjoined status as wife and mother.

Although status is often discussed in terms of wealth or power, women's jural
status has implications for ethical research. As married partners, or political
actors, women may not have full jural status and have to effect their claims and
rights through their husbands, brothers, natal family, clan elders, or the state.
This gender-specific jural status makes the interpretation of informed consent
difficult, and has challenged both ethicists and social scientists (Ekunkwe and
Kessel 1984; Schoepf 1991).[1] Schoepf demonstrates how ethnographic data are
misused to justify these decisions (1991:758).

The application of the principle of beneficence creates dilemmas as well.
First, the researcher must ask if the informant is harmed by her selection and
participation in research activities. Second, the researcher must guarantee that
the release of information during or on completion of the study is not harmful
to participants. It is easy to visualize how unanticipated consequences of participating in research could be harmful. For example, reports of the percentage of
women with STDs, age at initiation of intercourse, number of partners (for the
wife or her husband), or HIV/AIDS status can have negative effects on women in
study communities.[2]

Justice is the ethical principle most closely associated with society and social
ethics, and discussion of justice in research moves rapidly beyond the level of the
individual. Concerns for justice, such as the need to identify specific interven-

tions for women, can be in conflict with the principles of autonomy and beneficence. When these principles conflict, it may be difficult to identify an ethically
appropriate position.

Given these constraints in the analysis of ethically appropriate positions, and
the Euro-American framework of this discourse, it is surprising that local participation in the design, implementation, and analysis of research is not more
widely pursued (Fabrega 1989). Beyond issues of informed consent, clearly an
improved understanding of the research, and an improved manner of identifying potentially unanticipated consequences, as well as improved research outcomes would be the product of more complete participation on the part of the
researched community in designing and implementing the research (cf. Melton
et al. 1988; Merton 1990).

Participation is also a response to the call for interventions that promote the
empowerment of women. As Krieger and Margo (1991:127) argue: "Women
with the least control over their bodies and their lives are at greatest risk of
acquiring AIDS." How better to understand one's position, encourage a group
identity, and gain ammunition for the political struggle than to conduct research
that clearly articulates the problem to be addressed?

The Ethics of Targeting Research

In their review article on HIV and women, Hankins and Handley (1992:957)
note, "Seemingly little attention has been paid thus far to the unique features of
human immunodeficiency virus (HIV) infection in women." They also report a
focus on pregnancy in the study of HIV disease in women when such research
was undertaken. Ironically, that is also the reason why many women have been
excluded from drug trials and other research that might potentially damage a
fetus (Levine 1991:96).

Many researchers have voiced concern about too little and poorly targeted
research on women (Faden, Geller, and Powers 1991; Herdt and Boxer 1991).
Although there will continue to be concerns about women of childbearing age
participating in drug trials and trials of interventions with physical or biological agents, such as the female condom or vaginal viricides, there is little evidence that this participation is dangerous or that the benefits do not far outweigh the risk (Levine 1991). Few, if any, grounds exist for excluding women
from research with biologically active agents, and there should be even fewer
concerns for excluding women from social and behavioral research. Discussing
HIV progression to disease and other epidemiological and clinical research,
Hankins and Handley make an eloquent plea with ramifications for social and
behavioral science research:

> A concerted effort on the part of clinicians, researchers, funding agencies, and decision makers is required for redressing the inequities in both gender-specific knowledge of the natural history, progression, and outcome of HIV disease and the adequacy of medical and psychosocial care for women with HIV infection. The unique features of HIV infection in women have been subject to both scientific neglect and policy void, situations that can and should be rectified with dispatch. (Hankins and Handley 1992:967)

It appears that opinion is shifting strongly, at least for research in the developed world, for increased targeting of research for women. It is time, then, to consider other (nonbiological) concerns that need to be addressed about the unwanted consequences of targeting women.

Just as gender-based inequalities, such as powerlessness, lack of wealth, and inferior status, make women more vulnerable to the inducements of participation in unsafe sex (Mays and Cochran 1988), they may also be more vulnerable to the inducements of research participation and more at risk to the consequences of the research (Schoepf 1991). For example, with respect to sero-testing, Asia Watch (1993) documents that Myanmar prostitutes are being tested in Thailand for HIV without their knowledge, not informed of their status, and returned to Myanmar to face an uncertain future and even death. Schoepf (1991:756) details many of these risks for women in Zaire and lays out scenarios of how the status of women interacts with AIDS research in gender-specific ways, including accusations of witchcraft, scapegoating, and repudiation.

Women's perceived vulnerability has even had an effect on trials of behavioral interventions. Traditionally researchers argue that it is the male partner, interested in multiple partners, dyadically, domestically, and culturally dominant, that drives infection and therefore should be the target of research. The consequence of this approach is all too apparent, however: STD programs for men, condom programs for prostitutes and men, and partner reduction programs for men.

Even when programs are targeted at women, they often do not address women's real issues or concerns but instead focus on certain roles women play. As Herdt and Boxer (1991:178) note:

> Thus far in the epidemic, women have been primarily viewed as vectors (e.g., as sex partners of IDUs [injecting drug users], bisexual men, or men patronizing prostitutes) or transmitters (e.g., perinatal infection), rather than as a distinct category requiring specialized approaches and culturally sensitive knowledge.

Feminist scholars have also identified the effects of dominant paradigms on research about women:

> The official conceptions of sexuality and models of behavior . . . were largely based on a view of behavior as a matter of choice by free individuals . . . Women's ability to choose safer sexual practices, or to refuse unsafe (or any other) sexual activity, was not a question of free choice among equals, but one of negotiation within structurally unequal social relationships. (Holland et al. 1994:223)

The authors' solution is to "focus on young women's expressions of their experience, rather than on the facts of their behavior" (ibid., 224). This will be discussed later in the article.

Gender-specific approaches that focus on women themselves, on women's subjective experience, and on the multitudinous facets of women and women's roles seem too diffuse and impractical for health researchers. Many epidemiologists are skeptical of indirect effects and their accompanying indirect interventions, as well as cultural and social structural research frameworks that require qualitative research.

At the same time, approaching the general population, especially women, about interrupting HIV transmission has angered many gatekeepers. Discussions of women's sexuality may be more loaded and treated with more denial than discussions of men's needs and desires. Women, in their roles as preservers and bearers of culture, and as socializers, are often viewed as the sacred moral core of many cultures, and many people are made uncomfortable by confounding their roles as wives and mothers.

One result of the concern to balance distinct rights of patients and society in the clinical encounter has been the development of a narrative approach to bioethics, analyzing the interaction of the clinic visit (Carson 1990; Brody 1987; Hunter 1986).[3] Narrative approaches argue for ethnography and naturalistic observation, and provide a mechanism for incorporating ethical viewpoints of individuals and the community studied in research. Here, feminist and ethicist issues are conjoined. Although there is a growing literature discussing the issues addressed in the first sections of this article, the ethics of the application of particular research methods on gender and AIDS have not been well discussed. In the next section I explore the ethical implications of various research approaches. In reviewing different popular behavioral research methods used in the study of AIDS, I draw on my own personal experiences of conducting survey and qualitative research for more than twenty years in diverse locales.

The Ethics of Research Methods

Gender concerns about specific methods have implications for research in two senses. First, the particular format and most common interview sites for research may both bias responses and put women at risk. These kinds of concerns are remediable in research that is sensitive to gender (Holland et al. 1994). A more subtle concern is that embedded in particular research methods are unstated theoretical assumptions about the topics being discussed which may be biased against women's concerns (Holland et al. 1994; Bhattacharyya 1993). Both these issues are considered in analyzing different research methods.

KABP Surveys

Knowledge-Attitude-Practice (KAP) studies, and Knowledge-Attitudes-Beliefs and Practices (KABP) studies[5] have become the sine qua non for behavioral research on AIDS. The World Health Organization's Global Program on AIDS, for example, created a worldwide system of KABP studies that are still being analyzed today (Carael, Cleland, and Adeokun 1991). Additionally, the behavioral research on AIDS conducted by the National Institutes of Health (NIH) is overwhelmingly KAP research. Although these research organizations are increasingly turning away from this research and exploring qualitative research methods, KAP approaches still dominate.

As the nomenclature implies, these research activities are meant to collect information about respondents knowledge, motivation, and self-reported practices. K, A, and P have been identified because of an implicit theory of behavioral change: If someone has knowledge about a given problem, and is motivated to do something about it, then behavior will change.[6] This model has been superseded in the behavioral sciences because of concerns about environmental influences on behavior such as social structure and culture (Hornik 1988). Analyses from such research often lose sight of specific practices and individuals by confounding cultural norms and normative persons. Additional difficulties with this method include problems of response bias of self-reported data (Catania et al. 1990), including sociodemographic and socioeconomic variables that are collected as predictors of these KAP variables. In fact, KAP studies are misnamed. These KABP studies are structured interview surveys, often household interview surveys, and share the strengths and weaknesses of this approach (Bulmer and Warwick 1983; Huntington, Berman, and Kendall 1989; Bernard 1994; Stone and Campbell 1984;). As Carael, Cleland, and Adeokun (1991:S65) point out: "By themselves, the survey data, removed as they are from their social and cultural context, cannot furnish satisfactory explanations of patterns of sexual behavior."

Researchers produce a special form of information from household interview surveys using structured instruments with close-ended items. The reasons for the adoption of these approaches are both for research efficiency and for quantifiability, that is, the ability to collect and analyze rapidly information about a relatively large number of informants across wide areas for often quite specific purposes. The K, A, and Ps collected in this research are used in AIDS research to identify risk factors for transmission, and to identify individuals or groups that are "high risk."

Leaving aside, for the moment, issues of reliability and validity, one must ask who owns the data so constructed and what is it used for? Correlations may only be found with items included in the questionnaire, and variables related to women and gender issues may be inappropriately operationalized in these instruments. For example, does class or relations of power within a relationship determine condom use? If relative power is not measured, or insensitively measured, then gender might not count for much in analysis.

Feminists observe, hidden under the guise of research objectivity, false assumptions about women. Data, stripped of the context of embedded gender relations and analyzed with "neutral," rational, but patriarchal models of decision making, create an entire discourse that often blames women for sexual misconduct (Holland et al. 1994).

Researchers need to be concerned about this stigmatization and false labeling of research subjects (Schoepf 1991). Women, identified either as prostitutes or vectors, are considered a "high-risk group," when, in fact, specific behaviors are high risk. These behaviors are embedded in socially constructed sexual roles. Indirect links, for example, between workforce participation, maternal responsibility, and sexuality may force women to engage in high-risk acts. Closely targeted research that does not develop an understanding of these issues will lead to interventions that fail.

A parallel may be found in the discussion of selective and integrated primary health care. As Berman (1982) points out, water and sanitation interventions, such as piped water in the home, which have multiple and diffuse benefits for women, were ruled out of "selective primary health care" because of the difficulty of demonstrating the link between water availability and quality to disease in risk factor studies. On the other hand, piped water in or near a home has multiple and important impacts on women's time and work. If these multiple and diffuse benefits—such as the extra time for food preparation or child care are not measured—then they fall out of the cost/benefit equation. More open-ended research approaches might identify more of these indirect benefits.

Because structured interviews are proposed for their efficiency, questionnaires are often put together too quickly to provide real opportunities to consider these issues. Often other questionnaires are used as models, perpetuating the same questions and topics. When the goal is to attempt comparisons across cultures, regions, and even nations, as often is the case for KABPs on AIDS, there is even less opportunity for developing instruments that are locally appropriate. Here, researchers must force local knowledge and categories into pigeonholes designed by outsiders. In the case of KABPs on sexual practices, categories such as "regular" or "casual" partners may be used in instruments, regardless of whether these categories have a locally meaningful referent.

Gender Issues in the Research Setting

Survey research interviews are often conducted in settings or under conditions that may differentially influence reporting by gender. For example, women's activities outside the home may be sharply constrained, and so most often interviews take place in the home. When this occurs it is difficult to maintain privacy and uninterrupted interview time. Such interviews are an invasion of privacy and create real costs. Since women's time is so constrained by household responsibilities this creates an additional burden beyond that often experienced by men. Among the costs of interviewing about AIDS is the explicit discussion of sexuality or STDs with a stranger, which is uncommon anywhere in the world. A woman holding a three year old or in the presence of other adult family members will, of course, not be perfectly frank about these topics. Precisely because women are often held to high or idealized standards of comportment, these interviews create particular problems for women.

Even when these issues are addressed, and women are found who do not feel particularly constrained by these topics, processes of reinterpretation make the collection and interpretation of results problematic. Stone and Campbell (1984) describe these processes with respect to family planning surveys in Nepal. When asked if a women knows "of" abortion as a family planning method, many women who knew perfectly well about abortion replied no. The question had been reinterpreted, according to Stone and Campbell, to mean "Did you have an abortion?" or "Do you approve of abortion?" Items concerning sexuality or STDs are likely to initiate a similar response.

Inequities of power and status are also magnified when women are informants. Interviewers, men or women, are often professionals, and having the job of interviewer already means cash income, which may be scarce. Status differential may be even greater when women are informants, and consequently courtesy bias and other difficulties of interviews in this setting may be enhanced. Some of these difficulties may be overcome if interviewers are selected so as to reduce these status differentials.

Random selection of participants also may create stigma. If a group of interviewers is visiting a town to conduct a survey on AIDS, then why did they stop at Dona Marta's house? Random sampling methods are not well understood by the lay public. Informants may be quite suspicious of the overt explanation provided by the interviewer.

Survey researchers in industrialized countries have devised alternative strategies to enhance reliability and validity. Telephone surveys, mail questionnaires, respondent answer sheets filled out away from the interviewer, and computer-administered questionnaires all provide, to informants who understand the privacy provisions and anonymity built into the system, a degree of privacy. These methods can be used in nonindustrialized countries among literate populations familiar with questionnaire culture; however, most often they are not.

"Neutral" settings, such as health clinics, are sometimes chosen for the administration of interviews. Although the setting may be neutral in a geographical sense, a family planning or STD clinic is hardly neutral in a social sense. Local (folk) health systems deliberately do not disentangle identification, cause, treatment, and blame in health seeking behavior. The health setting will condition responses precisely because informants fear that this is true for cosmopolitan medicine as well, or because the health interviewer will share information with health staff or other informants.

The previous paragraphs have focused on issues when women are informants. However, constraints on women's behavior may also affect their ability to serve as interviewers. From many points of view, same-sex interviewers are preferable for the discussion of intimate topics, but the use of female interviewers in household interview surveys may be limited by physical and social risk to the interviewer.

Focus Group Research

Focus groups are designed to overcome many of the difficulties of structured interviews (Bernard 1994; Kitzinger 1994). Focus group research has a long history in marketing and communication studies (Kitzinger 1994) that both demonstrates their usefulness and makes them controversial for some scholars.

Multiple respondents and group dynamics are meant to overcome the status differentials inherent in much research and to foster discussions, so that informants' natural language can be collected and analyzed. Because the interviews are open-ended, informants' own categories can be identified. Same-sex groups, in the same age categories, should permit open interaction and promote consensus. In fact, focus groups are often conducted in small community settings, and the informants do know each other. Young informants may be particularly constrained in talking about intimate topics in public. Sometimes snowball sampling techniques are used to recruit participants (bring a friend) or random or quota sampling may be used. Each sampling approach creates uncertainty for the interpretation of results, as discussed below.

In front of strangers who are nonetheless peers (in the case of random recruitment), personal and intimate disclosure is constrained. Culturally approved responses and expressed idealized norms may be the only research outcome. In front of friends and acquaintances recruited through snowball techniques, this outcome may be modified to reflect the justification of individual behaviors of participants in the focus group. In other words the language used and the general circumstances described by participants may make reference to a discrete event, unknown to the focus group leaders. For example, if the topic of oral sex is introduced into the discussion, does that mean that the researchers know, or think they know, that the participants practice oral sex? Does this mean that other members of the community know that the participants practice oral sex?

Clearly the questions asked by the group leader may be reinterpreted to refer to discrete events. The puzzled looks on the faces of informants in such groups may reflect an internal dialogue along the lines of "How did they hear about that?" Needless to say, focus group research on sexuality must be interpreted in light of the political and social interactions found among informants, which is not routinely collected in focus group research. Participation in focus groups on AIDS-related topics may also call unwanted attention to women and generate gossip.

Because focus group research has so recently become popular in general research, it does not have a substantial literature focusing on method, and focus group interviews are often inappropriately conducted. Sites for focus group research are often public and crowded, presenting constraints in discussion. Sometimes multiple focus groups are even conducted at the same time. Additionally, the analysis of focus group data is not well defined. Exactly how are the verbatim transcripts to be analyzed? Are word counts and content analysis appropriate? Should the data be treated as a special kind of ethnographic interview or a kind of structured interview? What information is included in the final report; what information is to be discarded? What theoretical models are appropriate?

Focus group research may also be highly reactive, a reason why focus group approaches are used as interventions. For these reasons focus group research is easily disparaged and dismissed by researchers familiar with more formal and rigorous methods. Presenting the findings of focus group research on women may paradoxically undercut and denigrate the authority and views of participants. There is certainly no scientific or ethical justification for conducting poor research.

Ethnographic Research/Participant Observation

A number of anthropologists have explored the relationship of anthropology and ethics (Kundstadter 1980; Lieban 1990; Marshal 1992a). Ethnographic research is particularly distinct from the methods previously described. Although short-term ethnographic research—labeled as rapid assessment, rapid ethnographic research, focused ethnographic surveys, or targeted intervention research—resembles focus group and survey research, ethnography does not. For example, protocols and research guides are developed only after substantial fieldwork; sampling of sites and research participants is anything but random; and the research site includes every possible locale, from homes through bars, shooting galleries, the local YMCA, and gay saunas. Ethnography is inherently participatory, because in a very real sense, informants define the subject matter, categories, and treatment. Most often the ethnographer is wholly dependent on the goodwill of informants, substantially changing the power relationship between researcher and research subject.

Ethnography also lends itself to more complete descriptions of the complex interaction of gender, sex, and AIDS, and to building empathy and understanding. Evaluating information provided by informants, the ethnographer must place that datum into a local context, judging its reasonableness, veracity, and other features by recourse to local conditions. Complex and diffuse issues for intervention, such as power and empowerment, lend themselves to these context-based approaches.

At the core of local interpretation are the categories defining local culture and society, and at the center of one of these categories lies gender. Gender issues can never be avoided in ethnographic fieldwork (although they were often not well discussed), and are rarely an afterthought. In the current literature on AIDS, anthropologists have made a substantial contribution to understanding AIDS prevention (e.g., Herdt and Lindenbaum 1991, or Peter Aggleton's edited series "Social Aspects of AIDS"), prevention programs for women (Worth 1989; Farmer, Lindenbaum, and Good 1993; Sobo 1993), treatment concerns (Schiller 1993), and ethical issues related to research on AIDS (in addition to works previously cited, Antoniello 1993; Goldsmith 1994; MacQueen 1993; McGrath and Marshall 1993; Singer 1994).

Surprising, then, is the finding that few long-term ethnographies have been conducted about the epidemic. Although lengthy fieldwork seemed a luxury at the beginning of the epidemic, a decade later we still know relatively little about sexuality, its development, negotiating sex, promoting changes in sexual practices, condom use, and a host of other issues related to the epidemic. Without this understanding, prevention is likely to be much less successful than it might be, and miscasting the prevention issues for women is likely to continue (Ward 1993).

Although rapid assessment tools and formal qualitative methods have been developed, and are a substantial improvement over survey research methodologies, they suffer from some of the same drawbacks as survey research. For example, questionnaires may be administered by interviewers just like close-ended survey instruments. Because Rapid Assessment Procedures (RAPS) may be completed in as short a time as six weeks, they do not permit rapport to be developed in the study communities. Informants have to be sampled, as in other quantitative studies, and the best and most reliable informants may not be identified. Finally, analysis of the responses to open-ended questions is problematic.

Even if traditional ethnography has clear methodological advantages, ethical issues still bedevil ethnographic research (Wight 1993; Marshall 1991, 1992a, 1992b; Schoepf 1991; Singer 1994; Fabrega 1989). Researchers understand the specific context in which ethical principles should be applied, and can translate these universal ethical principles into appropriate local practices. However local and universal ethical and legal principles may clash. Long duration and the researcher's gender can also place sharp restrictions on the kinds of questions that can be asked, and the validity of the responses. Additionally, long duration means that the researcher has access to truly intimate and potentially dangerous information about informants.

Informed consent is made difficult because the direction and scope of open-ended ethnography is difficult to detail. The ethnographer, inadvertently, may also transmit knowledge about informants to others, or act in ways that may be interpreted as providing information about others. The locales for study are no longer convenient "communities," but often complex urban environments where the ethnographer cannot be well known to the majority of residents. Additionally, the ethnographer may be associated with one or another faction or group. This identification can bring risk both to the ethnographer and the informants.

From the point of view of justice for informants, Schoepf (1991) details how ethnographic data may be misused in prevention activities. Early approaches to prevention activities in Africa highlighted sexual exotica, blaming the epidemic on "cultural" factors such as sexuality and promiscuity (Packard and Epstein 1991). As Packard and Epstein point out, this may represent real bias on the part of the observer and lead prevention research strategies astray.

Another issue related to the implications of exploring and understanding gender roles and high-risk behaviors is identifying closely with ill informants. Few anthropologists are prepared to confront extremely personal and painful information, especially when so little in the way of intervention knowledge and skills are included in their training. Researchers have called for the creation of a clinical anthropology to train researchers to cope with the weight of empathy and the relatively passive response expected in traditional anthropology (Chrisman and Maretzki 1982; Herdt and Stoller 1990).

Building true participation with the research community is a partial solution. Richard Parker (1991), an anthropologist in Brazil who participates in a democratically run nongovernmental organization, ABIA (Brazilian Interdisciplinary AIDS Association), involved with affected communities, demonstrates a model that resolves many of the ethical dilemmas posed above.

Through participatory research, both the goals and mechanisms of research can be jointly developed. The outcomes of participation can include different strategies for identifying and interviewing research subjects, the inclusion or exclusion of particular components of research, such as the drawing of blood for sero-testing, and continuous monitoring and feedback on the progress of research. Participatory research can also be a particularly effective intervention, as was the case with the "STOP AIDS" campaign in San Franciso's gay community. Many ethical concerns are built into the design and development of participatory research, and debate about participation and conduct of the study provides evidence for narrative approaches to bioethics.

A Research Agenda

Ethical issues clearly challenge current methodological approaches, both in terms of protecting informants and with respect to issues of justice associated with social science research. In an increasingly litigious and politicized world of research, action-oriented and participatory research models may be among the few permitted to continue. Certainly the justification for social science must address the question of benefits, and of who benefits. In this environment, ethical conundrums need to be addressed through research on enhancing participation in trials, and participation in research in general. Clearer models of informed consent, and the impact of conventional research approaches on women, need to be investigated, especially as they relate to research on sexuality and disease. Searching for sources of systematic gender bias in methods and instrumentation, and around themes related to sexuality and disease, is paramount if scientific as well as ethical goals are to be achieved. Much of this research needs to be initiated through intensive locally based and culturally informed research about the social, political, and economic status of women.

REFERENCES

Aggleton, Peter. 1992. *Social Aspects of AIDS*. Edited series. London: Falmer Press.

Antoniello, Patricia. 1993. Women, HIV, and Pregnancy Decisions: Ethical Issues and Anthropological Research. American Anthropological Association Annual Meeting, Washington, D.C.

American Psychological Association. Committee for the Protection of Human Participants in Research. 1986. Ethical issues in psychological research on AIDS. *IRB: A Review of Human Subjects Research* 8 (4): 8–10.

Asia Watch. 1993. The Women's Rights Project. *A Modern Form of Slavery: Trafficking of Burmese Women and Girls into Brothels in Thailand*. New York: Human Rights Watch.

Bankowski, Z., J. H. Bryant, and J. M. Last. 1991. *Ethics and Epidemiology: International Guidelines*. Proceedings of the Twentieth-fifth CIOMS Conference, Geneva.

Berman, Peter. 1982. Selective primary health care: Is efficient sufficient. *Social Science and Medicine* 16 (10): 1054–59.

Bernard, H. Russell. 1994. *Research Methods in Anthropology*. 2d ed. Newbury Park, Calif.: Sage.

Bertrand, Jane T., et al. 1991. AIDS-related knowledge, sexual behavior, and condom use among men and women in Kinshasa, Zaire. *American Journal of Public Health* 81 (1): 53–58.

Bhattacharyya, Karabi. 1993. *Understanding Acute Respiratory Infections: Culture and Method*. Ann Arbor, Mich.: University Microfilms.

Brody, H. 1987. *Stories of Sickness*. New Haven: Yale University Press.

Bulmer, M. and D. Warwick, eds. 1983. *Social Research in Developing Countries*. New York: Wiley.

Carael, Michel, John Cleland, and Lawrence Adeokun. 1991. Overview and selected findings of sexual behavior surveys. *AIDS* 5 (suppl.1): S63-S74.

Carovano, Katherine. 1991. More than mothers and whores: Redefining the AIDS prevention needs of women. *International Journal of Health Services* 21 (1): 131–42.

Carson, R. A. 1990. Interpretive bioethics: The way of discernment. *Theoretical Medicine* 11:51–59

Catania, J. A., D. R. Gibson, B. Marin, T. J. Coates, and R. Greenblatt. 1990. Response bias in assessing sexual behaviors relevant to HIV transmission. *Evaluation and Program Planning* 13:19–29.

Chrisman, Noel J. and T. Maretzki. 1982. *Clinically Applied Anthropology: Anthropologists in Health Science Settings*. Dordrecht, Holland: D. Reidel.

Christakis, Nicholas. 1988. The ethical design of an AIDS vaccine trial in Africa. *Hastings Center Report* 18 (3): 31–37.

Dickens, B. M., L. Gostin, and R. J. Levine. 1991. Research on human populations: National and international ethical guidelines. *Law, Medicine, and Health Care* 19 (3–4): 191–200.

Ekunkwe, Ebun O. and Ross Kessel. 1984. Informed consent in the developing world. Case study and commentaries. *Hastings Center Report* 14 (3): 22–24.

Fabrega, H. 1989. An ethnomedical perspective of medical ethics. *Journal of Medicine and Philosophy* 15:593–625.

Faden, R. R. and Thomas L. Beauchamp. 1986. *A History and Theory of Informed Consent*. New York: Oxford University Press.

Faden, R. R., G. Geller, and M. Powers. 1991. *AIDS, Women, and the Next Generation*. New York: Oxford University Press.

Farmer, P., S. Lindenbaum, and M-J. D. Good. 1993. Women, poverty, and AIDS: An introduction. *Culture, Medicine, and Psychiatry* 17 (4): 387–97.

Fuenzalida-Puelma, Hernan, et. al. 1992. Ethics and the Law in the Study of AIDS. Washington, D.C.: The Pan American Health Organization.

Goldsmith, Douglas. 1994. Confidentiality in Ethnography: Drugs, Sex, and AIDS in the Lives of Informants in New York City in the 1980s. Paper presented at the Society for Applied Anthropology Annual Meetings. Cancun, Mexico.

Gostin, Larry. 1991. Ethical principles for the conduct of human subject research: Population-based research and ethics. *Law, Medicine, and Health Care* 19 (3–4): 191–200.

Green, Edward C. 1992. The anthropology of sexually transmitted disease in Liberia. *Social Science and Medicine* 35 (12): 1457–68.

Hankins, Catherine A. and M. A. Handley. 1992. HIV disease and AIDS in women: Current knowledge and a research agenda. *Journal of Acquired Immune Deficiency Syndromes* 5:957–71.

Herdt, Gilbert and Andrew Boxer. 1991. Ethnographic issues in the study of AIDS. *Journal of Sex Research* 28 (2): 171–87.

Herdt, Gilbert and Shirley Lindenbaum. 1992. *The Time of AIDS: Social Analysis, Theory, and Method*. Newbury Park, Calif.: Sage.

Herdt, Gilbert and Robert J. Stoller. 1990. *Intimate Communications: Erotics and the Study of Culture*. New York: Columbia University Press.

Holland, J., C. Ramazanoglu, S. Scott, S. Sharpe, and R. Thomson. 1994. Methodological Issues in Researching Young Women's Sexuality. In M. Boulton, ed., *Challenge and Innovation: Methodological Advances in the Social Research on HIV/AIDS*, 219–39. London: Taylor and Francis.

Hornik, R. 1988. The knowledge-behavior gap in public information campaigns: A development communication view. Working Paper No. 110, pp. 113–38. Annenberg School for Communication, University of Pennsylvania.

Hunter, K. M. 1986. There was this one guy . . . : The uses of anecdotes in medicine. *Perspectives of Biological Medicine* 29:619–30.

Huntington, D., P. Berman, and C. Kendall. 1989. Health interview surveys for child survival programs: A review of methods, instruments, and proposals for their improvement. *Occasional Paper No. 6*, Institute for International Programs, The Johns Hopkins University, School of Hygiene and Public Health.

Kaufert, J. M. and J. D. O'Neil. 1990. Biomedical Rituals and Informed Consent: Native Canadians and the Negotiation of Clinical Trust. In G. Weisz, ed., *Social Sci-*

ence Perspectives on Medical Ethics, 41–64. Philadelphia: University of Pennsylvania Press.

Kitzinger, Jenny. 1994. Focus groups: Method or madness. In M. Boulton, ed., *Challenge and Innovation: Methodological Advances in the Social Research on HIV/AIDS*, 159–75. London: Taylor and Francis.

Krieger, Nancy and Glen Margo. 1991. Women and AIDS: Introduction. *International Journal of Health Services* 21 (1): 127–30.

Kundstadter, Peter. 1980. Medical ethics in cross-cultural and multi-cultural perspectives. *Social Science and Medicine* 14B:289–96.

Levine, Carol. 1991. AIDS and the Ethics of Human Subjects Research. In Frederic G. Reamer, ed., *AIDS and Ethics*, 77–104. New York: Columbia University Press.

Levine, Robert J. 1979. The Nature and Definition of Informed Consent in Various Research Settings. In the National Commission for the Protection of Biomedical and Behaviors Research, ed., *The Belmont Report: Ethical Principles and Guidelines for the Protection of Human Subjects*, vol. 1, appendix. Bethesda, Md.: Office of Protection from Research Risks, U.S. Public Health Service.

MacQueen, Kathleen M. 1993. Scientific Constraints: Issues in the Design of Large-Scale Preventive HIV Vaccine Trials. American Anthropological Association Annual Meetings. Washington, D.C.

Marshall, Patricia. 1991. Research Ethics in Applied Medical Anthropology. In Carole Hill, ed., *Training Manual in Applied Medical Anthropology*, 213–35. Washington, D.C.: America Anthropological Association.

Marshall, Patricia. 1992a. Anthropology and bioethics. *Medical Anthropology Quarterly* 6 (1): 49–73.

———. 1992b. Ethical Issues in Anthropological Research on HIV Risk Behavior. Conference on Culture, Sexual Behavior, and AIDS. University of Amsterdam, July 25.

Mays, V. and S. Cochran. 1988. AIDS risk and risk: Issues in the perception of reduction activities by black and Hispanic/Latina women. *American Psychologist* 43:949–57.

McGrath, Janet W. and Patricia A. Marshall. 1993. The Role of Anthropology in the Ethical Conduct of HIV/AIDS Vaccine Trials. American Anthropological Association Annual Meetings. Washington, D.C.

Mason, James. 1989. *Research Confidentiality Protection—Certificate of Confidentiality—Interim Guidance* (June 8). Washington, D.C.: Office of the Assistant Secretary of Health.

Melton, Gary B. and Joni N. Gray. 1988. Ethical dilemmas in AIDS research: Individual privacy and public health. *American Psychologist* 43 (1): 60–64.

Melton, Gary B., Robert J. Levine, Gerald P. Koocher, et al. 1988. Community consultation in socially sensitive research: Lessons from clinical trials of treatments for AIDS. *American Psychologist* 43 (7): 573–81.

Merton, Vanessa. 1990. Community-based AIDS research. *Evaluation Review* 14 (5): 502–37.

Packard, Randall M. and Paul Epstein. 1991. Epidemiologists, social scientists, and the structure of medical research on AIDS in Africa. *Social Science and Medicine* 33 (7): 771–94.

Parker, Richard G. 1991. Sexual diversity, cultural analysis, and AIDS education in Brazil. In Gilbert Herdt and Shirley Lindenbaum, eds., *The Time of AIDS: Social Analysis, Theory and Method*, 225–42. Newbury Park, Calif.: Sage.

Schiller, Nina Glick. 1993. The invisible women: Caregiving and the construction of AIDS health services. *Culture, Medicine, Psychiatry* 17 (4): 487–512.

Schoepf, Brooke Grundfest. 1991. Ethical, methodological, and political issues of AIDS research in Central Africa. *Social Science and Medicine* 33 (2): 749–63.

Singer, Merrill. 1994. Ethical challenges in street ethnography. *Anthropology Newsletter* 35 (4): 29–30.

Sobo, Elisa J. 1993. Inner-city women and AIDS: The psychosocial benefits of unsafe sex. *Culture, Medicine, Psychiatry* 17 (4): 455–85.

Stone, L. and J. Gabriel Campbell. 1984. The use and misuse of surveys in international development: An experiment from Nepal. *Human Organization* 43 (1): 27–37.

U.S. Department of Health and Human Services (DHHS). 1981. Final regulations amending basic HHS policy for the protection of human research subjects: Final rule: 45 CFR 46. *Federal Register: Rules and Regulations* 46 (16): 8366–92.

U.S. National Commission for the Protection of Human Subjects of Biomedical and Behavior Research. 1979. *The Belmont Report: Ethical Principles and Guidelines for the Protection of Human Subjects of Research*. Bethesda, Md.: Office of Protection from Research Risks, U.S. Public Health Service, April 18.

Ward, Martha C. 1993. A different disease: HIV/AIDS and health care for women in poverty. *Culture, Medicine, Psychiatry* 17 (4): 413–30.

WHO/CIOMS (World Health Organization/Council for International Organizations of Medical Sciences). 1982. *Proposed International Guidelines for Biomedical Research Involving Human Subjects*. Geneva: CIOMS.

Wight, Daniel and Marcia Bernard. 1993. The limit to participant observation in HIV/AIDS research. *Practicing Anthropology* 15 (4): 66–69.

World Medical Association. 1978. Declaration of Helsinki. In Warren T. Reich, ed., *Encyclopedia of Bioethics*, vol. 4, p. 1770. New York: The Free Press.

Worth, D. 1989. Sexual decision making and AIDS: Why condom promotion among vulnerable women is likely to fail. *Studies in Family Planning* 20 (6): 297–307.

Epilogue: What Next? A Policy Agenda

E. MAXINE ANKRAH AND LYNELLYN D. LONG

W e are at a critical juncture in our knowledge and action about women and HIV/AIDS. As the articles in this volume have shown, much is already known about the causes and consequences of this epidemic for women. But more remains to be learned about what women know about HIV/AIDS, what support they need in order to cope with it, and what they can do to avoid being infected. The authors in this book assume that such knowledge comes from understanding women's experiences as a valid basis for guiding research, policy, and programmatic efforts.

Throughout the world HIV/AIDS affects all phases of women's lives. To understand women's experiences, we must consider their entire life cycle—not just their sexual relationships and reproductive years (Chen, Amor, and Segal 1991). We must examine the effects of HIV/AIDS on women's situations and roles—not only those living with HIV—but also on their roles and responsibilities as caregivers, parents, workers, and so on. The failure to see women's different vulnerabilities and strengths because they do not readily fit into a neat category, such as a "high-risk group," or engage in "high-risk behavior" distorts many HIV/AIDS prevention efforts. Especially in times of economic and social instability, most women confront HIV/AIDS in some aspect of their lives.

Women's experiences are extremely diverse (Herdt and Lindenbaum 1992). Programs, policies, and research must consider the role that socioeconomic factors—age, residence, class, and ethnicity—play in creating different experiences and outcomes. But women's experiences with HIV/AIDS also follow some common patterns. Poor women worldwide are most at risk and generally have less support regardless of their age, who they are, what they do, or where they live. Yet simple dichotomies between First- and Third-World women, "good" and "bad" women, or rich and poor women are seriously misleading. As the epidemic escalates, every woman becomes increasingly exposed to the possibility of being infected or affected by HIV/AIDS at some time in her life—either through friends, neighbors, children, partners, or through her own circumstances. Therefore prevention efforts must be by and for all women. Understanding how HIV/AIDS affects the lives of women in one country or one society can also inform the design of interventions for women elsewhere.

HIV/AIDS is not only a medical problem; it is also a social phenomena. HIV/AIDS prevention cannot be based solely on new medical technologies directed toward finding a cure for the disease. Research into new technologies must also consider the social and cultural factors in women's lives that contribute to their vulnerability. Interventions need to address women's particular circumstances and the constraints they face. The microbicide trials discussed by Elias and Heise in article 19 respond to this need. Yet even without effective female-controlled technologies, several authors relate how women are taking on the issues of prevention and care, assessing their risks, and making significant changes in their lives.

An Agenda for Action

The authors' views are derived not only from their knowledge and years of involvement with HIV/AIDS. Their reflections also come from listening and learning from other women. This volume represents a collective sharing among women and men, living with and without HIV/AIDS. From these multiple experiences and positions, an agenda emerges for HIV/AIDS research, policy, and programs for women. The sections below focus on ten issues that are critical to protecting women against HIV/AIDS.

The Socioeconomic Dimensions

As a social phenomenon, HIV/AIDS presents unique concerns and dilemmas for women. In part, this reflects the various situations in which women live that make them susceptible. Yet HIV/AIDS prevention strategies tend not to effect changes in the environmental conditions that render women highly vulnerable. For example, social transformations—such as structural adjustment and the transition to a market economy, as are now occurring in Africa, Eastern Europe, and parts of Asia and Latin America—are having a potentially devastating effect on women. The effect of these conditions may be more profound on women than on men. Deteriorating economic circumstances, rising nationalism, and a conservative backlash—a politics of reversion and regression—are eroding women's positions in many societies. These effects are witnessed in the widespread feminization of poverty. Poverty alone places many women at greater risk as they frequently must exchange sex to meet the basic needs of their family members and themselves. Because of traditional inequities, men often control women's behaviors. Thus decision making and autonomous choice in sexual activity are removed from many women. In many societies, being a virgin is also becoming a risk factor because men may be seeking presumably safer, younger sexual partners. Women's vulnerability is further exacerbated by their increasing unemployment and their need to provide for their children and households. Despite these trends, the structural, macroeconomic, and social contributors to the effects of HIV/AIDS on women have yet to be fully indicated and factored into HIV/AIDS prevention programs. We must therefore include strategies to address structural and environmental change on the agenda of HIV/AIDS prevention.

Information for Women

Women need access to information in order to make informed choices. Experience demonstrates, for example, that we should avoid two-tiered paternalistic systems on issues such as breast-feeding, contraceptives, and pregnancy for HIV-positive women. We should also avoid talking down to women or offering information that has little value and that cannot be implemented, given the particular circumstances of women's lives. As adults, women will and should be expected to calculate their own risks. Because the issues are complex and the knowledge base is incomplete, women need a great deal of information beyond such simple messages as "AIDS kills!" As a result of poorly conceived messages, many women worldwide believe that the disease does not affect them personally and that Information-Education-Communication (IEC) campaigns apply only to the "high-risk groups."

Access to technical and culturally relevant information is needed; we must avoid canned messages. Women can create their own relevant slogans and admonitions. Women talking to women can be an effective part of AIDS prevention and knowledge. Focus groups can also be a very constructive mechanism in this effort in circumstances where women feel safe and at ease talking with others. However, these groups need to be organized by the networks or communities of women themselves. Messages must also be presented in a culturally appropriate language. Both research and prevention activities to understand women's parameters of action and choice should focus on finding ways to enlarge these parameters.

Lessening Women's Vulnerability

Women and young girls in many countries are subject to increased sexual violence and abuse. A "culture of silence" about such incidents is often imposed on women, especially in countries where their status is particularly low. Globally, current measures of protecting women and girls, psychologically as well as physically, are inadequate. Such legal measures that are enacted are rarely sufficiently enforced to guarantee women's protection. Violence against women takes various forms; forced sex is but one of them. Many women in regions of conflict suffer both domestic and state-sanctioned forms of violence, but all types potentially increase their risk of HIV/AIDS if the perpetrator of abuse is HIV-infected. Women living in poverty, in situations of political turmoil, in conditions of military occupation, in refugee camps, and in households without a male figure are likely to be prime targets of men who prey on women. International human rights protective measures, as well as their implementation, do not adequately attend to women's increased risk of HIV/AIDS that derives from coercive situations. Relief and development programs often fail to provide adequate safeguards. Therefore, in the design of programs and policies, AIDS prevention activities must consider the issue of violence, or threat of violence, as major contributors to women's vulnerability.

Health Care Reform

Health care programs must be informed by locally specific knowledge and practices. But lessons can also be derived from similarities in women's experiences. Even though women and their children are often the primary clients in health care systems, they share a common experience of being patronized, dictated to, ignored, or denied access to many systems by health care providers. There are structural similarities, too, in women's experiences, vis-à-vis policies and programs that result in women having little opportunity to participate in policy formation, information, and biomedical research, and to gain funding for their concerns. Nor is much attention accorded to health care needs that are specific to the problems of AIDS in women.

Women can benefit from knowledge about their bodies, how HIV/AIDS is transmitted, and from available technologies such as barrier methods to prevent HIV transmission. Informed choice depends on having access to the latest information about new technologies and methods. Yet much health care provided for HIV/AIDS ignores this fundamental need. Health policies and programs must therefore be informed by greater gender sensitivity. Every woman should be assured of at least minimal provision through comprehensive health care systems in their respective countries.

Involving Men and Boys

Men and boys need to be educated and made more aware of the issues affecting
women if they are to demonstrate greater sexual responsibility toward women
and girls. Male sexual responsibility is key to both men and women's freedom
from HIV/AIDS. Research needs to look at how education and communication
interventions address boys and men and what messages are being conveyed
about their role in combating HIV transmission to women. Prevention and
research programs must also examine how to incorporate gender analyses into
programs. Too often HIV prevention and research efforts directed toward
women are not incorporated into overall HIV/AIDS programming but are
treated as small, insignificant, and peripheral activities. Resource constraints
are frequently cited as the excuse of why even the smallest of efforts go unas-
sisted. Funding priorities should aim to reach men and women rather than only
women. Women's concerns must be integrated into the major programs such as
STD control, as well as those designed to affect policies and appropriate behavioral change.

Women-Controlled Technologies

The development of female barrier methods and microbicides should rank high
among the priorities of pharmaceutical companies, donors, governments, and
nongovernmental organizations. Nowhere can we depend on existing prevention strategies (condom promotion, partner abstinence, and STD prevention and
control) or even new technologies alone to address women's risks of HIV transmission. Given the social, economic, and biological complexity of HIV/AIDS,
there are no simple technological "fixes." However, a technology that women
themselves can control is empowering to women and can help to lessen their
vulnerability.

Many issues surrounding the control and prevention of HIV/AIDS are not new
phenomena. Lessons from family planning and educational programs may provide insights for clinical trials and the adoption of new technologies. Lessons can
also be learned from successful mass education and literacy programs. In addition, HIV/AIDS and STD prevention should be included in family planning services and school curricula.

Research Priorities

Currently much of the HIV/AIDS research focuses primarily on women's behaviors rather than on the situations that inform those behaviors. Research on

HIV/AIDS should include situational as well as behavioral issues in their design. Research should be more participatory and involve women in the design, implementation, reporting, and dissemination of results. Women and men who are not necessarily researchers but know the local contexts and have a stake in the results should be involved in defining critical questions. Local NGOS can play a major role in involving local constituencies, in training local research collaborators, and in disseminating relevant results.

Donors and funding agencies should also support intervention or action-oriented research and provide more funding for research that considers women's socioeconomic circumstances. Increased international collaboration between researchers from the South and North is also needed. The dichotomy between domestic and international research in many societies keeps important lessons and findings from being transferred to inform new research and interventions.

Advancing Women's Legal and Political Status

Prevention strategies need to be cast more broadly to encompass women's legal status. HIV/AIDS prevention requires long-term strategies and will ultimately require political, economic, and social restructuring of relationships through legal reforms. Issues such as unequal access to resources, stereotypical roles and responsibilities that are disadvantageous to women, the care of children, property and inheritance rights, and differential legal rights all constrain women's ability to prevent HIV/AIDS.

Women's NGOS and community groups can play a critical advocacy to advance women's legal and political status. Two recent international conferences held in 1995—the Conference on Population and Development (ICPD) in Cairo and the Conference on the Status of Women in Beijing—exemplify the degree to which women's NGOS and networks are gaining power and space to increase local and global responsiveness to their issues and concerns. At the ICPD women's NGOS were instrumental in guiding the international debate to address issues such as abortion, women's reproductive health, and women's sexual rights and decision making. At the Beijing conference women's NGOS received worldwide attention for such issues and concerns as sexual orientation, women's work as work for pay, women's rights as human rights, and the exploitation of many females around the world. The conference platform also advocated equality of the sexes as a basis for global development and peace.

Beyond these international forums, women worldwide are enlarging their roles and responsibilities. They are also responding to care and services when these are provided. For example, many support services, focus groups, and counseling programs are already having a significant impact on improving women's status, rights, and authority in their communities. Where women are already in positions of responsibility and power, they can use their influence to benefit other women. Enlarging women's choices and options and advancing their legal and political status are HIV/AIDS interventions and, in turn, should be incorporated into all intervention strategies.

Building Solidarity against HIV/AIDS

HIV-negative as well as -positive women should be involved in prevention and control campaigns. HIV/AIDS is not "their" problem but "ours." HIV/AIDS prevention and control efforts need to enlist women in key positions and mobilize all women politically where this would strengthen measures promoted by governments to increase attention given to the impact of AIDS on women. Political mobilization efforts should enlist men to make them more aware of how HIV/AIDS can affect the lives of their daughters, wives, mothers, kin, and friends. Men also need to be aware of how their behaviors can affect their primary relationships.

A Sense of Urgency

The rise of HIV/AIDS in women must be seen as an urgent matter. But instead public attention is diminishing. Policy makers and the donor world community appear to be losing a sense of urgency just when women are beginning to constitute the highest percentage of new AIDS cases worldwide.

Governments and international organizations must treat HIV/AIDS in women as a medical, social, economic, and political priority and seek comprehensive, integrative approaches for addressing this issue. The public can no longer depend on laissez faire approaches. All nations need to move quickly on all fronts beyond "business as usual" in order to stop the escalation of HIV/AIDS. Governments, the private sector, and communities must act quickly to develop new programs, policies, and procedures and new collaborative approaches. Everyone must be willing to devote more resources to addressing all aspects of this problem.

Implicit in the recommendations of this proposed agenda is the need to address women's empowerment, honestly and realistically. The rhetoric about women's empowerment has become meaningless at best and disempowering at worst. Too often development and social service agencies, and women's organizations focus their efforts on "empowering women"—a contradiction in terms. One person cannot empower another. Notions of empowerment are also meaningless when interventions designed to address women's lack of empowerment do not take into account the everyday realities of their lives. Women use strategies to survive. But strategies that are needed to ensure their immediate survival may be at variance with women's health and long-term wellbeing. To address empowerment in any meaningful way, women themselves must gain more power over many aspects of their lives and must have the support of men in doing so.

Knowing and accepting women's varied experiences with HIV/AIDS enlarges our current policies, programs, and research in new, creative, and promising directions. Such knowledge not only empowers women who are vulnerable to the disease but also those living with it. By taking women's experiences seriously, governments, donors, institutions, NGOs, and individuals will be better prepared to meet the challenge of HIV/AIDS in all people's lives.

REFERENCES

Amor, J. S. and Sheldon J. Segal, eds. 1991. *AIDS and Women's Reproductive Health*. New York: Plenum.
Herdt, Gilbert and Shirley Lindenbaum, eds. 1992. *The Time of AIDS: Social Analysis, Theory, and Method*. Newbury Park, Calif.: Sage.

Notes

Introduction: Counting Women's Experiences

1. These examples were suggested by Barbara de Zalduondo based on her own observations and research.

3. Women Who Sleep with Women

1. Indeed, Hunter's therapist encouraged her to marry and have children, saying that the "problem" would thereby resolve itself. Alexander was in a therapy group in the 1960s in which at least two people, a man and a woman, were each trying to establish a heterosexual identity for themselves, one overtly (the man) and one without ever discussing it (the woman), encouraged by the therapist who in other ways was extremely supportive of unconventional positioning of the self in society.

2. While she was at the World Health Organization (WHO), Alexander talked with many African AIDS experts about the probable existence of homosexuality in Africa, despite the overwhelming denial of its existence. After one such discussion, Nzila Nzilambi, a Zairean physician, went home and asked some women sex workers if they knew any men who had sex with men, and they said, "Of course," and pointed to some men at the other end of the bar.

5. Making a Living: Women Who Go Out

1. Not all who ply the sex trade are women, some are men or in between: *hijra*, *kthooey*, *travesti*, hustlers, rent boys, *michis*. And all too often, other men necessary to this trade, the clients, are forgotten. At the Ninth International Conference on AIDS (1993), 134 abstracts were concerned with prostitution, of which only 18 considered male pros-

titutes and only 37 considered clients. No entries were listed for managers. Since this book is about women's relationship to AIDS, this article will focus on the women sex workers. Although there are female clients, as well as female managers, no research has looked at the first group, and very little has been concerned with the second.

2. Filgueras (1993) told me that in her opinion the young women working in clubs or bars were much safer than the girls on the street and were in a much better position to insist on condom use or to get help if a client became violent. In addition, they were less vulnerable to the random violence at the hands of police.

3. At the European Prostitutes Congress in Frankfurt in December 1991, a discussion was held concerning the age at which a woman's right to work as a prostitute should be recognized in the European Community. Women from the northern European countries assumed twenty-one was the appropriate age; women from Italy made the point that in some parts of Italy, girls get married at fourteen and begin having children at fifteen. There is some discordance, they felt, between saying that a woman is old enough to marry and raise children but only several years later is old enough to make the decision about whether to work as a prostitute.

4. Sex workers and their allies tried to work out an agreement regarding the Tenth International Conference on AIDS, held in Yokohama, Japan, in August 1994. However, the Japanese government refused to either modify the law or issue waivers for the conference (they made one well-publicized exception); as a result, sex workers—the subject of 134 abstracts at the Ninth International Conference on AIDS—had to lie on their visa applications if they wished to attend the conference. Migrant prostitutes, who may enter and leave the country several times over the course of a few years in order to work in the well-recognized and acknowledged, although illegal, red-light districts in Tokyo, for example, receive temporary visas to do so. No effort was made to bar clients from entry into Japan to attend the conference which, if it was like all the previous AIDS conferences, provided substantial business for prostitutes working in Yokohama. Sex workers who wanted to attend the Fourth World Conference on Women in Beijing, in 1995, faced the same problem.

5. Privileged communication with a woman who worked as a prostitute in San Francisco, 1989.

6. The states, some of which also enacted felony legislation and are preceded by an asterisk, include *California, *Colorado, *Florida, *Georgia, Iowa, Idaho, Illinois, *Kentucky, Louisiana, Maryland, Michigan, *Nevada, Oklahoma, Rhode Island, *South Carolina, *Tennessee, *Utah, Virginia, Washington, and West Virginia. The stiffest sentence for felony prostitution is in Nevada, with a maximum of twenty years.

7. Privileged communication with sex workers' rights advocates who met with District Attorney Arlo Smith to discuss this issue in 1994 (see also Kingston 1993). In late 1994, under pressure from the Department of Public Health, COYOTE, and the San Francisco Board of Supervisors, the district attorney ended the practice on a six-month trial basis. In mid-1995 the revised policy had not been formally extended.

8. Gloria Lockett, with whom I founded the California Prostitutes Education Project (CAL-PEP), used to tell me about police taking condoms from her during the sev-

enteen years she worked on the street, puncturing them with keys or a ballpoint pen, and handing them back to her, saying, "Now, go out and work!" (personal communications, 1983–89). In 1987, under pressure from the Department of Public Health, the police department issued a directive that police would no longer confiscate either condoms or bottles of bleach; the order was silent on the issue of "evidence," and police proceeded to photocopy the condoms in order to use the photocopies as evidence (the impact of the heat from the photocopying machine on condom reliability is not known). The work order expired in 1993, and negotiations for a new directive have yet to result in a permanent agreement (Leigh 1993, personal communication; Stuart 1994, personal communication). As of this writing (June 1995), many street prostitutes in New York City complain that when police arrest them, they confiscate condoms and fail to return them when the women get out of jail (Raphael 1995, personal communication).

9. When I was a child my father worked as a housepainter. Once he was on a job to paint a bank, and the only time they could work there was on Sundays, which at the time was illegal. On the days that he worked the police officer who walked the beat came by, and my father, who was the supervisor of the crew, gave him $10. Then a patrol car came by, and my father gave that officer $15, quite a bit of money in the 1940s. Then the captain of the police station came by, and my father called his boss, who came down and worked out an arrangement with the captain, and the crew worked undisturbed for the rest of the day.

10. Privileged communication with a woman who worked independently in New York City, 1993. During the 1993 hearings on police corruption in New York City, I scanned the *New York Times* every day looking for this aspect to be discussed. Day after day, nothing. Then one day Anna Quindlen (1993) wrote a column about the hearings, and there it was, a reference to police entering brothels and raping the women. On 15 March 1995 the local NBC television affiliate aired a videotape on its 11:00 P.M. news program, showing a member of the Public Morals Division undressed and receiving fellatio performed by a woman identified as a prostitute. Despite this serious violation of department regulations and the law, the officer was merely suspended without pay for ten days. Although the videotape was aired again a number of times in March, and again in May, no further action had been taken by the police department as of June 1995.

11. Privileged communication with women working in a poor neighborhood in Kisumu, Kenya, May 1993.

12. Privileged communication, May 1995. Exaggeration, perhaps, but other women have told me that many police officers are also clients, some decent, some abusive, all in violation of the laws they are sworn to uphold.

13. Meurig Horton of the World Health Organization, Global Programme on AIDS, told me in 1990 that while he was in the Philippines, he visited a clinic where sex workers were examined. He noticed that the doctors used one speculum for all the women in succession, merely swishing it around in a pail of water between women. Around the same time, King Holmes, of the University of Washington, Seattle, told me that he had made the same observation twenty years earlier. Jill Harsin (1985:272) commented on the likelihood of the spread of gonorrhea from one woman to another, during the nine-

teenth-century regulatory system in Paris, through the use of a speculum that was not sterilized, as did Allan Brandt (1985) commenting on the same system in the second decade of this century. He also cited contemporary reports of doctors examining fifty-nine women an hour in Bordeaux, and fifteen women in thirteen minutes in Cherbourg (1985:101).

14. This discussion of Thailand is based on conversations with many individuals, including representatives of private and governmental Thai organizations that work with, organize, provide services to, or do research about prostitutes in Thailand.

15. Personal communications with women in Kisumu and Mombasa, May 1993. I also noticed, in Ethiopia in 1991, that older women often paired with younger women, something a number of researchers have found in other countries, so that if the older women were able to teach skills of control to the newer sex workers, the younger women might be better able to protect themselves from HIV.

16. Personal communications with representatives of sex work projects in the Philippines, Kenya, and Thailand. This has implications for AIDS prevention as well, since the women who have incorporated lower-risk activities into their work-styles could share their self-protective skills with other sex workers, and in fact with non-prostitute women as well.

17. This includes members of the organization WHISPER, some of whom are former prostitutes, and the Coalition against Trafficking in Women, an organization that has organized a number of conferences on the subject and that has been working to get the United Nations to declare prostitution per se, voluntary as well as forced, a violation of women's human rights. Human Rights Watch, which says it takes no stand on prostitution, in fact reiterates the Coalition's demand for greater enforcement of laws against every participant in prostitution except those prostitutes who are "innocent" victims of "traffickers."

18. These prostitutes, who include both women and men, are affiliated with such organizations as COYOTE, PONY, and HIRE, in the United States; SWAT and SWAV, in Canada, affiliated with the U.S. based North American Task Force on Prostitution; the prostitutes' collectives in each state in Australia and New Zealand, affiliated with the Scarlet Alliance; De Rode Draad, in the Netherlands; Comitato per i diritti civili delle prostitute, in Italy; HYDRA, HWG, and Phoenix, in Germany; Scot-PEP, in Scotland; and Aspasie and Xenia, in Switzerland. All these organizations are affiliated with the International Committee for Prostitutes Rights, based in the Netherlands. In addition, members of these groups helped to establish the Network of Sex Work Projects, which focuses primarily on HIV/AIDS prevention, based in the United Kingdom.

19. I want to thank Karen Booth for this particular way of framing the whore-madonna dichotomy.

14. Women, Children, and HIV/AIDS

1. The vignettes are based on the author's clinical case notes. Names and other identifying information have been changed to protect the confidentiality of those involved.

16. Dilemmas for Women in the Second Decade

1. The 1993 U.S. Public Health Service budget for HIV/AIDS prevention equaled $600 million, as compared to the USAID HIV/AIDS prevention budget for 1993 of $80 million. In 1990 the world's total expenditures on AIDS care costs came to $3.5 billion, of which $2.4 billion was spent in North America. In that same year, of the $1.4 billion spent on prevention worldwide, $1.3 billion was spent in the industrialized world.

2. A nongovernmental organization (NGO) is defined as an indigenous private organization that pursues activities to relieve suffering, promote the interests of the poor, or undertake community development for the benefit of individuals outside the organization, and does not intend to yield a profit.

3. A private voluntary organization (PVO) is defined as a nongovernmental, nonprofit organization engaged in voluntary foreign aid, humanitarian efforts, and long-term development programs.

18. Talking about Sex: A Prerequisite for AIDS Prevention

1. The Women and AIDS Research Program of the International Center for Research on Women, with support from the U.S. Agency for International Development, supported seventeen studies worldwide to identify ways to reduce women's risk of HIV infection.

20. The Ethics of Social and Behavioral Research on Women and AIDS

1. An individualist approach would posit that steps need to be taken to elevate the status of women so they can provide informed consent, but until that time it is difficult to see, from a technical point of view, how a woman who does not enjoy full and separate jural status can provide consent to participate. Even if she does, moreover, she may be subject to considerable sanction.

2. At the same time release of information on women who use condoms with their partners, although controversial, might help women negotiate condom use.

3. Although not explicitly directed at ethical issues, Herdt and Stoller (1990) explore privacy issues with respect to the ethnographic exploration of sex and gender among the Sambia (cf. 391ff.).

4. Design issues for randomized placebo-controlled trials have received attention (q.v. Grodin et al. 1988). Holland et al. (1994) also discuss the implications of research methods. Several of their positions are discussed in this article.

5. The acronyms KAP and KABP are used interchangeably in this article.

6. The B in KABP is often added when cultural knowledge is collected in surveys.

About the Contributors

Priscilla Alexander

Priscilla Alexander is the co-coordinator of the National Task Force on Prostitution, a voluntary association of sex workers and sex workers' rights supporters in North America. Previously she worked for the World Health Organization's Global Program on AIDS. She is also the coeditor of the book *Sex Work:Writings by Women in the Sex Industry* (San Francisco: Cleis, 1987) and has written numerous articles on various aspects of prostitution.

Luiza Klein Alonso

Luiza Klein Alonso has a doctoral degree from Harvard Graduate School of Education, is currently a professor at the University of São Paulo, and does consulting work for Family Health International/AIDSCAP in Brasil. Her major research is in the field of women, behavioral change, and qualitative evaluation.

E. Maxine Ankrah

Dr. Ankrah is currently the associate director for the Women's Initiative at Family Health International (FHI) AIDSCAP. Before joining AIDSCAP, Dr. Ankrah, who has a Ph.D. in sociology, was an associate professor at Makerere University in Uganda, where she spearheaded the establishment of a women's studies department. Dr. Ankrah has extensive experience in HIV/AIDS research, has served on several national AIDS boards, has served as a consultant to several international organizations, and has authored several publications.

Carrie Auer

Carrie Auer is currently working on early childhood development for Save the Children. Previously Dr. Auer worked as an American Association for the Advancement of Science (AAAS) Fellow in the Office of Education in the U.S. Agency for International Development. She has also worked in a pediatric infectious diseases clinic at a major medical center.

Katherine C. Bond

Katherine C. Bond received her Sc.D. in International Health at The Johns Hopkins University School of Hygiene and Public Health. She has worked as field director of the Social Mobility, Sexual Behavior, and HIV in Northern Thailand Project (SOM-SEX), supported by The Johns Hopkins University in Baltimore and Chiang Mai University in Thailand. Her current research focuses on social and sexual networks of urban migrants in northern Thailand.

Jeanine M. Buzy

Jeanine M. Buzy, Ph.D., was an AAAS (American Association for the Advancement of Science) Fellow and Nongovernmental Organizations (NGO) Coordinator for the U.S. Agency for International Development. She now resides in Australia.

Kathleen Cash

Kathleen Cash, Ed.D., has worked as an educator, researcher, project planner, and materials development specialist in Asia, Africa, and the United States. She is the principal investigator for an AIDS prevention research and education project for Northern Thai female migratory laborers as part of the Women and AIDS Project at the International Center for Research on Women. Dr. Cash is also currently working with psychosocial programs for refugees and displaced persons in Croatia and Bosnia.

Michel Cayemittes

Michel Cayemittes, M.D., M.S., is a pediatrician and the director of the Haitian Child Health Institute in Petion Ville, Haiti.

David D. Celentano

David D. Celentano, Sc.D., M.H.S., is a professor of social and behavioral sciences in the Department of Health Policy and Management at The Johns Hopkins School of Hygiene and Public Health. He is also a professor of international health and of epidemiology. A behavioral epidemiologist, he was the principal investigator (PI) of the FHI/AIDSCAP study, "Social Mobility, Human Sexuality, and HIV in Northern Thailand," from which the data in his article were drawn.

Christopher J. Elias

Christopher J. Elias, M.D., M.P.H., is currently a senior associate and country representative with the Population Council, Bangkok, Thailand. In Asia he coordinates a program concerned with reproductive health, research in family planning operations, expansion of contraceptive choice, gender and development research, and institutional strengthening in Thailand, Myamar, and the Lao P.D.R. He is also responsible for coordinating, in conjunction with the Population Council's Center for Biomedical Research, efforts to develop a female-controlled vaginal microbicide.

Helene D. Gayle

Helene D. Gale is associate director of the Centers for Disease Control (CDC), directing CDC's Washington, D.C., office. She received her M.D. from the University of Pennsylvania and her M.P.H. from The Johns Hopkins University in 1981. She has served as a consultant to international agencies including the World Health Organization. Before assuming her current position, Dr. Gayle served as the AIDS Coordinator and Chief of the HIV/AIDS Division for the U.S. Agency for International Development (USAID). She has published numerous articles on public health and has received many awards for her scientific and public health contributions. She is also a captain in the commissioned Corps of the United States Public Health Service.

Robert Gringle

Robert Gringle, M.Ed., is with the Communication Department of International Projects Assistance Services, Carrboro, North Carolina.

Geeta Rao Gupta

Geeta Rao Gupta is the vice president of the International Center for Research on Women (ICRW). She has a Ph.D. in social psychology from Bangalore University, India, and has worked for the last fourteen years on issues related to women's health and women in development.

Lori L. Heise

Lori L. Heise directs the Violence, Sexuality, and Health Rights Program of the Pacific Institute for Women's Health, a nonprofit organization with offices in Los Angeles, California, and Washington, D.C. The program undertakes research and provides technical assistance to help integrate concern for sexuality, gender violence, and human rights into public health policy and practice.

Joyce Hunter

Joyce Hunter has her M.S.W. from Hunter College, School of Social Work, and received her doctorate in social welfare from the Graduate School and University

Center of the City University of New York. She is the director of the Community
Liaison Program, HIV Center for Clinical and Behavioral Studies, NYSPI/NY; pres-
ident of the National Lesbian and Gay Health Association; co-chair of the Global
AIDS Action Network; and serves on the advisory board of the International AIDS
Society.

Carl Kendall

Carl Kendall is an associate professor of international health and development at the
Tulane School of Public Health and Tropical Medicine. Formerly director of the
Center for International Community-based Health Research at The Johns Hopkins
University School of Hygiene and Public Health, he collaborated on the AIDS in
Street Kids Project in Belo Horizonte, Brazil. He is the principal investigator for the
Evaluation of the USAID-supported Zambia HIV/AIDS Prevention Project, a mem-
ber of the Panel on Data and Research Priorities for Arresting AIDS in sub-Saharan
Africa of the National Academy of Sciences, and a member of the Commission on
AIDS and Education of the American Anthropological Association.

Mubina Hassanali Kirmani

Mubina Hassanali Kirmani received her doctorate in education from Harvard University, Cambridge, Massachusetts. She is currently a professor of education at
Trenton State University in New Jersey. She works as a consultant for the World
Bank, Women in Development Unit. Dr. Kirmani has worked on women's issues in
education and health in developing countries, mainly sub-Saharan Africa.

Lynellyn D. Long

Lynellyn D. Long, Ph.D., is the Population Council Representative in Vietnam and an
adjunct professor at Johns Hopkins University School of Hygiene and Public Health.
She was formerly the project officer for the U.S. Agency for International Development (USAID) Trauma and Humanitarian Assistance Program for the Balkans and a
senior health and population advisor for USAID's Office of Women in Development.

Purnima Mane

Purnima Mane is a former associate professor in the Department of Medical and
Psychiatric Social Work at the Tata Institute of Social Sciences, Bombay. She is currently Gender and Behavioral Science Advisor at the Joint United Nations Programme on HIV/AIDS (UNAIDS) in Geneva. Her special area of interest is women
and AIDS, specifically in terms of the analysis of factors enhancing their risk and
needed policy and programmatic interventions. Her recent publications include
AIDS Prevention: The Sociocultural Context in India (with Shubhada Maitra, TISS, 1992)
and *Mental Health in India* (with Katy Gandevia, TISS, 1993)

Anna C. Martin

Anna C. Martin worked at Wellstart International as Senior Program Associate for Francophone Africa. At Wellstart she managed the Expanded Promotion of Breast-feeding Program's activities in Rwanda, Cameroon, and Senegal. Previously she had lived and worked in Kenya with CARE International. Ms. Martin is currently pursuing a Ph.D. in social and behavioral sciences at The Johns Hopkins University School of Hygiene and Public Health.

Jaclyn Miller

Jaclyn Miller, M.S.S.W., Ph.D., Associate Professor and Director of Field Instruction, has been on the faculty of the Virginia Commonwealth University, School of Social Work, for sixteen years. There she has taught clinical practice, mental health policy, group work, and women's issues. Her publications appear in *Social Work*, *American Journal of Orthopsychiatry*, and *Journal of Social Work Education*. She is president-elect of the Virginia-National Association of Social Workers.

Dorothy Munyakho

Dorothy Munyakho is a Bachelor of Arts graduate from the University of Nairobi. She has worked as a journalist for the last seventeen years, nine of them with Nation Newspapers, publishers of East Africa's leading daily. She has written extensively on health and development issues, notably for the Panos Institute in London and also the World Health Organization. She is currently the executive director of Interlink Rural Information Service (IRIS), a nongovernmental media organization concerned with rural development and urban slum issues.

Chloe O'Gara

Chloe O'Gara's work focuses on women's issues and public health education. Dr. O'Gara conducted research, taught, and designed programs in Central America for six years, and directed Wellstart International's Expanded Promotion of Breast-feeding Program. She is now a senior fellow at the University of Michigan, working in the U.S. Agency for International Development (USAID) Office of Population.

Anne Outwater

Anne Outwater, who earned her M.A. in nursing administration, was acting resident adviser of the Tanzania Country Office under the Family Health International (FHI) AIDS Control and Prevention Program.

Barbara Parker

Barbara Parker is a medical anthropologist with maternal, child health/family planning experience in Bangladesh, Nepal, and other developing countries. She has served as a Health and Child Survival Fellow, providing management and technical support to the U.S. Agency for International Development (USAID) Mother Care, maternal and neonatal health project, as a social science consultant for the World Bank, and as a program officer for Medical Care Development, International (MCDI). She is currently an independent consultant based in Durban, South Africa.

David Patterson

David Patterson is project manager for Medical Care Development, International's Ndwedwe District Child Survival Project in South Africa. Before joining MCDI he provided technical assistance as a consultant to USAID-funded projects, the World Health Organization, the World Bank, and the International Centre for Diarrhoeal Diseases Research, Bangladesh (ICDDR, B).

Elizabeth A. Preble

Elizabeth A. Preble, presently director of technical support for the AIDS Control and Prevention (AIDSCAP) Project of Family Health International, has worked as a public health specialist in the fields of international maternal and child health, family planning, and HIV/AIDS for the past twenty years. In the early years of the AIDS epidemic, as senior adviser to UNICEF, she developed UNICEF's first AIDS policy and program to address problems related to women and children.

Debbie Runions

Debbie Runions became hiv-positive in 1992. A year later she left her career in corporate America to become an HIV/AIDS educator and professional speaker. Ms. Runions has more than twenty years of experience writing articles for magazines, newspapers, and trade publications. She has been chosen for the National Leadership Coalition on AIDS for President Clinton's HIV/AIDS Advisory Council.

Martin Schwartz

Martin Schwartz is a professor of social work at Virginia Commonwealth University where he teaches advanced social work practice and an elective on AIDS. He has a private practice and works with HIV-infected persons and their families. He is a licensed clinical social worker, a board-certified diplomate in clinical social work, and a member of the National Academy of Social Work Practice.

Galia D. Siegel

Galia D. Siegel works with the Policy Unit of the AIDS Control and Prevention (AIDSCAP) project of Family Health International. The international focus of her current work with gender analysis and women and AIDS policy issues at AIDSCAP follows two years in New York City, where she worked as a counselor, case manager, and

HIV/AIDS educator in a drug treatment and HIV/AIDS services program for women and their families.

Christine Thomas

Christine Thomas, who became HIV-positive sometime between 1985 and 1989, has three children and lives in Washington, D.C. She currently is a member of the Management Committee Board for the Whitman Walker Clinic and is a board member for the Pediatric Care Program of Washington, D.C., where she organizes a stress management group for mothers living with HIV or AIDS. She was a receptionist at the Department of Human Services from 1989 to 1991.

Priscilla R. Ulin

Priscilla R. Ulin, Ph.D., is a medical sociologist and deputy director of the Women's Studies Division, Family Health International, Research Triangle Park, North Carolina.

Chayan Vaddhanaphuti

Chayan Vaddhanaphuti, Ph.D., is currently director of the Social Research Institute of Chiang Mai University, Chiang Mai, Thailand. Dr. Chayan is also the principle investigator of the "Social Mobility, Sexual Behavior, and HIV in Northern Thailand Project" (SOMSEX). He is actively involved in a range of development issues in northern Thailand.

Ellen Weiss

Ellen Weiss is the project manager of the Women and AIDS Research Program of the International Center for Research on Women (ICRW). She has an M.Sc. in maternal and child health from the University of London and has worked with health, nutrition, and development programs for the last sixteen years.

Index